Critical Essays on Virginia Woolf

Critical Essays on Virginia Woolf

Morris Beja

G. K. Hall & Co. · Boston, Massachusetts

94-416

Library of Congress Cataloging in Publication Data

Beja, Morris.
    Critical essays on Virginia Woolf.

    (Critical essays on modern British literature)
    Includes index.
    1. Wolf, Virginia, 1882–1941 — Criticism and interpretation —
Addresses, essays, lectures. I. Title. II. Series.
PR6045.072Z544   1985   823'.912   85–914
ISBN 0-8161-8753-3

To the student of literature

*". . . and I make it real by putting it
into words."*

— Virginia Woolf, Moments of Being

CRITICAL ESSAYS ON MODERN BRITISH LITERATURE

The critical essays series on modern British literature attempts to provide a variety of approaches to both the modern classical writers of Britain and Ireland, and the best contemporary authors. In general, the series seeks to represent the best in published criticism, augmented, where appropriate, by original essays by recognized authorities. The goal of each volume is to suggest a new perspective on its particular author.

Morris Beja has attempted to reconcile several disparate schools of Woolf criticism. Beja's thesis is that although Woolf is one of the great figures of "modernism" she makes an equal appeal to the "postmodern" critic. Her highly stylized "art novel" or "avant-garde novel" is part of the great experimentation that went on during the first third of the twentieth century, and her innovations and refinements are also pertinent to self-conscious contemporary artists such as John Barth. Her frank treatment of female sexuality makes an appeal to the contemporary audience, though her characters are timeless and her situations universal. The same is true regarding Woolf's interest in contemporary social reform and criticism, apparent in some of her works and missing in others. Large segments of her diaries that make an appeal to contemporary structuralist criticism are not reflected in her other works, and the androgyny, so much commented on in recent criticism, is but a part of the heterogeneity apparent in the scope of her work. (Two new essays by Ellen Carol Jones and Barbara Hill Rigney reflect the thought of the contemporary androgynous and feminist schools of modern criticism.) Beja's final point is that although Woolf is claimed by several ages and many schools of criticism, she cannot be pigeonholed in any. Virginia Woolf was "unique and all alone, even as she has become part of our inheritance."

Zack Bowen, GENERAL EDITOR

University of Delaware

CONTENTS

INTRODUCTION

Virginia Woolf is one of the great figures of "the modern novel," and like all those figures — names like Joyce, Faulkner, Kafka, and Proust come immediately to mind — she is a figure out of the past. That is an odd situation for people whom we persist in calling "modern" anyway. If "Modernism" reflects more than mere chronology, then we can assume with most critics that we have left "Modernism" behind, and that we are in a phase that is called, rather awkwardly, "Post-Modernism." But one point is obvious: although it is almost touching to see how frequently it is forgotten, the fact is that Virginia Woolf is no longer a contemporary writer, and it is almost half a century since she was.

That is not to say that her work is not vital, or that it does not create excitement among the most "contemporary" of our own contemporaries — the young. For many of them, indeed, she is the figure among the "classic moderns" to whom they most intimately respond. That development is intriguing to anyone who remembers how much resistance to her work there was among college students, for example, not so long ago — or, for that matter, to one who recalls how an attempt to talk about Woolf might well lead to the discovery that few of one's friends and colleagues were familiar with much of her work, and that many were surprised that anyone was "still" interested in it. On the other hand, such phenomena produce a cynical awareness that fashions continue to shift — away from writers as well as to them. In any case, whether one is a contemporary has little to do with whether one is currently popular. But perhaps not nothing to do with it, at least not nowadays.

According to the influential critic Leslie Fiedler, for example, our true contemporaries among writers of fiction are those who are writing Pop Art for the marketplace, while "the Art Novel or Avant-Garde Novel is in the process of being abandoned wherever fiction remains alive, which means that that sub-genre of the novel is dying if not dead."[1] No one aimed more unashamedly at creating "the Art Novel" than Virginia Woolf, so if Fiedler is right, her work is historical, not contemporary (or immortal, not dead). Some of it was very popular in her lifetime and sells extremely well now, but nevertheless her basic appeal is to people who — to use John

1

Barth's distinction in "The Literature of Exhaustion" — may enjoy "pop art" but prefer "the kind of art that not many people can *do*: the kind that requires expertise and artistry as well as bright aesthetic ideas and/or inspiration."[2] In that sense Barth and Woolf are "contemporaries" — although that may remind us of how frequently Barth speaks with bemused irony of himself and his calling as anachronistic. To be a true contemporary, one supposes, one would have to be a filmmaker, not a bookwriter.

If I seem overly concerned with terms like "modern" and "contemporary," I can only plead that I take my clue from Woolf herself, and from her own concern: two of her most important essays were entitled "Modern Fiction" and "How It Strikes a Contemporary." In a famous passage in "Modern Fiction" she looked at three of the most prestigious novelists in England of the time, 1919 — Arnold Bennett, H. G. Wells, and John Galsworthy — and said of their work, "Is life like this? Must novels be like this?" The answer of course was no. But she also admitted that she could not predict with certainty what the "life" in the new fiction *would* be like. Nevertheless, she was willing to venture to say:

> However this may be, the problem before the novelist at present, as we suppose it to have been in the past, is to contrive means of being free to set down what he chooses. He has to have the courage to say that what interests him is no longer "this" but "that": out of "that" alone must he construct his work. For the moderns "that," the point of interest, lies very likely in the dark places of psychology.[3]

That prophecy was certainly corroborated by subsequent developments in the so-called "modern novel." Is it still true? Some would argue that the mind and its dark places are no longer the central interest of contemporary literature, which may spend at least as much energy in explorations of the body.

Many discussions contrast Virginia Woolf with contemporary women writers who explore or depict female sexuality with the loving frankness and subjective interest that used to be restricted to male sexuality. The idea that her art does not fit into such a context is a very old cliché about Woolf's work: in 1924 even her friend Clive Bell remarked that "an oversexed person will never appreciate the art of Virginia Woolf; nor will a fundamentally stupid."[4] Enthusiasts for her art who feel disconcerted by the implications of Bell's first point will presumably have to take what comfort they can from his second. Or they may realize that her work is by no means as "sexless" as many critics have assumed it to be. Yet even that is not to claim, obviously, that she is the "contemporary" of Erica Jong or Judith Krantz.

Which brings us to a relevant question: with which of our contemporaries should Woolf be compared? Or, if you will, who precisely *are* our contemporaries? The question recalls Woolf's lament in her essay, "How It

Strikes a Contemporary," that in the literature of her time no names dominated all the rest.[5] When we reflect that she was speaking at a time when Joyce, Yeats, Eliot, and Lawrence were all already well known, we may feel that her words suit our day better than hers, but no doubt readers fifty years from now will find our inability to agree about our contemporaries equally incomprehensible.

Probably the aspect of Woolf's career that most immediately strikes us as notably contemporary is her feminism, although it would be a massive miscalculation to explain the current intensity of interest in Woolf as simply a manifestation of feminist interest in feminist writers. (And of course in some quarters explaining it in those terms amounts to explaining it away.) Our interest in the title character of *Mrs. Dalloway*, for example, is the result of many complex forces, and surely prominent among them are her vague stirrings of unrest at what she calls "this being Mrs. Dalloway; not even Clarissa any more; this being Mrs. Richard Dalloway"—a psychic situation which she connects with what she thinks of as "the oddest sense of being herself invisible; unseen; unknown."[6] But we do not let our awareness of those stirrings cause us to start thinking of Mrs. Dalloway as *Ms.* Dalloway. We should I believe try to be as aware as Clarissa Dalloway herself is that to categorize people is to distort them: "she would not say of Peter, she would not say of herself, I am this, I am that."[7]

Similar restraint is advisable in regard to attempts to categorize Woolf's art. Consequently, it would be a mistake to let her involvement in feminism as a social issue—important as that issue was and is, and pervasive as its presence in her art may be—blind us to her depiction of other social controversies as well, in the mistake so many of her own contemporaries made. Nor should we blind ourselves to the reasons why someone might have made that mistake about Woolf, for her work was tremendously varied. In some of that work, we *do* get a sense that the world of causes, of society, of issues, is elsewhere. In *The Waves*, for example, the kind of detailed depiction of the real world around us every day that makes one still seek out the sights encountered by Clarissa Dalloway in London is completely missing. Nobody stalks Bernard's world with a Kodak Instamatic; not even a Canon or a Nikon would help.

Nor is it merely that places are vague. As she put it in her Diary while contemplating the book that was to become *The Waves*, she wished to see what would happen if she avoided "writing exteriorly"; she could realize that "even externality is good," but in this experiment she was determined "to eliminate all waste" and the "appalling narrative business of the realist." So even events hardly exist in the resulting novel. *The Waves* is indeed, as Virginia Woolf contemplated it, an "abstract" and "eyeless" book.[8] It might seem easy, then, to charge the book with solipsism. Considering that it was after all the "damned egotistical self,"[9] which Woolf felt intruded upon the stream of consciousness fiction of Joyce and

Dorothy Richardson, that she so wanted to avoid, the charge is an ironic one—but (given her quite deliberate refusal in that novel to portray the external world), a difficult charge to refute—difficult, but perhaps not impossible. In any case, her work is not monolithic, and *The Waves* is not "representative"; for others of her works had very different approaches, and she could be no less insistent than the most socially conscious of our contemporaries in showing the problems of her society. One of the ironies in the history of criticism of Virginia Woolf is that the perspective from which she was so frequently attacked or at best dismissed during her own time—the social or political perspective, as critics failed to recognize its fundamental presence in her own art—became in the 1980s the perspective from which she was to be most vociferously praised, especially by feminist critics.

Woolf's similarity to writers of our time who present indictments of society is obvious, for example, in such a novel as *The Years*, but surely not much less so in a novel like *Mrs. Dalloway*, in which a prime aim, as recorded in her Diary, is "to criticise the social system, & to show it at work, at its most intense"[10]—a goal at which the novel admirably succeeds. In the psychotherapeutic relationship between Septimus Warren Smith and Sir William Bradshaw, for instance, we see at work what R.D. Laing calls "the politics of experience," and we are shown how "exploitation must not be seen as such. It must be seen as benevolence."[11] Woolf also shares with Laing and legions of contemporary writers a fascination with the divided self, the disintegrated, dissociated personality—what the Diary calls "states of consciousness" or "second selves."[12] Like such writers as Joyce and Lawrence in her time and Nabokov, Durrell, Lessing, Fowles, and Heller in ours, Woolf rejects the notion of totally integral personality as not merely inaccurate but unhealthy as well, since "unity" seems so often to entail having a single, overriding but partial and distorted self. An analogy is to the sense of the androgynous self as healthier than one that is "solely" male or "solely" female.

All such talk about personality makes literary sense only if you assume that novels have characters as well as words and pages. Although the essay "Mr. Bennett and Mrs. Brown" is justly famous as a revolutionary document, its basic assumption is one that has, as Woolf immediately acknowledges, "the sanction of Mr. Arnold Bennett": "That men and women write novels because they are lured on to create some character."[13] The 1920s were a time when critics could unashamedly speak of "characters," as in E.M. Forster's influential discussion in *Aspects of the Novel*. It was in this realm, in fact, that both Bennett and Forster felt that Woolf's work fell short.[14] Part of her defense was to write "Mr. Bennett and Mrs. Brown," the final version of which appeared in 1924. But in her Diary she was already thinking in terms more reminiscent of ones we hear from our contemporaries among the structuralists, and, as Robert Scholes has expressed it, one effect of "structuralist thinking on the contemporary novel . . . has naturally been a decline of fictional individuation of character."[15] Similar trends have appeared within the *nouveau roman*: according to Nathalie Sarraute, for example, writers after Dostoevsky learned that " 'the psychological' . . . did not exist."[16] Woolf too thinks in terms of what she calls the "post-Dostoevsky argument" that "character is dissipated into shreds now."[17] I have remarked that in *The Waves* the external world and events hardly seem to exist — and at least outside the six chief characters and maybe Percival, *people* are hardly there. We get more of Bernard's being than anyone else's in that book, but we never for example get the foggiest notion about what sort of woman he married — and we even begin to wonder about *his* status as a "character." In her *Diary*, Woolf responds to a favorable review of *The Waves* by reflecting, "Odd, that they (The Times) shd. praise my characters when I meant to have none."[18]

Are her contemporaries, then, the novelists we call the Post-Modernists? They often write books that are not so much novels as anti-novels — books, let us say, like *The Waves*. Actually, *The Waves*, which once seemed to be the epitome of "Modernism" (whatever that was) now seems not to have been that at all, but to have looked forward to much of what has been typical of "Post-Modernism" (whatever that is). Certainly, too, the most interesting and compelling of contemporary novelists still tend to be those who have felt challenged by the great moderns, not those who have ignored them or who have seemed to pretend they never existed or who regard them as aberrations. A seminal essay like Barth's "The Literature of Exhaustion," with its sense that "the used-upness of certain forms or exhaustion of certain possibilities" is a source of opportunity rather than "a cause for despair,"[19] has been doing for fiction in Barth's time largely what her essay "Modern Fiction" did for it in Woolf's. Moreover, when Barth in his own novels (like Nabokov, Pynchon, and others in theirs) constantly draws our attention to the "artificiality" of his created world, we may be reminded not only of Woolf's *The Waves* but at least of her *Between the Acts* and *Orlando* as well. In this respect, Woolf surely seems closer to many of our contemporaries than the E.M. Forster who asserts in *Aspects of the Novel* that "the novelist who betrays too much interest in his own method can never be more than interesting; he has given up the creation of character and summoned us to help analyse his own mind."[20]

Virginia Woolf always summons us to that task. That is so true that one may well feel that her true contemporaries are the novelists (among those coming to mind are Beckett, Mailer, Nin, Robbe-Grillet and Spark) who possess a gift that Woolf felt to be "as rare a gift as any — the gift of an entirely personal vision of life of which one's books are the more or less complete embodiment."[21] Yet she also realized the "danger" of "the damned egotistical self" that she saw exemplified in Joyce. Joyce himself sensed that danger and in *A Portrait of the Artist as a Young Man* had

Stephen Dedalus praise the artist who could be like "the God of the creation," remaining "within or behind or beyond or above his handiwork, invisible, refined out of existence, indifferent, paring his fingernails."[22] But in the end the work of each of them, Joyce *and* Woolf, embodies an intensely and pervasively "personal vision." As an important element in her criticism as well as her fiction, her feelings about the centrality of this vision bring her close in essential ways to the "critics of consciousness" of the Phenomenological Geneva School, who feel "that an author, throughout his works, takes part in a personal adventure, and that the works themselves represent the author's continual progress toward self-recognition."[23]

If the conclusion to which I seem to have been leading is that Virginia Woolf is the contemporary of all the living novelists whose names have come up even in this short introduction — Barth, Beckett, Durrell, Fowles, Heller, Jong, Krantz, Lessing, Mailer, Pynchon, Robbe-Grillet, Sarraute, Spark — then my purpose has not been clear. For while she is in some figurative sense their contemporary, it is finally truer that she is the contemporary of none of them. Denying that does injustice both to her and to them. Attempts to make Woolf one of us are no less tempting and ultimately no more valuable than all those past critical attempts to connect her to Jane Austen or Marcel Proust or Roger Fry. Virginia Woolf was unique — all alone — even as she was part of a tradition. She is still unique and all alone, even as she has become part of our inheritance. She is not our contemporary. But that is all right, neither was she her contemporaries' contemporary.

Morris Beja

The Ohio State University

Notes

1. "The Death and Rebirth of the Novel," in *The Theory of the Novel*, ed. John Halperin (New York: Oxford Univ. Press, 1974), p. 194.

2. *Atlantic*, 220 (Aug. 1967), 30.

3. *The Common Reader: First Series* (London: Hogarth Press, 1957), pp. 189, 192.

4. "Virginia Woolf," *Dial*, 77 (Dec. 1924), 461.

5. *Collected Essays* (London: Hogarth Press, 1966), II, 155–56.

6. *Mrs. Dalloway* (New York: Harcourt, 1925), p. 14.

7. *Mrs. Dalloway*, p. 11.

8. *The Diary of Virginia Woolf, III: 1925–1930*, ed. Anne Olivier Bell, with Andrew McNeillie (New York: Harcourt Brace Jovanovich, 1980), pp. 203, 209.

9. *The Diary of Virginia Woolf, II: 1920–1924*, ed. Anne Olivier Bell with Andrew McNeillie (New York: Harcourt Brace Jovanovich, 1978), p. 14.

10. *Diary, II*, p. 248.

11. *The Politics of Experience* (1967; rpt. New York: Ballantine, 1968), p. 57. On the relationship between Laing's ideas and Woolf, see Barbara Hill Rigney, *Madness and Sexual Politics in the Feminist Novel* (Madison: Univ. of Wisconsin Press, 1978).

12. *Diary, III*, p. 12.

13. *Collected Essays* (London: Hogarth Press, 1966), I, 319.

14. See Robin Majumdar and Allen McLaurin, eds., *Virginia Woolf: The Critical Heritage* (London: Routledge and Kegan Paul, 1975), e.g., pp. 53, 113, 176–77.

15. Robert Scholes, *Structuralism in Literature: An Introduction* (New Haven: Yale Univ. Press, 1974), p. 193.

16. *The Age of Suspicion*, trans. Maria Jolas (New York: George Braziller, 1963), p. 14.

17. *Diary, II*, p. 248.

18. *The Diary of Virginia Woolf, IV: 1931–1935*, ed. Anne Olivier Bell, with Andrew McNeillie (New York: Harcourt Brace Jovanovich, 1982), p. 47.

19. "The Literature of Exhaustion," p. 29.

20. (1927; rpt. London: Edward Arnold, 1958), p. 77.

21. "Lady Ritchie," *TLS*, No. 894 (6 Mar. 1919), 123.

22. (New York: Viking, 1964), p. 215.

23. Sarah N. Lawall, *Critics of Consciousness* (Cambridge: Harvard Univ. Press, 1968), p. 197. A full discussion of the questions I have raised would have to confront the complex question of the "implied" narrator or author. For an examination of that topic, see J. Hillis Miller, "*Mrs. Dalloway*: Repetition as the Raising of the Dead," reprinted in the present volume.

REVIEWS

Notes on Novels [*Jacob's Room*]   Rebecca West*

There is an expression, one of those unused phrases that nest in the tall tree-top of the idiom book. "I would rather have his room than his company." One learned its French equivalent, which was not less excluded from common speech (strange and beautiful it is, like one of Swinburne's nature poems, this mating of unuttered phrases with their alien fellow-outcast over frontier seas and mountains, through the kind ponderous idiom-book), and it was forgotten, till it should be recalled by Mrs. Woolf's last book. Very strongly has Mrs. Woolf preferred Jacob's room to his company. Jacob lives, but that is hearsay. Jacob dies; there could be nothing more negative than the death of one who never (that we could learn for certain) lived, reported by a mouth that makes every human event she speaks of seem as if it had not happened. But his room we know. "The eighteenth century has its distinction. These houses were built, say, a hundred and fifty years ago. The rooms are shapely, the ceilings high; over the doorways a rose or a ram's skull is carved in wood. Even the panels, painted in raspberry-coloured paint, have their distinction." We know so much about it; how his mother's letter, in its pale blue envelope, lay waiting for him by the biscuit-box; how the *Globe* looked pinkish under the lamplight and was stared at, but not read, one cold night; how the room heard, at hours when the elderly lie abed, young men disputing on whether this or that line came in Virgil or Lucretius; and how, Jacob dead in the war, it felt his absence. "Listless is the air in an empty room, just swelling the curtain; the flowers in the jar shift. One fibre in the wicker arm-chair creaks, though no one sits there. . . ."

Mrs. Woolf has again provided us with a demonstration that she is at once a negligible novelist and a supremely important writer. The novel may be exactly what it likes. It may be fifteen thousand words, or five hundred thousand; it may be written as simply as a melody in one part or as elaborately as a symphony. But it must, surely, submit to one limitation. It must primarily concern itself with humanity. Only the long drive of the human will can be fitly commemorated in the long drive of the novel

*Reprinted from the *New Statesman*, 20 (4 Nov. 1922), 142.

form. Now from that point of view *Jacob's Room* is a failure. The fault of it is not that it is about commonplace people—that, indeed, is never a fault—but that it is not about individuals at all but about types as seen through the refractions of commonplace observers' eyes. Jacob's mother, Betty Flanders, is based on the conventional exclamations that such a figure of bluff maternity would evoke from a commonplace observer; so, too, Florinda the whore; so, too Mother Stuart, her *entrepreneuse*; so, too, Clara Durrant, the nice girl; and Sandra Wentworth Williams, humorous but wholly a reported thing, dredged up from the talk of some cosmopolitan tea party.

But take the book not as a novel but as a portfolio, and it is indubitably precious. A portfolio is indeed an appropriate image, for not only are Mrs. Woolf's contributions to her age loose leaves, but they are also connected closely with the pictorial arts. Though she may have read Jane Austen and the Russians and James Joyce with more than common delight and intelligence, it is nothing in literature that has made her. She can write supremely well only of what can be painted; best of all, perhaps, of what has been painted. Take, for example, one of the rare occasions when the people in the book evoke emotion, the short and subtle and extremely funny conversation between Miss Edwards and Mr. Calthorp at the Durrants' party. The temptation is to ascribe it (since it plainly hardly came of itself) to the influence of Jane Austen. But if that had been the source the conversation would have had some high lights of verbal amusingness on it instead of being simply a success in suggestion, in the evocation of a prim social atmosphere. The derivation is surely a drawing in *Punch*, a pre-Du Maurier drawing of discreet ladies in spread skirts and young men with peg-top trousers and curling beards, sitting at parties glorious with the innocent pretentiousness of hired pineapples and *ad hoc* waiters from the pastrycook's.

There is dull stuff near the beginning about the Scilly Isles; none of the old people whose hints Mrs. Woolf can take, painted those parts. There is a good outing with the foxhounds in Essex, to which Morland and the old hunting prints have given their jollity. But best of all are Mrs. Woolf's London series. There was a gentleman who lived in the prime of the nineteenth century, when it was at once prim and fresh and artificial like a newly-plucked gardenia, named Mr. Boys, who made many lithographs of London. It was all as lovely then as Nash's Quadrant when we were young. Exquisitely did the industrious Mr. Boys capture its beauty, looking through an eye clear and bright as a dewdrop, wielding a neat hand as neatly as any old maid at her embroidery, to record the near-classicism of those stately streets, the pediments which were usually mitigated in their Latinity by emblems of Britannia and sculptural allusions to the Royal Family, the proud pillars that were painted the colour of pale soup and marbled, as likely as not, with pink veinings. Taste was his absolutely. He was, one remembers, not so good with his people, save with such oddities as sweeps and hurdy-gurdy men. Yet it was not all masonry. He knew God as well as Nash. Above his streets there were limitless skies (by them alone you may know whether your copy is coloured by his hand or a hireling's) full of light, full of real sailing clouds.

His talent was blood-brother to that of Mrs. Woolf. Always and whimsically enough, since her tale is of this day, she suggests that young virgin-spirited London of his time. Her eye, too, is clear and bright as a dewdrop, her industry immense and humble, her taste as final. She can tell how dawn comes to London. "The Bank of England emerges; and the Monument with its bristling head of golden hair; the dray-horses crossing London Bridge show grey and strawberry and iron coloured. There is a whir of wings as the suburban trains rush into the terminus. And the light mounts over the faces of all the tall blind houses, slides through a chink and paints the lustrous bellying crimson curtains; the green wineglasses; the coffee cups; and the chairs standing askew." She tells how Rotten Row looks on a sweet afternoon; how the leather curtain flaps at the door of St. Paul's; how the morning army looks pouring over Waterloo Bridge. She is less successful with her considered characters than with her odd vignettes, less successful with Jacob than Mrs. Grandage. Yet this is no brick-counting, no extension of the careful cataloguing "Nature Notes" method to the phenomena of town. It is authentic poetry, cognisant of the soul.

A Day in London Life
[*Mrs. Dalloway*]
Richard Hughes*

To the poet the visible world exists: it shines with an intense brilliance, not only to the eye but to the touch, ear, smell, inward vision. (To the man-of-the-world, the visible world is unreal: his reality is a spiritual one: the only things which exist for him are his desires, and—in a lesser degree—his beliefs.) In Mrs. Woolf's new novel, "Mrs. Dalloway," the visible world exists with a brilliance, a luminous clarity. In particular, it is London: to the reader, London is made, for the first time (this will probably surprise him) to exist. It emerges, shining like crystal, out of the fog in which all the merely material universe is ordinarily enveloped in his mind: it emerges, and stays. The present writer has "known" London all his life: but Mrs. Woolf's evocation of it is of a very different quality from his own memories: a quality which answers the farmer's question, when he was puzzled as to why folk should pay five hundred guineas for a painting of his farm, when they could have the house itself for two hundred. To Mrs. Woolf London exists, and to Mrs. Woolf's readers

*Reprinted from *Saturday Review of Literature* (16 May 1925), 755.

anywhere and at any time London will exist with a reality it can never have for those who merely live there.

Vividness alone, of course, is not art: it is only the material of art. But Mrs. Woolf has, I think, a finer sense of form than any but the oldest living English novelist. As well as the power of brilliant evocation she has that creative faculty of form which differs from what is ordinarily called construction in the same way that life differs from mechanism: the same quality as Cézanne. In the case of the painter, of course, this "form" is purely visual; the synthesis — relation — rhythm — whatever you call it, is created on this side the eye; while in the case of the poet the pattern is a mental one, created behind the eye of the reader, composed directly of mental processes, ideas, sensory evocation — not of external agents (not of the words used, I mean). So, in the case of Mrs. Woolf, and of the present novel, it is not by its vividness that her writing ultimately stays in the mind, but by the coherent and processional form which is composed of, and transcends, that vividness.

Philosophy as much as smell of violets is grist to the artist's mill: in actual practice, it is generally more so. Here, Mrs. Woolf touches all the time the verge of the problem of reality: not directly, like Pirandello, but by implication. (She is not so prone to emphasis as Pirandello.) In contrast to the solidity of her visible world there rises throughout the book in a delicate crescendo *fear*. The most notable feature of contemporary thought is the wide recognition by the human mind of its own limitation; *i.e.*, that it is itself not a microcosm (as men used to think) but the macrocosm: that it cannot "find out" anything about the universe because the terms both of question and answer are terms purely relative to itself: that even the key-words, *being* and *not-being*, bear no relation to anything except the mind which formulates them. (This is at least as old as Tao Tse, but until now has seldom been recognized by the ordinary man.) In short, that logical and associative thinking do not differ in ultimate value — or even perhaps in kind. So, in this book each of the very different characters — Clarissa Dalloway herself, the slightly more speculative Peter, the Blakeian "lunatic," Septimus Warren Smith, each with their own more or less formulated hypothesis of the meaning of life — together are an unanswerable illustration of that bottomlessness on which all spiritual values are based. This is what I mean by fear.

To come to the matter of chronicle, this novel is an account of a single day in London life; its sole principal event is the return from India of Mrs. Dalloway's rejected suitor; the other characters are in many cases not even acquainted with the principals — sometimes simply people they pass in the street, or even people who merely see the same aeroplane in the sky. Towards the end, one of these strangers flings himself from a window; and Mrs. Dalloway, after spending most of the morning wandering about Bond Street, gives a party in the evening. But then, Chronicle is an ass;

this is an unusually coherent, lucid, and enthralling book, whatever he may suggest to the contrary.

The Novel as Work of Art [*To the Lighthouse*]
Conrad Aiken*

Among contemporary writers of fiction, Mrs. Woolf is a curious and anomalous figure. In some respects, she is as "modern," as radical, as Mr. Joyce or Miss Richardson or M. Jules Romains; she is a highly self-conscious examiner of consciousness, a bold and original experimenter with the technique of novel-writing; but she is also, and just as strikingly, in other respects "old-fashioned." This anomaly does not defy analysis. The aroma of "old-fashionedness" that rises from these highly original and modern novels — from the pages of *Jacob's Room, Mrs. Dalloway*, and now again from those of *To the Lighthouse* — is a quality of attitude; a quality, to use a word which is itself nowadays old-fashioned, but none the less fragrant, of spirit. For in this regard, Mrs. Woolf is no more modern than Jane Austen: she breathes the same air of gentility, of sequestration, of tradition; of life and people and things all brought, by the slow polish of centuries of tradition and use, to a pervasive refinement in which discrimination, on every conceivable plane, has become as instinctive and easy as the beat of a wing. Her people are "gentle" people; her houses are the houses of gentlefolk; and the consciousness that informs both is a consciousness of well-being and culture, of the richness and luster and dignity of tradition; a disciplined consciousness, in which emotions and feelings find their appropriate attitudes as easily and naturally — as *habitually*, one is tempted to say — as a skilled writer finds words.

It is this tightly circumscribed choice of scene — to use "scene" in a social sense — that gives to Mrs. Woolf's novels, despite her modernity of technique and insight, their odd and delicious air of parochialism, as of some small village-world, as bright and vivid and perfect in its tininess as a miniature: a small complete world which time has somehow missed. Going into these houses, one would almost expect to find antimacassars on the chair-backs and daguerreotype albums on the tables. For these people — these Clarissa Dalloways and Mrs. Ramsays and Lily Briscoes — all are vibrantly and saturatedly conscious of background. And they all have the curious innocence that accompanies that sort of awareness. They are the creatures of seclusion, the creatures of shelter; they are exquisite

*Reprinted from Conrad Aiken, A *Reviewer's ABC: Collected Criticism of Conrad Aiken from 1816 to the Present* (Meridian Books, 1958), pp. 389–92; originally published as "The Novel as Work of Art" in *Dial*, 83 (July 1927), 41–44.

beings, so perfectly and elaborately adapted to their environment that they have taken on something of the roundness and perfection of works of art. Their life, in a sense, is a sea-pool life; unruffled and secret: almost, if we can share the cool illusion of the sea-pool's occupants, inviolable. They hear rumors of the sea itself, that vast and terrifying force that lies somewhere beyond them, or around them, but they cherish a sublime faith that it will not disturb them; and if it does, at last, break in upon them with cataclysmic force, a chaos of disorder and undisciplined violence, they can find no language for the disaster: they are simply bewildered.

But if, choosing such people and such a *mise en scène* for her material, Mrs. Woolf inevitably makes her readers think of *Pride and Prejudice* and *Mansfield Park*, she compels us just as sharply, by her method of evoking them, to think of *Pilgrimage* and *Ulysses* and *The Death of a Nobody*. Mrs. Woolf is an excellent critic, an extremely conscious and brilliant craftsman in prose; she is intensely interested in the technique of fiction; and one has at times wondered, so vividly from her prose has arisen a kind of *self-consciousness* of adroitness, whether she might not lose her way and give us a mere series of virtuosities or *tours de force*. It is easy to understand why Katherine Mansfield distrusted "Mr. Bennett and Mrs. Brown." She felt a kind of sterility in this dexterous holding of the raw stuff of life at arm's length, this playing with it as if it were a toy. Why not be more immediate — why not surrender to it? And one did indeed feel a rather baffling aloofness in this attitude: it was as if Mrs. Woolf were a little afraid to come to grips with anything so coarse, preferred to see it through a safe thickness of plate-glass. It was as if she could not be quite at ease with life until she had stilled it, reduced it to the mobile immobility of art — reduced it, even, to such comfortable proportions and orderliness as would not disturb the drawingroom. In *Jacob's Room*, however, and *Mrs. Dalloway*, Mrs. Woolf began to make it clear that this tendency to sterile dexterity, though pronounced, might not be fatal; and now, in her new novel, *To the Lighthouse*, she relieves one's doubts, on this score, almost entirely.

For, if one still feels, during the first part of this novel almost depressingly, and intermittently thereafter, Mrs. Woolf's irritating air as of carrying an enormous technical burden: her air of saying "See how easily I do this!" or "This is incomparably complex and difficult, yet I have the brains for it": nevertheless, one's irritation is soon lost in the growing sense that Mrs. Woolf has at last found a complexity and force of theme which is commensurate with the elaborateness and self-consciousness of her technical "pattern." By degrees, one forgets the manner in the matter. One resists the manner, petulantly objects to it, in vain: the moment comes when at last one ceases to be aware of something persistently artificial in this highly feminine style, and finds oneself simply immersed in the vividness and actuality of this world of Mrs. Woolf's — believing in it, in fact, with the utmost intensity, and feeling it with that completeness of surrender with which one feels the most moving of poetry. It is not easy to say whether this abdication of "distance" on the reader's part indicates that Mrs. Woolf has now achieved a depth of poetic understanding, a vitality, which was somehow just lacking in the earlier novels, or whether it merely indicates a final triumph of technique. Can one profitably try to make a distinction between work that is manufactured, bitterly and strenuously, by sheer *will* to imagination, and work that is born of imagination all complete — assuming that the former is, in the upshot, just as convincing as the latter? Certainly one feels everywhere in Mrs. Woolf's work this will to imagine, this canvassing of possibilities by a restless and searching and brilliant mind: one feels this mind at work, matching and selecting, rejecting this color and accepting that, saying, "It is this that the heroine would say, it is this that she would think"; and nevertheless Mrs. Woolf's step is so sure, her choice is so nearly invariably right, and her imagination, even if deliberately willed, is so imaginative, that in the end she makes a beautiful success of it. She makes her Mrs. Ramsay — by giving us her stream of consciousness — amazingly alive; and she supplements this just sufficiently, from *outside*, as it were, by giving us also, intermittently, the streams of consciousness of her husband, of her friend Lily Briscoe, of her children: so that we are documented, as to Mrs. Ramsey, from every quarter and arrive at a solid vision of her by a process of triangulation. The richness and copiousness and ease, with which this is done, are a delight. These people are astoundingly real: they belong to a special "class," as Mrs. Woolf's characters nearly always do, and exhale a Jane-Austenish aroma of smallness and lostness and incompleteness: but they are magnificently real. We live in that delicious house with them — we feel the minute textures of their lives with their own vivid senses — we imagine with their extraordinary imaginations, are self-conscious with their self-conscious-ness — and ultimately we know them as well, as terribly, as we know ourselves.

Thus, curiously, Mrs. Woolf has rounded the circle. Apparently, at the outset of her work, avoiding any attempt to present life "immediately," as Chekhov and Katherine Mansfield preferred to do; and choosing instead a medium more sophisticated and conscious, as if she never for a moment wished us to forget the *frame* of the picture, and the fact that the picture *was* a picture; she has finally brought this method to such perfection, or so perfectly allowed it to flower of itself, that the artificial has become natural, the mediate has become immediate. The technical brilliance glows, melts, falls away; and there remains a poetic apprehension of life of extraordinary loveliness. Nothing happens, in this houseful of odd nice people, and yet all of life happens. The tragic futility, the absurdity, the pathetic beauty, of life — we experience all of this in our sharing of seven hours of Mrs. Ramsay's wasted or not wasted existence. We have seen, through her, the world.

New Novels [A *Room*
of *One's Own*]

V. Sackville-West*

I am going to begin by talking about a book which is not a novel at all. My excuse for doing this, if excuse I must have, is a double one. In the first place, this book which is not a novel is by one of the most distinguished living novelists, and in the second place it is in some degree concerned with fiction. The book I refer to is called *A Room of One's Own*, and it is by Virginia Woolf. (Hogarth Press, 58).

Mrs. Woolf, as you probably know, is a critic as well as a novelist; but this little book, which is not a novel, is not pure criticism either. In so far as it is "about" anything at all, it is a study of women, their circumstances (especially in the past), and the effect of those circumstances upon their writing. Why did women not take to writing earlier? Why did they take to novels rather than to poetry or plays? What will they turn to in the future? Such are some of the questions which Mrs. Woolf propounds. If one is to write, she says, one must have five hundred a year and a room of one's own—but here be on your guard, for she is not a writer whom it is safe to take too literally. A room of one's own, yes; but beyond the actual, four-walled room there is the room of one's peculiar character, woman's peculiar character, which is not the same as man's character.

"One goes into the room," says Mrs. Woolf, "but the resources of the English language would be much put to the stretch, and whole flights of words would need to wing their way illegitimately into existence before a woman could say what happens when she goes into a room. The rooms differ so completely; they are calm or thunderous; open on to the sea, or, on the contrary, give on to a prison yard; are hung with washing; or alive with opals and silks; are hard as horsehair or soft as feathers—one has only to go into any room in any street for the whole of that extremely complex force of femininity to fly in one's face." And then she goes on to say, "It would be a thousand pities if women wrote like men, or lived like men, or looked like men, for if two sexes are quite inadequate, considering the vastness and variety of the world, how should we manage with the one only? Ought not education to bring out and fortify the differences rather than the similarities?"

Thus you see that the burden of Mrs. Woolf's exhortation to women is that they should be themselves, and should exploit their own peculiar gifts instead of trying to emulate the gifts proper to the masculine mind; and you will see also from these quotations that the book is not only full of ideas but also of commonsense. Mrs. Woolf has perhaps never been given sufficient credit for her commonsense. Airy, fantastic, brilliant—all these adjectives have been lavished on her, till you might think her work as

*Reprinted from *Listener*, 2 (6 Nov. 1929), 620.

coloured but as empty as an iridescent bubble; you might overlook the fact that the fluttering leaves on the tree to which I compared her just now are tethered to solid boughs which in their turn are tethered to a solid trunk; you might forget that her extravagances, if they have imagination and poetry for grandparents on the maternal side, have also sense and erudition for grandparents on the paternal. I make this allusion to the ancestry of Mrs. Woolf's creative genius all the more confidently because she herself, in this essay, indicates the need for something of the sort in reference to literature. No less a critic than Coleridge, she reminds us, said that a great mind is androgynous. She tells us a little parable of a man and a woman getting into a taxi and driving off together, and then she adds, "Certainly when I saw the couple get into the taxi-cab, the mind felt as if, after being divided, it had come together again in a natural fusion. The obvious reason would be that it is natural for the sexes to co-operate." Mrs. Woolf is too sensible to be a thorough-going feminist. There is no such thing as a masculinist, she seems to say, so why a feminist? And she goes on to wonder (amateurishly, she says) whether there are two sexes in the mind corresponding to the two sexes in the body, and whether they also require to be united in order to get complete satisfaction and happiness? I know of no writer who fulfils this condition more thoroughly than Mrs. Woolf herself. She enjoys the feminine qualities of, let us say, fantasy and irresponsibility, allied to all the masculine qualities that go with a strong, authoritative brain; and it is precisely this combination added to her profound knowledge of literature which fits her so admirably to discuss women in general, and women who write in particular. I hope all men will read this little book; it will do them good. I hope all women will read it; it will do them good, too.

[Review of *The Waves*]   Anonymous*

What kind of book does one write after "Orlando"? That was an exception and a prodigy in more ways than one. Here, in "The Waves," is something visibly in the line of Mrs. Woolf's novels, and a return to the life we live, yet so singularly unconventional in its texture and form that one might fancy "Orlando's" vivid flashes of the past were the real, and this the dream and the prodigy.

For the book is, as it were. a piece of subtle, penetrating magic. The substance of life, as we are accustomed to see it in fiction, is transposed and the form of the novel is transmuted to match it. The six characters, a band of friends — three of each sex — reveal themselves from childhood's

*Reprinted from *Times Literary Supplement*, 7 Oct. 1931, p. 773.

spring to the autumn or winter of their lives; but all they feel or do is given to us from their own lips, each taking up the one before in a kind of tranced, yet impetuous soliloquy. Each is alone with himself and yet aware of the others; in the middle and again at the end we see them reunited as a group, and finally Bernard, the man of words and contacts, gathers up the whole perspective. Such, in the barest words, is its scheme, which, fluid as it appears in the reading, has the nicest symmetry of arrangement. Its substance is not to be divided from its form; the form has been evoked by the essence — for substance seems too ponderous a word for the gleaming, darting drops of light which these lives are, as one sees them. As one of the girls says in an excited moment: —

> I see every blade of grass very clear. But the pulse drums so in my forehead, behind my eyes, that everything dances — the net, the grass; your faces leap like butterflies; the trees seem to jump up and down. There is nothing staid, nothing settled, in this universe. All is rippling, all is dancing; all is quickness and triumph.

It is a glittering rain of impressions and reactions, then, to which Mrs. Woolf has reduced the experience of her characters? Not quite, though she seldom or never eschews the medium of the five senses. Their moods and selves are shown by a gesture, an image, a perception, but these are filaments in the consciousness of each speaker. Each of them is much more conscious than we habitually are — this sharpened and dramatized consciousness is the "convention" of the novel — and utters not merely his sense of the moment, but, again and again, his secret individuality. Here, for instance, one of them enters a room: —

> I smoothed my hair when I came in, hoping to look like the rest of you. But I cannot, for I am not single and entire as you are. I have lived a thousand lives already. . . . What you see beside you, this man, this Louis, is only the cinders and refuse of something once splendid.

And here another: —

> The leaves might have hidden me still. But I did not hide behind them. I walked straight up to you instead of circling round to avoid the shock of sensation as I used. But it is only that I have taught my body to do a certain trick. Inwardly I am not taught; I fear, I hate, I love, I envy and despise you, but I never join you happily.

One might say that in Mrs. Woolf's novel life has turned into what she once described it as being — "a luminous halo, a semi-transparent envelope surrounding us from the beginning of consciousness to the end." And the novel has turned into something very like a poem. This incisive and unflagging prose is as rapid as verse, and the utterances follow one another with a sort of rhythmical incantation. Sometimes they are frankly antiphons, and one always has that sense of a response; the book moves to that measure. This formal effect recurs with the further settings which have given it its title; prefixed to each movement of it there is a background of the sea, with changes from dawn to sunset. Here, it seems to us, the effect of a complete detachment does not quite succeed. It may be because Mrs. Woolf does not keep our eyes on the sea, but diverts them to birds and fields and gardens; or it may simply be that these elaborate, often exquisite, passages are too deliberate altogether.

A poetic novel, as it certainly is, it is still—however peculiarly—a novel. The six people all have their idiosyncrasy of nature; Bernard, with his communicative, affable receptiveness; Louis, very conscious of humiliations, but with a kind of ruthless romanticism below his business efficiency; Neville, who lives with a concentrated inwardness and makes, we infer, a name; and the women—Jinny, who lives for her body and the sparkle of life; Susan, embedded in the country rhythm and motherhood; and Rhoda, a flying nymph of solitude. We watch them unfolding, and are aware of the silence under their speech, movement without action, and the flickering of that inmost flame of personality—call it spirit or ego—whose place is often vacant even in a novel of character. Mrs. Woolf's uncommon achievement is to have made this visible, and it is hardly less of a feat, perhaps, to have shown life in a texture which matches it. It seems a proof by example that the matter of fiction can be changed and distilled to a new transparency. Yet there is as certainly a cost in the process. The book, with all its imaginativeness and often poignant feeling, leaves some sense of a void behind, if not of an actual desolation. It is not merely, perhaps, that we have been deprived of the usual comfortable upholsterings but that creative experience in life is of a closer tissue than this and demands a fuller view of its attachments. Alive as the novel is with the vividness of things, one feels in more than one sense that its spirits roam through empty places. Yet it is simpler, after all, to be grateful for a book that achieves its own aim and that no one else could have written.

[Review of *The Years*]   Edwin Muir*

The title of Mrs. Woolf's new novel probably indicates what she wishes us to look for in it—that is, not so much a picture of manners as a graph of time; but if that was the problem she does not give the impression of having solved it with her usual skill. The years, we know, are indifferent to us; we grow old whether we are ambitious or lazy, married or single, good or bad. In leaving so much out of her story, in ignoring love, for instance, a striking omission in a novel containing about a score of characters, Mrs. Woolf ignores what the years ignore, and this might seem

*Reprinted from *Listener* (31 Mar. 1937), 622.

right if the years did not ignore everything: they have no story. There is certainly a change in the life of everybody which is not merely the change brought about by his own experience, by what he has felt and thought and what has been done to him by the world; a change which comes over us at moments, or at least that is how we feel it and that is the only way in which we can describe it. This feeling is very strongly conveyed in *War and Peace*, and it is conveyed mainly by Tolstoy's unique apprehension of the simultaneity of life. His picture shows us all the generations at once, childhood, youth, middle age, old age, a changeless picture modified by ceaseless change: and it is this completeness that gives us the measure and the sensation of the passing of time. It also gives time its continuity. Mrs. Woolf does not attempt continuity. She shows her characters in 1880, 1891, 1907, 1908, 1910, 1911, 1913, 1914, 1917, 1918, and at the present day. One cannot say whether in doing this she wishes to say that life is discontinuous; the recurring pattern of the story seems to indicate the opposite; but the effect, in spite of that, is one of discontinuity. Almost everything has been abstracted from these characters except the fact that at certain dates they are certain ages. To make them feel and think in accordance with their ages (they hardly act at all) required a fine and discriminating imagination. But they do not become real, they only become old. One has the feeling that Mrs. Woolf has almost left them out.

There are brilliant scenes in the story such as only Mrs. Woolf could have written, the scene, for instance, where Eleanor reads a letter from her brother Martin in India while she is driving to the Law Courts in London: Mrs. Woolf is incomparable when she is evoking a sense of simultaneity in time. But the pattern which she stretches over the story strikes one as cold and artificial, and mainly external. Sometimes it is employed with fine effect:

> "Can't one live in more places than one?" Rose asked, feeling vaguely annoyed, for she had lived in many places, felt many passions, and done many things.
> "I remember Abercorn Terrace," said Maggie. She paused. "There was a long room; and a tree at the end; and a picture over the fireplace, of a girl with red hair."

Where this comes it has the effect of poetry, perhaps because we know the long room and the tree and the picture only from Mrs. Woolf's own description of them, and when Maggie speaks of them she recreates them in another dimension. But the necessity to complete the pattern drives Mrs. Woolf on to follow Rose's thoughts past this stage:

> She saw them sitting round a table; and a detail that she had not thought of for years came back to her — how Milly used to take her hair-pin and fray the wick of the kettle. And she saw Eleanor sitting with her account books; and she saw herself go up to her and say: "Eleanor, I want to go to Lamley's."

The first passage describes a natural memory, and being a natural memory it can surprise us; but the second is a careful fragment of Mrs. Woolf's pattern, and it merely makes us wonder why, out of thousands of memories, Rose should be made to remember the particular one which was needed for that pattern: the natural surprise is gone. But we feel the pattern more persistently here than in any of Mrs. Woolf's other books. The long last chapter on the present day is by far the best; but after *The Waves* this is a disappointing book.

England Under Glass [*Between the Acts*]
Malcolm Cowley*

American travelers in England before this war often felt that they were strolling — no, were being wheeled in comfortable chairs — past the neat showcases of a museum. These trains that always ran on time were obviously toy trains, built and kept in order by some retired millionaire. These fields were covered with excelsior dyed green; no grass was ever so free from weeds. These earthen dykes that surrounded the fields — and kept them from being worked by machinery — were preserved as a relic of Saxon times; and the wild flowers that grew on the dykes were planted there by the same pious hands that had thatched the cottages and painted a soft mist over the horizon. Even the people sometimes looked like wax figures dressed in authentic costumes and labeled Mine Host or Farmer Hobbs or The Costermonger. And the general supervision of this country was by a political subcommittee of the Society for the Preservation of British Antiquities; one pictured them as kindly men who met on the steps of the British Museum with their umbrellas raised to protect them from the gentle rain. The oldest of them would say, "We must break no glass," and the next-to-oldest, "We must shatter no illusions," while even the pigeons would be cooing, "Peace in our time."

This England under glass, this England where people of breeding were sometimes not quite sure whether they were themselves or their family portraits, is the subject of Virginia Woolf's last novel (Harcourt, Brace, $2.50). The local scene is Pointz Hall, outside an English village; the time is a summer's day in 1939. The plot — well, "Between the Acts" has no plot, strictly speaking, but the action is concerned with a pageant given for the benefit of the local church. This pageant deals with the history of England from the earliest times. It is brilliantly written, and while it lasts it holds the audience together, after a fashion. When it ends, the spectators and the actors disperse to their homes, their daily papers

*Reprinted from *New Republic* (6 Oct. 1941), 440.

and their daily quarrels; for each of them, "the curtain rises." A summer day has passed and much has been revealed, but nothing has been changed.

It has often been pointed out that Mrs. Woolf's method has little to do with that of the ordinary novel. There is no conflict in her books; no sense of drama or dialectic; there is no progress through difficulties toward marriage or a deathbed. There is not even a story, in the usual sense of the word. Mrs. Woolf in her heart did not believe in stories; she thought of herself as living in a world where nothing ever happened; or at least nothing that mattered, nothing that was real. The reality was outside the world, in the human heart. And her literary method, based on this philosophy, was not to deal explicitly with a situation, but rather to present the shadows it cast in the individual consciousness. When the last shadows had moved across the screen, and when the attentive reader had caught a glimpse of something motionless behind them — "this peace, this rest, this eternity" — Mrs. Woolf had nothing more to say. Her story had ended without having begun.

This method — as I think William Troy was the first to observe — is that of lyric poetry rather than fiction. And "Between the Acts" is the most lyrical of all her books, not only in feeling but also in style. The historical pageant is written chiefly in verse; the characters in their private meditations are always breaking into verse; and even the narrative passages have an emotional intensity and a disciplined freedom in the use of words that one does not associate with prose. Moreover, Mrs. Woolf uses almost as many symbols as Yeats does in his later work. The first scene in the book is a meeting to discuss a new cesspool for the village — nobody could overlook her meaning here — and the pageant is being held to buy a new lighting system for the church. It is enacted by the villagers themselves as if to indicate the continuity of English life; Queen Elizabeth after all must have looked like Mrs. Clark the tobacconist. The village idiot wanders across the scene, playing no one but himself. In the last tableau, entitled "The Present Time — Ourselves," the characters bring mirrors on the stage and hold them up to the audience, while a voice howls from a megaphone that they are nothing but "scraps, orts and fragments."

The coming war is scarcely mentioned. Once a dozen airplanes fly overhead in military formation; twice the heroine finds herself thinking — she doesn't know why — about a newspaper story she had just read of a girl raped by soldiers. Yet the spirit of war broods over the novel, and one feels at every moment that bombs will soon be crashing through the museum cases. Factories will rise on the site of the wrecked cottages; the green lawns will be an airfield; the "scraps, orts and fragments" will be swept away.

Virginia Woolf herself would soon become a war casualty, though not in the simple manner that was suggested by the first accounts of her suicide. A phrase in the coroner's report led to an exchange of letters in The Sunday Times; a bishop's wife was superior, and Leonard Woolf wrote a frank and dignified answer. It seems that Mrs. Woolf had suffered a mental breakdown during the First World War and, after her recovery, had been haunted by the fear of relapsing into madness. This fear was especially vivid during the period of tension that always followed the completion of a novel. In other words, it was the mental strain of writing "Between the Acts" and not the physical strain of living under bombardment that caused her death. But the book itself is her comment on the war, or rather her elegy for the society the war was destroying, and so we are back at our starting point. When the bombs crashed through the glass that covered England, she was one of the people—and they were not the weaklings or the cowards—who were too finely organized for life in the wind and the rain.

Her books, too, are not written for this new age. If one rereads several of them in succession, as I did recently, one is more likely to be impressed by their narrow range of characters and emotions than by their cool wit and their warm imagination. The outside world has made itself real to us as it never was to the people in her novels. But it would be wrong to treat the judgment of our moment in time as if it were that of history. The days will come again when people have leisure to appreciate her picture of the inner world and her sense of the living past. The spirit if not the body of Georgian England survives in her novels.

ESSAYS

Virginia Woolf, and Feminine Fiction

Herbert J. Muller*

1

The novels of Virginia Woolf, supplemented by her numerous critical essays, make an excellent primer for the study of the advanced technique of modern fiction. Her early novels, *The Voyage Out* (1915) and especially *Night and Day* (1919), were more or less conventional in form; *Jacob's Room* (1922) made a bold departure that has been confirmed and extended by all her later work, and rationalized in an explicit, consistent creed. She protests in the first place against the materialism of the great Edwardians (Bennett, Galsworthy, Wells) — the sea of *things* in which their characters are drowned. But with their detail she rejects their methods and their whole conception of the art of fiction: the externalized description and analysis, the tight, symmetrical plots, the trim patterns of character — in sum the solidity and rigidity of life as they portray it. Life is not a "series of gig lamps" but a "luminous halo"; and this halo cannot be rendered by mere inventory or analysis. In "Mr. Bennett and Mrs. Brown" she admitted that enlightened contemporaries have themselves not yet created a great character, but she is confident that in time they will catch the elusive Mrs. Brown. Then will begin "one of the most important, the most illustrious, the most epoch-making" chapters in the history of the novel.

For this glorious cause Virginia Woolf has accordingly done her bit, with as great conscientiousness as modesty. She has made it her whole business to reproduce in purer form the actual sensation of living: to render immediately the essence of experience by subtle intimation and not by analysis or comment, by the evocation of atmosphere and not by formal narrative, by innumerable quick snapshots and not by set pictures of studio poses. In short, she is one of the most thoroughgoing impressionists. The Edwardians, she declares, give "a vast sense of things in general, but a very vague one of things in particular"; and life does not necessarily exist

*Reprinted from Herbert J. Muller, *Modern Fiction: A Study of Values* (New York: Funk and Wagnalls, 1937), pp. 317-28.

more fully in apparently big than in apparently small things. "Let us record the atoms as they fall upon the mind in the order in which they fall, let us trace the pattern, however disconnected and incoherent in appearance, which each sight and incident scores upon consciousness."

Hence the minimizing of plot in her novels, as in so much modern fiction. Matthew Josephson once announced that the novel is approaching the saturation point because of the limited number of "situations" available, the sameness of most story material (the statisticians of criticism have reduced the number of basic plots to a distressingly low figure); he finds the chief significance of Mrs. Woolf, Joyce, and others in that they are confronting the problem of "how to write a novel without telling a story." This is a new version of a complaint as old as Horace. But Josephson not only overlooks the endless possibilities of variation and combination; he forgets that the same objection might be made to life itself — yet people go on living, and apparently find life on the whole as strange and exciting as ever. The invincible popularity of the risqué anecdote is in itself enough to make nonsense of the notion that we have grown weary of familiar situations. The real reasons for the contemporary's exaggerated distrust of "story," his sophisticated contempt for "mere story-tellers," are rather those implied by Virginia Woolf: an interest in states of mind more than in actions, an impression of enormous complexity impossible to fit into simple molds, above all a feeling that neither the deeper truths nor the actual *feel* of life can be adequately rendered by tidy narratives with a definite beginning, middle, and end. It is an insistence, once more, that life itself does not narrate. Plot has gone the way of the other trappings of conventional realism, and for similar reasons; all have come to be regarded as superficial, artificial, or *unreal.*

This central intention explains all the striking characteristics of Mrs. Woolf's methods: the myriad sensory impressions, the stream of consciousness, the deliberate discontinuity and the liberties with chronology, what Professor Beach calls the composite picture or Gide the "breadthwise cutting" of the slice of life; and all have many parallels in modern fiction. She is especially indebted to James Joyce, most obviously in her use of the interior monologue. She differs from Joyce in that she filters and canalizes the stream of consciousness, selecting, distilling, and then projecting by a very personal style a blend of sensations and conscious and subconscious thoughts that gives a vivid illusion of mental experience without being a literal picture of it; but like him she is interested in the endless flux of consciousness, and presents the outside world only as refracted through it. She remains almost entirely within the minds of her characters. In *The Waves*, indeed, she never gets out.

All this is best illustrated in *Mrs. Dalloway*, the most successful of her novels. Like *Ulysses*, it is the record of a single day, a day in London; and like Joyce, Virginia Woolf introduces unconnected characters and incidents, and develops a number of themes whose relation is primarily symphonic. She gives as vivid an impression of a dense cross-section, and a distinctly more vivid impression of the flow of time, the passing of a day. Many readers have admired the subtle, continuous interpenetration of consciousness and background — London at every moment suffusing the minds of her characters until it becomes a living presence. In a sense Clarissa Dalloway presides over this scene. She is on the forefront of the stage most of the time, thinking about her old lover and the party she is to give. Her relations with Peter establish a kind of dramatic conflict, her party finally winds up the day. Yet there is no real dénouement, no real plot, for nothing is resolved. These more prominent characters provide a focus and a point of view, but they are not Mrs. Woolf's whole interest. Nor does she, like Joyce, introduce purely artificial devices to unify her scattered material. She apparently has more confidence in the legitimacy of her intention and is free from his uneasy feeling that without such devices he could not convey a whole and single impression. She is content to give the full sensation of living during her day; and without all his organs, her novel is more clearly organic and has a more distinct configuration. She succeeds in establishing a subtle kind of unity and completeness that satisfies all readers but those who must have a full stop to their symphony, a resounding chord that leaves no doubt as to the propriety of clapping and reaching for their hats.

2

As I am not an ardent admirer of the work of Virginia Woolf, simple justice demands a prefatory tribute to her many admirable qualities. Almost all readers are impressed by her exquisite artistry. It is revealed immediately in a prose style that has few equals in modern fiction. Always delicate, supple, shimmering, cadenced, it is at once lovely in itself and splendidly expressive. Inevitably one speaks of "nuances," the precision with which she renders the elusive shades of thought and feeling, sight and sound. With so fine an instrument at her command, Mrs. Woolf hence achieves brilliantly the end she set for herself: the imaginative re-creation rather than the formal dissection of human experience.

By her highly selective art, moreover, she manages to skirt the more obvious dangers implicit in her methods and materials. She gains all the intimacy and immediacy of the mental soliloquy at the minimum cost of triviality, incoherence, irrelevance, or mere messiness. Above all, she does not explore consciousness and record sensation for its own sake. If she presents no dramatic struggle, she always refers the sensations of her leading characters to fundamental problems of conduct: the joy and the sorrow, the mystery of the meaning of life with which they are all intensely preoccupied.

Finally, one should be grateful for the mellowness of Mrs. Woolf — a mellowness, unlike that of some of her British contemporaries, neither self-conscious nor premature. She is one of the few important literary personalities of this age that seem in no way maimed or poisoned by it. Her art is no sublimation of her private woes or compensation for her private frustration; it offers no excuse to call in the psychoanalyst lurking around the corner. Although contemporary novelists are less prone to a cold hate of their characters than they are reputed to be, none remains on more affable terms with his characters while yet keeping so clear of them. She has all the easy familiarity of the great Victorians without their habit of taking liberties with it. In short, her fiction like her criticism consistently displays a spirit serene, tolerant, humane, civilized.

So much, at least, must be granted Virginia Woolf. She is on one of the forefronts of modern fiction; she is one of the most distinguished of living women writers. Yet this very eminence sharpens a somewhat embarrassing issue. What finally impresses me in her fiction is its insubstantiality. This exquisite art somehow runs thin, this "luminous halo" somehow grows wraithlike. Her novels have nothing of the elemental force of Dostoyevsky, Hardy, or Dreiser; among their own impressionistic kind they have little of the intensity and glow of Conrad, Proust, or Lawrence. Behind all their subtlety and vividness is no real passion or energy. With her unfailing acuteness Mrs. Woolf has stated exactly the limitations of the art of Arnold Bennett; Bennett was himself as just when he remarked, with masculine bluntness, that her novels "seriously lack vitality."

This deficiency is in part the price of her method and creed. To "record the atoms as they fall," to "trace the pattern . . . which each sight and incident scores upon consciousness," is inevitably to give disproportionate emphasis to separate moments, and hence likely to leave an effect of inconsequence. Mrs. Woolf flits about her subject, throws a flashing light from many angles, darts in to capture bright bits of truth; but by the very nature of this method she never comes to grips with a situation. She does not confront steadily a deep emotion or really plunge into it. A brilliant butterfly, swift in flight, she settles unerringly on the choicest flowers and extracts their choicest essence; but she never gets to the roots. Hence even the lovely style—dipping, sparkling, rippling, at any given moment a marvel of expressiveness—ultimately palls. The constant flutter and glimmer becomes monotonous; at the end it suggests preciosity or mere fussiness.

Similarly Mrs. Woolf pays the penalty of her too constant immersion in the inner life—which is not the whole of life. In reacting against the excesses of laborious documentation, she has contracted a kind of horror of externals—which are after all *real*. Too often we are straining our eyes at a mist. In actual experience, the halo that is her constant concern surrounds a solid, earthy substance; but of this substance she gives us only fleeting, sidelong glimpses. Hence, as Elizabeth Drew remarks, "we feel rather as if we were trying to construct the plot of a Greek play from nothing but the remarks of the chorus." Fragile and anemic to begin with, her characters come finally to seem disembodied spirits—wispy, evanescent, despite their spiritual essence perishable. One has only to set the fragile Clarissa Dalloway beside Mrs. Morel of *Sons and Lovers* to perceive the difference between characterization that is subtle and sharp and characterization that is also solid. And this refining away of the solid substance of character becomes even more fastidious in the later novels of Mrs. Woolf. *Mrs. Dalloway* is set against the living background of London; in *The Waves* the outside world fades into a backdrop, leaving six minds quivering in a sensitized vacuum, six characters in search of an author: an author to give them flesh, blood, dress, a home, a world—anything to clothe their precious spirits.

What sucks the blood out of Virginia Woolf's novels is not entirely, however, this ultra-refined technique. Even her early, more conventional novels, written before she had arrived in this rarefied realm where material circumstance is a kind of vulgar illusion, are wanting in vitality. They are less memorable, in fact, than her later novels, and plainly suggest that her later manner is more natural and becoming to her. And so one must look into her temperament, her whole equipment as a novelist, to discover the final explanation of her limitations.

In reviewing *To the Lighthouse*, Conrad Aiken paid a poet's tribute to the old-fashioned fragrance of Mrs. Woolf's spirit, the odor of old lavender that comes off her work despite the ultramodernity of her technique and her insight. Her characters are all gentle folk framed in a beautiful little picture in a cloistered gallery; and this tightly circumscribed scene is what gives her novels "their odd and delicious air of parochialism, as of some small village-world, as bright and vivid and perfect in its tininess as a miniature: a complete world which time has somehow missed." Here is the charm of her work—and it is much the charm of Mrs. Gaskell's *Cranford*. Here is also the reason why it is little more than charming. As creatures of shelter, her characters are too delicate to participate in a really big or intense drama. They never have to worry about vulgar necessity or the intrusion of rude, elemental emotion. They hear only as off-stage rumbles and rumors the great, terrifying, destructive forces of the outside world— as Clarissa Dalloway experiences the World War, a very horrid thing for a lady to have to think about. "I am all fiber. All tremors shake me," declares one of the six soliloquists of *The Waves*. "I dance. I ripple. I am thrown over you like a net of light," says another. "Now," exclaims less fortunate phantom No. 3, "I will wrap my agony inside my pocket-handkerchief." This is an almost complete summary of the perfected art of Virginia Woolf. These are indeed children speaking, but when they are grown up as ladies and gentlemen their accents are as highly mannered, their responses as tremulous, their feelings as refined. None has an emotion that cannot be wrapped up in a pocket-handkerchief.

This is not to say that Mrs. Woolf is herself tender-minded and merely genteel—she clearly sees through her Mrs. Dalloway. Neither is it to deny her the right to her materials — the world is infested with Mrs. Dalloways. Yet one may fairly comment that out of such material at most only minor classics can be woven. In the world she has chosen to create, neither robust comedy nor deeply moving tragedy is possible. And what clearly defines her limitations is that this is apparently the only kind of world she is able to create. In *Mrs. Dalloway*, to be sure, she introduces one Septimus Smith, a shell-shocked veteran, to supplement the narrowness of Clarissa's range of experience. His madness and suicide would appear to symbolize the brutal realities of the outside world, set Clarissa's party in its right perspective, provide the complement necessary for a whole picture of London. But even this madness has been toned down, purged of all terrifying elements. It is a very gentle, tender, wistful madness, nothing like that represented by Shakespeare and Dostoyevsky. It is merely touching, at worst disturbing. It is indeed almost pretty.

To this extent at least Mrs. Woolf shares the frailty of her characters: like them she never surrenders herself to life. She is seemingly as afraid to pull out all the stops and let go. The penalty of her culture and refinement is a too highly self-conscious art, an almost fearful aloofness, in Aiken's words a "dexterous holding of the raw stuff of life at arm's length." Conrad was equally concerned with the "semi-transparent envelope" about human experience, but he strove to penetrate it, sink his teeth in the solid emotional experience from which it emanates; she gives us simply the envelope. She shies away from any experience so uncouth that it cannot be reduced to the tidy proportions of her drawing-room world, so powerful that it might break through the gossamer web of her art. It is, once more, a brilliantly woven web; but it is too finespun to contain any big emotion, any violent conflict, any profound or tumultuous experience.

3

In *A Room of One's Own* Virginia Woolf wrote a notable preamble to a kind of feminine Declaration of Independence. She asked that women writers be granted the same freedom as men, the same right to follow their calling in retirement without being asked to perform more mundane duties. Although her very well-mannered plea scarcely created a furor, it was still a challenge; and no doubt it helped to secure a privilege already more generally taken for granted. Mrs. Woolf now has a room of her own. But what does she do in it? She sits and embroiders. She does water colors in pastel shades. She plays minor chords with the soft pedal down. In short, her room might as well be the drawing-room of a parsonage, and she serving tea to the ladies of the parish. Essentially, she writes like that busy housewife, mother, and soft-eyed model of Victorian womanhood, Mrs. Elizabeth Cleghorn Gaskell.

Now, this is a quite legitimate occupation, today as before. I would not join the rude pack howling outside her window and demand of Mrs.

Woolf that she go out and rub elbows with the workers, give us a strike with bloody riots, hail the coming Revolution. Yet one wonders at the persistence of this fragile femininity. One wonders why so many other women novelists in rooms of their own write in the same key, and why their works are greeted so rapturously by other emancipated women critics. One is finally tempted to generalize the contribution of women to modern fiction, to group them in a single chapter as the Society of the Daughters of Henry James.

The first of the nine volumes of Dorothy Richardson's *Pilgrimage*, a continuous record of the atoms that fell upon the consciousness of one Miriam Henderson, was greeted with some enthusiasm; the discontinuance of this record saddened few readers—was in fact scarcely noticed. At first attracted by the novelty of the method—a mere association of sensation and ideas without dramatic issue and social or philosophical theme—most readers had all they wanted of Miriam and her sensitive impressions long before the ninth volume. In *The House of Mirth* Edith Wharton made what in its day (1905) seemed a daringly realistic study of high society, and in *Ethan Frome* she wrote a poignant, if too perfectly chiseled and "artistic," tragedy of New England life; but the bulk of her work concerns the doings of pallid gentlefolk and soon acquires the mustiness that has already sent *The House of Mirth* to the attic. In her early work, especially *My Antonia*, Willa Cather wrote simply, robustly, almost grandly the epic of the Mid-Western pioneers; she has since withdrawn into a kind of nunnery to give herself up to wistful reminiscence, and now employs her beautiful prose in the embroidery of such wispy stuff as *Shadows on the Rock* and *Lucy Gayheart*. Ellen Glasgow has still a vein of iron and irony; but the author of the starkly realistic *Barren Ground* recently gave way to a rather petulant outburst against the school of novelists that has been portraying the cruder, harsher realities of Southern life, and now seems more at home among the refined emotions of the decayed gentility in *The Sheltered Life*. Similarly one could tick off the names and generalize the achievements of Anne Sedgwick, Rosamond Lehmann, Dorothy Canfield Fisher, and innumerable lesser practitioners of this delicate art. At their worst they seem simply remote, hovering fussily over the fringes of modern life. At their best they have a rare sensitiveness, they write beautifully, they render with a nice precision the subtle gradations of perception and sensation—but in this delicious banquet the mere man still yearns for a little red beef and port wine.

There are, of course, many significant exceptions to this generalization. In an earlier age, George Eliot's work has a quality that men are pleased to call masculine; *Wuthering Heights* seethes with an unladylike passion. Among contemporaries, Sigrid Undset writes in a major key; Pearl Buck's *The Good Earth* has a simple strength, as do the novels of Henry Handel Richardson; Evelyn Scott is, if not first-rate, at least not fluttery; and a number have caught fire from the class war. Yet most of the more conspicuous women novelists are like Virginia Woolf still specialists in the wistful, fragile, filmy, dainty. They are Mrs. Gaskells in modern dress. Even the sophisticates, like Tess Slesinger in *The Unpossessed*, do not penetrate to the roots of the dilemma of the disenchanted, and they display in their cynicism a quality that a Victorian would instantly recognize as feminine.

The simplest explanation of this quality is that women have for centuries been insulated against the larger, more abstract problems, conditioned to a more direct dependence upon their immediate human environment; and ingrained attitudes cannot be changed overnight by new fashions or even by new legislation. Probably, too, women are biologically adapted to different modes of experience. In his fascinating studies of child psychology, Jean Piaget observed that little girls have no single game with as many rules as the little boys themselves have elaborated for marbles, no game with "as fine and consistent an organization and codification." Their ingenuity in hopscotch, for example, is displayed chiefly in the invention of new figures; rules they revise freely, having less regard for their authority and less interest in general concepts. At any rate the fact as we now have it is that women writers concern themselves primarily with the more concrete and intimate problems of human relationships, less with large issues or ultimate meanings. As Elizabeth Drew remarks, it is difficult to imagine a woman writing a novel like *Lord Jim*, *The Brothers Karamazov*, or *Arrowsmith*, based on the hero's necessity of harmonizing his soul with some ideal concept apart from the practical problems of everyday living. And as Edwin Muir admits after a eulogy of Virginia Woolf, "The one important quality of the critic which she lacks is the power of wide and illuminating generalization." In short, the explanation of their work in the novel is also the explanation of why there are women columnists but few philosophers, of why there are women singers and musicians but few composers, of why—though for centuries, they have been trained to paint—there are few great women painters. They reproduce with consummate sensitiveness; they seldom create on a large scale or in the light of a large ideal concept.

I repeat—and not out of chivalry—that all this by no means justifies a contemptuous attitude toward the women novelists. Their province is a legitimate one in the midst of whatever crises or revolutions; and if it is difficult, in the face of *Remembrance of Things Past* or *Death in Venice*, to continue romantically to attribute to them a delicacy and sensitiveness beyond the experience of men, it is foolish to scorn the charm of their work or deny its validity within their range. If they seldom produce more than minor classics, only the portentously solemn reader would spend all his time among masterpieces. Moreover, they have generally a sureness and directness, a balance and poise, that are restful in a restless age. If at times they settle into a superficial and depressing "soundness"—as in the Maine school recently becoming popular—at best they have the sanity that comes from a clear perception of the simple realities and simple values of ordinary existence. Precisely because they are chiefly concerned with immediate realities, the women writers are less likely to be distracted or thwarted by the profound uncertainties of this era. Yet for this same reason they are less significant for the purposes of this study. The deeper issues of modern literature and life have no doubt given to many men a sickly and oppressive self-consciousness; but they are nevertheless urgent, they must somehow be met. Virginia Woolf and her sisters contribute little but their incidental refinements of method and manner.

Characters and Human Beings   Joan Bennett*

Mr. E. M. Forster[1] writes of Virginia Woolf

> she could seldom so portray a character that it was remembered afterwards on its own account, as Emma is remembered, for instance, or Dorothea Casaubon, or Sophia and Constance in *The Old Wives' Tale*.

Nor is Mr. Forster alone in feeling that Virginia Woolf's mature novels fail to provide a gallery of memorable portraits, such as can be derived from the works of other great novelists. However that may be, it is certain that she developed a different method of characterization from theirs, and one that produces a different effect. In her first two books some, but not all, of the characters are first introduced in the traditional way. Mr. Hilbery, who plays a minor role in *Night and Day*, is sketched for the reader at his first appearance:

> He was an elderly man, with a pair of oval, hazel eyes which were rather bright for his time of life, and relieved the heaviness of his face. He played constantly with a little green stone attached to his watch chain, thus displaying long and very sensitive fingers, and had a habit of moving his head hither and thither very quickly without altering the position of his large and rather corpulent body, so that he seemed to be providing himself incessantly with food for amusement and reflection with the least possible expenditure of energy. One might suppose that he had passed the time of life when his ambitions were personal, or that he had gratified them as far as he was likely to do, and now employed his considerable acuteness rather to observe and reflect than to attain any result.
>
> [*Night and Day*]

The fault here is a slight overloading with detail, and the physical traits are made to carry an undue burden of psychological significance, a

*Reprinted from Joan Bennett, *Virginia Woolf: Her Art as a Novelist* (Cambridge: Cambridge Univ. Press, 1964), pp. 19–41. Originally published 1945.

common fault with this type of presentation. The essential characteristics of an outline portrait are there, the key to the character is given, Mr. Hilbery is an individual not merely a type, his main characteristics are easily remembered and can be developed and confirmed by his subsequent behaviour, thus giving the reader the self-gratulatory feeling of having understood him from the first. Mary Datchet, a more important character in the book, the complement of the more elusive heroine, Katharine Hilbery, is introduced by the same method:

> She was some twenty-five years of age, but looked older because she earned, or intended to earn, her own living, and had already lost the look of the irresponsible spectator and taken on that of the private in the army of workers. Her gestures seemed to have a certain purpose; the muscles round eyes and lips were set rather firmly, as though the senses had undergone some discipline, and were held ready for a call upon them. She had contracted two faint lines between her eyebrows, not from anxiety but from thought, and it was quite evident that all the feminine instincts of pleasing, soothing and charming were crossed by others in no way peculiar to her sex. For the rest she was brown-eyed, a little clumsy in movement, and suggested country-birth and a descent from hard-working ancestors, who had been men of faith and integrity rather than doubters or fanatics.
>
> [*Night and Day*]

But the presentation of Rachel, in *The Voyage Out*, and of Katharine Hilbery, in *Night and Day*, is of a different kind; the reader discovers them gradually, and incompletely, in part from their own speech and reflections, in part from their effect upon other people. They are more elusive than Mr. Hilbery or Mary Datchet, just as, in real life, the people we know intimately are more elusive than our acquaintance — we are aware that there is always something more to be discovered. The first picture we have of Rachel is a picture in the mind of Helen Ambrose:

> Helen looked at her. Her face was weak rather than decided, saved from insipidity by the large enquiring eyes; denied beauty, now that she was sheltered indoors, by the lack of colour and definite outline. Moreover, a hesitation in speaking, or rather a tendency to use the wrong words, made her seem more than normally incompetent for her years. Mrs. Ambrose, who had been speaking much at random, now reflected that she certainly did not look forward to the intimacy of three or four weeks on board ship which was threatened. Women of her own age usually boring her, she supposed that girls would be worse. She glanced at Rachel again. Yes! how clear it was that she would be vacillating, emotional, and when you said something to her it would make no more lasting impression than the stroke of a stick upon water. There was nothing to take hold of in girls — nothing hard, permanent, satisfactory.
>
> [*The Voyage Out*]

But the book, instead of developing and confirming this impression, contradicts it at many points; Helen has not taken the place of an omniscient narrator and given the reader a clue to Rachel's character; she has revealed a little of herself and of the first impression Rachel makes on a critical observer, but no more. Katharine in *Night and Day* is introduced as Denham first sees her, and there also we are not given the illusion that the picture is complete, nor even necessarily correct. Even in these first two books the people who most interest the reader cannot be summed up. When Mary Datchet attempts to find a label for Katharine, the reader is left in no doubt of its inadequacy:

> Mary felt herself baffled, and put back again into the position in which she had been at the beginning of their talk. It seemed to her that Katharine possessed a curious power of drawing near and receding, which sent alternate emotions through her far more quickly than was usual, and kept her in a condition of curious alertness. Desiring to classify her, Mary bethought her of the convenient term "egoist."
>
> "She's an egoist," she said to herself and stored that word up to give to Ralph one day when, as it would certainly fall out, they were discussing Miss Hilbery.
>
> *[Night and Day]*

The irrelevance of the classifying word is obvious both in its immediate context and in relation to the rest of our knowledge of Katharine. The word "egoist" tells us little about Katharine, but it expresses a need of Mary's, the need to define her and so be able to control her own reactions to Katharine's dynamic personality. She can only do this by holding her at a distance and so getting her as it were into focus. Virginia Woolf came to believe that all definition of character involved such a refusal to come near and that *character* in the sense in which the word is used of persons in fiction or, as often as not in biography, does not exist in real life. It is possible that the impression that she does not create clear or memorable characters is due to the fact that her portraits are of a different kind from those to which the reader of fiction is accustomed. The experience of reading fiction is analogous to the experience of looking at a painting. The painter's vision of his subject, his selection, placing and apportioning of objects or his interpretation of colour relations, are not only delightful in themselves, they also invite the beholder to see similar objects in nature in a new way, incorporating as much of the artist's vision as he has been able to assimilate. When a painter sees very differently from his predecessors, he will depart from the established conventions and, in all probability, he will paint in such a way that the majority of his public will at first be unable to discern any relation between his canvas and their own vision of the object in nature. Virginia Woolf's account of the first reception by the London public of the post-impressionist painters supplies an historical instance:

It is difficult in 1939, when a great hospital is benefiting from a centenary exhibition of Cézanne's works, and the gallery is daily crowded with devout and submissive worshippers, to realize what violent emotions those pictures excited less than thirty years ago. The pictures are the same; it is the public that has changed. But there can be no doubt about the fact. The public in 1910 was thrown into paroxysms of rage and laughter. They went from Cézanne to Gauguin and from Gauguin to Van Gogh, they went from Picasso to Signac, and from Derain to Friesz, and they were infuriated. The pictures were a joke, and a joke at their expense. One great lady asked to have her name removed from the Committee. One gentleman, according to Desmond MacCarthy, laughed so loud at Cézanne's portrait of his wife that "he had to be taken out and walked up and down in the fresh air for five minutes. Fine ladies went into silvery trills of laughter." The secretary had to provide a book in which the public wrote down their complaints. Never less than four hundred people visited the gallery daily. And they expressed their opinions not only to the secretary but in letters to the director himself. The pictures were outrageous, anarchistic, and childish. They were an insult to the British public and the man who was responsible for the insult was either a fool, an imposter or a knave.

[*Roger Fry: A Biography*]

Gradually, however, a new school of painting, if it arises out of a genuine visual perception, extends the vision of the beholders and ceases to seem odd. Nature may even be thought to have been faithfully represented for the first time by the new school. This conclusion is as false as the original rejection, since "the mind is not a mirror in which the world is reflected." A great number of patterns can, with equal fidelity, be elicited from the multiple impressions offered to the eye by a single scene or one human face. Thus it is also with the serious novelist:

since he is a single person with one sensibility the aspects of life in which he can believe with conviction are strictly limited.

[*The Common Reader: First Series*]

After 1919 the aspects of life in which Virginia Woolf could "believe with conviction" ceased to include the clearly definable human character. The people in her later books frequently express her own unwillingness to circumscribe human beings within the compass of a *character*. Mrs. Dalloway, for instance:

She would not say of anyone in the world now that they were this or that.

[*Mrs. Dalloway*]

Or Mrs. Ramsay, reflecting on the nature of the self:

. . . one after another, she, Lily, Augustus Carmichael, must feel, our apparitions, the things you know us by, are simply childish. Beneath it is all dark, it is all spreading, it is unfathomably deep; but now and again we rise to the surface and that is what you see us by.

[*To the Lighthouse*]

Or Bernard:

> We are not simple as our friends would have us to meet their needs. Yet love is simple.
>
> [*The Waves*]

Or Eleanor:

> These little snapshot pictures of people left much to be desired, these little surface pictures that one made, like a fly crawling over a face, and feeling, here's the nose, here's the brow.
>
> [*The Years*]

Or Peggy Pargiter:

> I'm good, she thought, at fact collecting. But what makes up a person — (she hollowed her hand), the circumference — no, I'm not good at that.
>
> [*The Years*]

When Virginia Woolf became fully conscious that the traditional method of characterization could not interpret her own vision of human beings, she sought for other means of communicating it. *Jacob's Room* is the first of her novels which wholly rejects the old method; but in it her new technique is not yet used with the ease and assurance she was later to acquire. Jacob Flanders is never directly described, and he rarely reveals himself to the reader by what he says or does. Instead we derive our impression of him from the effect he produces on other people in the novel, for instance, upon Mrs. Norman who travels in a train to Cambridge with him:

> Nobody sees anyone as he is, let alone an elderly lady sitting opposite a strange young man in a railway carriage. They see a whole — they see all sorts of things — they see themselves. . . . Mrs. Norman now read three pages of one of Mr. Norris's novels. Should she say to the young man (and after all he was just the same age as her own boy): "If you want to smoke, don't mind me?" No: he seemed absolutely indifferent to her presence . . . she did not wish to interrupt.
>
> But since, even at her age, she noted his indifference, presumably he was in some way or other — to her at least — nice, handsome, interesting, distinguished, well built, like her own boy? One must do the best one can with her report. Anyhow, this was Jacob Flanders, aged nineteen. It is no use trying to sum people up. One must follow hints, not exactly what is said, not yet entirely what is done. . . .
>
> [*Jacob's Room*]

This, relatively to the later novels, is a crude piece of work. It betrays uneasiness. The writer obtrudes herself in a way in which she will not do in her more mature books; by doing so she disturbs the illusion. But the foundation of the new technique is laid. The impact of one personality upon another continues in all her books to be an important means of composing the portrait of a human being. Throughout *Jacob's Room* we observe Jacob through the eyes of others:

> "I like Jacob Flanders," wrote Clara Durrant in her diary. "He is so unworldly. He gives himself no airs, and one can say what one likes to him, though he's frightening because. . . ." But Mr. Letts allows little space in his shilling diaries. Clara was not the one to encroach upon Wednesday. Humblest, most candid of women! "No, no, no," she sighed, standing at the green-house door, "don't break — don't spoil" — what? Something infinitely wonderful.
>
> But then, this is only a young woman's language, one, too, who loves, or refrains from loving. She wished the moment to continue for ever precisely as it was that July morning. And moments don't.

Then we are given a glimpse of what Jacob is actually doing at that moment and, to offset Clara's romantic impression, he is exchanging stories and rather coarse jokes with his male friends at an inn. There follows a series of reflections of Jacob in the minds of other people, including his mother:

> Betty Flanders was romantic about Archer and tender about John; she was unreasonably irritated by Jacob's clumsiness in the house.
>
> Captain Barfoot liked him best of the boys; but as for saying why. . . . It seems then that men and women are equally at fault. It seems that a profound, impartial, and absolutely just opinion of our fellow-creatures is utterly unknown. Either we are men, or we are women. Either we are cold, or we are sentimental. Either we are young, or growing old. In any case we are but a procession of shadows, and God knows why it is that we embrace them so eagerly, and see them depart with such anguish, being shadows. And why, if this and much more is true, why are we yet surprised in the window corner by a sudden vision that the young man in the chair is of all things in the world the most real, the most solid, the best known to us — why indeed? For the moment after we know nothing about him.
>
> Such is the manner of our seeing. Such the conditions of our love.
>
> [*Jacob's Room*]

From the conviction here expressed about the incompleteness of our knowledge of one another; and from the certainty here communicated that our fellow-beings do nevertheless arouse in us profound and valued feelings, springs Virginia Woolf's individual art of creating human beings. The method is cumulative, and it is therefore impossible to isolate from her books a portrait which epitomizes a particular character, either by means of description or dramatization. Nevertheless, it seems to me false to suggest, as Mr. Forster does, that the beings she creates are less memorable than the persons in other great works of fiction. Mrs. Ramsay, Mrs. Dalloway, Eleanor Pargiter, each of the main personalities in *Between the Acts*, and many others from her books, inhabit the mind of the reader and enlarge the capacity for imaginative sympathy. It is sympathy rather than judgment that she invokes, her personages are apprehended rather than comprehended. Increasingly the writer eliminates herself from her books, the illusion of the all-seeing eye is replaced by the illusion that we are seeing by glimpses, with our own imperfect vision. Far more, however, is set before our eyes in the books than in normal experience. Not only are we given the impression made upon other minds, but also the impressions received and formulated by the divers persons whose lives are interwoven for us and from the pattern of the book.

In creative power Virginia Woolf can bear comparison with the great masters of prose fiction. Despite the difficulty of isolating a detail from the whole picture it is worth while to make the attempt. Even if injustice is done to the modern writer by this method it will at least serve to illustrate the difference in kind between hers and the traditional draughtsmanship. In full consciousness of the risk run, I am prepared to juxtapose a passage from *Emma*, which I believe to be Jane Austen's masterpiece, a passage moreover of consummate art, and a passage from *To the Lighthouse.*

When Emma first becomes acquainted with Harriet, Jane Austen presents the situation in such a way as to give the reader a clear insight into Emma's character. And with her customary precision and what Virginia Woolf calls her "impeccable sense of human values," she guides the reader's judgment.

> Harriet Smith's intimacy at Hartfield was soon a settled thing. Quick and decided in her ways, Emma lost no time in inviting, encouraging, and telling her to come very often; and as their acquaintance increased, so did their satisfaction in each other. As a walking companion, Emma had very early foreseen how useful she might find her. . . . She had ventured alone once to Randalls, but it was not pleasant; and a Harriet Smith, therefore, one whom she could summon at any time to a walk, would be a valuable addition to her privileges. But in every respect as she saw more of her, she approved her, and was confirmed in all her kind designs.
>
> Harriet certainly was not clever, but she had a sweet, docile, grateful disposition, was totally free from conceit, and only desiring to be guided by anyone she looked up to. Her early attachment to herself was very amiable; and her inclination for good company, and power of appreciating what was elegant and clever, showed that there was no want of taste, though strength of understanding must not be expected. Altogether she was quite convinced of Harriet Smith's being exactly the young friend she wanted — exactly the something which her home required.

The first sentence of this passage merely states certain facts; but the second sentence dissects Emma's motives with surgical precision and with subtle artistry.

". . . Emma had very early foreseen how *useful . . . a* Harriet Smith"; by the turn of a phrase, the choice of an indefinite article, Jane Austen guides the reader's judgment and prepares the way for the ironic close of the paragraph: "confirmed in all her kind designs." The opening of the second paragraph can be read as statement of fact by the omniscient narrator; but it is principally an account of Emma's impression of Harriet, "not clever . . . sweet, docile, grateful . . . desiring to be guided. . . ." It is Emma, not Jane Austen, who finds Harriet's easily won affection "amiable," and Emma who thinks of herself as "good company . . . elegant, clever." In the last sentence the effect of the whole paragraph is summed up, and the obtuse egotism with which Emma has chosen a friend is wholly in the reader's grasp for his enjoyment, amusement and judgment, — "exactly the something which her home required."

In the following passage from Virginia Woolf's *To the Lighthouse*, as in the passage from *Emma*, two persons are presented, Mr. Tansley and Lily Briscoe. Mr. Tansley is a young man researching in a philosophical subject, a disciple of Mr. Ramsay, introduced by him into the house party which includes, besides the Ramsay family, several of their intimates. Tansley is comparatively a stranger among them. Lily is a painter and is preoccupied with the painting at which she has been working during the day. The visit to the Lighthouse mentioned in the passage refers back to a proposed expedition on the morrow, which is of considerable importance in the book. The scene is a dinner party and Lily is sitting opposite Mr. Tansley.

> Mr. Tansley was really, Lily Briscoe thought, in spite of his eyes, but then look at his nose, look at his hands, the most uncharming human being she had ever met. Then why did she mind what he said? Women can't write, women can't paint — what did it matter, coming from him, since clearly it was not true to him but for some reason helpful to him, and that was why he said it? Why did her whole being bow, like corn under a wind, and erect itself again from this abasement only with a great and rather painful effort? She must make it once more. There's the sprig on the tablecloth; there's my painting; I must move the tree to the middle; that matters — nothing else. Could she not hold fast to that, she asked herself, and not lose her temper, and not argue; and if she wanted a little revenge take it by laughing at him.
>
> "Oh, Mrs. Tansley," she said, "do take me to the Lighthouse with you. I should so love it."
>
> She was telling lies he could see. She was saying what she did not mean to annoy him, for some reason. She was laughing at him. He was in his old flannel trousers. He had no others. He felt very rough and isolated and lonely. He knew that she was trying to tease him for some reason; she didn't want to go to the Lighthouse with him; she despised him: so did Prue Ramsay; so did they all. But he was not going to be made a fool of by women, so he turned deliberately in his chair and looked out of the window and said, all in a jerk, very rudely, it would be too rough for her tomorrow. She would be sick.
>
> [*To the Lighthouse*]

The most obvious difference between this passage and the one from *Emma* is that the writer seems to have vanished, we are no longer aware of a mind directing our judgment. Certainly we discern an overassertive ego, both in Mr. Tansley and in Lily; but equally certainly we do not judge them. The spirit of comedy pervades this scene as it does the other; but it is not here satiric comedy. In the passage from *Emma* we were given certain indications of what went on in Emma's mind; but it was unmistakably Jane Austen who selected them and governed our response to them. In the passage from *To the Lighthouse* we attend exclusively to the thoughts and the words of Lily and Mr. Tansley. But there is a further and perhaps more significant difference between the two passages. The extract from Jane Austen is curiously complete in itself. It almost seems as though the book could be reconstructed from these paragraphs. Emma's attitude to Harriet at this point in the story epitomizes the error of judgment and the flaw in her character from which all the complications in the story and the whole development of the character arise. The attentive reader has, in this single passage, a key to the whole situation. The passage is centripetal. The passage from Virginia Woolf is centrifugal. Everything in it implies or demands extension out into the rest of the book. More knowledge of the way Lily looks at the world is implied than is given; sufficient understanding of it can only be gathered from the whole book. The remark "Women can't write, women can't paint" recalls not only a particular utterance but the reader's sense of Lily's self-consciousness which has been gradually formed in preceding episodes and will be extended until the final page. The degree in which she is right in supposing "it was not true to him but for some reason helpful to him," can only be known by reading all that has preceded. The way in which she recovers her balance by forming a new conception of her picture can only be fully appreciated in relation to earlier and later impressions of Lily at work. The visit to the Lighthouse, as has already been suggested, is far richer in significance than the single passage would imply. Similarly with all the impressions of Tansley gained in the last paragraph, none of them can be fully appreciated except in relation to the whole impression of Tansley, which cannot be isolated from the pattern of personalities in which we become aware of him. In this sense it is true to say that the art of Virginia Woolf is not applied to the drawing of single characters.

She was impelled by her own "vision of life" to emphasize the fluidity of human personality rather than its fixity. She perceived the variety of impressions made by one person upon the people round him and his own ever-changing consciousness of the surrounding world. Consequently, instead of defining an identity or epitomizing it in a particular incident, she invites us to discover it by living in the minds of her characters, or in the minds of others with whom they come into contact. The discovery can only be made by a gradually acquired intimacy. Understanding is cumulative. In *Jacob's Room* no very clear picture of Jacob as an individual emerges, because neither he himself nor the minds in which he is reflected are developed sufficiently for us to become intimate with them. On the other hand, in each scene or incident the quality of experience is fully communicated, our interest is concentrated upon modes of feeling that are common to many, rather than on those modes of feeling which define an individual. The power of communicating with profound insight and discriminating exactness experiences which are widespread and produce in the reader a sense of recognition is an essential part of Virginia Woolf's creative gift; though it is not the whole. It is developed to its fullest extent in *The Waves.* In that book she denies herself not only the outlined or summarized character seen from a point of view outside the book, but also the differentiated style in thought or speech, which is an alternative way of demarcating individuality. The six principal characters, from the nursery to old age, express themselves in the same subtle and imaginative idiom. Interest is focused upon their inward experience. Nevertheless, because of the small number of persons presented and the gradual unfolding of their minds, the reader becomes intimate with each and the six are clearly differentiated both from one another and from themselves at the different periods of their lives. The vocabulary, imagery and rhythms with which they are all alike endowed, is an unrealistic convention, which the reader has to accept. But the content of the consciousness expressed by each is always consistent both with the individual and with the time of life. Here, for instance, is the voice of Susan at the end of her school time; looking forward to being at home:

> I shall throw myself on a bank by the river and watch the fish slip in and out among the reeds. The palms of my hands will be printed with pine needles. I shall there unfold and take out whatever it is that I have made here; something hard. For something has grown in me here, through the winters and summers, on staircases, in bedrooms. I do not want, as Jinny wants, to be admired. I do not want people, when I come in, to look up with admiration. I want to give, to be given, and solitude in which to unfold my possessions.
>
> [*The Waves*]

And here is the voice of Susan in middle age:

> Now I measure, I preserve. At night I sit in the arm-chair and stretch my arm for my sewing; and hear my husband snore; and look up when the light from a passing car dazzles the windows and feel the waves of my life tossed, broken, round me who am rooted; and hear cries, and see others' lives eddying like straws round the piers of a bridge while I push my needle in and draw my thread through the calico.
>
> I think sometimes of Percival who loved me. He rode and fell in India. I think sometimes of Rhoda. Uneasy cries wake me at dead of night. But for the most part I walk content with my sons. I cut the dead petals from hollyhocks. Rather squat, grey before my time, but with clear eyes, pear-shaped eyes, I pace my fields.
>
> [*The Waves*]

But the voice of Rhoda is different. Here is Rhoda at school:

> "That is my face," said Rhoda, "in the looking glass behind Susan's shoulder — that face is my face. But I will duck behind her to hide it, for I am not here. I have no face. Other people have faces; Susan and Jinny have faces; they are here. Their world is the real world. The things they lift are heavy. They say Yes, they say No; whereas I shift and change and am seen through in a second. If they meet a housemaid she looks at them without laughing. But she laughs at me. They know what to say if spoken to. They laugh really; they get angry really; while I have to look first and do what other people do when they have done it."
>
> [*The Waves*]

And this is the voice of Rhoda, the woman:

> Oh, life, how I have dreaded you . . . oh, human beings how I have hated you! How you have nudged, how you have interrupted, how hideous you have looked in Oxford Street, how squalid sitting opposite each other staring in the Tube! . . . How you snatched from me the white spaces that lie between hour and hour and rolled them into dirty pellets and tossed them into the waste paper basket with your greasy paws. Yet those were my life.
>
> But I yielded. Sneers and yawns were covered with my hand. I did not go out into the street and break a bottle in the gutter as a sign of rage. Trembling with ardour, I pretended that I was not surprised. If Susan and Jinny pulled up their stockings like that, I pulled mine up like that also. So terrible was life that I held up shade after shade. Look at life through this, look at life through that; let there be rose leaves, let there be vine leaves — I covered the whole street, Oxford Street, Piccadilly Circus, with the blaze and ripple of my mind, with vine leaves and rose leaves.
>
> [*The Waves*]

The disadvantage of the convention adopted in *The Waves*, as regards character creation, is not that the six persons are undifferentiated, but rather the reverse. Because they are all endowed with an idiom suited to the expression of a subtle self-awareness, and so cannot be recognized by their accent nor by the form of their thought, the distinguishing quality of their personality has to be strongly emphasized; each is attached to his or her own symbol. Bernard is tied to his curiosity, his phrase-making, his desire to find a "story"; Susan to her need to strike roots, to possess, "to give, to be given"; Rhoda to her dreams and her fear of life; Jinny to her sensuousness and need for admiration; Neville to his love of order and intellectual clarity; Louis to his social insecurity, his "Australian accent and his father a banker in Brisbane," but also to "the great beast stamping," to his sense of identity with the past history of the race:

> What has my destiny been, the sharp-pointed pyramid that has pressed on my ribs all these years? That I remember the Nile and the women carrying pitchers on their heads; that I feel myself woven in and out of

the long summers and winters that have made the corn flow and have frozen the streams. I am not a single and passing being. My life is not a moment's bright spark like that on the surface of the diamond. I go beneath ground tortuously, as if a warder carried a lamp from cell to cell. My destiny has been that I remember and must weave together, must plait into one cable the many threads, the thin, the thick, the broken, the enduring of our long history, of our tumultuous and varied day. . . .

[*The Waves*]

It does not matter that, in this book, the characters have depth rather than width. The narrowing *leit-motif* helps to keep each distinct and also to weave the pattern of the whole. The reader is not disturbed by the emphasis on a defining attitude to life, because he is not, for the time being, attending to characterization but to human experience. He is attending to what it feels like to be young, or middle aged, or old; to be in the country or at school or in a London street; to rejoice, or to suffer, to strive or to be serene. The six personalities, with their differences of temperament, are the vehicles by which the experience is brought to him. The excitement of reading *The Waves* is due to an extension of ourselves, a quickening of memory and a deepening of perception, rather than to an addition to that gallery of human portraits to which fiction usually contributes.

But, although this subjective element is always important, it is not elsewhere so predominant as in *The Waves*. Virginia Woolf, in her other books, expresses more fully the diversity within unity of individual human beings, and differentiation of character is not elsewhere confined to a symbolic hall mark. The peculiar quality of *The Waves* required this device; with it she succeeded in communicating the gradual unfolding of human consciousness from youth to age in modern men and women with a similar cultural background and a similar endowment of sensibility and intelligence. She sacrificed some aspects of her vision so that the reader might live more fully within the minds of her six characters from youth to age. In all her novels, after the first two, personality is revealed as much by the record of an inner monologue as by action and conversation; but elsewhere the characters are more completely given. This is achieved by a continual shifting from mind to mind, so that we as often observe the experience given by one to another as the experience each receives. Also certain scenes are selected which throw a character into high relief, the scenes between Mrs. Dalloway and Miss Kilman, for instance, or between Lucy Swithin and William Dodge in *Between the Acts*. But in *The Waves* certain characters and events that affect the central six are in partial or complete shadow; Susan's husband, Bernard's wife, Neville's male and Louis's female lovers (other than those from among the six) are completely unknown to the reader. Even Percival, who plays so important a part in all their lives, is given only as a type. In *To the Lighthouse*, on the other hand, our considerable knowledge of Mr. Ramsay is an important factor in our understanding of his wife; Mrs. Ramsay's effect upon Lily, Mr. Bankes, Mr. Carmichael, Mr. Tansley or her own children forms an integral part of the reader's impression of her personality. Similarly, Mrs. Dalloway emerges as a fully rounded character because we know her husband, and Peter Walsh, Miss Kilman and Sally Seton and several others in whose minds we see her reflected. And we are present, either directly or by sharing the memories of divers people, at a number of crucial moments in her life, in which her personality expresses itself. Lucy Swithin in *Between the Acts* is known by her relation with her brother, with her daughter-in-law, with William Dodge and others, because we also know them. So it is with other characters in these books. It is not, I think, true of them that "they cannot be remembered afterwards on their own account." It is partially true of the characters in *The Waves* because the human value of that book is of a different kind.

The Waves is the fullest expression of the subjective aspect of Virginia Woolf's creative genius; in it the attention is wholly concentrated upon six people, and human experience is revealed from within their minds. In that book minor characters are very nearly nonexistent. In *The Years*, which followed next and was published six years later, there are a larger number of minor characters than in any other of her books. Just as, in life, people less intimately known to us are more easily defined, so it is with the minor character in fiction. As with comparative strangers, so with these background characters, the more distant viewpoint obscures the finely shaded, ever-varying quality of human personality — what is seen is the firm contour, the typical appearance and behaviour. The older method of character drawing, whose linear ancestor is the Theophrastian character, is here appropriate. Such characters can be conveyed by description and by a selection of typical speech and action. So, in *The Years*, whereas we live within the minds of the principals, the host of other people who surround them and contribute to the pattern of their lives are described from without. Colonel Abel Pargiter visits his mistress and her *character* and physical environment are firmly and quickly sketched:

> Nobody was there; he was too early. He looked round the room with distaste. There were too many little objects about. He felt out of place, and altogether too large as he stood upright before the draped fireplace in front of a screen upon which was painted a kingfisher in the act of alighting on some bulrushes. Footsteps scurried about hither and thither on the floor above. Was there somebody with her? he asked himself listening. Children screamed in the street outside. It was sordid; it was mean; it was furtive. One of these days, he said to himself . . . but the door opened and his mistress, Mira, came in.
>
> "Oh Bogy, dear!" she exclaimed. Her hair was very untidy; she was a little fluffy-looking; but she was very much younger than he was and really glad to see him, he thought. The little dog bounced up at her.

> "Lulu, Lulu," she cried, catching the little dog in one hand while
> she put the other to her hair, "come and let Uncle Bogy look at you."
> [*The Years*]

The Years is not wholly successful because, with so large a canvas and so
many background and foreground characters, the reader's attention is
insufficiently centred. As in *Jacob's Room*, the first experiment in the new
form, so here, in the first attempt to combine the advantages of the new
presentation of character with those of the old, individual scenes and
experiences are vivid, rich and delicately observed; but the book, even
after several readings, does not give the reader the sense of a single,
organized whole. In her next and last book, *Between the Acts*, the
problem of combining, without confusion, subjective revelation of personality with definition of minor characters is solved by the invention of a
subtle and complex form. Within that form both methods of characterization are successfully used; Mrs. Manresa, for instance, is shown directly by
the author, or reflected in the minds of the other characters, or by her
words and actions — at moments even, though much more rarely than with
the people we know more intimately, we live in her own mind:

> Then they went in to lunch, and Mrs. Manresa bubbled up,
> enjoying her own capacity to surmount, without turning a hair, this
> minor social crisis — this laying of two more places. For had she not
> complete faith in flesh and blood? and aren't we all flesh and blood?
> and how silly to make bones of trifles when we are all flesh and blood
> under the skin — men and women too! But she preferred men — obvi-
> ously.
> "Or what are your rings for, and your nails, and that really
> adorable little straw hat?" said Isa addressing Mrs. Manresa silently and
> thereby making silence add its unmistakable contribution to talk. Her
> hat, her rings, her finger nails red as roses, smooth as shells, were there
> for all to see. But not her life history. That was only scraps and
> fragments to all of them, excluding perhaps William Dodge, whom she
> called "Bill" publicly — a sign perhaps that he knew more than they did.
> Some of the things that he knew — that she strolled the garden at
> midnight in silk pyjamas, had the loud-speaker playing jazz, and a
> cocktail bar, of course they knew also. But nothing private; no strictly
> biographical facts."
> [*Between the Acts*]

There follows a paragraph, still expressing what goes on in Isa's mind,
giving a few conjectural details of Mrs. Manresa's biography. After which
Mrs. Manresa speaks:

> "All I need," said Mrs. Manresa ogling Candish, as if he were a real
> man, not a stuffed man, "is a corkscrew."
> "Look, Bill," she continued, cocking her thumb — she was opening
> the bottle — "at the pictures. Didn't I tell you you'd have a treat?"
> Vulgar she was in her gestures, in her whole person, over-sexed,

over-dressed for a picnic. But what a desirable, at least valuable, quality it was — for everybody felt, directly she spoke, "She said it, she's done it, not I," and could take advantage of the breach of decorum, of the fresh air that blew in, to follow like leaping dolphins in the wake of an ice-breaking vessel. Did she not restore to old Bartholomew his spice islands, his youth?

"I told him," she went on, ogling Bart now, "that he wouldn't look at our things" (of which they had heaps and mountains) "after yours. And I promised him you'd show him the — the — " here the champagne fizzed up and she insisted upon filling Bart's glass first. "What is it all you learned gentlemen rave about? An arch? Norman? Saxon? Who's the last from school? Mrs. Giles?"

She ogled Isabella now, conferring youth upon her; but always when she spoke to women, she veiled her eyes, for they, being conspirators, saw through it.

So with blow after blow, with champagne and ogling, she staked out her claim to be a wild child of nature.

[*Between the Acts*]

With such variety and flexibility of method Mrs. Manresa is presented; a minor character in the sense that we do not wholly identify ourselves with her, yet a memorable and important character who plays an essential part in the whole composition.

Like most novelists, Virginia Woolf can only fully communicate the experience of a limited number of human types. Some great novelists have a wider, some a narrower range than hers. By enriching her technique of character drawing in *Between the Acts*, she was able to extend her range; but in the main, because she focused her vision of human beings upon the indefinable, fluid personality, rather than on the definite and settled *character*, she concentrated upon those kinds of people into whose minds she could most fully enter and through whose eyes she could imagine herself looking out upon the world. For her central characters she limits herself to one large social class, the class of those who have incomes or earn salaries. Around that centre she creates the poor whom Eleanor visits in *The Years*, Mrs. Potter, old, deaf and bedridden, or Mrs. Dempster and other typical Londoners in *Mrs. Dalloway*, and they are often created with the same insight and sureness of touch as the central characters, though with less fullness. Mrs. Dempster has a long monologue, of which the following is a sample:

> For it's been a hard life, thought Mrs. Dempster. What hadn't she given to it? Roses; figure; her feet too. (She drew the knobbed lumps beneath her skirt.)
>
> Roses, she thought sardonically. All trash m'dear. For really, what with eating, drinking, and mating, the bad days and good, life had been no mere matter of roses, and what was more, let me tell you, Carrie Dempster had no wish to change her lot with any woman's in Kentish Town. . . .

[*Mrs. Dalloway*]

And Virginia Woolf creates also those who are in more direct touch with her centre; Mrs. Dalloway's maid Lucy; Crosby, the faithful retainer in *The Years*; the two charwomen in *To the Lighthouse*; the butler, the cook and the villagers in *Between the Acts*. She lives centred, as most people do, in one social sphere and looks outward from it, with sympathy and understanding, but with inevitably diminishing vision, to the spheres outside it.

Like many other novelists, Virginia Woolf also creates a limited range of intellectual and moral types. Jane Austen, for instance, has her intelligent, quick-witted young women, of Elizabeth Bennet's sisterhood, and also those who like Anne Elliot and Fanny Price are more notable for their gentle thoughtfulness; and she has her silly girls and silly women; her vulgarians and her social snobs, both of the climbing and of the condescending, variety. It would be possible also to classify her male characters under some half-dozen heads. Yet she never repeats herself; no individual within the class is mistakable for another. Similarly with Virginia Woolf. There are the disinterested scholars, like Mr. Ramsay, Mr. Hilbery or Edward Pargiter; there are the intellectuals, who cannot fall in love with the other sex, Bonamy in *Jacob's Room*, Neville in *The Waves*, Nicholas in *The Years* and William Dodge in *Between the Acts*; there are the women with a gift for creating harmony, women of exquisite tact and sensibility like Mrs. Ramsay, Mrs. Dalloway and Mrs. Hilbery; and there are those who create works of art, like Lily Briscoe or Miss La Trobe; and those who work for a cause, like Rose Pargiter in *The Years* and Lady Bruton in *Mrs. Dalloway*. These and some few other kinds of persons recur in different books; but though they can be roughly classified in this way the individuals within each kind are more unlike than they are like one another. Her range is limited in so far as she sees most clearly, because she sympathises most fully, with men and women who are either sensitive or intelligent or both, and the dimmer wits and, above all, blunter sensibilities are further removed from her centre of vision.

Notes

1. *Virginia Woolf*, by E. M. Forster, Cambridge University Press, 1942.

Mrs. Dalloway: Repetition as the Raising of the Dead
J. Hillis Miller*

The shift from the late Victorian or early modern Thomas Hardy to a fully modernist writer like Virginia Woolf might be thought of as the transition to a new complexity and a new self-consciousness in the use of devices of repetition in narrative. Critics commonly emphasize the newness of Virginia Woolf's art. They have discussed her use of the so-called stream-of-consciousness technique, her dissolution of traditional limits of plot and character, her attention to minutiae of the mind and to apparently insignificant details of the external world, her pulverization of experience into a multitude of fragmentary particles, each without apparent connection to the others, and her dissolution of the usual boundaries between mind and world.[1] Such characteristics connect her work to that of other twentieth-century writers who have exploded the conventional forms of fiction, from Conrad and Joyce to French "new novelists" like Nathalie Sarraute. It might also be well to recognize, however, the strong connections of Woolf's work with the native traditions of English fiction. Far from constituting a break with these traditions, her novels are an extension of them. They explore further the implications of those conventions which Austen, Eliot, Trollope, and Thackeray exploited as the given conditions of their craft. Such conventions, it goes without saying, are elements of meaning. The most important themes of a given novel are likely to lie not in anything which is explicitly affirmed, but in significances generated by the way in which the story is told. Among the most important of those ways is Woolf's organizing of her novels around various forms of recurrence. Storytelling, for Woolf, is the repetition of the past in memory, both in the memory of the characters and in the memory of the narrator. Mrs. Dalloway (1925) is a brilliant exploration of the functioning of memory as a form of repetition.

The novel is especially fitted to investigate not so much the depths of individual minds as the nuance of relationship between mind and mind. If this is so, then a given novelist's assumptions about the way one mind can be related to others will be a generative principle lying behind the form his or her novels take. From this perspective the question of narrative voice can be seen as a special case of the problem of relations between minds. The narrator too is a mind projected by a way of speaking, a mind usually endowed with special access to other minds and with special powers for expressing what goes on there.

*Reprinted from Fiction and Repetition: Seven English Novels (Cambridge: Harvard Univ. Press, 1982), pp. 176–202, 240. Originally published as "Virginia Woolf's All Souls' Day: The Omniscient Narrator in Mrs. Dalloway," in The Shaken Realist: Essays in Modern Literature in Honor of Frederick J. Hoffman, ed. Melvin J. Friedman and John B. Vickery (Baton Rouge: Louisiana State Univ. Press, 1970).

The manipulation of narrative voice in fiction is closely associated with that theme of human time or of human history which seems intrinsic to the form of the novel. In many novels the use of the past tense establishes the narrator as someone living after the events of the story have taken place, someone who knows all the past perfectly. The narrator tells the story in a present which moves forward toward the future by way of a recapitulation or repetition of the past. This retelling brings that past up to the present as a completed whole, or it moves toward such completion. This form of an incomplete circle, time moving toward a closure which will bring together past, present, and future as a perfected whole, is the temporal form of many novels.

Interpersonal relations as a theme, the use of an omniscient narrator who is a collective mind rising from the copresence of many individual minds, indirect discourse as the means by which that narrator dwells within the minds of individual characters and registers what goes on there, temporality as a determining principle of theme and technique — these are, I have argued elsewhere,[2] among the most important elements of form in Victorian fiction, perhaps in fiction of any time, in one proportion or another. Just these elements are fundamental to Virginia Woolf's work too. It would be as true to say that she investigates implications of these traditional conventions of form as to say that she brings something new into fiction. This can be demonstrated especially well in *Mrs. Dalloway*. The novel depends on the presence of a narrator who remembers all and who has a power of resurrecting the past in her narration. In *Mrs. Dalloway* narration is repetition as the raising of the dead.

"Nothing exists outside us except a state of mind"[3] — this seemingly casual and somewhat inscrutable statement is reported from the thoughts of the solitary traveler in Peter Walsh's dream as Peter sits snoring on a bench in Regent's Park. The sentence provides an initial clue to the mode of existence of the narrator of *Mrs. Dalloway*. The narrator is that state of mind which exists outside the characters and of which they can never be directly aware. Though they are not aware of it, it is aware of them. This "state of mind" surrounds them, encloses them, pervades them, knows them from within. It is present to them all at all the times and places of their lives. It gathers those times and places together in the moment. The narrator is that "something central which permeate[s]," the "something warm which [breaks] up surfaces" (p. 46), a power of union and penetration which Clarissa Dalloway lacks. Or, to vary the metaphor, the narrator possesses the irresistible and subtle energy of the bell of St. Margaret's striking half past eleven. Like that sound, the narrator "glides into the recesses of the heart and buries itself." It is "something alive which wants to confide itself, to disperse itself, to be, with a tremor of delight, at rest" (p. 74). Expanding to enter into the inmost recesses of each heart, the narrator encloses all in a reconciling embrace.

Though the characters are not aware of this narrating presence, they are at every moment possessed and known, in a sense violated, by an invisible mind, a mind more powerful than their own. This mind registers with infinite delicacy their every thought and steals their every secret. The indirect discourse of this registration, in which the narrator reports in the past tense thoughts which once occurred in the present moments of the characters' minds, is the basic form of narration in *Mrs. Dalloway*. This disquieting mode of ventriloquism may be found on any page of the novel. Its distinguishing mark is the conventional "he thought" or "she thought," which punctuates the narrative and reveals the presence of a strange one-way interpersonal relation. The extraordinary quality of this relation is hidden primarily because readers of fiction take it so much for granted. An example is the section of the novel describing Peter Walsh's walk from Clarissa's house toward Regent's Park: "Clarissa refused me, he thought"; "like Clarissa herself, thought Peter Walsh"; "It is Clarissa herself, he thought"; "Still the future of civilisation lies, he thought"; "The future lies in the hands of young men like that, he thought" (pp. 74–76) — and so on, page after page. If the reader asks himself where he is placed as he reads any given page of *Mrs. Dalloway*, the answer, most often, is that he is plunged within an individual mind which is being understood from inside by an ubiquitous, all-knowing mind. This mind speaks from some indeterminate later point in time, a point always "after" anything the characters think or feel. The narrator's mind moves easily from one limited mind to another and knows them all at once. It speaks for them all. This form of language generates the local texture of *Mrs. Dalloway*. Its sequential structure is made of the juxtaposition of longer or shorter blocks of narrative in which the narrator dwells first within Clarissa's mind, then within Septimus Smith's, then Rezia Smith's, then Peter's, then Rezia's again, and so on.

The characters of *Mrs. Dalloway* are therefore in an odd way, though they do not know it, dependent on the narrator. The narrator has preserved their evanescent thoughts, sensations, mental images, and interior speech. She rescues these from time past and presents them again in language to the reader. Narration itself is repetition in *Mrs. Dalloway*. In another way, the narrator's mind is dependent on the characters' minds. It could not exist without them. *Mrs. Dalloway* is almost entirely without passages of meditation or description which are exclusively in the narrator's private voice. The reader is rarely given the narrator's own thoughts or shown the way the world looks not through the eyes of a character, but through the narrator's private eyes. The sermon against "Proportion" and her formidable sister "Conversion" is one of the rare cases where the narrator speaks for her own view, or even for Woolf's own view, rather than by way of the mind of one of the characters. Even here, the narrator catches herself up and attributes some of her own judgment of Sir William Bradshaw to Rezia: "This lady too [Conversion] (Rezia Warren Smith divined it) had her dwelling in Sir William's heart" (p. 151).

In *Mrs. Dalloway* nothing exists for the narrator which does not first exist in the mind of one of the characters, whether it be a thought or a thing. This is implied by those passages in which an external object — the mysterious royal motorcar in Bond Street, Peter Walsh's knife, the child who runs full tilt into Rezia Smith's legs, most elaborately the skywriting airplane — is used as a means of transition from the mind of one character to the mind of another. Such transitions seem to suggest that the solid existing things of the external world unify the minds of separate persons because, though each person is trapped in his or her own mind and in his or her own private responses to external objects, nevertheless these disparate minds can all have responses, however different they may be, to the same event, for example to an airplane's skywriting. To this extent at least we all dwell in one world.

The deeper meaning of this motif in *Mrs. Dalloway* may be less a recognition of our common dependence on a solidly existing external world than a revelation that things exist for the narrator only when they exist for the characters. The narrator sometimes moves without transition out of the mind of one character and into the mind of another, as in the fourth paragraph of the novel, in which the reader suddenly finds himself transported from Clarissa's mind into the mind of Scrope Purvis, a character who never appears again in the novel and who seems put in only to give the reader a view of Clarissa from the outside and perhaps to provide an initial demonstration of the fact that the narrator is by no means bound to a single mind. Though she is bound to no single mind, she is dependent for her existence on the minds of the characters. She can think, feel, see only as they thought, felt, and saw. Things exist for her, she exists for herself, only because the others once existed. Like the omniscient narrators of *Vanity Fair, Middlemarch,* or *The Last Chronicle of Barset,* the omniscient narrator of *Mrs. Dalloway* is a general consciousness or social mind which rises into existence out of the collective mental experience of the individual human beings in the story. The cogito of the narrator of *Mrs. Dalloway* is, "They thought, therefore I am."

One implication of this relation between the narrator's mind and the characters' minds is that, though for the most part the characters do not know it, the universal mind is part of their own minds, or rather their minds are part of it. If one descends deeply enough into any individual mind one reaches ultimately the general mind, that is, the mind of the narrator. On the surface the relation between narrator and individual goes only one way. As in the case of those windows which may be seen through in a single direction, the character is transparent to the narrator, but the narrator is opaque to the character. In the depths of each individual mind, this one-way relationship becomes reciprocal. In the end it is no longer a relationship, but a union, an identity. Deep down the general mind and the individual mind become one. Both are on the same side of the glass, and the glass vanishes.

If this is true for all individual minds in relation to the universal mind, then all individual minds are joined to one another far below the surface separateness, as in Matthew Arnold's image of coral islands which seem divided, but are unified in the depths.[4] The most important evidence for this in *Mrs. Dalloway* is the fact that the same images of unity, of reconciliation, of communion well up spontaneously from the deep levels of the minds of all the major characters. One of the most pervasive of these images is that of a great enshadowing tree which is personified, a great mother who binds all living things together in the manifold embrace of her leaves and branches. This image would justify the use of the feminine pronoun for the narrator, who is the spokeswoman for this mothering presence. No man or woman is limited to himself or herself, but each is joined to others by means of this tree, diffused like a mist among all the people and places he or she has encountered. Each man or woman possesses a kind of immortality, in spite of the abrupt finality of death: "did it not become consoling," muses Clarissa to herself as she walks toward Bond Street, "to believe that death ended absolutely? but that somehow in the streets of London, on the ebb and flow of things, here, there, she survived, Peter survived, lived in each other, she being part, she was positive, of the trees at home; of the house there, ugly, rambling all to bits and pieces as it was; part of people she had never met; being laid out like a mist between the people she knew best, who lifted her on their branches as she had seen the trees lift the mist, but it spread ever so far, her life, herself" (p. 12; see also pp. 231, 232). "A marvellous discovery indeed — " thinks Septimus Smith as he watches the skywriting airplane, "that the human voice in certain atmospheric conditions (for one must be scientific, above all scientific) can quicken trees into life! . . . But they beckoned; leaves were alive; trees were alive. And the leaves being connected by millions of fibres with his own body there on the seat, fanned it up and down; when the branch stretched he, too, made that statement" (p. 32). "But if he can conceive of her, then in some sort she exists," thinks the solitary traveler in Peter Walsh's dream, "and advancing down the path with his eyes upon sky and branches he rapidly endows them with womanhood; sees with amazement how grave they become; how majestically, as the breeze stirs them, they dispense with a dark flutter of the leaves charity, comprehension, absolution . . . let me walk straight on to this great figure, who will, with a toss of her head, mount me on her streamers and let me blow to nothingness with the rest" (pp. 85–87). Even Lady Bruton, as she falls ponderously asleep after her luncheon meeting, feels "as if one's friends were attached to one's body, after lunching with them, by a thin thread" (p. 170).

This notion of a union of each mind in its depths with all the other minds and with a universal, impersonal mind for which the narrator speaks is confirmed by those notations in A *Writer's Diary* in which, while writing *Mrs. Dalloway*, Woolf speaks of her "great discovery," what she calls her "tunnelling process,"[5] that method whereby, as she says, "I dig out beautiful caves behind my characters: I think that gives exactly what I want; humanity, humour, depth. The idea is that the caves shall connect" (WD, p. 59).

Deep below the surface, in some dark and remote cave of the spirit, each person's mind connects with all the other minds, in a vast cavern where all the tunnels end. Peter Walsh's version of the image of the maternal tree ends nevertheless on an ominous note. To reach the great figure is to be blown to nothingness with the rest. This happens because union with the general mind is incompatible with the distinctions, the limitations, the definite edges and outlines, one thing here, another thing there, of daylight consciousness. The realm of union is a region of dispersion, of darkness, of indistinction, sleep, and death. The fear or attraction of the annihilating fall into nothingness echoes through *Mrs. Dalloway*. The novel seems to be based on an irreconcilable opposition between individuality and universality. By reason of his or her existence as a conscious human being, each man or woman is alienated from the whole of which he or she is actually, though unwittingly or at best half-consciously, a part. That half-consciousness gives each person a sense of incompletion. Each person yearns to be joined in one way or another to the whole from which he or she is separated by the conditions of existence as an individual.

One way to achieve this wholeness might be to build up toward some completeness in the daylight world, rather than to sink down into the dark world of death. "What a lark! What a plunge!" (p. 3) — the beginning of the third paragraph of *Mrs. Dalloway* contains in miniature the two contrary moments of the novel. If the fall into death is one pole of the novel, fulfilled in Septimus Smith's suicidal plunge, the other pole is the rising motion of "building it up," of constructive action in the movement, fulfilled in Clarissa Dalloway's party. Turning away from the obscure depths within them, the characters, may, like Clarissa, embrace the moment with elation and attempt to gather everything together in a diamond point of brightness: "For Heaven only knows why one loves it so, how one sees it so, making it up, building it round one, tumbling it, creating it every moment afresh"; "what she loved was this, here, now, in front of her"; "Clarissa . . . plunged into the very heart of the moment, transfixed it, there — the moment of this June morning on which was the pressure of all the other mornings, . . . collecting the whole of her at one point" (pp. 5, 12, 54). In the same way, Peter Walsh after his sleep on a park bench feels, "Life itself, every moment of it, every drop of it, here, this instant, now, in the sun, in Regent's Park, was enough" (pp. 119–120).

(This echoing from Clarissa to Peter, it is worth noting, is proof that Clarissa is right to think that they "live in each other.")

"The pressure of all the other mornings" — one way the characters in *Mrs. Dalloway* achieve continuity and wholeness is through the ease with which images from their pasts rise within them to overwhelm them with a sense of immediate presence. If the characters of the novel live according to an abrupt, discontinuous, nervous rhythm, rising one moment to heights of ecstasy only to be dropped again in sudden terror or despondency, nevertheless their experience is marked by profound continuities.

The remarkably immediate access the characters have to their pasts is one such continuity. The present, for them, is the perpetual repetition of the past. In one sense the moment is all that is real. Life in the present instant is a narrow plank reaching over the abyss of death between the nothingness of past and future. Near the end of the novel Clarissa thinks of "the terror; the overwhelming incapacity, one's parents giving it into one's hands, this life, to be lived to the end, to be walked with serenely; there was in the depths of her heart an awful fear" (p. 281). In another sense, the weight of all the past moments presses just beneath the surface of the present, ready in an instant to flow into consciousness, overwhelming it with the immediate presence of the past. Nothing could be less like the intermittencies and difficulties of memory in Wordsworth or in Proust than the spontaneity and ease of memory in *Mrs. Dalloway*. Repeatedly during the day of the novel's action the reader finds himself within the mind of a character who has been invaded and engulfed by a memory so vivid that it displaces the present of the novel and becomes the virtual present of the reader's experience. So fluid are the boundaries between past and present that the reader sometimes has great difficulty knowing whether he is encountering an image from the character's past or something part of the character's immediate experience.

An example of this occurs in the opening paragraphs of the novel. *Mrs. Dalloway* begins in the middle of things with the report of something Clarissa says just before she leaves her home in Westminister to walk to the florist on Bond Street: "Mrs. Dalloway said she would buy the flowers herself" (p. 3). A few sentences later, after a description of Clarissa's recognition that it is a fine day and just following the first instance of the motif of terror combined with ecstasy ("What a lark! What a plunge!"), the reader is "plunged" within the closeness of an experience which seems to be part of the present, for he is as yet ignorant of the place names in the novel or of their relation to the times of Clarissa's life. Actually, the experience is from Clarissa's adolescence: "For so it had always seemed to her, when, with a little squeak of the hinges, which she could hear now, she had burst open the French windows and plunged at Bourton into the open air" (p. 3).

The word "plunge," reiterated here, expresses a pregnant ambiguity.

If a "lark" and a "plunge" seem at first almost the same thing, rising and falling versions of the same leap of ecstasy, and if Clarissa's plunge into the open air when she burst open the windows at Bourton seems to confirm this identity, the reader may remember this opening page much later when Septimus leaps from a window to his death. Clarissa, hearing of his suicide at her party, confirms this connection by asking herself, "But this young man who had killed himself—had he plunged holding his treasure?" (p. 281). If *Mrs. Dalloway* is organized around the contrary penchants of rising and falling, these motions are not only opposites, but are also ambiguously similar. They change places bewilderingly, so that down and up, falling and rising, death and life, isolation and communication, are mirror images of one another rather than a confrontation of negative and positive orientations of the spirit. Clarissa's plunge at Bourton into the open air is an embrace of life in its richness, promise, and immediacy, but it is when the reader encounters it already an image from the dead past. Moreover, it anticipates Septimus's plunge into death. It is followed in Clarissa's memory of it by her memory that when she stood at the open window she felt "something awful was about to happen" (p. 3). The reader is not surprised to find that in this novel which is made up of a stream of subtle variations on a few themes, one of the things Clarissa sees from the window at Bourton is "the rooks rising, falling" (p. 3).

The temporal placement of Clarissa's experiences at Bourton is equally ambiguous. The "now" of the sentence describing Clarissa's plunge ("with a little squeak of the hinges, which she could hear now"), is the narrator's memory of Clarissa's memory of her childhood home brought back so vividly into Clarissa's mind that it becomes the present of her experience and of the reader's experience. The sentence opens the door to a flood of memories which bring that faraway time back to her as a present with the complexity and fullness of immediate experience.

These memories are not simply present. The ambiguity of the temporal location of this past time derives from the narrator's use of the past tense conventional in fiction. This convention is one of the aspects of the novel which Woolf carries on unchanged from her eighteenth- and nineteenth-century predecessors. The first sentence of the novel ("Mrs. Dalloway said she would buy the flowers herself"), establishes a temporal distance between the narrator's present and the present of the characters. Everything that the characters do or think is placed firmly in an indefinite past as something which has always already happened when the reader encounters it. These events are resurrected from the past by the language of the narration and placed before the present moment of the reader's experience as something bearing the ineradicable mark of their pastness. When the characters, within this general pastness of the narration, remember something from their own pasts, and when the narrator reports this in that indirect discourse which is another convention of *Mrs. Dalloway*, she has no other way to place it in the past than some version of the past tense which she has already been using for the "present" of the characters' experience: "How fresh, how calm, stiller than this of course, the air was in the early morning" (p. 3). That "was" is a past within a past, a double repetition.

The sentence before this one contains the "had" of the past perfect which places it in a past behind that past which is the "present" of the novel, the day of Clarissa's party. Still Clarissa can hear the squeak of the hinges "now," and the reader is led to believe that she may be comparing an earlier time of opening the windows with a present repetition of that action. The following sentence is in the simple past ("the air was"), and yet it belongs not to the present of the narration, but to the past of Clarissa's girlhood. What has happened to justify this change is one of those subtle dislocations within the narration which are characteristic of indirect discourse as a mode of language. Indirect discourse is always a relationship between two distinguishable minds, but the nuances of this relationship may change, with corresponding changes in the way it is registered in words. "For so it had always seemed to her" — here the little word "had" establishes three identifiable times: the no-time or time-out-of-time-for-which-all-times-are-past of the narrator; the time of the single day of the novel's action; and the time of Clarissa's youth. The narrator distinguishes herself both temporally and, if one may say so, "spatially," from Clarissa and reports Clarissa's thoughts from the outside in a tense which she would not herself use in the "now" of her own experience. In the next sentence these distances between the narrator and Clarissa disappear. Though the text is still in indirect discourse in the sense that the narrator speaks for the character, the language used is much more nearly identical with what Clarissa might herself have said, and the tense is the one she would use: "How fresh, how calm, stiller than this of course, the air was in the early morning." The "was" here is the sign of a relative identity between the narrator's mind and the character's mind. From the point of view the narrator momentarily adopts, Clarissa's youth is at the same distance from the narrator as it is from Clarissa, and the reader is left with no linguistic clue, except the "stiller than this of course," permitting him to tell whether the "was" refers to the present of the narration or to its past. The "was" shimmers momentarily between the narrator's past and Clarissa's past. The subtly varying tense structure creates a pattern of double repetition in which three times keep moving together and then apart. Narration in indirect discourse, for Woolf, is repetition as distancing and merging at once.

Just as a cinematic image is always present, so that there is difficulty in presenting the pastness of the past on film (a "flashback" soon becomes experienced as present), so everything in a conventional novel is labeled "past." All that the narrator presents takes its place on the same plane of time as something which from the narrator's point of view and from the reader's is already part of the past. If there is no past in the cinema, there is no present in a novel, or only a specious, ghostly present which is generated by the narrator's ability to resurrect the past not as reality but as verbal image.

Woolf strategically manipulates in *Mrs. Dalloway* the ambiguities of this aspect of conventional storytelling to justify the power she ascribes to her characters of immediate access to their pasts. If the novel as a whole is recovered from the past in the mind of the narrator, the action of the novel proceeds through one day in the lives of its main characters in which one after another they have a present experience, often one of walking through the city, Clarissa's walk to buy flowers, Peter Walsh's walk through London after visiting Clarissa, Septimus and Rezia's walk to visit Sir William Bradshaw, and so on. As the characters make their ways through London the most important events of their pasts rise up within them, so that the day of *Mrs. Dalloway* may be described as a general day of recollection. The revivification of the past performed by the characters becomes in its turn another past revivified, brought back from the dead, by the narrator.

If the pressure of all the other moments lies on the present moment which Clarissa experiences so vividly, the whole day of the action of *Mrs. Dalloway* may be described as such a moment on a large scale. Just as Proust's *A la recherche du temps perdu*, a book much admired by Woolf, ends with a party in which Marcel encounters figures from his past turned now into aged specters of themselves, so the "story" of *Mrs. Dalloway* (for there is a story, the story of Clarissa's refusal of Peter Walsh, of her love for Sally Seton, and of her decision to marry Richard Dalloway), is something which happened long before the single day in the novel's present. The details of this story are brought back bit by bit for the reader in the memories of the various characters as the day continues. At the same time the most important figures in Clarissa's past actually return during the day, Peter Walsh journeying from India and appearing suddenly at her door, then later coming to her party; Sally Seton, now married and the mother of five sons, also coming to her party.

The passage in *A Writer's Diary* about Woolf's "discovery," her "tunnelling process," takes on its full meaning when it is seen as a description of the way *Mrs. Dalloway* is a novel of the resurrection of the past into the present of the characters' lives. The tunnelling process, says Woolf, is one "by which I tell the past by instalments, as I have need of it" (WD, p. 60). The "beautiful caves" behind each of the characters are caves into the past as well as caves down into the general mind for which the narrator speaks. If in one direction the "caves connect" in the depths of each character's mind, in the other direction "each [cave] comes to daylight at the present moment" (WD, p. 59), the present moment of Clarissa's party when the important figures from her past are present in the flesh.

Woolf has unostentatiously, even secretly, buried within her novel a clue to the way the day of the action is to be seen as the occasion of a resurrection of ghosts from the past. There are three odd and apparently irrelevant pages in the novel (pp. 122–124) which describe the song of an ancient ragged woman, her hand outstretched for coppers. Peter hears her song as he crosses Marylebone Road by the Regent's Park Tube Station. It seems to rise like "the voice of an ancient spring" spouting from some primeval swamp. It seems to have been going on as the same inarticulate moan for millions of years and to be likely to persist for ten million years longer:

ee um fah um so
foo swee too eem oo

The battered old woman, whose voice seems to come from before, after, or outside time, sings of how she once walked with her lover in May. Though it is possible to associate this with the theme of vanished love in the novel (Peter has just been thinking again of Clarissa and of her coldness, "as cold as an icicle"; pp. 121–122), still the connection seems strained, and the episode scarcely seems to justify the space it occupies unless the reader recognizes that Woolf has woven into the old woman's song, partly by paraphrase and variation, partly by direct quotation in an English translation, the words of a song by Richard Strauss, "Allerseelen," with words by Hermann von Gilm.[6] The phrases quoted in English from the song do not correspond to any of the three English translations I have located, so Woolf either made her own or used another which I have not found. Here is a translation more literal than any of the three published ones I have seen and also more literal than Woolf's version:

Place on the table the perfuming heather,
Bring here the last red asters,
And let us again speak of love,
As once in May.

Give me your hand, that I may secretly press it,
And if someone sees, it's all the same to me;
Give me but one of your sweet glances,
As once in May.

It is blooming and breathing perfume today on every grave,
One day in the year is free to the dead,
Come to my heart that I may have you again,
As once in May.

Heather, red asters, the meeting with the lover once in May, these are echoed in the passage in *Mrs. Dalloway*, and several phrases are quoted directly: "look in my eyes with thy sweet eyes intently"; "give me your hand and let me press it gently"; "and if some one should see, what matter they?" The old woman, there can be no doubt, is singing Strauss's song.

The parts of the song not directly echoed in *Mrs. Dalloway* identify it as a key to the structure of the novel. "One day in the year" is indeed "free to the dead," "Allerseelen," the day of a collective resurrection of spirits. On this day the bereaved lover can hope that the beloved will return from the grave. Like Strauss's song, *Mrs. Dalloway* has the form of an All Soul's Day in which Peter Walsh, Sally Seton, and the rest rise from the dead to come to Clarissa's party. As in the song the memory of a dead lover may on one day of the year become a direct confrontation of his or her risen spirit, so in *Mrs. Dalloway* the characters are obsessed all day by memories of the time when Clarissa refused Peter and chose to marry Richard Dalloway, and then the figures in those memories actually come back in a general congregation of persons from Clarissa's past. The power of narrative not just to repeat the past but to resurrect it in another form is figured dramatically in the action of the novel.

Continuity of each character with his own past, continuity in the shared past of all the important characters—these forms of communication are completed by the unusual degree of access the characters have in the present to one another's minds. Some novelists, Jane Austen or Jean-Paul Sartre, for example, assume that minds are opaque to one another. Another person is a strange apparition, perhaps friendly to me, perhaps a threat, but in any case difficult to understand. I have no immediate knowledge of what he is thinking or feeling. I must interpret what is going on within his subjectivity as best I can by way of often misleading signs — speech, gesture, and expression. In Woolf's work, as in Trollope's, one person often sees spontaneously into the mind of another and knows with the same sort of knowledge he has of his own subjectivity what is going on there. If the narrator enters silently and unobserved into the mind of each of the characters and understands it with perfect intimacy because it is in fact part of her own mind, the characters often, if not always, may have the same kind of intimate knowledge of one another. This may be partly because they share the same memories and so respond in the same way to the same cues, each knowing what the other must be thinking, but it seems also to be an unreflective openness of one mind to another, a kind of telepathic insight. The mutual understanding of Clarissa and Peter is the most striking example of this intimacy: "They went in and out of each other's minds without any effort," thinks Peter, remembering their talks at Bourton (p. 94). Other characters have something of the same power of communication. Rezia and Septimus, for example, as he helps her make a hat in their brief moments of happiness before Dr. Holmes comes and Septimus throws himself out of the window: "Not for weeks had they laughed like this together, poking fun privately like married people" (p. 217). Or there is the intimacy of Clarissa and her servant Lucy: " 'Dear!' said Clarissa, and Lucy shared as she meant her to her disappointment (but not the pang); felt the concord between them" (p. 43).

In all these cases, there is some slight obstacle between the minds of the characters. Clarissa does after all decide not to marry Peter and is falling in love with Richard Dalloway in spite of the almost perfect communion she can achieve with Peter. The communion of Rezia and Septimus is intermittent, and she has little insight into what is going on in his mind during his periods of madness. Clarissa does not share with Lucy the pang of jealousy she feels toward Lady Bruton. The proper model for the relations among minds in *Mrs. Dalloway* is that of a perfect transparency of the minds of the characters to the mind of the narrator, but only a modified translucency, like glass frosted or fogged, between the mind of one character and the mind of another. Nevertheless, to the continuity between the present and the past within the mind of a given character there must be added a relative continuity from one mind to another in the present.

The characters in *Mrs. Dalloway* are endowed with a desire to take possession of these continuities, to actualize them in the present. The dynamic model for this urge is a movement which gathers together disparate elements, pieces them into a unity, and lifts them up into the daylight world in a gesture of ecstatic delight, sustaining the wholeness so created over the dark abyss of death. The phrase "building it up" echoes through the novel as an emblem of this combination of spiritual and physical action. Thinking of life, Clarissa, the reader will remember, wonders "how one sees it so, making it up, building it round one" (p. 5). Peter Walsh follows a pretty girl from Trafalgar Square to Regent Street across Oxford Street and Great Portland Street until she disappears into her house, making up a personality for her, a new personality for himself, and an adventure for them both together: "it was half made up, as he knew very well; invented, this escapade with the girl; made up, as one makes up the better part of life, he thought — making oneself up; making her up" (p. 81). Rezia's power of putting one scrap with another to make a hat or of gathering the small girl who brings the evening paper into a warm circle of intimacy momentarily cures Septimus of his hallucinations and of his horrifying sense that he is condemned to a solitary death: "For so it always happened. First one thing, then another. So she built it up, first one thing and then another . . . she built it up, sewing" (pp. 219, 221). Even Lady Bruton's luncheon, to which she brings Richard Dalloway and Hugh Whitbread to help her write a letter to the *Times* about emigration, is a parody version of this theme of constructive action.

The most important example of the theme is Clarissa Dalloway's party, her attempt to "kindle and illuminate" (p. 6). Though people laugh at her for her parties, feel she too much enjoys imposing herself, nevertheless these parties are her offering to life. They are an offering devoted to the effort to bring together people from their separate lives and combine them into oneness: "Here was So-an-so in South Kensington; some one up in Bayswater; and somebody else, say, in Mayfair. And she felt quite continuously a sense of their existence; and she felt what a waste; and she felt what a pity; and she felt if only they could be brought together; so she did it. And it was an offering; to combine, to create" (pp. 184–185). The party which forms the concluding scene of the novel does succeed in bringing people together, a great crowd from poor little Ellie Henderson all the way up to the Prime Minister, and including Sally Seton and Peter Walsh among the rest. Clarissa has the "gift still; to be; to exist; to sum it all up in the moment" (p. 264).

Clarissa's party transforms each guest from his usual self into a new social self, a self outside the self of participation in the general presence of others. The magic sign of this transformation is the moment when Ralph Lyon beats back the curtain and goes on talking, so caught up is he in the party. The gathering then becomes "something now, not nothing" (p. 259), and Clarissa meditates on the power a successful party has to destroy the usual personality and replace it with another self able to know people with special intimacy and able to speak more freely from the hidden depths of the spirit. These two selves are related to one another as real to unreal, but when one is aware of the contrast, as Clarissa is in the moment just before she loses her self-consciousness and is swept up into her own party, it is impossible to tell which is the real self, which the unreal: "Every time she gave a party she had this feeling of being something not herself, and that every one was unreal in one way; much more real in another . . . it was possible to say things you couldn't say anyhow else, things that needed an effort; possible to go much deeper" (pp. 259–260).

An impulse to create a social situation which will bring into the open the usually hidden continuities of present with past, of person with person, of person with the depths of himself, is shared by all the principal characters of *Mrs. Dalloway*. This universal desire makes one vector of spiritual forces within the novel a general urge toward lifting up and bringing together.

This effort fails in all its examples, or seems in part to have failed. It seems so implicitly to the narrator and more overtly to some of the characters, including Clarissa. From this point of view, a perspective emphasizing the negative aspect of these characters and episodes, Peter Walsh's adventure with the unknown girl is a fantasy. Lady Bruton is a shallow, domineering busybody, a representative of that upper-class society which Woolf intends to expose in her novel. "I want to criticise the social system," she wrote while composing *Mrs. Dalloway*, "and to show it at work, at its most intense" (WD, p. 56). Rezia's constructive power and womanly warmth does not prevent her husband from killing himself. And Clarissa? It would be a mistake to exaggerate the degree to which she and the social values she embodies are condemned in the novel. Woolf's attitudes toward upper-class English society of the nineteen-twenties are ambiguous, and to sum up the novel as no more than negative social satire is a distortion. Woolf feared while she was writing the novel that Clarissa would not seem attractive enough to her readers. "The doubtful point," she wrote in her diary a year before the novel was finished, "is, I think, the character of Mrs. Dalloway. It may be too stiff, too glittering and tinselly" (p. 60). There is in fact a negative side to Clarissa as Woolf presents her. She is a snob, too anxious for social success. Her party is seen in part as the perpetuation of a moribund society, with its hangers-on at court like Hugh Whitbread and a Prime Minister who is dull: "You might have stood him behind a counter and bought biscuits," thinks Ellie Henderson, " – poor chap, all rigged up in gold lace" (p. 261).

Even if this negative judgment is suspended and the characters are taken as worth our sympathy, it is still the case that, though Clarissa's party facilitates unusual communication among these people, their communion is only momentary. The party comes to an end; the warmth fades; people return to their normal selves. In retrospect there seems to have been something spurious about the sense of oneness with others the party created. Clarissa's power to bring people together seems paradoxically related to her reticence, her coldness, her preservation of an area of inviolable privacy in herself. Though she believes that each person is not limited to himself, but is spread out among other people like mist in the branches of a tree, with another part of her spirit she contracts into herself and resents intensely any invasion of her privacy. It almost seems as if her keeping of a secret private self is reciprocally related to her social power to gather people together and put them in relationship to one another. The motif of Clarissa's frigidity, of her prudery, of her separateness runs all through *Mrs. Dalloway*. "The death of her soul," Peter Walsh calls it (p. 89). Since her illness, she has slept alone, in a narrow bed in an attic room. She cannot "dispel a virginity preserved through childbirth which [clings] to her like a sheet" (p. 46). She has "through some contraction of this cold spirit" (p. 46) failed her husband again and again. She feels a stronger sexual attraction to other women than to men. A high point of her life was the moment when Sally Seton kissed her. Her decision not to marry Peter Walsh but to marry Richard Dalloway instead was a rejection of intimacy and a grasping at privacy. "For in marriage a little licence, a little independence there must be between people living together day in day out in the same house; which Richard gave her, and she him . . . But with Peter everything had to be shared; everything gone into. And it was intolerable" (p. 10). "And there is a dignity in people; a solitude, even between husband and wife a gulf," thinks Clarissa much later in the novel (p. 181). Her hatred of her daughter's friend Miss Kilman, of Sir William Bradshaw, of all the representatives of domineering will, of the instinct to convert others, of "love and religion" (p. 191), is based on this respect for isolation and detachment: "Had she ever tried to convert any one herself? Did she not wish everybody merely to be themselves?" (p. 191). The old lady whom Clarissa sees so often going upstairs to her room in the neighboring house seems to stand chiefly for this highest value, "the privacy of the soul" (p. 192): "that's the miracle, that's the mystery; that old lady, she meant . . . And the supreme mystery . . . was simply this: here was one room; there another. Did religion solve that, or love?" (p. 193).

The climax of *Mrs. Dalloway* is not Clarissa's party but the moment when, having heard of the suicide of Septimus, Clarissa leaves her guests behind and goes alone into the little room where Lady Bruton has a few minutes earlier been talking to the Prime Minister about India. There she sees in the next house the old lady once more, this time going quietly to bed. She thinks about Septimus and recognizes how factitious all her attempt to assemble and to connect has been. Her withdrawal from her party suggests that she has even in the midst of her guests kept untouched the privacy of her soul, that still point from which one can recognize the hollowness of the social world and feel the attraction of the death everyone carries within him as his deepest reality. Death is the place of true communion. Clarissa has been attempting the impossible, to bring the values of death into the daylight world of life. Septimus chose the right way. By killing himself he preserved his integrity, "plunged holding his treasure" (p. 281), his link to the deep places where each man or woman is connected to every other man or woman. For did he not in his madness hear his dead comrade, Evans, speaking to him from that region where all the dead dwell together? "Communication is health; communication is happiness" (p. 141) — Septimus during his madness expresses what is the highest goal for all the characters, but his suicide constitutes a recognition that communication cannot be attained except evanescently in life. The only repetition of the past that successfully repossesses it is the act of suicide.

Clarissa's recognition of this truth, her moment of self-condemnation, is at the same time the moment of her greatest insight:

> She had once thrown a shilling into the Serpentine, never anything more. But he had flung it away. They went on living . . . They (all day she had been thinking of Bourton, of Peter, of Sally), they would grow old. A thing there was that mattered; a thing, wreathed about with chatter, defaced, obscured in her own life, let drop every day in corruption, lies, chatter. This he had preserved. Death was defiance. Death was an attempt to communicate; people feeling the impossibility of reaching the centre which, mystically, evaded them; closeness drew apart; rapture faded, one was alone. There was an embrace in death. (Pp. 280–81)

From the point of view of the "thing" at the center that matters most, all speech, all social action, all building it up, all forms of communication, are lies. The more one tries to reach this centre through such means the further away from it one goes. The ultimate lesson of *Mrs. Dalloway* is that by building it up, one destroys. Only by throwing it away can life be preserved. It is preserved by being laid to rest on that underlying reality which Woolf elsewhere describes as "a thing I see before me: something abstract; but residing in the downs or sky; beside which nothing matters; in which I shall rest and continue to exist. Reality I call it" (WD, pp. 129–130). "Nothing matters" — compared to this reality, which is only defaced, corrupted, covered over by all the everyday activities of life, everything else is emptiness and vanity: "there is nothing," wrote Woolf during one of her periods of depression, " — nothing for any of us. Work, reading, writing are all disguises; and relations with people" (WD, p. 141).

Septimus Smith's suicide anticipates Virginia Woolf's own death. Both deaths are a defiance, an attempt to communicate, a recognition that self-annihilation is the only possible way to embrace that center which evades one as long as one is alive. Clarissa does not follow Septimus into death (though she has a bad heart, and the original plan, according to the preface Woolf wrote for the Modern Library edition of the novel, was to have her kill herself). Even so, the words of the dirge in *Cymbeline* have been echoing through her head all day: "Fear no more the heat o' th' sun/ Nor the furious winter's rages." Clarissa's obsession with these lines indicates her half-conscious awareness that in spite of her love of life she will reach peace and escape from suffering only in death. The lines come into her mind for a last time just before she returns from her solitary meditation to fulfill her role as hostess. They come to signify her recognition of her kinship with Septimus, her kinship with death. For she is, as Woolf said in the Modern Library preface, the "double" of Septimus. In *Mrs. Dalloway*, Woolf said, "I want to give life and death, sanity and insanity" (WD, p. 56). The novel was meant to be "a study of insanity and suicide; the world seen by the sane and the insane side by side" (WD, p. 51). These poles are not so much opposites as reversed images of one another. Each has the same elemental design. The death by suicide Woolf originally planned for Clarissa is fulfilled by Septimus, who dies for her, so to speak, a substitute suicide. Clarissa and Septimus seek the same thing: communication, wholeness, the oneness of reality, but only Septimus takes the sure way to reach it. Clarissa's attempt to create unity in her party is the mirror image in the world of light and life of Septimus's vigorous appropriation of the dark embrace of death in his suicide: "Fear no more the heat of the sun. She must go back to them. But what an extraordinary night! She felt somehow very like him — the young man who had killed himself. She felt glad that he had done it; thrown it away" (p. 283). For Woolf, as for Conrad, the visible world of light and life is the mirror image or repetition in reverse of an invisible world of darkness and death. Only the former can be seen and described. Death is incompatible with language, but by talking about life, one can talk indirectly about death.

Mrs. Dalloway seems to end in a confrontation of life and death as looking-glass counterparts. Reality, authenticity, and completion are on the death side of the mirror, while life is at best the illusory, insubstantial, and fragmentary image of that dark reality. There is, however, one more structural element in *Mrs. Dalloway*, one final twist which reverses the polarities once more, or rather which holds them poised in their irreconciliation. Investigation of this will permit a final identification of the way Woolf brings into the open latent implications of traditional modes of storytelling in English fiction.

I have said that *Mrs. Dalloway* has a double temporal form. During the day of the action the chief characters resurrect in memory by bits and pieces the central episode of their common past. All these characters then come together again at Clarissa's party. The narrator in her turn embraces both these times in the perspective of a single distance. She moves forward through her own time of narration toward the point when the two times of the characters come together in the completion of the final sentences of the novel, when Peter sees Clarissa returning to her party. Or should one say "almost come together," since the temporal gap still exists in the separation between "is" and "was"? "It is Clarissa, he said. For there she was" (p. 296).

In the life of the characters, this moment of completion passes. The party ends. Sally, Peter, Clarissa, and the rest move on toward death. The victory of the narrator is to rescue from death this moment and all the other moments of the novel in that All Souls' Day at a second power which is literature. Literature for Woolf is repetition as preservation, but preservation of things and persons in their antithetical poise. Time is rescued by this repetition. It is rescued in its perpetually reversing divisions. It is lifted into the region of death with which the mind of the narrator has from the first page been identified. This is a place of absence, where nothing exists but words. These words generate their own reality. Clarissa, Peter, and the rest can be encountered only in the pages of the novel. The reader enters this realm of language when he leaves his own solid world and begins to read *Mrs. Dalloway*. The novel is a double resurrection. The characters exist for themselves as alive in a present which is a resuscitation of their dead pasts. In the all-embracing mind of the narrator the characters exist as dead men and women whose continued existence depends on her words. When the circle of the narration is complete, past joining present, the apparently living characters reveal themselves to be already dwellers among the dead.

Clarissa's vitality, her ability "to be; to exist," is expressed in the present-tense statement made by Peter Walsh in the penultimate line of the novel: "It is Clarissa." This affirmation of her power to sum it all up in the moment echoes earlier descriptions of her "extraordinary gift, that woman's gift, of making a world of her own wherever she happened to be": "She came into a room; she stood, as he had often seen her, in a doorway with lots of people round her . . . she never said anything specially clever; there she was, however; there she was" (pp. 114–115); "There she was, mending her dress" (p. 179). These earlier passages are in the past tense, as is the last line of the novel: "For there she was." With this sentence "is" becomes "was" in the indirect discourse of the narrator. In that mode of language Clarissa along with all the other characters recedes into an indefinitely distant past. Life becomes death within the impersonal mind of the narrator and within her language, which is the place of communion in death. There the fragmentary is made whole. There all is assembled into one unit. All the connections between one part of the novel and another are known only to the agile and ubiquitous mind of the narrator. They exist only within the embrace of that reconciling spirit and through the power of her words.

Nevertheless, to return once more to the other side of the irony, the dirge in *Cymbeline* is sung over an Imogen who is only apparently dead. The play is completed with the seemingly miraculous return to life of the heroine. In the same way, Clarissa comes back from her solitary confrontation with death during her party. She returns from her recognition of her kinship with Septimus to bring "terror" and "ecstasy" to Peter when he sees her (p. 296). She comes back also into the language of the narration where, like Imogen raised from the dead, she may be confronted by the reader in the enduring language of literature.

It is perhaps for this reason that Woolf changed her original plan and introduced Septimus as Clarissa's surrogate in death. To have had a single protagonist who was swallowed up in the darkness would have falsified her conception. She needed two protagonists, one who dies and another who dies with his death. Clarissa vividly lives through Septimus's death as she meditates alone during her party. Then, having died vicariously, she returns to life. She appears before her guests to cause, in Peter Walsh at least, "extraordinary excitement" (p. 296). Not only does Clarissa's vitality come from her proximity to death. The novel needs for its structural completeness two opposite but similar movements, Septimus's plunge into death and Clarissa's resurrection from the dead. *Mrs. Dalloway* is both of these at once: the entry into the realm of communication in death and the revelation of that realm in words which may be read by the living.

Though *Mrs. Dalloway* seems almost nihilistically to recommend the embrace of death, and though its author did in fact finally take this plunge, nevertheless, like the rest of Woolf's writing, it represents a contrary movement of the spirit. In a note in her diary of May 1933, Woolf records a moment of insight into what brings about a "synthesis" of her being: "how only writing composes it: how nothing makes a whole unless I am writing" (WD, p. 201). Or again: "Odd how the creative power at once brings the whole universe to order" (p. 213). Like Clarissa's party or like the other examples of building it up in *Mrs. Dalloway*, the novel is a constructive action which gathers unconnected elements into a solidly existing object. It is something which belongs to the everyday world of physical things. It is a book with cardboard covers and white pages covered with black marks. This made-up thing, unlike its symbol, Clarissa's party, belongs to both worlds. If it is in one sense no more than a manufactured physical object, it is in another sense made of words which designate not the material presence of the things named but their absence from the everyday world and their existence within the place out of place and time out of time which are the space and time of literature. Woolf's writing has as its aim bringing into the light of day this realm of communication in language. A novel, for Woolf, is the place of death made visible. Writing is the only action which exists simultaneously on both sides of the mirror, within death and within life at once.

Though Woolf deals with extreme spiritual situations, her work would hardly give support to a scheme of literary history which sees twentieth-century literature as more negative, more "nihilistic," or more "ambiguous" than nineteenth-century literature. The "undecidability" of *Mrs. Dalloway* lies in the impossibility of knowing, from the text, whether the realm of union in death exists, for Woolf, only in the words, or whether the words represent an extralinguistic realm which is "really there" for the characters, for the narrator, and for Woolf herself. Nevertheless, the possibility that the realm of death, in real life as in fiction, really exists, is more seriously entertained by Woolf than it is, for example, by Eliot, by Thackeray, or by Hardy. The possibility that repetition in narrative is the representation of a transcendent spiritual realm of reconciliation and preservation, a realm of the perpetual resurrection of the dead, is more straightforwardly proposed by Virginia Woolf than by most of her predecessors in English fiction.

Notes

1. See, for one well-known example of this, "The Brown Stocking," an essay on a passage in *To the Lighthouse,* in Erich Auerbach, *Mimesis,* trans. Willard R. Trask (Princeton: Princeton University Press, 1953), pp. 525–553.

2. In *The Form of Victorian Fiction* (Notre Dame, Ind.: University of Notre Dame Press, 1968).

3. Virginia Woolf, *Mrs. Dalloway* (New York: Harcourt, Brace, 1925), p. 85. Further citations from this novel will be identified by page number from this edition.

4. See "Written in Butler's Sermons" and "To Marguerite—Continued," *The Poems of Matthew Arnold,* ed. Kenneth Allott (London: Longmans, Green, 1965), pp. 51–52, 124–125.

5. *A Writer's Diary* (New York: Harcourt, Brace, 1954), p. 60. Henceforth cited in the text as WD.

6. Opus 10, no. 8. For the score and von Gilm's text see Richard Strauss, *Lieder für Mittlere Stimme mit Klavierbegleitung,* Universal Edition, III (Leipzig: Jos. Aibl-Verlag; London: Boosey and Hawkes, 1907), 9–11.

[Woolf and Androgyny]   Carolyn Heilbrun*

Writing of Virginia Woolf in 1932, Winifred Holtby suggested that while the doctrine of androgyny was not peculiar to Virginia Woolf, "no one, perhaps, has dramatized it so effectively, nor explained it with such confidence." Like Blake, Holtby points out, Virginia Woolf knew that:

> When the Individual appropriates universality
> He divides into Male and Female, and when the
>   Male and Female
> Appropriate Individuality they become an Eternal
>   Death.[1]

Were we to forget that phenomenon which Millett has called the "counter-revolution" and which she dates from 1930 until 1960, we might wonder that Holtby should be, until the 1960s, almost alone in perceiving the importance of androgyny to Woolf's vision.[2] Not that Holtby, in what is certainly the best book on Woolf written prior to 1960, guesses at the androgyny which hides behind the great novels. But sharing, as she did in 1932, Woolf's pre-counterrevolutionary mind, she was able to see what the critics in the dark years were unable or unwilling to find. It is indeed questionable whether any of the criticism on female and androgynous writers written in this period will, with rare exceptions, endure. The work of most male critics on the Brontës, for example, will probably with time seem simply an aberration of the critics' cultural bias.

Holtby, then, is vital to a discussion of Woolf's androgyny, because she recognized Woolf's uniqueness in perceiving how symbols of responsibility and prestige call out, in England's daughters, "the manliness of their girlish hearts," but even more because she saw how arbitrary is the assignment of male and female characteristics in the first place:

> For we have to fix the labels after an intellectual process which is at its best guesswork. We cannot recognize infallibly what characteristics beyond those which are purely physical are "male" and "female." Custom and prejudice, history and tradition have designed the fashion plates; we hardly know yet what remains beneath them of the human being. When writers like D. H. Lawrence and Wyndham Lewis talk about "masculine values" and "a masculine world" we can guess pretty much what they mean. . . . Yet looking round upon the world of human beings as we know it, we are hard put to say what is the natural shape of men or women, so old, so all-enveloping are the molds fitted by history and custom over their personalities. We do not know how much of sensitiveness, intuition, protectiveness, docility and tenderness may not be naturally "male," how much of curiosity, aggression, audacity and combativeness may not be "female." We might as well call the

*Reprinted from Carolyn Heilbrun, *Toward a Recognition of Androgyny* (New York: Alfred A. Knopf, 1973), pp. 151–67, 188–89.

conflicting strains within the human personality black and white, negative and positive, as male and female. The time has not yet come when we can say for certain which is the man and which the woman, after both have boarded the taxi of human personality.[3]

"Some collaboration has to take place in the mind between the woman and the man before the act of creation can be accomplished." The words are Woolf's, from *A Room of One's Own*: "To think, as I have been thinking these last two days, of one sex as distinct from the other is an effort," she continues. Yet Holtby alone seems clearly to have understood that this androgynous ideal never led Woolf to underestimate the importance of sexuality; in fact, her recognition of sex's actual place in life, in *Jacob's Room*, for example, is quite astonishing for a woman writer of her time. Admiration for virility, pleasure in the contemplation of it, was something she easily recognized and confirmed; nor did she ever confuse the attractions of virility with her distaste for male oppression. She understood the beauty of young men.

It has been Virginia Woolf's peculiar destiny to be declared annoyingly feminine by male critics at the same time that she has been dismissed by women interested in the sexual revolution as (*A Room of One's Own* apart) not really eligible to be drafted into their ranks. Is this another example of the cultural displacement which occurs when one age attempts to criticize the age that has just preceded it? Holtby's obvious advantage was a shared point of view: not that she and Woolf shared any detail of their backgrounds, but they were both women, both deeply intelligent, both the victims of the Georgians who, as Holtby said,

> had discovered the Nerves. . . . Particularly they had discovered sex. At the very moment when an artist might have climbed out of the traditional limitations of domestic obligation by claiming to be a human being, she was thrust back into them by the authority of the psychologist. A woman, she was told, must enjoy the full cycle of sex-experience, or she would become riddled with complexes like a rotting fruit. . . . The full weight of the Freudian revelation fell upon [the woman writer's] head. . . . The confusion and conflict were immeasurably disturbing. The wonder is that any woman continued to write novels at all.[4]

Holtby's particular contribution as a critic of Woolf is to have perceived Woolf's central vision as embodying less an inner tension between masculine and feminine inclinations than a search for a new synthesis and an opportunity for feminine expression. Woolf saw as profoundly as anyone the need for our energy to flow in new directions, and she and her reputation suffered frightfully in the over-manly years as she struggled against the male-oriented world. The sight of two people, a man and a woman, in a taxi, which seemed to Woolf a metaphor for the conjoining of the two sexes rather than the separation of them into antagonistic forces, was seized upon by Holtby to stand for Woolf's androgynous vision. The other two androgynous symbols are the lighthouse and the snail, both of them reaching from her earliest to her latest work.[5] The "Mark on the Wall" is discovered, at the end of that story, to be a snail, a living thing, as Marder has written, "that may be said to combine the opposites within itself — the shell, the hard, inanimate outer structure protecting and concealing a dark, evasive, living center." In *The Waves*, Bernard speaks of a shell forming "upon the soft soul, nacreous, shiny, upon which sensations tap their beaks in vain."

Even those critics who are sympathetic to Woolf's vision often misunderstand it; for them, the idea of androgyny is less a union representative of the range of human possibility than an agreed-upon division. Marder, for example, speaks of Mrs. Ramsay as androgynous,[6] while clearly Mrs. Ramsay lacks all the "masculine" powers of logic, order, ratiocination; in the same way James Hafley and others suggest Mrs. Ramsay's completeness, since she appears to fathom with her intuition what intelligence falsifies; she becomes an antidote to "mere intellect." Since Virginia Woolf is "feminine," we are to assume that she is championing the "feminine" vision of Mrs. Ramsey against the life-denying "masculine" vision of Mr. Ramsay. In truth, it is only in groping our way through the clouds of sentiment and misplaced biographical information that we are able to discover Mrs. Ramsay, far from androgynous or complete, to be as one-sided and as life-denying as her husband. Readers have seldom been clear as to whether her son and daughter reach the lighthouse because her spirit survived her death, or because her death has liberated her children.

One criticizes Mrs. Ramsay at one's peril. One of the first critics to suggest in print that Mrs. Ramsay was less than wholly admirable was Mitchell Leaska, whose study of the voices in *To the Lighthouse* was greeted with howls of protest, the most penetrating from the anonymous critic in the *Times Literary Supplement* who seemed uncertain whether to be indignant at the suggestion that Mrs. Ramsay was less than ideal because it was a new reading, or because doubt had been cast upon Mrs. Woolf's relation to the Fourth Commandment.[7] To be sure, the effect of biographical criticism has encouraged readers to see the portrait of Mr. Ramsay as venial, that of Mrs. Ramsay as adoring, although Leonard Woolf and Quentin Bell, Virginia Woolf's biographer, thought Mr. Leaska's study more central to the author's vision than any other which had yet been made.

To the Lighthouse is Mrs. Woolf's best novel of androgyny. *The Waves*, to be sure, as Harvena Richter says, presents all the six characters as part of Bernard's androgynous whole.[8] But as in the end Bernard's voice subsumes all the others, one can recognize in this novel a revolution in technique and a revelation of consciousness which, while it includes the androgynous vision, surpasses it. *To the Lighthouse* enables us to see that, just as Flaubert said: "I am Emma Bovary," so Virginia Woolf has, in a fashion, said: "I am Mr. Ramsay." For so she is. The Mrs. Ramsays not only cannot write novels, they do not even read them. What Mrs. Ramsay marks is the return of the earth mother who, deprived for centuries of all power, position, major influence, may now again be worshiped in a vein which, giving women all adoration, gives them no ability but that of "knowing," in some vaguely mystical way. Beautiful and loving, Mrs. Ramsay has thrust herself into the midst of our impoverished world and seduced us into worshiping her.

As a mother goddess, she has not only sought her power by the seduction of her sons and the denial of her daughters, she has turned over to the undiluted male power the ordering of the world: "Indeed, she had the whole of the other sex under her protection; for reasons she could not explain, for their chivalry and valour, for the fact that they negotiated treaties, ruled India, controlled finance; finally for an attitude towards herself which no woman could fail to feel or to find agreeable, something truthful, childlike, reverential; which an old woman could take from a young man without loss of dignity, and woe betide the girl — pray Heaven it was none of her daughters! — who did not feel the worth of it, and all that it implied, to the marrow of her bones!" Her husband meanwhile envisions the world in the masculine order she has condoned: ". . . if thought is like the keyboard of a piano, divided into so many notes, or like the alphabet is ranged in twenty-six letters all in order, then his splendid mind had no sort of difficulty in running over those letters one by one, firmly and accurately, until it had reached, say, the letter Q. He reached Q. Very few people in the whole of England ever reach Q. Here, stopping for one moment by the stone urn which held the geraniums, he saw, but now far, far away, like children picking up shells, divinely innocent and occupied with little trifles at their feet and somehow entirely defenceless against a doom which he perceived, his wife and son, together in the window. They needed his protection; he gave it them. But after Q?"

It has often been noticed that this masculine ordering of the world is deficient, and most readers and critics suppose Woolf to be condemning her father, or Mr. Ramsay, for this "masculine" order, while exalting the "feminine" order of Mrs. Ramsay. But surely, if his division of truth into so artificial an order as the alphabet is life-denying, no less so is her moody and dreamy mistiness which, unable to distinguish objects on the sea, comparing itself to a wedge of darkness, demands the protection of men while undermining what truths they find. So that for her and her children the truth about the weather, one of the few determinable truths available, is turned into a "masculine" aggression. James, protected by her excessive maternalism, hates his father, hates his "masculinity" which, so the boy is led to feel, attacks her, his mother. It is only after her death that, with the parental blessing each child will always wish for — "Well done!" — James can recognize, not just the feminine quality of the lighthouse, its light, but also the masculine, the tower, stark, straight, bare — the vision he and his father share. Cam, who had as a child been attracted to the story Mrs. Ramsay was reading James, is sent away so that Mrs. Ramsay may continue the love affair with her son, the chief temptation of devoted mothers: the making of their sons into lovers.

No one has shown forth, more swiftly, more surely than Woolf the reward to women for subjection: "Insinuating, too, as she did the greatness of man's intellect, even in its decay, the subjection of all wives . . . to their husband's labours, she made him feel better pleased with himself than he had done yet, and he would have liked, had they taken a cab, for example, to have paid for it." Thus the reward for female humility is to have one's cab paid for, the effect of it is to encourage male aggression in men like Charles Tansley, so that brotherly love will come to be expressed by him "by denouncing something, by condemning somebody." It is Lily Briscoe who will know where he fails, who will burn with his words that women can't write, women can't paint, but who will remember, honorably, much to his credit. Lily, the nonmaternal artist, is the one who must come to the rescue of Mrs. Ramsay, the artist of life, when her dinner party is about to be doomed by Charles Tansley's sulking, and though for Mrs. Ramsay's sake Lily rescues the dinner party by flattering him, and playing the dependent role he expects of women, she privately moves the salt cellar to remind her of her painting and thinks with relief that she need not marry anyone.

Throughout *To the Lighthouse*, Mrs. Ramsay is presented as the mother goddess, the earth mother in all her beauty. So Molly Bloom will represent the earth mother in all her fecund promiscuity. But if Molly Bloom is scarcely ideal even as the fecund earth mother — do earth mothers practice coitus interruptus? — so Mrs. Ramsay is not ideal either. She must always assure herself of her fascination, and cannot bear either to express love or to be faced with men like Mr. Carmichael, whom she does not fascinate. Yet her beauty is such that all recognize it, adore it, protect it, love particularly her ineptitude with logical thought. Mr. Ramsay likes women to be vague, misty in thought. Certainly she is enchantingly beautiful. Charles Tansley regards her: "With stars in her eyes and veils in her hair, with cyclamen and wild violets — what nonsense was he thinking? She was fifty at least; she had eight children. Stepping through fields of flowers and taking to her breast buds that had broken and lambs that had fallen; with the wind in her hair." William Bankes telephones her about trains: "He saw her at the end of the line very clearly Greek, blue-eyed. How incongruous it seemed to be telephoning to a woman like that. The Graces assembling to have joined hands in meadows of asphodel to compose that face." As mother goddess, she is in the midst of what has come to be called the feminine mystique: "Why, she asked, pressing her chin on James's head, should they grow up so fast. Why should they go to school? She would have liked always to have had a baby. She was happiest carrying one in her arms. Then people might say she was tyrannical, domineering, masterful, if they chose; she did not mind. And, touching his hair with her lips, she thought, he will never be so happy again." (One may notice parenthetically that Woolf understood what we have seen Priestley observe in other connections: that no surrender to the "feminine" role protects a woman from being accused of seeking domination.)

Yet Mrs. Ramsay, with part of her being, longs to be more than the source of life for others. "All the Being and the doing, expansive, glittering, vocal, evaporated; and one shrunk, with a sense of solemnity, to being oneself, a wedge-shaped core of darkness, something invisible to others. . . . She praised herself in praising the light, without vanity, for she was stern, she was searching, she was beautiful like that light." Her destiny, after all, is inevitable. "It was odd, she thought, how if one was alone, one leant to inanimate things; trees, streams, flowers; felt they expressed one; felt they became one; felt they knew one, in a sense were one; felt an irrational tenderness thus (she looked at that long steady light) as for oneself. There rose, and she looked and looked with her needles suspended, there curled up off the floor of the mind, rose from the lake of one's being, a mist, a bride to meet her lover."

It is just after this moment that Mr. Ramsay looks "into the hedge, into its intricacy, its darkness." But neither his impulse nor hers can bridge their inevitable polarization; they are entrapped, he is in his "masculine" order, she in her femaleness, her mother-goddess quality. Yet he, after her death, will be able to offer his children androgyny, will discover he did not need her devouring, speechless love to affirm his children's being. She, divine in her beauty, is fatal because though she has nourished and been adored, she has withheld the femininity which might have prevented the war, the terror of "Time Passes." Mrs. Ramsay, in the first section of the novel, has "presided with immutable calm over destinies [she has] completely failed to understand."

In trying to counter the enormous beauty of Mrs. Ramsay, in trying to reveal the dangers inherent in that marvelous femininity, one must be careful not to seem wholly to condemn her. The genuine wonder of her beauty reveals the miracle of Woolf's art. As the mother of young children, at certain moments, Mrs. Ramsay is perfection; but it is the spontaneous perfection of a moment, not the accumulated understanding of a lifetime. Her knowledge is all instinctive. When James will not have the boar's head removed, and Cam cannot sleep with its bony reminder of death, Mrs. Ramsay succeeds in fudging reality: she covers the head; it is still there, she can tell James. But now it is a beautiful sight, a nest, she tells Cam, reminding the little girl of stars falling and parrots and antelopes and gardens and everything lovely. Mrs. Ramsay, leaving the room when the children are finally asleep, feels a chill and reaches to draw her shawl about her. She has used it to cover the boar's head, given the children her own protection. This is not the sort of act of which it is possible to make a lifetime's occupation.

"Time Passes," the middle and shortest section of *To the Lighthouse*, presents the hell man has made of his world; not alone hell in general, but a particular hell, the hell of World War I. As the section opens, five characters appear, all unmarried, two of them to die young. Andrew and Prue, the doomed Ramsay children, announce that it is almost too dark to see, that one can hardly tell the sea from the land. (When Mrs. Ramsay agreed to marry Mr. Ramsay, she stepped from a boat onto the land, guided by his outstretched hand.) Lily questions about a burning light, and they put it out; Mr. Carmichael, the poet, alone leaves his candle burning, since he is reading Virgil. He, the poet, is the only one in "Time Passes," the terrible period of the war, who will do something life-enhancing: he will publish a book of poems. That Mr. Carmichael should be reading Virgil is significant: Dante chose Virgil for his guide in hell.

In the hell which follows, death is both from childbirth and war; mercy is apparent only insofar as it bestows swift death. Prue, "given" in marriage on her father's arm, is sacrificed in her female role; Andrew, taken in war, is sacrificed to his male role. And Mrs. Ramsay, in a sentence of significant syntax, turns out to have died, leaving Mr. Ramsay with his arms empty: "Mr. Ramsay, stumbling along a passage one dark morning, stretched his arms out, but Mrs. Ramsay having died rather suddenly the night before, his arms, though stretched out, remained empty." Mr. Ramsay, the subject of this sentence, stretches out his arms which remain empty, the same action which followed his desire to be told she loved him, the same distress which followed his seeing the stern look on her face when he looked into the intricacy of the hedge. Mrs. Ramsay exists only in a subordinate clause, the object of his needs. At the end of the section Lily returns; the artist awakens. It is she who asks the first question in the last section, "The Lighthouse," and it is she who, in the final sentence, has her vision. It is she who joins the mother and child in the window — a purple patch — with the tiny boat that has reached the lighthouse; it is she who, by drawing a line in her drawing (the tree of the dinner party: the lighthouse?), completes her picture. She and Mr. Carmichael, the poet, the man whose marriage had failed and who had not needed anything from Mrs. Ramsay, together understand the significance of the occasion. "They had not needed to speak," Lily thinks. "They had been thinking the same things and he had answered her without her asking him anything. He stood there as if he were spreading his hands over all the weakness and suffering of mankind; she thought he was surveying, tolerantly and compassionately, their final destiny." Mr. Carmichael lets his hand fall slowly, crowning the occasion with a blessing, and she has had her vision which only androgynous art can bestow.

As to marriage, certainly that is not held forth in the novel as an ideal. The eight children, the bill for the greenhouse, the loss of friendship, and a man no longer able to do his best work: these are the aspects of marriage we view with sentiment and have, until recently, been expected naturally to condone. But what is the marriage? Mr. Ramsay has asked her life from Mrs. Ramsay, and has paid with his own professional life for her love and beauty. But when he asks Lily to have his soul comforted, she praises his boots and discovers (and how few readers with her) that it is enough. She had not needed to sacrifice herself. In homage, he ties her laces. He had borne down upon her, threatening her sense of self, but she had not offered him submission, and he had been revived with what she did offer, an understanding of the proper shape of shoes. So Mr. Bankes, with whom she was friends though they did not marry, had admired her shoes which gave her feet room. A moment's understanding between a man and a woman may be enough: one of them need not offer her whole life, nor demand a major part of his.

If in the first section, "The Window," the female impulse, attractive and enslaving, is presented, it is in the last section that the male impulse dominates, before the androgynous vision which ends the book. We applaud the father's blessing, the boy's identification with, his acceptance of, his father and his male body. But we see what happens when the female impulse is lacking: fishes, bait cut from their living bodies, are left to die slowly out of water; when the light from the lighthouse fails, ships are wrecked and men die clinging to a mast. Because Mr. Ramsay can rescue James from his unhealthy devotion to his mother, the androgynous visions which follow are possible. Cam, seeing the island now from the boat, thinks: "It was like that then, the island," and sees her home with a double vision. And as she experiences this, there spurts up "a fountain of joy," the same fountain associated with her mother throughout the first section; Cam, like her, cannot tell the points of a compass but, unlike her, does not wish to stop time, nor to step forever from a boat onto the land of femaleness. She affirms her father in his being. James, echoing her words, thinks: "So it was like that, the lighthouse one had seen across the bay all these years; it was a stark tower on a bare rock. It satisfied him. It confirmed some obscure feeling of his about his own character." But, James had thought earlier, "the other was also the Lighthouse. For nothing was simply one thing. The other Lighthouse was true too. It was sometimes hardly to be seen across the bay."

For, as Lily Briscoe thinks, "Love has a thousand shapes. There might be lovers whose gift it was to choose out the elements of things and place them together and [give] them a wholeness not theirs in life. . . ."

Marriage as it had existed through the ages, with the male and female joining but not changing their preordained images, fails in Virginia Woolf's ideal androgynous world. To put it another way, marriages accepted as "successful" doom their members. Prue is given in a "fitting" marriage, but she dies, though everything had "promised so well." The Rayleys' marriage, which Mrs. Ramsay had engineered (as is the wont of womanly women), failed as a success, but succeeded as a failure, when they had other lovers and she handed him his car tools in friendship. Mr. Carmichael and Lily Briscoe, one with a failed marriage and other with none at all, alone learn the single vision.

Mrs. Dalloway is, among much else, a collection of failed marriages; it almost questions the value of marriage itself. Septimus's wife cannot save him, nor, it is to be supposed, could Richard Dalloway have saved Clarissa from the death Woolf tells us was originally to be hers. People seem so alive when young, but they end, like Sally Seton and Peter Walsh, either married to a success in Manchester, the mother of five enormous boys, or involved in sordid flirtations with married women. Clarissa, as narrower and narrower grows her bed, remembers the moments when "she did undoubtedly then feel what men felt." Septimus, her double or mirror image, who has been able to feel in a way not recognized as certainly "masculine," goes to the war and "develops manliness," as a result of which he cannot feel, cannot mourn his dead friend, and must destroy himself. Clarissa has denied the manliness, Septimus the femininity within.

The constant recurrence of the First World War in Virginia Woolf's books is perhaps her most pointed and damning condemnation of the "masculine" world. Leaving aside the stridency of *Three Guineas*, we still have the repeated use of the war as the great destructive element — destructive of androgyny as of much else. *Jacob's Room*, the first of her technically innovative novels, is a war book, little recognized as such but one of the greatest: the civilian *All Quiet on the Western Front*. The war persists through *Mrs. Dalloway*, *To the Lighthouse*, *Orlando*, and, skipping *The Waves*, reappears in *The Years*. *Between the Acts*, written when the terrors of the Second World War were daily expected, is about war as about much else: the acts of the title, meaning many things, mean the wars also. Looking back now, we can see how prophetic Woolf was in her condemnation. To the androgynous view, war is indefensible.

In *Mrs. Dalloway*, the marriages are all life-denying, from Mrs. Dalloway's own marriage to Richard (who cannot say he loves) to the dreadful Bradshaws. Only Elizabeth Dalloway, whose Chinese eyes Lily Briscoe will share, seems to contemplate the possibility of not being a wife. Evading Miss Kilman on one side, her mother on the other, not caring for the men who find her lovely, Elizabeth, in a new world, may find her way.

Orlando ends with the marriage of the future, a marriage of the androgynous world. "In every human being," Virginia Woolf writes in that book of wonders where the hero is a woman half of his lifetime, "a vacillation from one sex to the other takes place, and often it is only the clothes that keep the male or female likeness, while underneath the sex is the very opposite of what is above." As to Orlando and her husband, Marmaduke Bonthrop Shelmerdine, Esquire:

"You're a woman, Shel," she cried.

"You're a man, Orlando!" he cried.

"Are you positive you aren't a man?" he would ask anxiously, and she would echo, "Can it be possible you're not a woman?" and then they must put it to the proof without much ado. For each was so surprised at the quickness of the other's sympathy, and it was to each such a revelation that a woman could be as tolerant and free-spoken as a man, and a man as strange and subtle as a woman, that they had to put the matter to the proof at once.

In a perceptive passage, Delattre has noticed the connection between Woolf's *Orlando* and Shakespeare's *As You Like It*:

l'*Orlando* de Virginia Woolf, dont le nom est précisément celui d'un des personnages principaux de *Comme il vous plaira*, semble combiner en lui les deux caractères shakespeariens d'Orlando et de Rosalinde. Il est, comme l'Orlando élizabéthain, un modèle de courage et de noblesse, de respect filial et de courtoisie. Il a, comme lui encore, l'esprit prompt et le sang vaillant, et il n'a aucune peine à gagner, par son élégante bravoure, tous les coeurs féminine qui l'approchent. Comme Rosalinde elle-même, d'autre part, Orlando devenue femme continue de manifester un penchant à la raillerie rieuse, voire à la repartie espiègle, une expérience, en même temps, fort avertie du train du monde, mais parfois aussi un éblouissement total devant l'amour. La beauté, dans la "biographie" de Virginia Woolf comme dans la comédie de Shakespeare, ne va pas sans caprices, l'amour sans brusqueries inexpliquées, le burlesque, l'excentricité même, y jouant leur rôle. L'atmosphère qui règne dans les deux oeuvres est toute de paix heureuse, elle des soirs d'été si propices aux songes, "comme si toute la fertilité et l'activité amoureuse de la nuit y avaient tissé leur toile." On retrouve dans *Orlando* le "clair obscur continuel" qui baigne *As you like it*, "avec ses imprévus, ses suggestions, ses échappées spirituelles."[9]

Virginia Woolf recognized the nineteenth century as the age when everything was covered up or disguised, except the sexes, which became more divided than they had ever been, more distinguishable. But in Elizabeth's England, it had been different, as Woolf's first sentence signifies: "He—for there could be doubt of his sex, though the fashion of the time did something to disguise it—was . . ." In the age of Elizabeth II, as the merest glance around with verify, the same "disguise" has returned.

In a story entitled "A Society," published in 1921 and never reprinted, Virginia Woolf foresaw that we must stop having so many children, and must stop having wars as well. Is the great division of the sexes responsible for our sorry world? It would seem so. "Oh, Cassandra," a lady cries, "for heaven's sake let us devise a method by which men may bear children."

"It is too late. . . . We cannot provide even for the children that we have."

"And then you ask me to believe in intellect." The ladies regard a small girl, the daughter of one. "Once she knows how to read there's only one thing you can teach her to believe in—and that is herself." "Well," the other answers, "that would be a change."[10] It was a change about which Virginia Woolf whispered all her life, through all her works. For "love — as the male novelists define it — and who, after all, speak with greater authority? — has nothing whatever to do with kindness, fidelity, generosity, or poetry. Love is slipping off one's petticoat and — but we all know what love is."

Of course we do not know, nor do we know what androgyny is. Woolf writes of a signal, no noisier than a single leaf detaching itself from a plane tree, but a "signal pointing to a force in things which one has overlooked." For by the turn of the century, or earlier, virility had become self-conscious — men were writing "only with the male side of their brains," as indeed, with the exception of those already mature by the First World War, they have been writing until this very time. Woolf sees that unless some collaboration takes place "in the mind between the woman and the man before the act of creation" we will have war, the Forsytes, the *Old Wives' Tale*, the women's rights movement, but we will not have love nor, perhaps, life.

When Holtby chose the symbol of *Two in a Taxi* for Woolf's androgynous vision, she saw that for Woolf some mysterious impulse had led humanity to this moment. As Woolf watched from her window, this mysterious impulse brought "from one side of the street to the other diagonally a girl in patent leather boots, and then a young man in a maroon overcoat"; the mysterious impulse brought a taxicab also, and as all three came together at a point directly beneath the window, the taxi stopped, "and the girl and the young man stopped; and they got into the taxi; and then the cab glided off as if it were swept on by the current elsewhere." For the mind too, Woolf thought, after being divided, can be reunited in just so natural a fusion. There was always the possibility of so natural a fusion, of a force in things overlooked, which might lead "elsewhere."[11]

Notes

1. Winifred Holtby, *Virginia Woolf* (London: Wishart & Co., 1932), pp. 184, 185.

2. For a recent book which does much to illuminate Woolf's views on androgyny, see Herbert Marder, *Feminism and Art: A Study of Virginia Woolf* (Chicago: University of Chicago Press, 1968). Another early study which is of interest is Ruth Gruber, *Virginia Woolf* (Leipzig: Verlag von Bernhard Tauchnitz, 1935).

3. Holtby, *Virginia Woolf*, pp. 182–3.

4. *Ibid.*, pp. 29–30.

5. The remarks of even so astute a critic as Irma Rantavaara, who has written the best history of Bloomsbury to date by an outsider, indicates clearly the subtle bias which no critic could escape in the fifties. Thus Rantavaara refers to Woolf's "physical hermaphroditism," her "bisexuality which was perhaps too evenly balanced; the tension helped to create a state of neurosis." That the tension might be the secret of the great artist, the neurosis (in part, at least) produced by cultural forces, is not absolutely faced. Nonetheless, Rantavaara has

understood how the epithet "feminine" is hurled at Woolf again and again, and it is this quality, Rantavaara suggests, which is responsible for the critical diatribes of Daiches, Troy, Aiken, Muller, among others. "Their view of her is colored by their social vision," Rantavaara adds, although in 1953 she could not know how colored. Unfortunately, in this highly intelligent study, "androgynous mind" is used as the description of a morbid state, though perhaps essential to the artist. Irma Rantavaara, *Virginia Woolf and Bloomsbury* (Helsinki: Annales Academae Scientiarum Fennicae, 1952), pp. 116, 148, 149.

6. Marder, *Feminism and Art*, p. 133. Marder has an extended discussion of these androgynous symbols.

7. Mitchell A. Leaska, *Virginia Woolf's Lighthouse: A Study in Critical Method* (New York: Columbia University Press, 1970).

8. Harvena Richter, *The Inward Voyage* (Princeton, N.J.: Princeton University Press, 1970), pp. 247–8.

9. Floris Delattre, *Le Roman psychologique de Virginia Woolf* (Paris: Librairie Philosophique J. Vrin, 1932), pp. 189–90. George Sand chose to translate *As You Like It*, but not, as one might have supposed, because of the androgynous heroine; what interested George Sand was the character of Jaques. See also J. K. Johnstone, *The Bloomsbury Group*, p. 321, where he suggests that "Rachel Vinrace and Terrence Hewet, of *The Voyage Out*, who become engaged to one another and achieve complete and perfect union for a moment as Rachel dies, express the two different sides of their creator's character."

10. Virginia Woolf, "A Society," *Monday or Tuesday* (New York: Harcourt, Brace and Company, 1921), pp. 39, 40.

11. The quotations in the final two paragraphs are from Virginia Woolf, *A Room of One's Own*, in this order: pp. 167, 176, 181, 167, 169.

The "Orts and Fragments" in
Between the Acts   James Naremore*

Between the Acts is, technically at least, an unfinished work, since Virginia Woolf never made whatever final revisions she might have considered necessary — the novel was published posthumously. Until recently it has received comparatively little attention, and it has never enjoyed the comfortable niche in undergraduate literature courses sometimes accorded *Mrs. Dalloway* and *To the Lighthouse*.[1] Probably Mrs. Woolf would be disappointed by its reputation. In November 23, 1940, the day she finished the manuscript, she wrote in her *Diary*, "I am a little triumphant about the book. I think it's an interesting attempt at a new method."[2]

But the "new method," when it has been discussed at all, has usually been looked on with disfavor. Thus Dr. Leavis has written that Mrs. Woolf's "mannerisms" are characterized by an "extraordinary vacancy and pointlessness," and Melvin Friedman has described the book as a "stream of consciousness novel" that fails because it does not adopt "the system

*Reprinted from James Naremore, *The World without a Self* (New Haven: Yale Univ. Press, 1973), pp. 219–39.

itself."[3] *Between the Acts*, however, is not an impressionistic hodgepodge, and it should not be attacked for failing to conform to a rather amorphous genre. It is, in fact, a successful experiment which contains some of Mrs. Woolf's best writing.

The criticisms that have been applied to *Between the Acts* may grow out of the book's somewhat disjointed quality, which is characteristic of modernist classics like *The Waste Land* and *Ulysses* but not of Mrs. Woolf's other novels. There are no chapters, but the text is divided into what might be called "scenes" of various lengths, separated from one another by blank spaces. Those idiosyncratic and artful transitions that one finds everywhere in *Mrs. Dalloway, To the Lighthouse,* and *The Waves* are conspicuously absent in this novel. *Mrs. Dalloway* also lacks chapters and has blank spaces to mark some transitions, but the spaces serve only to break up an otherwise unceasing flow of words; and an image or idea that precedes a space is nearly always repeated at the beginning of the next scene to maintain the rhythm and help us bridge the gap. In *Between the Acts* the rhythm is not continuous; we have only fragments of action and character, little vignettes strung together, calling to mind the "orts and fragments" of which (we are told) life seems to be composed. Though the order of these passages is probably not arbitrary, and though they are held together loosely by the time sequence, one could rearrange several of the scenes without any noticeable change in the effect.

Let us consider a relatively innocuous example of such a scene. It occurs early in the book, and begins with this paragraph:

> The nurses after breakfast were trundling the perambulator up and down the terrace; and as they trundled they were talking—not shaping pellets of information or handing ideas from one to another, but rolling words, like sweets on their tongues; which, as they thinned to transparency, gave off pink, green, and sweetness. This morning that sweetness was: "How cook had told 'im off about the asparagus; how when she rang I said: how it was a sweet costume with blouse to match"; and that was leading to something about a feller as they walked up and down the terrace rolling sweets, trundling the perambulator.[4]

The paragraph is in many ways typical of Mrs. Woolf. It illustrates her almost hypnotic rhythms, a certain air of grace and cultivation, and a distance from the nurses that is suited to an English lady of the upper middle class. It also reflects her love of fragile, pretty, feminine images: "They thinned to transparency, gave off pink, green, and sweetness." Furthermore, one is struck by the paragraph's artfully symmetrical structure. It is made up of two compound-complex sentences of almost exactly equal length, so that the first period divides the paragraph neatly in half. Two phrases from the first sentence, "trundling the perambulator" and "rolling words, like sweets on their tongues," are picked up and repeated in the last sentence, with only a slight variation, as if they were part of a refrain which served to round off the picture neatly: "rolling sweets, trundling the perambulator." This affection for repeated phrases and symmetry has been, in previous novels, a pronounced characteristic of Mrs. Woolf's style.

What is interesting about the paragraph is not, however, its virtuosity or neatness, but rather that the effect of neatness has been accomplished in spite of a scene based largely on tenuous and fragmentary elements. The nurses have no particular destination in mind as they trundle, and we are allowed to hear only trivial snatches of their conversation; phrases, as usual in Mrs. Woolf's novels, have become detached from their immediate contexts, so that we catch only vague and poetic fragments; they are pieces, "sweets," which seem to be blown to us on the wind. What gives this scene its wholeness, what connects all the fragments, is the rhythm; which the artist (in a manner reminiscent of La Trobe and her gramophone) renders through a little prose-poem.

The paragraph stands at the opening of a scene about two pages long, a scene containing almost all of the mannerisms that are typical of Mrs. Woolf's style. In the paragraph which follows, for example, the narrator presents a descriptive commentary on the grounds around Pointz Hall. It is characterized by the peculiar voice that dominates texts as diverse as *The Voyage Out* and *To the Lighthouse*, where the author becomes at times a ghostly observer, speaking almost as if she were one of her characters: "It was a pity that the man who had built Pointz Hall had pitched the house in a hollow . . . The terrace was broad enough to take the entire shadow of one of the great trees laid flat. There you could walk up and down, under the shade of the trees." The reader is almost hypnotized by the view, until the narrator breaks the spell by turning again to the nurses, who are calling out to the child George. Suddenly, without any apparent transition, we assume George's sensibility as he grubs among the flower-beds. The hypersensitive imagery here is reminiscent of the opening of *The Waves*. Indeed a "monster" appears, in the form of old Oliver, coming out from behind a bush with a newspaper wrapped round his nose. Lyricism gives way to terror and then comedy as Mrs. Woolf shifts the reader's perspective. Faced with Oliver and his big Afghan, Sohrab, the child bursts into tears. Oliver, in some ways reminiscent of Mr. Ramsay, walks away muttering to himself, " 'A cry-baby—a cry-baby.' " As he tries to read his newspaper we see into his mind:

> He tried to find his line in the column, "A cry-baby—a cry-baby." But the breeze blew the great sheet out; and over the edge he surveyed the landscape—flowing fields, heath and woods. Framed, they became a picture. Had he been a painter, he would have fixed his easel here, where the country, barred by trees, looked like a picture. Then the breeze fell.
>
> "M. Daladier," he read, finding his place in the column, "has been successful in pegging down the franc . . ." [pp. 18–19]

At this ellipsis, the scene ends. There is, in fact, no other novel by Mrs. Woolf that uses the ellipsis so freely. In *Between the Acts* it appears everywhere, as if to emphasize the tenuous and fragmentary quality of life.

There is nothing exceptional about this episode; though it is a fine scene in itself, though it furthers the delineation of setting and character in minor ways, though it suggests (as do many other scenes) that war broods over the horizon, in retrospect it is not one of the most important moments in the novel. Furthermore it has no clear relationship with what follows — a blank space and shift to Isa, who is in her room combing her hair and contemplating her face in the mirror. One aspect of the technique used here needs emphasis, however, because there are very few examples of it in Mrs. Woolf's earlier work. I am speaking of her frequent quotations. These bits of dialogue, nearly always partially freed from their context, point to the apparent aimlessness and the disconnected quality of life; at the same time, the normal banality of everyday language is replaced by that oddly disembodied, poetic effect I have mentioned already:

> "How cook had told 'im off about the asparagus; how when she rang I said: how it was a sweet costume with blouse to match."
> "Come along, George."
> "Good morning, sir," a hollow voice boomed at him from a beak of paper.
> "Say good morning, George; say 'Good morning, Grandpa.' "
> "Heel! . . . heel, you brute! . . . Heel! . . . You wild beast . . . you bad beast."
> "A cry-baby — a cry-baby."
> "M. Daladier . . . has been successful in pegging down the franc . . ." [pp. 15–19]

This peppering of fragmentary quotations throughout the scenes is perhaps the most distinctive attribute of the novel. Nearly every page is filled out with just such "orts and fragments"; the one I have quoted, in fact, is a relatively mild example of the sort of mixture found every-where — lines of poetry, orders to the grocer, comments on the weather, quotes from newspapers, etc. The effect is distinctly analogous to that " 'stream of broken dreams, nursery rhymes, street cries, half-finished sentences and sights' " that Bernard describes in *The Waves*. Here, however, the stream is not simply talked about but rendered — it is plain that it exists neither in an individual consciousness nor in any objective situation: it is made of the whole context of a given scene, and developed into a kind of harmony by the author. Perhaps here, for the first time, Virginia Woolf was able to make her technique evoke the sense of unity that concerned her all along — without the correlated sense of retreat from being and doing, of immersion in water with only muffled sounds audible from above. *Between the Acts* does not sacrifice the "outside" world, either to the narrative voice or to the sensibilities of the characters.

Objective events are shown to have the same texture as internal monologues, so that everything, inside and out, in this person and that,
combines to make what Mrs. Ramsay called a "single stream."

We might consider how this technique works at another place in the
novel — the conversation between Isa, Mrs. Swithin, and Oliver, on pp.
22–40. Actually these pages contain two scenes, since the conversation in
the library is briefly interrupted with a shift to the villagers working in the
barn; for my purpose, however, I will treat only the scene in the library. It
opens with Old Oliver alone, drowsing in an armchair, dreaming of youth
and India:

> The dream hand clenched; the real hand lay on the chair arm, the veins
> swollen but only with a brownish fluid now.
>   The door opened.
>   "Am I," Isa apologized, "interrupting?" [p. 24]

This technique, this moment, is again characteristic of Virginia Woolf: the
author steps back from the character whose dream she has described to
view him from the outside, like a ghostly but unprivileged observer; then,
as quietness descends, and just as the dreamer seems to be on the verge of
extinction, there is a sudden intrusion. The scene goes on with Oliver
contemplating his daughter-in-law.

> Many old men had only their India — old men in clubs, old men in
> rooms off Jermyn Street. She in her striped dress continued him,
> murmuring, in front of the book cases: "The moor is dark beneath the
> moon, rapid clouds have drunk the last pale beams of even. . . . I have
> ordered the fish," she said aloud, turning, "though whether it'll be fresh
> or not I can't promise. But veal is dear, and everybody in the house is
> sick of beef and mutton. . . . Sohrab," she said, coming to a standstill in
> front of them. "What's *he* been doing?" [pp. 24–25]

Oliver's meditation, as described in this passage, has an ordered quality,
but Isa's remarks are as disordered and fragmentary as any internal
monologue. Oliver observes that Isa's son is a crybaby. Isa only turns to the
bookshelves and says, " 'The library's always the nicest room in the
house.' " Now she picks up the *Times* and reads an item about the rape of a
girl — the shock is compounded because the item intrudes on her meditations about *The Faerie Queene*, Keats, the *Kreutzer Sonata*, and the relics
of English civilization that the library holds. Mrs. Swithin comes in with a
hammer and nails, and more casual remarks on the weather follow,
interwoven with Isa's thoughts and a paragraph by the narrator, who
seems to look up at the sky with her characters: "There was a fecklessness,
a lack of symmetry and order in the clouds, as they thinned and thickened.
Was it their own law, or no law, they obeyed?"

The clouds, however, are no more "feckless" than the apparently
random play of conversation in the library. " 'It'll rain, I'm afraid,' " Mrs.
Swithin says. " 'We can only pray.' " Oliver sniffs, " 'And provide umbrel-

las.' " Seeing the nurses out the window, and wanting to avoid another quarrel over religion, Mrs. Swithin abruptly starts talking about Isa's children:

> "Oh there they are — the darlings!"
> The perambulator was passing across the lawn.
> Isa looked too. What an angel she was — the old woman! Thus to salute the children; to beat up against those immensities and the old man's irreverences her skinny hands, her laughing eyes! How courageous to defy Bart and the weather!
> "He looks blooming," said Mrs. Swithin.
> "It's astonishing how they pick up," said Isa.
> "He ate his breakfast?" Mrs. Swithin asked.
> "Every scrap," said Isa.
> "And baby? No sign of measles?"
> Isa shook her head. "Touch wood," she added, tapping the table.
> [pp. 31–32]

The expression "Touch wood" makes Mrs. Swithin curious: "What's the origin — the origin — of that?" " 'Superstition,' " says Oliver, still brooding over how Lucy Swithin's skull could hold a "prayable being." He looks under "Superstition" in the encyclopedia, while Lucy flushes and begins talking about the fish with Isa — would they be fresh? This topic leads to thoughts and observations about the sea:

> "Once there was no sea," says Mrs. Swithin. "No sea at all between us and the continent. I was reading that in a book this morning. There were rhododendrons in the Strand; and mammoths in Piccadilly."
> "When we were savages," said Isa.
> Then she remembered; her dentist had told her that savages could perform very skillful operations on the brain. Savages had false teeth, he said. False teeth were invented, she thought he said, in the time of the Pharaohs.
> "At least so my dentist told me," she concluded.
> "Which man d'you go to now?" Mrs. Swithin asked her.
> "The same old couple; Batty and Bates in Sloane Street."
> "And Mr. Batty told you they had false teeth in the time of the Pharaohs?" Mrs. Swithin pondered.
> "Batty? Oh not Batty. Bates," Isa corrected her.
> Batty, she recalled, only talked about Royalty. Batty, she told Mrs. Swithin, had a patient a Princess.
> "So he kept me waiting well over an hour. And you know, when one's a child, how long that seems."
> "Marriages with cousins," said Mrs. Swithin, "can't be good for the teeth." [pp. 38–39]

Mrs. Woolf has been accused of being humorless; certainly there are critics, Dr. Leavis among them, who are not amused by *Orlando*. A passage like this one, however, is full of such gentle and subtle comedy that it is hard to see how anyone could fail to enjoy it. Yet I suspect that passages like this encouraged Leavis to charge the book with "vacancy." The point to be emphasized is that the conversation in the library has become more than ever a stream directed by accident and association. Mrs. Swithin stops. " 'How did we begin this talk' she counted on her fingers. 'The Pharaohs. Dentists. Fish . . . Oh yes, you were saying, Isa, you'd ordered fish. And I said, "That's the problem . . ." ' "

So the scene ends, trailing off into another ellipsis. The conversation has doubled back upon itself, as conversations have a way of doing, and is ready to start out again on another aimless course, determined by those "pellets of information" dropped casually by this person or that. Perhaps this effect is what Melvin Friedman refers to when he says that the "devices" of stream of consciousness have been applied from the "outside."[5] The form of the inner life, with all its random play of associations and images, is here shown to be the form of life itself, and the novel reveals that we inhabit neither private nor public worlds, but rather some hazy, shifting ground in between. Furthermore, beneath all the apparent triviality, important issues are being raised: Lucy Swithin's brave little defiance of the weather and her remarks on dinosaurs in Piccadilly have profound ramifications. One could list at length the triumphs of this scene—the fine, quiet comedy between Lucy and Oliver; the daydreams, which seem to be spun out at a moment's notice and then abruptly shattered; the inane, easy chatter of relatives in a library, chatter which keeps verging on poetry. Virginia Woolf was not without her limitations as a novelist, but in moments like this she truly was extending the boundaries of Jane Austen's work. Few writers in English fiction can reveal so dramatically the quiet and sometimes terrible power and beauty that lie beneath everyday domestic relationships.

Mrs. Woolf's artistry in such a scene has something in common with La Trobe's theatrical, that odd conglomeration of doggerel, scraps of verse, and parodies of British drama. Built upon "orts and fragments" itself, the pageant is not only an interpretation of history but also a means by which harmony is created. It merges people, brings the fragments together and makes them "all one stream." That is why so many of the descriptions of the audience are a synthesis of bits and pieces; even when the play is over and the audience leaves there is a sense of community:

> "And what about the Jews? The refugees . . . the Jews . . . People like ourselves, beginning life again . . . But it's always been the same. . . . My old mother, who's over eighty, can remember. . . ."
> [p. 145]

The method here is very different from that used to convey the height of the audience's emotion, as they think about the music in unison at the close of the play. But even here, where the style is intended to give a sense of dispersion, the passage intimates a kind of harmony. Art, then, if we may take La Trobe as a type of the artist, has an affirmative end; it bridges gaps, holds things together, merges people, and its greatest enemy is the awful space between acts.

Virginia Woolf's anxiety over discontinuity and fragmentation and her attempts to depict unity in the face of this anxiety are equally implicit in the title of her book. She had originally planned to call it *Pointz Hall* (to represent the continuity of history through an English country estate, as in *Orlando*), but the title she finally chose is more appropriate. From the first, Mrs. Woolf was in love with inaction, and throughout her novels she asserts the value of that "embrace" of the world which, as Bernard says, is " 'impossible to those who act.' " This novel purports to be about what happens — or exists — in the space between actions; but here there is not so much a weariness with life as an uneasy incipience, as if some great event were hovering, about to take place. Leonard Woolf describes a somewhat similar mood in his account of the months before World War II: "There was in those days an ominous and threatening unreality, a feeling that one was living in a bad dream and that one was on the point of waking up from this horrible unreality into a still more horrible reality . . . There was [an] incessant feeling of . . . impending disaster."[6] He pictures war itself as "a cosmic rail station waiting-room, with nothing to do but wait endlessly for the next catastrophe" (p. 10).

Most of the characters in the novel seem to be aware that some new act is about to begin, and that it threatens what had appeared to be the permanent round of their lives, just as a flight of military aircraft suddenly interrupts Reverend Streatfield's request for contributions to the local chapel. But this impending something — the war — is usually presented quite indirectly. Thus in the scene I have just described, Isa Oliver dreamily browses over the newspaper in the library (in the same disengaged way that Mrs. Ramsay reads poetry), and the words suddenly take on meaning; the vision of horror that leaps out of the paper is specifically military in character:

> as her father-in-law had dropped the *Times*, she took it and read: "A horse with a green tail . . ." which was fantastic. Next, "The guard at Whitehall . . ." which was romantic and then, buildings word upon word, she read: "The troopers told her the horse had a green tail; but she found it was just an ordinary horse. And they dragged her up to the barrack room where she was thrown upon a bed. Then one of the troopers removed part of her clothing, and she screamed and hit him about the face. . . ."
>
> That was real; so real that on the mahogany door panels she saw the Arch in Whitehall; through the Arch the barrack room; in the barrack room the bed, and on the bed the girl was screaming and hitting him about the face, when the door (for in fact it was a door) opened and in came Mrs. Swithin carrying a hammer. [p. 27]

As Mrs. Swithin chatters about the summer pageant and the weather, the hammer she holds becomes linked in Isa's mind with an impending terror:

Every summer, for several summers now, Isa had heard the same words; about the hammer and the nails; the pageant and the weather. Every year they said, would it be wet or fine; and every year it was — one or the other. The same chime followed the same chime, only this year beneath the chime she heard: "The girl screamed and hit him about the face with a hammer." [p. 29]

Giles, Isa's stockbroker husband, is acutely aware of the war in Europe, and he is furious at his immobility, at the absurdity of going on as usual when some decisive act is called for: "Had he not read in the morning paper, in the train, that sixteen men had been shot, others prisoned, just over there, across the gulf, in the flat land which divided them from the continent? Yet he changed [for dinner]." When Mrs. Swithin sits on the lawn and muses on the view (" 'It'll be there . . . when we are not.' "), Giles squirms, raging mentally at "old fogies who sat and looked at views over coffee when the whole of Europe — over there — was bristling . . . At any moment guns would rake that land into furrows; planes splinter Bolney Minster into smithereens and blast the Folly. He, too, loved the view. And blamed Aunt Lucy, looking at views, instead of — doing what?" By the end of the novel Giles himself has done no more than crush a garden snake and initiate a meaningless affair with Mrs. Manresa, that earthy, even gaudy visitor who arrives unexpectedly at the pageant.

The novel places the reader in a kind of limbo between historical events, and between two sexual acts as well: in the interludes between the acts of the pageant, Isa daydreams about the gentleman farmer Haines, and while her husband is lured off by Mrs. Manresa she makes half-hearted overtures to the effete William Dodge. There is relatively little indication that the marriage between Giles and Isa will be significantly affected by these flirtations, but the last page of the novel leaves us in suspense. The coming act — it is not explicitly described as sexual — is to be in some way a *first* act, or at least a repetition of all acts between men and women. In this sense it will determine the continuity of life:

> The great hooded chairs had become enormous. And Giles too. And Isa too against the window. The window was all sky without colour. The house had lost its shelter. It was night before roads were made, or houses. It was the night that dwellers in caves had watched from some high place among the rocks.
> Then the curtain rose. They spoke.

The fall of night in Virginia Woolf's novels is often made to suggest the beginning of history, but then history is never presented in her work as anything but a kind of fashion: "What you see us by," as Mrs. Ramsay says; hence the possibility of containing all history in one sexual relationship.

Between the Acts is built on that attempt at a masculine-feminine dialectic which is so much a part of Mrs. Woolf's fiction; the important historical events, if La Trobe can be taken as an authority, are not wars but loves. Hence the three plays that make up the "acts" of the summer pageant (they can be read as parodies of Shakespeare, Congreve, and Gilbert and Sullivan) are all at bottom the same play about love between the sexes. To underscore the sense of historical continuity, three sets of male-female relationships are established within the story proper, each representing a different period of history but each fundamentally the same. The first is contained in the eighteenth-century portraits which hang facing one another in Pointz Hall. On the one hand is an ancestor who holds the reins of his horse and seems to chafe at having to pose. (" 'If you want my likeness, dang it sir, take it when the leaves are on the trees.' ") Opposite him is an anonymous lady who leans elegantly on a pillar and leads the viewer's eye "through glades of greenery and shades of silver, dun and rose into silence." The male-female roles are characterized here as in Mrs. Woolf's other novels; even small details like the fact that the male figure "has a name" and is a "talk producer" are typical and significant. Reinforcing this statement about the elemental distinctions between the male and female, we have a nineteenth-century couple, Mr. Bartholomew Oliver, late of the Indian Civil Service, and his sister, Lucy Swithin:

> Old Bartholomew tapped his fingers on his knee in time to the tune. . . . He looked sardonically at Lucy, perched on her chair. How, he wondered, had she ever borne children? . . .
>   She was thinking, he supposed, God is peace. God is love. For she belonged to the unifiers; he to the separatists. [p. 140]

The third couple are, of course, the twentieth-century figures, Giles and Isa — she dreamy and always murmuring fragments of verse, he, like the other males, impatient to do something. The confrontation of these two at the end represents the major "act" of the novel, the next great historical event; but that act is only about to take place as the novel ends. Indeed, even their infidelity to one another is not yet an accomplished fact.

These, then, are two important implications of the title: we are between wars and between two decisive acts in the lives of an archetypal male and female; in both cases the security of Pointz Hall is threatened, and in both cases an important event seems imminent, so that Giles and Isa continually have the feeling that the future is "disturbing our present." But there is a third and perhaps transcendent implication that helps us understand more clearly the impulses behind Mrs. Woolf's experimentation with the form of the novel. The title suggests, as Geoffrey Hartman has noted, that the book is about unfilled spaces;[7] more specifically, it is about the anxiety that grows from an effort to discover a continuity and unity in life. The great problem that animates this novel, as indeed all Mrs. Woolf's novels, is whether to deny or accept the terrible sense of separation between things. What is threatened here is not only the continuity of English civilization and the continuity of the relationships at

Pointz Hall, but the continuity of life itself. By positing a world and a family hovering between acts, Virginia Woolf creates an air of uncertainty — and not only about metaphysics, for the voice that speaks like a mechanical god from the bushes at the end of La Trobe's pageant is hardly convinced of the moral value of human beings.

Nevertheless doubts are always being dispelled by vaguely affirmative notes. That "megaphonic, anonymous" voice, speaking to the audience at first in clipped sentences and then in doggerel, is pretty clearly the voice of Miss La Trobe, and it is not difficult to hear Virginia Woolf speaking too: "*All you can see of yourselves is scraps, orts and fragments? Well then listen to the gramophone affirming . . .*" (p. 220). What the gramophone affirms is harmony and unity, and it does this largely through the power of art, which unites the audience: "Compelled from the ends of the horizon; recalled from the edge of appalling crevasses; they crashed; solved; united. And some relaxed their fingers; and others uncrossed their legs." As the audience leaves, the gramophone mutters "*Dispersed are we,*" but it adds, "*let us retain whatever made that harmony.*"

But something more than La Trobe's art or Lucy Swithin's religion is needed to make a meaningful continuum out of our lives. We are told that there is a unity, a continuity extending from the dinosaurs to the Victorians to us. But there is an active element in history, and the absence of action, the paralysis that Giles Oliver feels, is made to seem a genuine evil. Some act is required, some means to crush the "monstrous inversion." Whether the act will take place is another matter, but the projected "act" between Giles and Isa seems to represent a hope for the continuity of humanity. Though Mrs. Woolf herself has more in common with Lucy Swithin and Miss La Trobe, with Isa the dreamy wife, it is clear that the harmony she seeks is incomplete without Giles and old Oliver, that some kind of androgynous synthesis is necessary.

Virginia Woolf's visions of unity and her peculiar sort of "feminine" aestheticism offer at best a limited compensation for the uncertainties of life. But *Between the Acts* recognizes the limitations of her philosophy more clearly than any of her previous novels. In spite of its warm comedy, in spite of its optimistic notes, it leaves us on the brink of an action; and the technique, even granting that the book is in some sense unfinished, indicates a certain unwillingness to improve on life by shaping its random flux into a neat pattern. I have said that the novel appears random and disjointed in contrast to her other, rather obviously symmetrical books. One thinks of the voyage out — voyage in symbolism of her first novel; of the almost improbably ordered day in the life of Clarissa Dalloway, ending as primly and neatly as a ballroom dance; of the single day described in *To the Lighthouse,* completed after the space of ten years during which "time passes"; and of still another day, marked by the rising and setting sun in the purple chapters of *The Waves. Between the Acts* is also concerned with the events of a single day — or at least it might easily have been. The first, very short scene, a little over a page and a half, describes a conversation during "a summer's night." All the rest of the narrative is devoted to the following day, as if the author were deliberately avoiding an easy symmetry.

And this slightly disordered, asymmetrical quality is carried over into the depiction of individual scenes, as I have noted already. Even Miss La Trobe's play leaves us with the feeling that the tidy structure had to collapse at the last minute. A prologue and a parody of an Elizabethan comedy; a prologue and a parody of a Restoration comedy; a prologue and a parody of a Victorian comedy — and then suddenly we come to the last act, which isn't there, and we have to make do with a mirror and a megaphone. It is as if the closer we get to "life itself," the life of the moment, the less consolation art has to offer. In other words, what Leavis and Friedman have taken to be the absence of structure is in fact a conscious faulting of structure, a questioning of the power of "significant form" that runs far deeper than Lily Briscoe's feeling that her vision is past or Bernard's criticism of words and compacted shapes — deeper because the criticism is embodied in the very form of the work, as in no other novel by Virginia Woolf.

Mrs. Woolf's whole art is aimed at creating or revealing a world where there are no discrete events and in that sense no "acts." To place the emphasis on acts is to become fragmented; therefore from the first her style was designed to affirm a continuity between things, to show that life cannot be arbitrarily divided, that we are not paralyzed, and that we only seem to be forever poised on the brink. In this novel, however, the plot, the style, and the structure reflect the tension of doubt. Imagine for a moment that time could become slow enough for us to sense a great gap between the ticks of the clock. In those spaces between ticks, between acts, as it were, it is quite possible and perhaps even inevitable to wonder, fearfully, whether or not the next tick will come — and if it comes, whether it will resemble the ones that preceded it, or herald a whole new order. In such a condition, all order, all meaning is in suspension, awaiting the next stroke, the next act. The problem is much the same if it is expressed in terms of space, for we do not know what is going on "over there," just as in the novel we do not know what is happening across the channel. There was a time, Mrs. Swithin keeps noting, when the channel was not there and England was joined to the continent. Not so now; all we get are items in the newspaper, country gossip, and an ominous swoop of military aircraft. Everybody is in some sense isolated, fragmentary, and words must not only be spoken, but also travel across space in order to be heard. The two characters who come nearest to representing Mrs. Woolf's own values are both "unifiers," but they are also slightly absurd figures, portrayed with an ironic objectivity. Thus Lucy Swithin, a whimsical, Victorian old lady, keeps fingering her crucifix; and Miss La Trobe sweats behind a tree, trying to bring her audience into a state of harmony, frustrated when the actor's words are blown away.

The novel does affirm the existence of meaning, continuity, unity, even if only in tenuous ways, as in the scene where Mrs. Swithin looks into a deep pool and broods on the nature of fish:

> "Ourselves," she murmured. And retrieving some glint of faith from the grey waters, hopefully, without much help from reason, she followed the fish; the speckled, streaked and blotched; seeing in that vision beauty, power, and glory in ourselves.
>
> Fish had faith, she reasoned. They trust us because we've never caught 'em. But her brother would reply: "That's greed." "Their beauty!" she protested. "Sex," he would say. "Who makes sex susceptible to beauty?" she would argue. He shrugged who? Why? Silenced, she returned to her private vision; of beauty which is goodness; the sea on which we float. Mostly impervious, but surely every boat sometimes leaks? [pp. 239–40]

The watery metaphor, that image of total unity so often employed by Mrs. Woolf, is not stressed in this novel; in fact in this passage she seems to regard it with somewhat wistful amusement. But a kind of stream is implied, nevertheless, in the orts and fragments that represent the substance of most of the individual scenes. It is Mrs. Swithin's view of history that the novel ultimately supports: history understood not as a cycle or even a significant progression, but as a framework for the constant play of what Isa describes as love, hate, and peace. Only the surfaces of our lives change; nature, as the villagers tell us, *"is always the same, summer, winter, and spring."* This view, of course, can be deduced from all of Mrs. Woolf's novels. In this last book, however, there is a happier sense of the importance of cultivation, the digging and delving that give the earth its serene, permanent aspect. This very recognition of the importance of action brings some fear and doubt with it. Mrs. Swithin's view is qualified by her amusing, genteel religiosity. Virginia Woolf herself made a habit of attacking the official Christianity of the Victorians, and Bartholomew Oliver is by no means an unsympathetic character when he snorts at Mrs. Swithin's crucifix. Art itself is brought into question more deeply than in any of Mrs. Woolf's other novels — even the artist La Trobe questions her own sincerity, and, when the pageant is over, finds herself in need of a drink. There is just enough doubt, in fact, to lend an air of suspense as the curtain rises at the end.

Notes

1. The book has had some distinguished advocates. Northrop Frye, for example, calls it Virginia Woolf's "most profound work (*Anatomy of Criticism* [New York: Atheneum, 1967], p. 67). See also Warren Beck's "For Virginia Woolf," *Forms of Modern Fiction*, ed. William Van O'Connor (Minneapolis: University of Minnesota Press, 1948), pp. 243–53; and Allen, *The English Novel*, p. 338. Two recent discussions of the novel's themes are useful: Ann Yanko Wilkinson, "A Principle of Unity in *Between the Acts*," *Criticism* 8 (Winter 1966): 53–63; and

Renee Watkins, "Survival in Discontinuity — Virginia Woolf's *Between the Acts*," *Massachu-setts Review* 10 (Spring 1969): 356–76.

2. Woolf, *A Writer's Diary*, p. 331.

3. F. R. Leavis, "After *To the Lighthouse*," *Scrutiny* 10 (January 1942): 295–97; Friedman, *Stream of Consciousness: A Study in Literary Method*, p. 208.

4. Virginia Woolf, *Between the Acts* (London: Hogarth Press, 1969), p. 15. Unless otherwise noted, all references are to this edition.

5. Friedman, *Stream of Consciousness: A Study in Literary Method*, p. 208.

6. Leonard Woolf, *The Journey Not the Arrival Matters: An Autobiography of the Years 1939–1969* (London: Hogarth Press, 1969), p. 53.

7. Geoffrey Hartman, "Virginia's Web," *Chicago Review* 14 (Spring 1961): 28.

[Woolf's *Orlando* and V. Sackville-West]

Joanne Trautmann*

In *The Waves* Neville observes that as a writer Bernard exploits his friends for his stories, a comment resembling Vita's charge that Virginia Woolf saw everything in her life as potential copy. "We are all," Neville says, "phrases in Bernard's story, things he writes down in his notebook under A or under B." When Bernard's creator read V. Sackville-West's *Passenger to Teheran* in 1926, she wrote its author: "I kept saying, 'How I should like to know this woman' and then thinking, 'But I do,' and then 'no, I don't — not altogether the woman who writes this.' I didn't know the extent of your subtleties. . . . The whole book is full of nooks and corners which I enjoy exploring." A vaguely sexual image for this G. E. Moore exercise in the cognition of the beautiful qualities of one's friend. By October 1927 Virginia was writing *Orlando: a Biography* in which she proposed to do her exploring. She wrote to Vita about the project, seeking her agreement and cooperation: "I should like to untwine and twist again some very odd incongruous strands in you." She had, she reported, been reading *Knole and the Sackvilles:* "Dear me, you have a rich dusky attic of a mind. Oh yes, I want very much to see you." An article published after the appearance of Virginia Woolf's diary made it clear that V. Sackville-West, her family, and home were the inspirations for *Orlando*. In *The Listener* for 27 January 1955, Vita reprinted this and several other letters relating to the book. She claims not to have been deceived by Virginia's "sudden, urgent desire" to see her. She repeats an old charge: "I realized that it was the author's form of cupboard love — in other words, I had become 'copy.' "

This was by no means the first time that a person from her private life had become the model for a character in Virginia Woolf's work. There had

*Reprinted from Joanne Trautmann, *The Jessamy Brides: The Friendship of Virginia Woolf and V. Sackville-West* (University Park: Pennsylvania State Univ. Press, 1973), pp. 38–48.

been the Lytton-like character in *The Voyage Out*, and the portraits of her parents in *To the Lighthouse*. Quentin Bell says that he and his aunt used to write little sketches of their mutual friends and relatives (thus the joke in *Orlando's* Preface, acknowledging the aid of her nephew as "an old and valued collaborator in fiction"). She noted in her diary for 18 September 1927, a plan to write contemporary history by using biographical sketches of all her friends. Already in this plan Vita was "Orlando, a young nobleman."

Virginia Woolf knew well the main problems of the biographer. She wrote to Vita about her mystery as the author of *Passenger to Teheran*: "Do we then know nobody? Only our own versions of them, which as likely as not, are emanations from ourselves?" In the case of her proposed biography-fantasy of a friend, this problem could be turned to an advantage, personal and aesthetic. She had already shown in *To the Lighthouse* Lily's intense desire to penetrate Mrs. Ramsay's mysteries, and in doing so become one with the object adored. "Could loving, as people called it, make her and Mrs. Ramsay one?" The device Lily chooses to manifest her desire for coalescence is her painting of Mrs. Ramsay in her natural environment. Lily would create her friend. Friendship, she thinks is "like a work of art."

After the experience of *Orlando*, Virginia Woolf had an even more profound understanding of friendships. *The Waves*, her next book, shows Bernard and his friends reflecting images of each other. "We use our friends to measure our own stature." Yet this is a painful process because it means mixing one's idea of oneself with another's idea. It means being "recalled," "mitigated," and "adulterated" (compare Sackville-West's "Solitude"). Bernard's relationship with the magnificently physical Percival is a mirror image in a specific way, and related in precisely this way to Virginia and Vita. Bernard is speaking: "I recover what he was to me: my opposite. . . . My own infirmities oppress me. There is no longer him to oppose them." The platonic relationship of Bernard with Neville, though Neville is exclusively homosexual in inclination, is like that between Virginia and Vita in that both are literary friendships. The friendship of Bernard the fiction writer and Neville the poet works on an obvious level when they compare, for example, their versions of Shakespeare and learn from each other's insights. The friendship works on the level examined by Lily Briscoe when, because of their special talents as artists, they can create each other. To Neville, Bernard addresses this offer of aesthetic love: "Let me create you. (You have done as much for me.)" Eventually, of course, all Bernard's friends are seen as emanations of himself. Indistinguishable from himself, they are only several of a thousand incongruous, male and female strands from all periods of time which twist together to form Bernard's multiple personality. Through those strands and their record in his own writing, Bernard, like Virginia Woolf, searches for a perfect unity: "Some people go to priests; others to poetry; I to my friends,

I to my own heart, I to seek among phrases and fragments something unbroken. . . ."

Orlando is a record of another of these searches, this time, more directly Virginia's. The book has been critically analyzed from several angles, as it requires. Among other categories, it may be seen as a parody of biography, an essay in the exotic, a mock-heroic novel of ideas, an imaginative literary and social history of England, and a biography of V. Sackville-West. Readers of Orlando have normally discussed the book without much more than superficial reference to the woman who inspired it. Irma Rantavaara lists some of the obvious biographical parallels, then adds: "These matter-of-fact biographical details are, however, the least important elements." Frank Baldanza has traced out many of the biographical parallels through a careful reading of Knole and the Sackvilles, from which Virginia Woolf took details, exaggerating them at will. Jean Guiguet is intrigued by the relationship between Woolf and Sackville-West and guesses that Virginia saw Orlando as a way of fulfilling herself through Vita.

I prefer to see the book as the symbolic story of the friendship between its author and the most important member of her audience, V. Sackville-West, to whom the book is dedicated. In "Mr. Bennett and Mrs. Brown" the author presses warmly for a coalition between writer and audience. Here the figure of Orlando is a coalition between Virginia and Vita.

This process begins with the genesis of the book. The first hint of the "Defoe narrative" that will become Orlando occurs in the diary entry for 14 March 1927. There Virginia Woolf sketches out a fantasy called "The Jessamy Brides": "Two women, poor, solitary at the top of a house." The ladies dream about Constantinople and golden domes. Virginia Woolf wants to have an extravagant fling with "satire and wildness." Furthermore, "sapphism is to be suggested." At its genesis, then, Orlando is the story, not of a single man, but of two romantic women, sapphic brides without men: Virginia and Vita out on a fantastic spree.

Orlando retains the fantasy originally planned, but it is based as well on truths about its subject and its author. Virginia Woolf admired a similar approach in other biographies. In an article on "The New Biography," written about the same time as she was beginning Orlando, she praised a certain biographer for doing what she was to do as she took both Vita and herself as subject: "he has devised a method of writing about people and about himself as though they were at once real and imaginary." (The biographer she refers to is Harold Nicolson.)

Vita Sackville-West did not see a word of Orlando until she received a printed copy. When she looked into the mirror held up for her by her friend, she saw a fantasy figure of heroic proportions. But she recognized enough details to be flattered. Some of them were private, signs between the two of them, but there are others which we can point to as part of what we know about Vita's life. We can see the distance between the design founded on fact and the heroic image filled in with emanations from her romantic creator.

Orlando's name is taken from *As You Like It*. Shakespeare's hero is the romantic young aristocrat, cut off from his father's fortune, as Vita was cut off from Knole. Floris Delattre's theory is that Woolf's Orlando is an amalgamation of Shakespeare's Orlando and Rosalind. This is very likely. Sprightly, imaginative Rosalind, who controls the events of Shakespeare's play, would certainly appeal to Virginia Woolf. In *Night and Day* the heroine's mother calls her a Rosalind type. The merging of the two "Jessamy Brides," Vita and Virginia figures, into Orlando is parallel to this merging of Orlando the nobleman and Rosalind the quick-witted controlling spirit.

But Rosalind is seen before her marriage. If Shakespeare had had a talented sister, Virginia Woolf hypothesizes in *Orlando*'s polemic, *A Room of One's Own*, she would not have had a chance to create anything except babies. So Woolf's talented young person of the sixteenth century must be male.

Fortuitously for Virginia Woolf, whose first literary loves were the Elizabethan prose writers, Elizabethan is the period in which the Sackville family produced the first of the men still remembered widely today. Starting with the first Sackville owner of Knole, Thomas, she builds her initial picture of Orlando from details of Thomas and Vita. Orlando's "fathers had been noble since they had been at all." They had been warriors. Their descendant now lives in a vast house decorated with heraldic leopards, Knole's most obvious decorative detail. This parallels Thomas Sackville's family history, which Vita traces in *Knole and the Sackvilles* back to a Norman nobleman who came over with William. "But what's 400 years of nobility, all the same?" — Virginia wrote in that first letter about *Orlando*. She may have tried to toss it off, but the impression remains that Virginia was highly romantic about this old family, and was impressed too, Quentin Bell believes. Thomas Sackville had, after all, written part of the first English tragedy. His descendants had also written and had patronized writers. There were Pope and Dryden manuscripts in the Knole library. Now, in Vita, Knole again had a resident poet. And her great friend was the writer Virginia Woolf, whose *Orlando* manuscript rests at Knole. The young Orlando sits in the attic, rapidly covering page after page with pompous poetry. This is as much Vita as Thomas, for as a young girl, she stole upstairs, her son relates, away from her unintellectual family and secretly wrote long historical novels, some in French and Italian, as Orlando's are. She had one early piece printed privately, as Orlando does.

Virginia caricatures other characteristics known to be Vita's — her sudden melancholy, her need for solitude, her love of nature. This exaggeration becomes part of the structure of the book. Virginia Woolf pictures Orlando alone on top of a hill from which he can see forty counties. Together the created Vita and her creator look at the vast view; first there in England, then in Constantinople, and then through several centuries, swooping down now and then to pick up the essential details of time and place.

Queen Elizabeth is introduced as Orlando's benefactress. She is useful because she was in fact a cousin of Thomas and did in fact make him her treasurer. Elizabeth is also valuable because her virginal attraction to Orlando is similar to the pose adopted by the author: the attracted but occasionally reticent and pedantic admirer. This stance provides a contrast with Orlando's own varied sexual adventures. Like the picaresque heroes he resembles, and also like several notorious Sackvilles, Orlando has an active love life. None of it sullies him; it merely promotes the image of a passionate, free-spirited young man. This was part of Virginia Woolf's original intention. She teases Vita about her amorousness in the letter of 9 October 1927, from which Vita delicately omitted a few words when she reprinted it in *The Listener.* Here, with my italics indicating the relevant phrase, is the line as it is found in Vita's script for the BBC broadcast on which the *Listener* article is based: "suppose Orlando turns out to be Vita, and it's all about you *and the lusts of your flesh* and the lure of your mind—heart you have none."

That last accusation, echoing Vita's charges against Virginia, takes form in Orlando's behavior during his first few affairs when he is, again like his picaresque forerunners, heartless. But he suffers when he meets Sasha because, modeled perhaps on Vita's great early love, Violet Trefusis, that princess is strange in several ways. She is, in the first place, a foreigner from a culture uncivilized in contrast to Elizabethan England. Their affair is conducted in French. Above all, Shasha's womanliness itself is mysterious to Orlando. That Virginia Woolf saw Sasha as a lesson in womanliness is suggested in part by her use of a photograph of her young niece, Angelica Bell, to stand for the princess as a child. In the midst of writing *Orlando*, Virginia described Angelica at a children's party as "so mature and composed; all grey and silver; such an epitome of all womanliness, such an unopened bud of sense and sensibility" (*Diary*, 20 December 1927). Soft one minute, savage the next, Sasha reminds Orlando of his pet white fox. (Orlando has Vita's love of animals.) Virginia Woolf enjoyed this joking imagery. At one point Sasha even howls like a wolf. Purity and a hint of the fang, Vita ascribed to her friend. Orlando is intrigued and confused by his lady's strangeness. But there are hints that he will one day understand. There may be qualities of the other in each of them, for their clothing, like the casual clothes Vita wore, makes no blatant announcement that the wearer is either one sex or the other.

His first major love encounter ended, Orlando falls into a trance. In fact Orlando experiences two trances. The second one is a Sleeping Beauty swoon, after which the author awakens Orlando to a new life. But the first resembles Virginia Woolf's depressed periods when she retired to her bed for days or weeks, and outward life, as far as she was concerned, stopped. During these periods she felt that something "partly mystical" happened to her (*Diary*, 16 February 1930). Just as Orlando undergoes his first trance because he has experienced a loss too painful to face directly, Virginia Woolf's mind "refuses to go on registering impressions. It shuts itself up. It becomes chrysalis." Toward the end of the illness described in this diary entry, Vita calls on Virginia, and she begins to revive. Something in "Vita's life so full and flush" has awakened her, and she begins to compose again.

Similarly, Orlando awakens from his trance to find that his adolescent affliction has become a disease: he must write. He reaches this knowledge after considering, in the manner of Thomas Sackville's "Induction" to *Mirror for Magistrates*, that "all pomp is built upon corruption" and after reading the "marvelously contorted" style of one of Virginia Woolf's favorites, Sir Thomas Browne. Now none of his inherited pomp means anything to the young nobleman. Vita rather liked the gatherings of aristocratic society as a young woman, but retreated more and more into a simpler life in order to write. And so does Orlando repudiate his courtly life style. He hopes that he has a calling and that his simple tastes and his humble greatgrandmother show that he belongs "to the sacred race rather than to the noble." So did Vita glory in her grandmother Pepita and emphasize the simplicity of her homes, in spite of the servants and the silver. Orlando seeks the friendship of the writer Nick Greene, a relationship which Virginia Woolf delights in writing about. Though the writing fraternity may be sacred, it is also human. Nick Greene is a snob; his wife has a yearly baby. Later Alexander Pope speaks three brilliant epigrams and slips back into dullness. Orlando, expecting gods, is dismayed. Knowing Vita's awe of Virginia Woolf's genius, it is easy to guess that Virginia is teasing Vita about the early period of their acquantance. Still, Nick Greene has a curious assortment of knowledge and a way with narrative which fascinates the entire household. Greene's satire against Orlando, foreshadowing, as Stephen Spender notes, Ray Campbell's *Georgiad*, drives Orlando into solitude again. He even burns his poetry, retaining only "The Oak Tree," another name for Sackville-West's "The Land," from which a few lines are quoted.

Greene's attack on Orlando's writing and Orlando's subsequent withdrawal to the contemplative life is a necessary step in his becoming a writer. Orlando here is Vita and Virginia and every writer. The external details are Vita's — Orlando trusts only dogs and roses — but the experiences are his creator's. Orlando's experiences with time seem a parody of Virginia Woolf's themes and techniques in other novels, particularly the "Time Passes" section of *To the Lighthouse*. Vita's ancient family adds depth to Virginia Woolf's sense that Orlando's past is there in every moment of the present. Eventually Orlando declares what Virginia did at age forty: he will write to please himself. Like Orlando reacting against Greene's attack, she reacts to an unfavorable review by stating that she has made a bargain with herself to be an unpopular writer (*Diary*, 17 and 18 February 1922). Virginia hopes to gain thereby "a sense of freedom," needing neither praise nor blame. Orlando chooses obscurity; even anonymity would be welcome.

In this new light he looks at his home as a work of art built over the centuries by anonymous noblemen. He determines to add what he can to this great impersonal art. This gives the author a chance to introduce more details about Knole, which she takes from the activities of Vita's ancestors in *Knole and the Sackvilles*. The author makes every attempt to understand her friend's love of Knole. In addition to Vita's book on her ancestral home, there was the evidence of several poems in *Orchard and Vineyard* (1921) about Vita's joy at returning to Knole. In *Orlando* there is something of Knole's personification for Vita. When Orlando returns home at the end of the novel and makes the customary walk through the house, the rooms are friends. Orlando and Knole have "known each other close on four centuries now. They had nothing to conceal." Virginia Woolf understands how Vita-Orlando feels now that Knole is beyond possessing. But in a way she consoles Vita for this loss through the recreation of Knole's past in *Orlando*. Woolf shows the way into the historical past which becomes simultaneous with Orlando's mental past, "the darkness where things shape themselves." In doing so, she satisfies her own sense of the continuity of events. Nigel Nicolson describes how Virginia Woolf would take his version of the events of the day and shape them imaginatively before handing them back to him, more permanently his. In *Orlando* she has played the same magical trick with Vita Sackville-West's version of Knole.

The middle part of Orlando's life is again based partly on the lives of the Sackvilles, some of whom served as ambassadors, and partly on Vita's own experiences. Only a short time before *Orlando* was written, Vita had been in Persia, surely the inspiration for much of the vaguely Middle Eastern details in this section of the book. But she had also been in Constantinople itself, to which Orlando goes as ambassador, when Harold Nicolson was on the diplomatic staff there during the war. Orlando is now "in the prime of life," and Virginia Woolf's description of his power over people is similar to Leonard's description of Vita in her prime. Orlando is said to have "the power to stir the fancy and rivet the eye. . . . The power is a mysterious one compounded of beauty, birth, and some rare gift, which we may call glamour and have done with it." The novel slips easily from this romance to a satiric evocation, in the manner of Sterne or Swift, of the life of an ambassador. In effect, this is a mock-heroic battle in Virginia's campaign to get Harold Nicolson to leave diplomacy. The story of Vita's grandmother comes in at this point, as does the debate between the aristocratic and gypsy strands in Vita's life style. Orlando, who has always romanticized the common, obscure people—a habit as much Virginia's as Vita's—marries Rosina Pepita, a dancer. This leads to Orlando's sojourn among the gypsies, where Virginia teases Vita about her family's being upstarts when compared to the gypsies' ancient heritage. More seriously, she shows Orlando's further education as a writer, an English writer with an English devotion to nature and an English aristocrat's reverence for tradition. The alliance with Rosina Pepita leads also to a comic version of the real life lawsuit following the death of Vita's grandfather, in which a son of his and Pepita's claimed inheritance of Knole.

But the most important event of Orlando's stay in Constantinople (the most important event, in fact, of his life) is his change from one sex to the other. This happens during one of those trance-retreats in which Orlando sees into "the dark hollow at the back of the head" and discovers, apparently, his womanliness. His body immediately makes the appropriate adjustments. Orlando's feminine traits will now dominate her life, though she retains all her masculine awareness as well.

Orlando becomes a woman at the age of thirty, approximately Vita's age when she first met Virginia. Thirty is also the age at which Virginia married. The age meant major new sexual experiences for both of them. At thirty Orlando is just beginning to operate fully, since until that time she has known only half of the complete, androgynous human nature.

Dressed at first in Turkish clothing of the sort which disguises the sex, Orlando must finally change to feminine clothing for her return to England, now in the eighteenth century. For a time the lady Orlando finds both sexes equally absurd. As the pursuer, she had thought Sasha's behavior incomprehensible. Now, as the pursued, she sneers at men because they are likely to trip over themselves if she shows a bit of leg. But soon she recognizes the advantages of being a woman with masculine experiences. As a woman, men will try to keep her in a position of poverty and ignorance; but she sees the pomposity of men playing at soldier and judge, and prefers those states that she thinks are more easily accessible to women: contemplation, solitude, love. She is capable of taking both masculine aggressive roles and feminine passive roles. She has a masculine knowledge of agriculture, riding, and drinking, yet she seeks no power over others. She is femininely tender, yet will not tie herself down to dull domestic chores. She discovers that her love for Sasha has now, if anything, deepened because they share a feminine consciousness. Sasha no longer seems an exciting, mysterious, but distant creature. To overcome the eighteenth-century limitations on women, Orlando, who is extraordinarily handsome, sometimes dresses in the clothing of a man and sallies forth to take in the night life. On one occasion, in a male disguise, she picks up a courtesan and is amazed to discover that she can see the girl's dishonest attempts to gratify her escort's masculinity. When Orlando drops her disguise, she and the girl quickly become close comrades, speaking freely as they can do with no man.

In her treatment of Orlando as an androgynous figure, Virginia Woolf is clearly glorifying those androgynous elements we have seen in Vita Sackville-West's appearance and values. Orlando even strides, as Vita was said to stride, and drives a car flamboyantly, as Vita did. Virginia Woolf investigates the emotional aspects of Vita's lesbian interests, and shows Orlando capable of knowing both men and women better. Like the female Orlando, Vita had, during her affair with Violet, disguised herself as a man. But I always have the sense that Vita provides the external details for what are, basically, Virginia Woolf's ideas and desires. V. Sackville-West has not written about woman-to-woman relationships as Virginia has. If she has them in mind—as I think she has in *The Edwardians*—Sackville-West treats such relationships very comfortably in male-female terms. We do not know, in short, much of what she thought about specifically womanly friendships. But Virginia has written frequently in her novels, her diary, and *A Room of One's Own* of the necessity for women to recognize their masculine qualities and men their feminine. Otherwise, she feels, the profound differences between the sexes will be further exaggerated and union prevented. What is more, through *Orlando* Virginia Woolf illustrates how one woman may understand her full, androgynous self by coming close to another. The women to whom Orlando feels close—Sasha and the prostitutes—help her find a wider definition of her own womanliness. On another level, the author feels close to Orlando. Virginia Woolf had been attracted to Katherine Mansfield because she had known prostitutes and other women whose life experiences were similarly exotic. Orlando becomes a strong, widely experienced woman, in some respects like, yet more likeable than, the hardened Katherine Mansfield.

As the nineteenth century approaches England, Orlando grows more and more into her womanliness. She begins to pick up something of that century's sense of coupleness and family. Like Vita, Orlando feels just enough of the spirit of her age to survive in society. Though she is naturally an adventurous sort, seeking life and lovers rather than a husband and domesticity, Orlando now yields to Victorianism and seeks a mate. In this way Virginia Woolf explains the situation of a woman like Vita who found the details of family life cloying in the extreme and yet married happily. I have already looked at the independence allowed her in her marriage to Harold Nicolson. For Orlando, Virginia Woolf provides another such marvelously suited husband. Every bit as romantic as his name, Marmaduke Bonthrop Shelmerdine caters to her moods as fast as they succeed each other. He encourages her passionate romantic attitudes; he plays to her acquiescent, quiet periods; and he leaves her to solitude whenever she needs it. They understand each other so well that each thinks the other may be of his own sex. Ugly Harriet, the Roumanian Archduchess, had been fraudulently androgynous: a man dressed, and dressed awkwardly, in women's clothing. He would not have done as a husband for Orlando.

Shelmerdine may be a fantasy husband—even his likeness in the book is taken from an anonymous, brightly colored painting, still hanging at Sissinghurst, of a romantic young man—but there are hints of Harold Nicolson about him. Shelmerdine's nature is mentally androgynous. One of Orlando's names for him, Mar, is a pet name used by the Nicolsons. Furthermore Shelmerdine, though an influential presence in Orlando's life, is actually away most of the time, as Harold Nicolson was before he resigned from the diplomatic service. But Marmaduke Bonthrop Shelmerdine is more like someone Orlando creates for her own purposes than like a real husband. His name and the imagery associated with it at the end of the book—glittering feathers—come to suggest the wild goose which Orlando has been pursuing with her net of words all her life.

Orlando may feel fulfilled on some level through her marriage and the birth of a son, but her more complex self wants desperately to write poetry. To accomplish this end, she needs to be unusually involved with herself. That is how we last see Orlando: she is trying to summon up a coherent picture of herself, composed of all the broken fragments in the book, in order to make another leap for the wild goose. Once again the external details are Vita's and the ideas a merging of Virginia's with what she imagines the created Vita's to be. Orlando receives The Burdett Coutts Memorial Prize for the simple nature poem she has been refining out of her experience for centuries. The Burdett Coutts is Vita's Hawthornden. But Orlando's thoughts about following the gleam, as Tennyson would have it, are expressed in imagery resembling what Virginia had used to explain her own mystical reason for writing. Orlando thinks about the wild goose: "Always it flies fast out to sea and always I fling after it words like nets. . . . And sometimes there's an inch of silver—six words—in the bottom of the net. But never the great fish who lives in the coral groves." Virginia writes in her diary: "It is not oneself but something in the universe that one's left with. It is this that is frightening and exciting in the midst of my profound gloom, depression, boredom, whatever it is. One sees a fin passing far out. . . . But by writing I don't reach anything" (30 September 1926). Orlando also expresses Virginia Woolf's disdain, as she spelled it out in *Three Guineas*, for that modern phenomenon the professional critic of literature, that inflated man who toadies to the writers and condescends to the readers.

Orlando is most nobly infused with Woolf ideas when Orlando calls upon herself and receives in reply the images of the multiple selves she has been, and therefore is. Just as Virginia Woolf addresses the "present owner of the name," her future self at age fifty (in her diary entry for 9 March 1920), and everywhere in the diary addresses a younger Virginia, so Orlando calls upon some of the selves, some of the "incongruous strands," we have seen. Many of the selves are identifiable with traits and experiences of Vita's. Orlando is snobbish about her family and home; she is truthful, generous, and spoiled; she has written some pieces which are romantic and facile: she has a passion for dogs, trees, peasant life, and night; she has loved both men and women. Virginia Woolf has spun these strands together, added certain emanations from herself, and pushed her necessarily incomplete work of art onto the stage at that terrifying time, the present moment: "the emerging monster," as she calls that moment in *The Waves*, "to whom we are attached."

So ends a book which could only have been written by an audacious genius. Like Lily Briscoe, Virginia Woolf had had her vision. She must have felt strangely close to Vita, for the Jessamy Brides had between them created Orlando. After writing her biography of Roger Fry, Virginia Woolf had a similar thought: "What a curious relation is mine with Roger at this moment — I who have given him a kind of shape after his death. Was he like that? I feel very much in his presence at the moment; as if I were intimately connected with him: as if we together had given birth to this vision of him: a child born of us" (*Diary*, 25 July 1940).

A Virgin Forest in Each   Avrom Fleishman*

Mrs. Dalloway (1925) has been analyzed widely and often well, perhaps because it is the one among Woolf's major works that most closely satisfies the traditional view of what a novel should be. Despite its manifest oddness and systematic technical innovation, this is in the first instance a novel, by virtue of its thorough absorption in social life and its close character study. There are, to be sure, passages of essay inserted in the text (especially the disquisition on Proportion and Conversion), but these may be regarded not as an attempt at a mixture of genres but rather as passionate intrusions by the author, based on personal experience. Indeed, the comparative absence here of the mixture of genres which was to enrich her later fiction requires that we look beneath the novelistic surface to grasp the work's uniqueness among portraits of high-society life.

As a series of experiments with the emergent techniques of perspectival narration, temporal discontinuity, and rhythmic juxtaposition of elements, *Mrs. Dalloway* may be considered the first important work of the literary period initiated by *Ulysses* — although hardly an advance upon it. Several critics have noted the resemblance between Mrs. Dalloway's walk and encounters on a single day in London and Leopold Bloom's equally busy June day in Dublin, but the extent of the resemblance has not

*Reprinted from Avrom Fleishman, *Virginia Woolf: A Critical Reading* (Baltimore: Johns Hopkins Univ. Press, 1975), pp. 69–95.

been appreciated.[1] The date of the former is as precise as the latter—a
Wednesday (19) in June (6), 1923 (80) (the Wednesday falling in mid-June,
1923, was the thirteenth). The day apparently begins at ten, as Clarissa
leaves her house to the sound of Big Ben striking the hour (6), for the next
hour struck is 11 A.M. (24), during the skywriting scene, when Clarissa is
returning home (and the Smiths are sitting in Regent's Park awaiting their
consultation with Sir William Bradshaw). Time moves to 11:30 as Peter
Walsh leaves the Dalloway house (53–55); to 11:45 as Walsh passes the
Smiths in Regent's Park (79) (but this is problematic, as Roll-Hansen has
shown, for Peter has not only walked to the park from Westminster in a
quarter-hour but has had his nap and dream too); to noon, the hour of the
Smiths' appointment, and also the moment when Clarissa lays her green
party dress on the bed (104); to 1:30 P.M., as the Smiths leave Sir William's
(113), near the time of Lady Bruton's lunch for Hugh Whitbread and
Richard Dalloway (113–15); to three, as Dalloway returns home (129–30),
arriving about 3:30, in the middle of Clarissa's nap (140); to six, when
Rezia hears the clocks after her husband's suicide (165); to shortly after
six, as Walsh reads Clarissa's letter (171). The day ends after three the
following morning, as Clarissa ruminates on Smith's suicide (204), before
returning to the end of her party. Time is a matter of concern to the
characters, who write odes to it, as does Smith (78, 162), personify it—or
its church bells—as does Clarissa (141), and approvingly connect it with
British institutions like Greenwich, as does Whitbread (113). It should be
noted, however, that all times given are not Greenwich mean time but
daylight saving time, as instituted by "the great revolution of Mr. Willett's
summer time" (178).

The homely particularity of these time indications implies a concept
of time as a series of "life junctures" rather than an impersonal scheme.
These life junctures are established by the presence of certain sensory
phenomena in different contexts, for example, the sound of Big Ben; by
common perceptions among unrelated observers, for example, those of the
Prime Minister's car or of a skywriting plane; and by convergences at
occasions of group activity, for example, Mrs. Dalloway's party. Time is
relativistic here, in the sense that it depends on the systems of measure-
ment, the state of motion of the bodies involved, and the degree of
simultaneity or divergence involved in the recording of disparate events.
But Woolf also entertained the current notions of time as *relative*,
subjective, and even personal. In a number of canceled passages—whose
deletion from the finished work does not diminish their interest—Woolf
mused on the personality that may be ascribed to various clocks, developing the notion of the personal life-time which they represent:

> In Westminster, where temples, meeting houses, conventicles &
> steeples of all kinds are congregated together, there is at all hours and
> halfhours, a round of bells, correcting each other, asseverating that time
> has come a little earlier, or stayed a little later, here or there. . . .

It might have been the seat of time itself, this island of Westminster, the forge where the hours were made, & sent out, in various tones and tempers, to glide into the lives of the foot passengers, of studious workmen [,] desultory women within doors, who coming to the window looked up at the sky as the clock struck, as if to say, What? or Why? They had their choice of answers; from the different sounds or [for "now"?] colliding, or running side by side, melting into each other, forming, for the moment, a trellis work of sound which, as it faced away, was suddenly renewed from some other steeple; St. Margarets, for example, saying two minutes after Big Ben how now, really & indeed, it was half past eleven. Yes, it was half past eleven, St. Margarets said, in her sad voice, upon hearing which, [it] was necessary to make haste, or again to loiter; or to attempt some kind of comparison, or to think how not merely that time differed but that the tone of it was possessed of the strangest power; now militant & masculine; now curtly prosaic, & now in the voice of St. Margarets *flower in the mind*, & had the power, like some breeze which visits a garden at dawn, to brush every flower and leaf in the minds territory, lifting, stirring, strangely, very strangely.[2]

These passages suggest that both clock-time — which had "come a little earlier, or stayed a little later" — and the men who live by it — "they had their choice of answers" — can endow temporality with the significance and even the personified appearance of human living. And this shaping process does not contest the claim that "now, really & indeed, it was half past eleven"; it merely records the fact with a note of amusement. There is in the final clauses, moreover, another dimension or intuition of time, at which Woolf could only hint and into which it is impossible to delve.

Equally precise and equally individual is the treatment of space in this novel. *Mrs. Dalloway* outdoes *Ulysses* in following its main characters' perambulations through the city, so that London becomes as powerfully charged a system of space as it is for more overtly urban novelists. Clarissa's route is best known: she crosses Victoria Street (6), passes Buckingham Palace to enter St. James's Park (9), crossed Piccadilly (10) on the way to Bond Street (11), and proceeds as far as Brook Street (20) before returning to Westminster. Her husband makes almost the same tour in reverse, starting at Lady Bruton's in Brook Street (124), walking with Hugh Whitbread down Conduit Street (124, 127), crossing Piccadilly and the Green Park (128), and passing through Dean's Yard (129) to his home. Their daughter strikes out at right angles to this Westminster-Mayfair axis, taking a bus eastward to the City (149) after tea with Miss Kilman in Victoria Street (138, 142); she pays an extra penny to proceed up the Strand (150), gets off at Chancery Lane (150) to explore the Temple (151), and then retreats via the Strand and a Westminster bus (153).

Peter Walsh's is the most extensive exploration, as befitting a Londoner just returned from India: on leaving Clarissa he crosses Victoria Street (54) but strikes out through the middle of the city, passing up Whitehall (56) and Trafalgar Square (58); he follows a girl up Cockspur

Street (59), across Piccadilly, up Regent Street, past Oxford and Great Portland Streets, and down a side street (60), where he loses her; he then goes on to Regent's Park (61), where he encounters the Smiths and has his dream, and back to Regent's Park tube station (91), where he takes a taxi to his solicitors' in Lincoln's Inn (52). He emerges from his divorce consultation, walks north past the British Museum (167) to his hotel in Bloomsbury (173), dines and dresses for the party, and walks down "Bedford Place leading into Russell Sq." (179) then on to Westminster by way of Whitehall (180). The Smiths follow a simpler route: from Regent's Park to Harley Street for their consultation and home to lodgings off the Tottenham Court Road (98). Thus each of the main characters traces a circle around himself, extending himself into space, moving through his characteristic part of London for personal services or on social rounds, and returning home for life or death — all except Walsh, the odd man out, who has not returned to his hotel by the end of the text, ending where we first saw him, at Clarissa's.

We may summarize these movements in space and time by indicating the narrative divisions so conspicuously *not* provided by the author in her effort to maintain the flow of living experience. *Mrs. Dalloway* may be divided into twenty-one sections, averaging ten pages each in length, as follows:

Section	Pages	Character-focus and situation	Time
I	5–16	Clarissa's shopping trip	10:00–11 A.M.
II	16–25 (30–33)	Londoners (including the Smiths and Clarissa) observing Prime Minister's car and skywriting	10:00 A.M.
III	25–30	Septimus in Regent's Park — fantasies	10:00–11 A.M.
IV	33–45	Clarissa at home	11:00 A.M.
V	45–54	Peter's visit to Clarissa	after 11:00 A.M.
VI	54–63	Peter's walk to the Park	after 11:30 A.M.
VII	63–72	Peter's dream and memories of Bourton	± 11:30 A.M.
VIII	72–79	Septimus and Rezia in Park — fantasies	± 11:30 A.M.
IX	79–92	Peter's memories of Bourton, etc.	after 11:45 A.M.
X	92–104	Smiths leaving Park — summary of Septimus's career	just before noon
XI	104–13	The Bradshaw consultation	12 noon–1:30 P.M.
XII	113–25	Lady Bruton's luncheon	1:30–3 P.M.
XIII	125–32	Richard's return home	arriving at 3 P.M.
XIV	132–41	Clarissa on Miss Kilman	before 3:30 P.M.
XV	141–48	Miss Kilman at tea and at church	after 3:30 P.M.
XVI	148–53	Elizabeth's bus ride	after 3:30 P.M.
XVII	153–66	Septimus's suicide	6:00 P.M.

This specificity of time and place has another effect beyond that of capturing the quality of life in an English upper-middle class setting. *Mrs. Dalloway*, like *Jacob's Room* and *To the Lighthouse*, is intimately tied to the England of the postwar years, not only recording the human losses and the moral atmosphere but probing at its basic institutions. It is no accident that this fiction is about the wife of a member of Parliament and was originally conceived as a short story to be called "The Prime Minister," for *Mrs. Dalloway* may be considered in part a political novel in the modern mode — updating Trollope's milieu, in effect.

Clarissa is the offspring of the Parrys, who were "courtiers once in the time of the Georges" (7) but who were not "very well off" (67) in Clarissa's time. They have seen their home, Bourton, descend to a distant relation, one Herbert, so that Clarissa sadly says, "I never go there now" (48). The family's social energies are summed up in Uncle William: "He had turned on his bed one morning in the middle of the War. He had said, 'I have had enough' " (13). Clarissa admires the grand ladies who carry on in heroic fashion after learning of the death of their sons (7, 12), rather scorns those like Miss Kilman who have been socially injured by the war (14), and remains ignorant of the war's influence on Smith's suicide, with which she does sympathize. She was a sentimental Radical in youth (169) but now concludes that "the most dejected of miseries sitting on doorsteps (drink their downfall) . . . can't be dealt with, she felt positive, by Acts of Parliament for that very reason: they love life" (6). Her husband is a Tory (planning to write Lady Bruton's family history if he becomes unemployed in the event of a Labour victory [122]), mildly progressive ("having championed the downtrodden and followed his instincts in the House of Commons" [127]), and in a position to tell Walsh what the "conservative duffers" meant "to do about India" (177). All have been numbed by the war's horror: Lucrezia Smith shrugs off her husband's loss of his friend Evans by thinking, "Every one has friends who were killed in the War" (74); a Mr. Bowley, who resides at the Albany, is moved at the sight of "poor women, nice little children, orphans, widows, the War — tut-tut" (23); and the narrator comments, "This late age of [the] world's experience had bred in them all, all men and women, a well of tears" (12).

Social class lines are, however, still well drawn: the crowds still respond to the symbols of authority and tradition, as a policeman responds to "something white, magical, circular, in the footman's hand, a disc inscribed with [the Prime Minister's] name" (20); "a Colonial insulted the House of Windsor" and meets with hostility in a pub (21); the men at White's "seemed ready to attend their Sovereign, if need be, to the cannon's mouth, as their ancestors had done before them" (21); and Hugh Whitbread is still "afloat on the cream of English society" (114). Lady Bruton pursues her favorite scheme of emigration (a social safety valve of long standing) and is favored with a *tête-à-tête* with the Prime Minister at Clarissa's party. But there have been profound changes that are only superficially apparent: ". . . something happened which threw out many of [Smith's employer's] calculations, took away his ablest young fellows, and eventually, so prying and insidious were the fingers of the European War, smashed a plaster cast of Ceres, ploughed a hole in the geranium beds, and utterly ruined the cook's nerves at Mr. Brewer's establishment at Muswell Hill" (95). For a recent arrival like Walsh, this subtle change can only be guessed at: "more than suspecting from the words of a girl, from a housemaid's laughter — intangible things you couldn't lay your hands on — that shift in the whole pyramidal accumulation which in his youth had seemed immovable" (178).

The consistently political ambience of *Mrs. Dalloway* is focused in the figure of the Prime Minister, which moves through the text from beginning to end. At the outset his car appears in Mayfair as Clarissa is doing her shopping, causing a stir of interest from many perspectives which anticipates the interest given to the skywriting airplane (16–22).[3] At the close the Prime Minister's visit helps knit together Clarissa's struggling party, providing a lift for the servants (181) as well as for the guests (189). This political symbol has long been associated with Clarissa, for early in life Walsh has berated her with it: "She would marry a Prime Minister and stand at the top of the staircase; the perfect hostess he called her . . ." (9). In the closing pages we see the prophecy partially fulfilled as the perfect hostess stands at the top of the stairs, and as for marrying the Prime Minister, her husband's career is not yet over. Smith's fate, too, is sketched with reference to this symbol of political eminence: he believes that his new religion must be conveyed urgently to the Prime Minister (75, 162).[4]

Even more powerful as a symbol of the state of society envisaged in this fiction is that of illness. All are ill: Clarissa, turned whitehaired since her bout of influenza (6), Evelyn Whitbread, chronically ill of an unspecified internal ailment (8), Smith, with his war psychosis, Ellie Henderson, subject to chills (185), and even the shamming Lady Lexham, who excuses herself from the party by pretending a cold (184). Attitudes toward sickness range from Dr. Holmes's policy of benign neglect to Elizabeth Dalloway's preference for the ill (150), with Sir William Bradshaw's Harley Street manner falling somewhere between. The most corrosive ailment in this society seems to be disease of the heart, and the condition takes on the symbolic proportions it had acquired in Ford's *The Good Soldier*: Clarissa's heart has been affected by her illness (6), and Walsh has always accused her of having no heart (10); he also declares this of Whitbread (9). Yet the unconventional Sally Seton, now Lady Rosseter, can reduce the symbol to a cliché — "What does the brain matter . . .

compared with the heart?" (213) — and Clarissa acknowledges that her daughter's affection for the objectionable Miss Kilman "proves she has a heart" (149). These sentimental pieties hint at the prevailing scarcity of the real thing in a society sick at heart.

The cumulative effect of such repeated notations and images is to establish a systematic network of social elements — human time, city space, personal relationships, professional and institutional activities, publicly shared symbols, political issues — so as to arrive at a vision of modern life on a national scale. This collective existence is not to be apprehended externally, as it would be by a social scientist or a naturalist novelist, but internally, as it is experienced by its participants. To this end, the internal monologues of the characters express their sense of relation to various social entities together with their sense of themselves as individuals distinct from these entities. Woolf's own notions of collective existence were highly developed,[5] but what is of most interest in *Mrs. Dalloway* is the form that such beliefs take in characters of different kinds, responding to situations that arise directly from the action.

Septimus Warren Smith maintains the most radical form of belief in a collective existence, joining not only people but also objects and even sensory phenomena in an organic unity:

> But they beckoned; leaves were alive; trees were alive. And the leaves being connected by millions of fibres with his own body, there on the seat, fanned it up and down; when the branch stretched he, too, made that statement. The sparrows fluttering, rising, and falling in jagged fountains were part of the pattern; the white and blue, barred with black branches. Sounds made harmonies with premeditation; the spaces between them were as significant as the sounds. A child cried. Rightly far way a horn sounded. All taken together meant the birth of a new religion — — (26)

The character of this religion is soon fleshed out with honored elements of mystical, pantheist, and antinomian creeds: "Men must not cut down trees. There is a God. . . . Change the world. No one kills from hatred . . . there is no crime . . . there is no death" (28).

Even more dramatic a consequence of Smith's religion is the relationship to society it entails:

> Look, the unseen bade him, the voice which now communicated with him who was the greatest of mankind, Septimus, lately taken from life to death, the Lord who had come to renew society, . . . suffering forever, the scapegoat, the eternal sufferer, but he did not want it, he moaned, putting from him with a wave of his hand that eternal suffering, that eternal loneliness. (29)

The ascription of these beliefs to Smith is remarkable less as an instance of psychological insight than as an application of modern anthropological knowledge of primitive religion and society.⁰ Woolf deepens her portrait of the outsider by relating him to the archetype of the scapegoat, which has traditionally accompanied the communal ideal. By the exclusion, sacrifice, or crucifixion of one of its members the group establishes or reaffirms its own organic ties. The image is first signaled when Rezia calls Septimus's attention to "a few sheep" grazing in the park (29). The role of Christ figure or lamb of God comes to him not merely out of religious hysteria or personal megalomania but from his sense of himself as a sacrificial object who affirms the collective existence by separating or sacrificing himself. Septimus thinks of himself as "this last relic straying on the edge of the world, this outcast, who gazed back at the inhabited regions . . ." (103). Thus his suicide is not the cowardly escape that Dr. Holmes names it (164) but is conceived as an act of martrydom: impaling himself on the spikes below, he cries to the world at large, "I'll give it you!" (164) — yielding his own life for mankind.⁷

In contrast to Smith, Peter Walsh espouses a humanist doctrine that connects him with people, not things: "I prefer men to cauliflowers" (5); ". . . he did not like cabbages; he preferred human beings" (211–12). But Walsh shares with Smith the warped personality and the status of the outcast: on his return, Clarissa finds in him "the same queer look; . . . a little out of the straight his face is" (46); "I know what I'm up against, he thought, running his finger along the blade of his knife" (52); ". . . he could not come up to the scratch, being always apt to see round things" (174–75). But Peter plays the social game, however badly and unwillingly: he becomes an imperial administrator in India, despite his youthful socialist beliefs (56); he is an easy mark for women, for "nobody of course was more dependent upon others. . . ; it had been his undoing" (174); and he decides to go to Clarissa's party despite his distaste for it.

For Clarissa Dalloway, unlike the principal males, the commitment to social unity conflicts with a vigorous sense of individuality, and in this tension lies her chief interest as the titular heroine. On the one hand, she believes in something like Smith's organic universe: ". . . somehow in the streets of London, on the ebb and flow of things, here, there, she survived, Peter survived, lived in each other, she being part, she was positive, of the trees at home; of the house there, ugly, rambling all to bits and pieces as it was; part of people she had never met; being laid out like a mist between the people she knew best, who lifted her on their branches as she had seen the trees lift the mist, but it spread ever so far, her life, herself" (11–12). This belief is of long standing, having been expressed to Peter during their youth, and it still retains some of the intimations of immortality which it then carried:

> . . . she felt herself everywhere; not "here, here, here"; and she tapped the back of the seat; but everywhere. She waved her hand, going up Shaftesbury Avenue. She was all that. So that to know her, or any one, one must seek out the people who completed them; even the places. . . .

It ended in a transcendental theory which, with her horror of death, allowed her to believe, or say that she believed (for all her scepticism), that since our apparitions, the part of us which appears, are so momentary compared with the other, the unseen part of us, which spreads wide, the unseen might survive, be recovered somehow attached to this person or that, or even haunting certain places, after death. Perhaps — perhaps. (168)

These fumblings for a belief in survival, amid images of the self's mixing with the people and places of one's life, bears a close resemblance to a number of meditative passages scattered through A *Writer's Diary*. Despite Clarissa's previous appearance as a superficial social butterfly in *The Voyage Out*, Woolf has been able to invest her with a depth that carries something of the author's own temper. It is a temper that leans toward a doctrine of collective existence, a fusion of selves in a community of love, an infusion of the marks of identity into the people one knows and into the earth, which endures.

But Woolf's self-projection has another side. Clarissa is an apostle of individuality, has a strong instinct of withdrawal from others, and is presented in the course of the narrative as vigorously preserving her sense of identity. Images of cloistral isolation and virginal inviolability attach to her (33, 35, 36, 45).[8] She admires the woman in the window across the way as a model of her own privacy.

> . . . she watched out of the window the old lady opposite climbing upstairs. Let her climb upstairs if she wanted to; let her stop; then let her, as Clarissa had often seen her, gain her bedroom, part her curtains, and disappear again into the background. Somehow one respected that — that old woman looking out of the window, quite unconscious that she was being watched. There was something solemn in it — but love and religion would destroy that, whatever it was, the privacy of the soul. (139–40)

The negative side of this individualism is recognized by Clarissa herself as egotism, expressed in her jealousy at Peter's new love affair and later at Lady Bruton's luncheon invitation to her husband: "But the indomitable egotism which for ever rides down the hosts opposed to it, the river which says on, on, on; even though, it admits, there may be no goal for us whatever, still on, on; this indomitable egotism charged her cheeks with colour . . ." (50–51). At its worst, egotism leads her to social conformity, strongly tinged by sexual prudery, as when in youth she had been horrified by gossip about a neighbor's adultery: ". . . it was her manner that annoyed [Peter]; timid; hard; arrogant; prudish. 'The death of the soul' " (66). At its best, egotism defines her as a unique being, an ultimate reality, as Peter sees her revealed at the close: "It is Clarissa. . . . For there she was" (213).[9]

Despite its grounding in social and political life, then, *Mrs. Dalloway* is designed as the fictional biography of a single character. Woolf's often-quoted introduction to the Modern Library edition has somewhat misled criticism into focusing on Clarissa and Septimus as a twin center, to the detriment of the novel's compelling unity. The work proceeds by a series of juxtapositions of the central figure and those who surround her: Peter Walsh, Sally Seton, Miss Kilman, and others besides Septimus. Its form suggests the model of a center with radial links to a number of points on the circumference rather than the polar opposition described in some readings.[10] Even a center/circumference model falsifies the dynamics of the work: Mrs. Dalloway is traced forward from morning to night on a given day and simultaneously back from the present into her past so as to fill in a potential biography. By catching up the entire course of a life still ongoing and directed toward the future, the narrative treatment parallels the deepening meditation of the heroine herself, so that her final acknowledgment of Septimus's relationship to her sheltered life is but the fulfillment of a gathering insight. Not only does the tale move toward Clarissa's enlightenment and imaginative expansion in the closing moments, but the elaboration of certain motifs and images throughout the work leads to a growing sense of the protagonist's permeation of the text. The experimentalism of *Mrs. Dalloway* is perhaps most unique in this: it used the conventions of the English social novel toward a metaphysical aim — the dawn of an individual's conviction of her own reality and the simultaneous evocation of that sense in the reader. In reaching toward the epiphany of a human subject rather than of a god, the fiction represents a "displacement" of previous literary modes, a transformation of myth into modern mythos, and a secularization of traditional religious concerns. This can be shown in the working of theme and action as the text moves from Peter's "It is Clarissa herself . . ." (56), through his sustained remembrance of her — ". . . there she was, however; there she was" (85) — to the manifestation of her at the close: "For there she was" (213).

The dialectic of communion and individuation that occurs in the narrative provides the justification for the fiction's elaborate experimentation with point of view. Although Woolf's use of the technique has been studied in detail by Richter and has been given philosophical depth by Auerbach, it has not generally been seen as an extension of the text's thematic concerns. The transition between Clarissa and Lucrezia by way of their perception of the Prime Minister's car (16, 18); between the London crowd and the Smiths by way of the skywriting airplane (23–25); between Peter and Lucrezia through their efforts to comfort a child, Elise Mitchell (72–73) (they later see each other directly, when the Smiths seem to be arguing [79]); between Walsh and Lucrezia again by way of the street singer (91–92); these carefully constructed perspectival situations are less exhibitions of experimental technique or epistemological theory than substantiations of the characters' personal experience. From these passing encounters and conjoint perceptions, human life is constituted.

The clearest indication that multiple points of view make up an underlying structure of experience—if not a group mind or unity of consciousness—are the instances of eerie coincidence. After Septimus's plunge from the window, Lucrezia dreams of passing through a window into a garden: "It seemed to her as she drank the sweet stuff that she was opening long windows, stepping out into some garden. But where?" (165). The movement of stepping from or leaping through a window into a garden, together with the hills and nearby sea of the surrounding landscape, place the dream at Bourton, where Clarissa had similarly "plunged" (5) (Bourton is set amid hills near the Severn [169]). Similarly, Clarissa's echoing of the motto "Fear no more" while taking her midday nap (45) is echoed by Septimus during his trancelike state before suicide (154).

The most extended and impressive example of a shared system of symbols in *Mrs. Dalloway* is the specter of an old woman. Early in the text, Clarissa thinks of Miss Kilman with distaste: "For it was not her one hated but the idea of her, which undoubtedly had gathered into itself a great deal that was not Miss Kilman; had become one of those spectres with which one battles in the night; one of those spectres who stand astride us and suck up half our life-blood, dominators and tyrants . . ." (14–15). Later, Clarissa and Peter share an unspoken image of a preternatural presence:

> "I am in love," he said, not to her however, but to some one raised up in the dark so that you could not touch her but must lay your garland down on the grass in the dark. . . . He had deposited his garland. Clarissa could make what she would of it.
> "In love!" she said. That he at his age should be sucked under in his little bow-tie by that monster! (50)

The ambiguity of this specter is emphasized not only by the varying reactions of Peter and Clarissa to its presidency over love but also by Clarissa's association of it with her image of a spiritual vampire like Miss Kilman.

The benign aspects of this figure are expanded soon after in Peter's dream:

> The grey nurse resumed her knitting as Peter Walsh, on the hot seat beside her, began snoring. In her grey dress, moving her hands indefatigably yet quietly, she seemed like the champion of the rights of sleepers, like one of those spectral presences which rise in twilight in woods made of sky and branches. The solitary traveller, haunter of lanes, disturber of ferns, and devastator of great hemlock plants, looking up suddenly, sees the giant figure at the end of the ride. (63)

The position of the figure in a forest, its statuelike aspect, its protective yet vaguely threatening influence mark this as an archetypal elaboration of the metaphoric images that had previously appeared in Peter's and Clarissa's minds.

A manuscript draft of these paragraphs employs phrases which further emphasize the psychological projection of a feminine archetype:

> And then a great brush swept smooth across his mind. . . . Again the great & benignant power took him into its keeping. (B.M., I, 24)

> In her white dress, moving her hands indefatigably yet quietly, she seemed like the champion of the rights of sleepers; like one of those spectral presences which, rise up in twilight, in woods, made of sky & branches yet endowed with a vast personality, *with benignity*, yet extremely aloof, & yet lure the solitary traveller to their arms by some promise of understanding — with a sense of power. An [word illegible], a voyager, to confide his suffering to them, to say, as he advances down the grassy ride, how they alone understand his immense weariness, which ceases to be weariness on the spot, & becomes luminous with the silver light of the sky between the branches, & deep, & romantic, & refreshing, as the leaves rustle & shake in the twilight wind. (B.M., I, 25)

> This figure in the sky is only a state of mind. She is my embodiment of an instinct. *She has no external existence.* She blesses my extreme weariness, & consents to take me up into her arms. . . . For if I can conceive of her, then, in some sense she exists. Thus guarding himself as well as he can, from ridicule, he is astonished, to find himself advancing towards the sky & leaves, as if they were the complement of his own person; as if they conspired [?] against an existence otherwise incomplete. (B.M., I, 26)

This was to be thought of, then, as a "great & benignant power," "a vast personality," who "blesses [man's] extreme weariness," a being endowed with divine afflatus and archetypal generality. It is also recognized not merely as a "state of mind" (as in G. E. Moore's philosophy) but as the "embodiment of an instinct," the Jungian projection of a universal impulse — in this case, toward completion and security with the feminine aspect of oneself, "the complement of his own person." Although these phrases are omitted in the published text, enough of their meaning is carried on in the specification of a "giant figure," emanating its "womanhood" and proffering "great cornucopias full of fruit" (63, 64).[11]

The crystallization of Peter's benign dream vision into the image of a nurturant female brings with it a new figure, which commands equal attention: the solitary traveler. Among the attributes ascribed to him — atheism (63), subjective idealism (63–64), tendencies toward withdrawal and extinction (64) — there is one that probably marks him as Peter himself: ". . . he is elderly, past fifty now" (64) (Peter is fifty-three [83]). Walsh as solitary traveler passes in his dream to a house where "coming to the door with shaded eyes, possibly to look for his return, with hands raised, with white apron blowing, is an elderly woman who seems (so powerful is this infirmity) to seek, over the desert, a lost son; to search for a rider destroyed; to be the figure of the mother whose sons have been killed in the battles of the world" (65). This apparition combines elements of Peter's imagination—the figure at the door, a landlady named Mrs. Turner (64), who serves him at his return (65)—with elements of Clarissa's—the bereaved Lady Bexborough and Mrs. Foxcroft, "eating her heart out because that nice boy was killed" (6–7). Peter wakes and associates his dream with a scene at Bourton at the time of his broken romance with Clarissa (65); moreover, he recalls "an old nurse, old Moody, old Goody, some such name they called her, whom one was taken to visit in a little room with lots of photographs, lots of bird-cages" (67). This old nurse is still going strong, doing service at the party: ". . . old Ellen Barnet, who had been with the family for forty years, . . . and remembered mothers when they were girls. . . . And they could not help feeling, Lady Lovejoy and Miss Alice, that some little privilege in the matter of brush and comb was awarded them having known Mrs. Barnet—'thirty years, milady,' Mrs. Barnet supplied her. . . . The dear old body, . . . Clarissa's old nurse" (183).

This configuration of images in Peter's and Clarissa's minds has obvious relations with the archetypes of the eternal feminine or *magna mater*, but it need not be pursued outside the text to reveal its powerful local significance. The solitary traveler is soon to be associated not only with Peter but also with Septimus: "He saw things too—he had seen an old woman's head in the middle of a fern" (74). Smith is even identified with the specter itself: "Septimus cried, . . . raising his hand like some colossal figure who has lamented the fate of man for ages in the desert alone . . ." (78). The old woman as repository of eternal loving is then elaborated in a street singer: ". . . the battered woman—for she wore a skirt—with her right hand exposed, her left clutching at her side, stood singing of love—love which has lasted a million years, she sang, love which prevails, and millions of years ago her lover, who had been dead these centuries, had walked, she crooned, with her in May . . ." (90).[12] A similar figure penetrates the awareness of Dalloway as he crosses the park, but he consigns her to his mental lumber room of social problems: "But what could be done for female vagrants like that poor creature, stretched on her elbow (as if she had flung herself on the earth, rid of all ties, to observe curiously, to speculate boldly, to consider the whys and the wherefores, impudent, loose-lipped, humorous), he did not know" (128). Finally, this old woman appears as the tutelary spirit who reveals Clarissa to herself:

> Oh, but how surprising—in the room opposite the old lady stared straight at her! . . . It was fascinating to watch her, moving about, that old lady, crossing the room, coming to the window. Could she see her? It was fascinating, with people still laughing and shouting in the drawing room, to watch that old woman, quite quietly, going to bed alone. (204)

Not only are the characters' imaginations stocked with collective images, drawn from a larger community of mind, but the narrative employs these images to further characterize them. In the most outstanding instance, the underlying affinity between Clarissa and Septimus is expressed by their persistent likening to birds. Both have noses "beaked like a bird's" (13) or are "beak-nosed" (17); both are attentive to the flight of birds, as seen in Clarissa's memory of "the rooks rising, falling" (5), and in Septimus's interest in "swallows swooping, swerving, flinging themselves in and out, round and round, yet always with perfect control . . ." (77); both are associated with birds in the minds of others, e.g., Scrope Purvis sees Clarissa with a "touch of the bird about her, of the jay, blue-green, light, vivacious" (6), and Septimus makes Rezia think of a "young hawk" (161). On the same page Septimus sees Rezia similarly: ". . . he could feel her mind, like a bird, falling from branch to branch, and always alighting, quite rightly." This image of the characters assumes more than metaphoric significance, however, as the bird becomes a complex symbol through repeated and diverse uses. It is a means of communication with the universe: "A sparrow perched on the railing opposite chirped Septimus, Septimus, four or five times over and went on, drawing its notes out, to sing freshly and piercingly in Greek words how there is no crime and, joined by another sparrow, they sang in voices prolonged and piercing in Greek words, from trees in the meadow of life beyond a river where the dead walk, how there is no death"(28).[13] The bird also is identified with the street singer (adding to her connections with an ancient spring and with the great mother archetype): ". . . with the bird-like freshness of the very aged, she still twittered 'give me your hand and let me press it gently' " (91). At Clarissa's moment of epiphany, she is marked by a renewed identification with the fragility and the creativity of birds: ". . . there was in the depths of her heart an awful fear. Even now, quite often if Richard had not been there reading the *Times*, so that she could crouch like a bird and gradually revive, send roaring up that immeasurable delight, rubbing stick to stick, one thing with another, she must have perished" (203).

Finally, the bird appears in a mythical guise but only to be rejected as too fanciful an intrusion into the direct contact of men and women at Clarissa's party: "The curtain with its flight of birds of Paradise blew out again. And Clarissa saw — she saw Ralph Lyon beat it back, and go on talking. So it wasn't a failure after all! it was going to be all right now — her party. . . . something now, not nothing, since Ralph Lyon had beat back the curtain" (187). The birds of Paradise, who can never come down to earth because they lack feet,[14] perhaps connote the imaginative designs which some of Woolf's characters entertain: beautiful, decorative, perhaps necessary illusions, they must be firmly beaten back for individuals to emerge and social life to proceed.

Another collective phenomenon that figures strongly in *Mrs. Dallo-*

way is the image of Shakespeare—although it does not have the central position that it takes in *Night and Day*. Clarissa alternates between quotations from *Cymbeline* and *Othello* to express her attitudes toward life and death: "Fear no more the heat o' the sun" (*Cymbeline*, act 4, scene 2); "If it were now to die,/'Twere now to be most happy" (*Othello*, act 2, scene 1). Septimus, on the other hand, has been imaginatively formed by "the intoxication of language—*Antony and Cleopatra*" (98; see also 94, 95, 99, 101). Even in his dying moments, this inspiration persists: "He was not afraid. At every moment Nature signified . . . standing close up to breath through her hollowed hands Shakespeare's words, her meaning" (154). By the same token characters are to be judged negatively to the degree to which they dislike or misread the poet: "Richard Dalloway got on his hind legs and said that no decent man ought to read Shakespeare's sonnets because it was like listening at keyholes (besides, the relationship was not one that he approved)" (84); in Septimus's room, Dr. Holmes "opened Shakespeare—*Antony and Cleopatra*; pushed Shakespeare aside" (101); Lady Bruton "never spoke of England, but this isle of men, this dear, dear land, was in her blood (without reading Shakespeare)" (198).[15]

Clarissa's repeated quotation of the dirge from *Cymbeline*—"Fear no more the heat of the sun"—has generally been taken as her self-encouragement to face life and the demands of the social world, in contrast to Septimus's escape from his fear by suicide. It will be recalled, however, that the dirge contains a biting ambiguity, which makes its way into the fiction: the singers are congratulating the (supposed) departed for escaping the rigors of nature, history, age—of life itself.[16] Thus Clarissa's affinity for the refrain may be taken as a mark of her strong propensity for death, which she indulges in imagination throughout the work: on her morning walk (12), during her midday activity (45), and on her withdrawal from the party (202-4). A passage from the manuscript version makes her drift toward death even clearer by ringing in another line of the dirge: "Thou thy worldly task hast done, Mrs. Dalloway read. Tears unshed, tears deep, salt, still, stood about her for all deaths and sorrows . . ." (B.M., II, 128). We can sense from this that Clarissa's tendency toward virginal coldness and withdrawal into chaste isolation is an expression of the universal reversion to the security of effortless stasis. And her temptation by death is furthered by her anxiety in face of the dangers of living. Summing up a number of marks of this fear, in a canceled passage, Clarissa is seen "thinking of her childhood all the time; the oddest ideas coming to her; fragments of poetry; & a sense of being out out far to sea, & alone; & blown on, very dangerously, for she never lost her sense that it is dangerous, living even one day. A rope walker, & beneath death; so she thought most people felt . . ." (B.M., II, 125).

It is at the end of this prolonged transaction with death that Clarissa chooses life, and her affirmation must be seen as the temporary resolution of a continuing ambivalence in the heroine—and in her creator. The extent of Clarissa's response to the authority of Septimus's act is suggested by another canceled passage: "She felt no pity for the young man who had killed himself; not for his wife; nor for herself; nothing but pride; nothing but joy; for to hear Big Ben strike Three, Four, Five, Six, seven, was profound & tremendous. . . . She must go back; she must breast her enemy; she must take her rose; Never would she submit—never, never!" (B.M., III, 99). Given this power of affirmation, a figure of satire in Woolf's earlier conception becomes in the course of the narrative a protagonist of life: she "forced herself with her indomitable vitality to put all that aside, there being in her a thread of life which for toughness, endurance, power to overcome obstacles and carry her triumphantly through he had never known the like of" (171).

From this standpoint, the contrast between the life-affirming Clarissa and the death-seeking Septimus may seem absolute, but the ambiguity in Clarissa's imagination—and her self-identification with the suicide—serves to align the two characters, even to blunt the distinction between life affirmation and death wish. The two main actions of the plot—suicide and party—are parallel in intention and effect despite their gross disparity in social acceptability. Both are designed as self-sacrifice for others—although both Clarissa and Septimus have an abiding bitterness about social life. Not only Septimus thinks of himself as making an act of sacrifice—Clarissa responds to her husband's, and her former lover's, criticism of her parties (133) with the impressive claim: ". . . it was an offering; to combine, to create; but to whom? An offering for the sake of offering, perhaps. Anyhow, it was her gift" (135).[17] This vision of a social ritual as creative and self-justifying elevates Clarissa above the stature of the social butterfly and endows her with some of the ironic qualities of the *pharmakos* that adhere to Septimus.

Clarissa's coming to consciousness in her contemplation of Septimus's self-sacrifice has long been acknowledged as the climax of the work and one of the great scenes of modern literature. In order to grasp its wider significance, we may recall a remark of Frye's: "An extraordinary number of comic stories, both in drama and fiction, seem to approach a potentially tragic crisis near the end, a feature that I may call the 'point of ritual death'. . . . In *Mrs. Dalloway* the actual suicide of Septimus becomes a point of ritual death for the heroine in the middle of her party."[18] While Frye describes the structure of the scene in generic terms—taking the work as a comedy, which entails a meeting with and release from the threat of death—it remains to be seen what role this potentially tragic interlude plays in the work's larger mythos.[19] In recent studies of myth and archetype, such movements of the hero are called patterns of "withdrawal and return"—a temporary removal from the active role, a pause for meditation and inspiration, and a rededication to the social group and its destiny. This pattern has less in common with the death and rebirth of the hero as sacred king or divine incarnation than it does with the hero as prophet or social leader. We may say, then, that there is a division of function within the conjoint protagonist of *Mrs. Dalloway*: while Septimus plays the role of sacrificial object — scapegoat or dying god — Clarissa plays the role of the social leader who temporarily withdraws for insight into the true significance of a leader's role and for rededication to it. Septimus as the outcast whose death reinvigorates his society is matched by Clarissa as social organizer who raises her activity from mindless social climbing to principled life affirmation.

The dramatic pattern of Septimus's sacrificial leap and Clarissa's meditative withdrawal and return parallels that of works manifesting the concept of a saving grace or way of redemption. If the joint protagonists are on the same side in the process of regaining health for their sick and perhaps moribund society, dramatic tension must be introduced in another opposition. It is not the hero of death and the heroine of life who are at odds but they, the healers, and others whom we may call the "forcers." Each is allotted his personal forcer, and for Clarissa it is Miss Kilman: "If only she could make [Mrs. Dalloway] weep; could ruin her; humiliate her; bring her to her knees crying, You are right. . . . It was to be a religious victory" (138). Similarly, the mordant portrayal of Septimus's forcer, Sir William Bradshaw, represents not merely a personal expression of the author's experience of psychiatrists[20] but an effort to exorcise a demonic power. Although the portrait is often wittily satirical, it is connected with the deepest themes of the work by being posed in mythic terms.

Sir William is seen not only by Septimus but by Clarissa, during her withdrawal and return, as a diabolic figure, a malevolent magus: "Suppose [Septimus] had had that passion, and had gone to Sir William Bradshaw, a great doctor, yet to her obscurely evil, without sex or lust, extremely polite to women, but capable of some indescribable outrage — forcing your soul, that was it — if this young man had gone to him, and Sir William had impressed him, like that, with his power, might he not then have said (indeed she felt it now), Life is made intolerable; they make life intolerable, men like that?" (203). The afflatus of these terms — "obscurely evil," "indescribable outrage," "his power" to make life intolerable — derives from something more than the immediate situation or from Clarissa's empathic leap to Septimus's point of view. They suggest a figure of some permanence in the human imagination, a figure which can inspire anxiety by its symbolic connection with bewitchment, hypnotism, and other ritual practices which depend on the surrender of the victim's will. Although these practices are often designed for medical ends, there is a tradition of rituals and superstitions involving control by a manipulative power who represents not a god but a demon — or, to put it in psychoanalytic terms, not the paternal ideal but the father in his threatening and coercive aspect. We are to regard Sir William, in common with Clarissa and Septimus, not merely as an authoritarian bully but as a shaman.[21] He is described as "the ghostly helper, the priest of science" (104) and as the executioner assigned to implement the ritual sacrifice of Septimus — who is reciprocally seen as "the criminal who faced his judges, the victim exposed on the heights" (107).

Of course, there is a humorous element in this identification, for Sir William is also a comic figure: the pedantic doctor who believes in the efficacy of his restoratives, his science, and his mealy-mouthed persuasion. Comedy is also conveyed through a satire of psychiatry and its banal vision of social improvement: "Worshipping proportion, Sir William not only prospered himself but made England prosper, secluded her lunatics, forbade childbirth, penalized despair, made it impossible for the unfit to propagate their views until they, too, shared his sense of proportion . . ." (110). The benevolence comes through finally as a pose; his real mode of operation is politically familiar: ". . . he had to support him police and the good of society, which, he remarked very quietly, would take care, [at a sanitarium] in Surrey, that these unsocial impulses . . . were held in control" (113). In sum, his domineering and sterilizing powers acquire the force of a blight on the land, rendering men infertile and enforcing the illness he is presumed to be curing. His medicine for England's feeble state is prosperity, in a modern rather than ancient sense of the term; its distance from true benevolence may be gauged from Elizabeth's idea of becoming a doctor because "she liked people who were ill" (150).

In contrast to Bradshaw's sterile influence, Septimus represents a potential force for revitalization. His name itself means "seventh" — an obvious reference to the seventh son of folklore, always lucky or gifted, often with occult powers, and with an instinctive knowledge of restorative powers that makes him a good doctor.[22] When the normal Clarissa is related to an abnormal Septimus, the one is too readily seen as queenly and socially competent (49), the other as "the eternal sufferer" (29), a social reject. Despite this sharp contrast, Septimus is not more deluded in thinking himself "lord of men" (75) than is Clarissa in finding it her vocation to "assemble" (205). The main difference between them is that he feels himself "in Hell" (69), while she repeatedly adverts to Heaven (6, 46, 52, etc.). Notwithstanding their very different points of view, they share certain essential attitudes, even using the same phrases: her formula for self-encouragement is "Fear no more the heat o' the sun" (12, 34, 204), and he takes up the refrain: "Fear no more, says the heart in the body; fear no more" (154). Clarissa finds a love of life in others (6), in the London air (9), in precious moments of the day (33), and in herself: "What she liked was simply life" (134). But Septimus, too, is aware of life in leaves and trees (26) and even at his death affirms, "Life was good. The sun hot" (164) (repeating his earlier view on page 103).[23]

Thus the exhortation to "fear no more the heat o' the sun" becomes an identification with the source of vitality central to mythologies from the primitive and classical to the scientific. Modern readers have little difficulty in acknowledging the heroine, who first appears with a promise to bear flowers and who stages her social triumph dressed in green, as a Flora figure. We are inclined to reject the hero's claim to be Jesus Christ, "lately taken from life to death, the Lord who had come to renew society" (29), but skepticism must deal more subtly with his claim to control the power of the sun. When the Prime Minister's car blocks traffic early in the text, Septimus relates all events to himself: "The world wavered and quivered and threatened to burst into flames. It is I who am blocking the way, he thought. Was he not being looked at and pointed at; was he not weighted there, rooted to the pavement, for a purpose?" (18). The suggestion of Septimus's powers is complex, for it carries the threat that the world will burst into flame — that his is not an infusion of divine energy but of "some horror . . . come almost to the surface" (18). Confirming part of his claim, it is stated that "the sun became extraordinarily hot because the motor car had stopped . . ." (17). It is, to be sure, a June day, "the sun was hot" (72) in Regent's Park and the newspaper reports that "there was a heat wave" (159).

The world does not receive its savior but Clarissa Dalloway does. The personification of Woolf's suicidism joins with the personification of her social self in a dramatic scene which we may take to be the manifestation of the artist in her text. That this scene — so often described in critical terms ranging from withdrawal and return to encountering the *Doppelgänger* — should bear all these and one more attribution is a mark of its symbolic universality. The one further model to be adduced is that of revelation, *anagnorisis*, or epiphany — the showing forth of the god and awed recognition of him by participants in the action or the audience. In her meditation in "the little room" (201) — like the prayer closet of devotional tradition — the heroine learns the identity, power, and value of a life thrown away for life itself.

The scene opens formally: "She went on, into the little room where the Prime Minister had gone with Lady Bruton. . . . There was nobody."

a) Her first associations are with the crucifixion, theologically vague but corporeally vivid: "Always her body went through it, when she was told, first, suddenly, of an accident; her dress flamed, her body burnt. He had thrown himself from a window. Up had flashed the ground; through him, blundering, bruising, went the rusty spikes." Since the authenticity of the hero's restorative act is so closely linked with physical suffering and death, it is necessary for the communicant to witness and empathize with those events.

b) "A thing there was that mattered; a thing, wreathed about with chatter, defaced, obscured in her own life, let drop every day in corruption, lies, chatter. This he had preserved." The "thing . . . that mattered" is here connected with a shilling once thrown in the Serpentine, which Clarissa had recalled on page 11 and now associates with Septimus's flinging away of his life. We remain unable to specify the object of sacrifice; what is emphasized is the contrast between the freedom of the sacrificial act and the "corruption" of daily life surrounding it.

c) "Death was defiance. Death was an attempt to communicate, people feeling the impossibility of reaching the centre which, mystically, evaded them; closeness drew apart; rapture faded; one was alone. There was an embrace in death." Despite the modern terminology—"an attempt to communicate," "reaching the centre," "one was alone"—these perceptions of death stand in a long tradition of mystical asceticism marked by the renunciation of worldly goods and human contacts, the movement toward death as release from the world and entry into a blessed state, the metaphoric substitution of a new order of being for earthly loves—"there was an embrace in death." But are we to dismiss Septimus's claims to threaten the earth with fire or to bring vital warmth as mere delusions of grandeur?

No final answer can be given, but it seems established that the tendency of this fiction is to assimilate its protagonists from their initially realistic mode to archetypal stature. The process is cumulative and cannot be hinged on any single detail, but on certain occasions there is a breakthrough from one stylistic level to the other. The most obvious example of this *Aufhebung* is the transformation of the street singer into "the voice of an ancient spring spouting from the earth" (90), singing in the words of a Strauss *Lied* the eternal tale of man and woman, life and death, earth and the cosmos: ". . . she laid her hoary and immensely aged head on the earth, now become a mere cinder of ice, she implored the Gods to lay by her side a bunch of purple heather, there on her high burial place which the last rays of the sun caressed; for then the pageant of the universe would be over" (90–91).[24] This is the final vision of reality in *Mrs. Dalloway*: the world has become a "mere cinder of ice," the eternal feminine has lost love, youth, and now life ("her high burial place"), and the sun has not only departed but may never come again. Such a world needs a savior, some return of vital force, some medicine for its illness or resurrection from its death. The official doctors, Holmes and Bradshaw, cannot help; Mrs. Kilman's assuagements by the balms of Christianity do not generally appeal.[25]

d) "Somehow it was her disaster—her disgrace. It was her punishment to see sink and disappear here a man, there a woman, in this profound darkness, and she forced to stand here in her evening dress." The next stage of religious experience is contrition—not only for her own life ("to stand here in her evening dress"), but for those of others ("here a man, there a woman")—and personal identification with the expiatory act of the one who takes on the world's faults: "Somehow it was her disaster—her disgrace."

e) "No pleasure could equal, she thought, straightening the chairs, pushing in one book on the shelf, this having done with the triumphs of youth, lost herself in the process of living, to find it, with a shock of delight, as the sun rose, as the day sank." The usually precise grammar of even Woolf's most difficult sentences fails at this point, and the text may be imperfect, but the impression is clear: the next sensation of the sequence is pleasure — indeed, "no pleasure could equal" it. Clarissa is referring to other experiences of sudden illumination and joy, and she goes on to recall some at Bourton and London; most significant is her inclusion of the present moment among the shocks of delight upon discovering what has all along been there.

f) Clarissa passes through a number of additional perceptions — of the old woman going to bed in her chaste isolation, of "the clock striking the hour, one, two, three," of the refrain "Fear no more the heat o' the sun" (and "If it were now to die, 'twere now to be most happy" on pages 202–3) — and now comes to her conclusion: "She felt somehow very like him — the young man who had killed himself. She felt glad that he had done it; thrown it away while they went on living." Her overt selfishness in feeling "glad that he had done it" is quickly evaporated by the ironies of the dying and reviving god motif (of which the scapegoat is a special case): he has "thrown it away while they went on living" — and their living on is linked to his leap of faith. At the spectacle of his heroism, she can identify herself with him, if not emulate him: "She felt somehow very like him. . . ."

g) "The clock was striking. The leaden circles dissolved in the air. But she must go back. She must assemble. . . . And she came in from the little room." The sounds of time passing serve to return her to the temporal world to which she is bound. But she can affirm her vocation within it: "She must assemble" — plan assemblies, bring people together, act for social cohesion. The scene ends as formally as it began: ". . . she came in from the little room."

The fiction expresses an opposition between two views of life that Woolf alternately entertained; these views are explicit in two essays of the period, couched in language closely related to the images of *Mrs. Dalloway*:

[Montaigne's] essays are an attempt to communicate a soul. . . . Communication is health; communication is truth; communication is happiness.[26]

That illusion of a world so shaped that it echoes every groan, of human beings so tied together by common needs and fears that a twitch at one wrist jerks another, where however strange your experience other people have had it too; where however far you travel in your own mind someone has been there before you — is all an illusion. We do not know our own souls, let alone the souls of others. Human beings do not go hand in hand the whole stretch of the way. There is a virgin forest in each; a snowfield where even the print of birds' feet is unknown. Here we go alone, and like it better so. Always to have sympathy, always to be accompanied, always to be understood would be intolerable. But in health the genial pretence must be kept up and the effort renewed — to communicate, to civilize, to share, to cultivate the desert, educate the native, to work together by day and by night to sport. In illness this make-believe ceases.[27]

Neither of these ultimate points of view is uppermost in Woolf; she entertained both, sometimes at the same time. We might dismiss them as the extremes of a manic-depressive psychosis; we had better regard them as pulses of a rhythm of response to reality — perhaps in tune with the rhythm of reality itself — one that will generate the structure and style of *To the Lighthouse* and *The Waves*.

Notes

1. Some of the raw data has been collected in Diderik Roll-Hansen, "Peter Walsh's Seven-League Boots: A Note on *Mrs. Dalloway*," *English Studies*, L (1968), 301–4. Other reflections on the choice of setting in a modern metropolis are given in Miroslav Beker, "London as a Principle of Structure in *Mrs. Dalloway*," *Modern Fiction Studies*, XVIII (1972), 375–85.

2. MS. in the British Museum, Vol. I, 5, 10. [Hereafter cited as B.M.] These passages correspond to pp. 6 and 55–56 of the text, respectively (the latter passage's focus on St. Margaret's is also picked up on p. 141).

3. That this is the Prime Minister's car and not the Queen's or the Prince of Wales's (as is supposed on p. 17) is suggested by the facts that its occupant is a male (17) and that it passes without stopping at St. James's Palace, the residence of the Prince (22).

4. The only other reference to the office is a joking one: Lady Bruton calls the obsequious Whitbread, "My Prime Minister" (122); the joke, of course, is that she is a travesty of a queen.

5. See my article, "Woolf and McTaggart," ELH, XXXVI (1969), 719–38; and J. Hillis Miller, "Virginia Woolf's All Souls' Day," in *The Shaken Realist: Essays in Modern Literature in Honor of F. J. Hoffman*, ed. O. B. Hardison, Jr., et. al. (Baton Rouge, 1970, pp. 10–27.

6. A rather idiosyncratic application; see, e.g. Jacqueline E. M. Latham, "Thessaly and the Collosal Figure in *Mrs. Dalloway*," *Notes and Queries*, XVI, (1969), 263: " 'Heaven was known to the ancients as Thessaly,' says a character in Virginia Woolf's short story, 'Kew Gardens,' first published in 1919. And in *Mrs. Dalloway* Septimus Warren Smith, sitting in Regent's Park, believes his friend Evans has returned to life from Thessaly. Although Thessaly was never used by the Greeks to mean heaven, it seems clear that it had this connotation for Virginia Woolf."

7. The primitive christological significance of the sacrifice is enhanced in a typescript passage: "He would kill himself. He would give his body to the starving Austrians" ("The Prime Minister," MS. of a story in the Berg Collection of the New York Public Library, p. 13). Cf. the notebook passage: "The whole world was clamouring Kill yourself, kill yourself, for our sake" (dated 22 Nov. 1924, Berg Collection, p. 25). In addition, Smith acquires properties of the drowned sailor in *The Waste Land*, who has a similar provenance in the *pharmakos* tradition: ". . . he himself remained high on his rock, like a drowned sailor on a rock" (77); he "lay like a drowned sailor, on the shore of the world" (103); "the most exalted of mankind, the criminal who faced his judges; the victim exposed on the heights; the fugitive; the drowned sailor; the poet of the immortal ode; the Lord who had gone from life to death" (107). These

terms associate Smith not only with the main themes of Eliot's poem but also with Leopold Bloom as persecuted savior (in his "Circe" fantasy) and eternal scapegoat (under the Cyclops's anti-Semitic attack).

8. This urge to chastity is accompanied by homosexual feelings, e.g., toward Sally Seton: ". . . she could not resist sometimes yielding to the charm of a woman. . . . she did undoubtedly then feel what men felt. . . . this falling in love with women" (36, 37).

9. One of the most curious but as yet unexplained aspects of the text is its *dédoublement* of one of the classic English novels, *Clarissa Harlowe*. Like the title figure of Richardson's work, Woolf's title figure is a lady of good family, "mistress of all the Accomplishments, natural and acquired, that adorn the Sex" but virginal, prudish, tending toward the frigid. Beyond the analogy of the heroines, there is a marked similarity between the two plots; in each, the heroine's family opposes her marriage to an ardent suitor, partly on mercenary, partly on personal, grounds — in the one case, because Lovelace is perhaps too fashionable, in the other, because Walsh is not fashionable enough. Here the parallel ends: Woolf's Clarissa does not allow herself to be carried off, does not suffer a crisis of conscience (although she has to keep on convincing herself that a marriage to Peter wouldn't have worked), and does not rise to tragic martyrdom. The relationship seems to have occurred to Woolf during the writing of *Mrs. Dalloway*: "And should I demolish Richardson? whom I've never read. Yes, I'll run through the rain into the house and see if *Clarissa* is there. But that's a block out of my day and a long long novel" (*Diary*, p. 64; 3 Aug. 1924). The fact that this comes almost as an after thought — and the suspicion that Woolf failed to follow up her impulse to read *Clarissa* — need not rule out the novel's relevance here. Certainly Woolf had some familiarity with *Clarissa* by 1922, when she wrote "On Re-reading Novels": Henry James "surmounts in *The Ambassadors* problems which baffled Richardson in *Clarissa*" (*Collected Essays*, II, 128). But she remained relatively indifferent to Richardson; e.g., in the retrospective essay, "Phases of Fiction" (1929), she admits that it contains "little reference or none to Fielding, Richardson, or Thackeray" (*Collected Essays*, II, 56).

10. A considerable literature has been built up on the varieties of polar significance to be accorded these characters: thus, for Keith Hollingworth, in *Studies in Honor of John Wilcox*, ed. A. D. Wallace and W. D. Ross (Detroit, 1958), p. 242, Septimus is the "incarnation of the death-instincts, Clarissa Dalloway of the instincts of life." For Alex Page, "A Dangerous Day: Mrs. Dalloway Discovers Her Double," *Modern Fiction Studies*, III (1961–62), 123, "he is the id to her ego." And for Francis L. Mollach, "Thematic and Structural Unity in *Mrs. Dalloway*," *Thoth*, V (1964), 62–73, her development is from repression to semiliberation at the close.

11. Reuben A. Brower, in *The Fields of Light: An Experiment in Critical Reading* (New York, 1951), p. 135, sees this as Peter's "vision of the consolatory woman who gives the kind of understanding which Peter had attributed to the girl [he follows on his walk] and which he had not found in Clarissa."

12. No further discussion of the song is necessary now that it has been identified and thematically related by Miller in *The Shaken Realist*, pp. 114–15, except to note that it remarkably reappears in Malcolm Lowry's *Under the Volcano* in the context of that work's setting on All Souls' Day.

13. The further use of the motif of birds speaking Greek will be discussed in connection with *The Years*. It is by now well known that the motif is drawn from Woolf's own hallucinations during her manic periods.

14. The *locus classicus* for the poetic use of this bit of "natural history" is Coleridge's "The Eolian Harp," ll. 20–25.

15. This use of the Bard as a symbolic criterion and focus of value is similar to that pursued by Mrs. Hilbery in *Night and Day*; it therefore comes as no surprise that Mrs. Hilbery not only appears in *Mrs. Dalloway* at a crucial point, toward the end of the party (209–10), but is also endowed with some of the *mana* ascribed to her in the earlier work: "And

up came that wandering will-o'-the-wisp, that vagous phosphorescence, old Mrs. Hilbery, stretching her hands to the blaze of [Sir Harry's] laughter . . . which, as [Clarissa] heard it across the room, seemed to reassure her on a point which sometimes bothered her. . . . : how it is certain we must die" (193). Mrs. Hilbery is also mentioned on p. 135.

16. For additional implications of the quotation, see Maud Bodkin, *Archetypal Patterns in Poetry: Psychological Studies of Imagination* (London, 1963 [1934]), pp. 87–88.

17. Clarissa's indelible attribute of party-giving is well summarized in Frank Baldanza, "Clarissa Dalloway's 'Party Consciousness,' " *Modern Fiction Studies*, II (1956–57), 24–30, which draws on the short stories where she functions similarly. Seven of these, including two hitherto unpublished, are collected in *Mrs. Dalloway's Party* (London, 1973).

18. *Anatomy of Criticism: Four Essays* (New York, 1968 [1957]), p. 179. For a number of suggestions on the myth and ritual motifs in this work, including its "rapprochement avec les rites religieux de 'purification,' 'libération du mal,' [et] rituel mystique," see Bernard Blanc, "La Quête de Mrs. Dalloway," *Le Paillon* (Nice), no. 3 (Dec.-Jan. 1972), pp. 10–13.

19. Another indication that the fiction was conceived in terms of classical genres is Woolf's plan for a continuing chorus of observers among the incidental characters, an idea developed in connection with her reading of the *Choephoroi* of Aeschylus; see Harvena Richter, *Virginia Woolf: The Inward Voyage* (Princeton, 1970), p. 139, for quotations from Woolf's notebook.

20. Leonard Woolf has movingly described his wife's pathological fear of and hostility to psychiatrists and has given one instance of a doctor resembling Bradshaw in insensitivity and humbug: *Beginning Again: An Autobiography of the Years 1911–1918* (London, 1963), p. 82.

21. This version of the magus or shaman lacks the anthropological sophistication of the later fictional use of the type by John Fowles in *The Magus*. Both novels are considerably adumbrated by E. M. Butler, *The Myth of the Magus* (Cambridge and New York, 1948).

22. See Funk and Wagnall's *Standard Dictionary of Folklore, Mythology and Legend*, S.V. "seventh son."

23. Others share the view: Walsh finds it "absorbing, mysterious, of infinite richness, this life" (180); and even Bradshaw answers his despondent patients: "Why live? they demanded. Sir William replied that life was good" (112). But Clarissa is aware that "life is made intolerable; they make life intolerable, men like that" (203). These and other general statements are given concrete associations in Marilyn S. Samuels, "The Symbolic Function of the Sun in *Mrs. Dalloway*," *Modern Fiction Studies*, XVIII (1972), 387–99.

24. The enormous importance of this figure here, and later in *The Years*, can be gathered from Woolf's description of a street encounter: "An old beggarwoman, blind, sat against a stone wall in Kingsway holding a brown mongrel in her arms and sang aloud. There was a recklessness about her; much in the spirit of London. Defiant—almost gay, clasping her dog as if for warmth. How many Junes had she sat there, in the heart of London? How she came to be there, what scenes she can go through, I can't imagine. O damn it all, I say, why can't I know all that too? Perhaps it was the song at night that seemed strange; she was singing shrilly, but for her own amusement, not begging." Quoted in Bell, *Virginia Woolf: A Biography* (London, 1971), II, 74, from the unpublished diaries in the Berg Collection, 8 June 1920.

25. In an essay published in the same year as *Mrs. Dalloway*, Woolf wrote: ". . . it is to the Greeks that we turn when we are sick of the vagueness, of the confusion, of the Christianity and its consolations, of our own age" (*Essays*, I, 13). This statement gives some inkling of a contributary motivation for Woolf's enterprise: it proceeds in part from her antipathy to Christianity and her high valuation of a healthier, classical culture. It is a judgment consistent with the marked strain of atheism running through *Mrs. Dalloway*: "Those ruffians, the Gods, shan't have it all their own way—her notion being that the Gods, who never lost a chance of hurting, thwarting and spoiling human lives, were seriously put

out if, all the same, you behaved like a lady. . . . Later she wasn't so positive, perhaps; she thought there were no Gods; no one was to blame; and so she evolved this atheist's religion of doing good for the sake of goodness" (87). There is some distance here between the author and her character's naive humanism, but their forms of rejecting conventional Christian solace are similar: "Why creeds and prayers and mackintoshes? [Miss Kilman's habitual garb] when, thought Clarissa, that's the miracle, that's the mystery; that old lady, she meant . . ." (140–41).

   26. "Montaigne," *Collected Essays*, III, 23–24; first published in 1924. These equations are given in *Mrs. Dalloway* on pp. 103–4.

   27. "On Being Ill," *Collected Essays*, IV, 196; first published in 1926.

Mrs. Dalloway and the Social System

Alex Zwerdling*

   "I want to criticise the social system and to show it at work, at its most intense."[1] Virginia Woolf's provocative statement about her intentions in writing *Mrs. Dalloway* has regularly been ignored, since it highlights an aspect of her work very different from the traditional picture of the "poetic" novelist interested in states of reverie and vision, in following the intricate pathways of individual consciousness. But Virginia Woolf was a prosaic novelist as well as a poetic one, a satirist and social critic as well as a visionary, and this element in her fiction is nowhere given more complete expression than in *Mrs. Dalloway.*[2] "Improving the world she would not consider," Forster says of Woolf; and Jean Guiguet insists that "the mechanical relations between individuals, such as are imposed by the social structure, dominated by concepts of class and wealth . . . are not her problem: as an artist, she refuses to consider them as within her competence."[3] But such cavalier dismissals of Woolf's social vision do not stand up under scrutiny. In novels like *Night and Day, Jacob's Room, Mrs. Dalloway, The Years,* and *Between the Acts,* Woolf is deeply engaged by the question of how the individual is shaped (or deformed) by his social environment, by how historical forces impinge on his life and shift its course, by how class, wealth, and sex help to determine his fate. All of these novels are rooted in a realistically rendered social setting and in most cases in a precise historical time. Woolf's attention was focused as sharply on society as on individual consciousness; what she saw there fascinated her and became a significant element in her work.

   This has not been generally recognized because of Woolf's intense dislike of any kind of propaganda in art. Her social criticism is usually expressed in the language of observation rather than in direct commentary. She detested what she called "preaching" in fiction and attacked writers who worked by this method, novelists like Lawrence ("It's the

*Reprinted from *PMLA*, 92 (Jan. 1977), 69–82.

preaching that rasps me. . . . I mean it's so barren; so easy: giving advice on a system") and Meredith ("Above all, his teaching is too insistent")[4] And the pictures of reformers in her novels are regularly satiric or sharply critical: for example, the deluded workers in the suffragette office in *Night and Day*, who are summed up by Mary Datchet in that novel as "eccentrics, undeveloped human beings, from whose substance some essential part had been cut away"; or Lady Bruton in *Mrs. Dalloway*, whose passionate dedication to the cause of emigration is described as liberating her "pent egotism . . . half looking-glass, half precious stone."[5] People anxious to reform their society and possessed of a message or a program are treated as arrogant and dishonest, unaware of how their political ideas serve their own psychological needs, and this is true even when Woolf is fundamentally sympathetic to their cause. In *Jacob's Room*, she describes a radical feminist writing her diatribes with "death and gall and bitter dust . . . on her pen-tip."[6] And in her diary, she compares the fraudulent political rhetoric of Mrs. Besant to artistic expression: "It seems to me more and more clear that the only honest people are the artists, and that these social reformers and philanthropists get so out of hand and harbour so many discreditable desires under the disguise of loving their kind, that in the end there's more to find fault with in them than in us" (*A Writer's Diary*, pp. 17–18).[7]

Woolf's own methods as a social critic, then, studiously avoid propaganda or direct statement. For her, fiction is a contemplative, not an active, art. She observes, describes, connects, provides the materials for a judgment about society and social issues; it is the reader's work to put the observations together and understand the coherent point of view behind them. Her own literary models were not Shaw and Lawrence but acute social observers like Chekhov and Chaucer. As she put it in *The Common Reader*, "It is safe to say that not a single law has been framed or one stone set upon another because of anything that Chaucer said or wrote; and yet, as we read him, we are absorbing morality at every pore."[8] As a moralist, Woolf works by indirection, subterraneously undermining the officially accepted code, mocking, suggesting, calling into question, rather than asserting, advocating, bearing witness: the satirist's art. Like the other Bloomsbury writers, Forster and Strachey, the target of her satire was essentially the English social system, with its hierarchies of class and sex, its complacency, its moral obtuseness. And also like them, her impulse was to understand as well as to judge, to know her society root and branch.

Mrs. Dalloway is in large measure an examination of a single class and its control over English society—the "governing class" (p. 86) as Peter Walsh calls it. But though Woolf's picture of Clarissa Dalloway's world is sharply critical, her book cannot really be called an indictment because it deliberately looks at its object from the inside. The very use of internal monologue is a form of sympathy, if not of exoneration. To know everything may not be to pardon everything, but it makes it impossible to judge simply and divide the world into heroes and villains. Though the governing class Woolf describes in the book is not strictly speaking her own, her connections with it are significant and are objectified in the technique she adopts. Like Forster's picture of the Wilcoxes in *Howards End*, Woolf's portrayal of the Dalloway set is an attempt to understand an alien, powerful class whose existence in some sense determines her own. As Margaret Schlegel puts it in Forster's novel, "More and more do I refuse to draw my income and sneer at those who guarantee it."[9] In contemplating her society along similar lines, Woolf is in effect continuing a tradition of the English intellectual aristocracy to which she firmly belonged, whose historic mission has been described by Noel Annan as "criticising the assumptions of the ruling class above them and forming the opinions of the upper middle class to which they belonged."[10]

Woolf examines the governing class of England at a particular moment in history. Unlike novels such as *The Waves*, *Mrs. Dalloway* has a precise historical setting, which it is important to understand. It takes place on a day in June 1923, five years after the end of the First World War. Jean Guiguet claims that Woolf's characters "are not bound to a social or historic context that would have dated them and rendered them outmoded" (p. 463), but it is notable that in this book she invents a major character, Peter Walsh, who has been out of England since the War, and allows him to comment on the transformation of society in that period: "Those five years — 1918 to 1923 — had been, he suspected, somehow very important. People looked different. Newspapers seemed different"; and morals and manners had changed (p. 80). There are a number of other topical references in the novel which its first readers would certainly have understood. The early 1920's brought to an end the Conservative-Liberal coalition in British politics; the elections of 1922 and 1923 marked the eclipse of the Liberals and the rise of Labour. For the first time the Labour Party became the official government opposition. It was only a matter of time before this "socialist" power, with its putative threat to the governing class examined in the novel, would be in office. Indeed, Conservative M.P.'s like Richard Dalloway are already making plans for that event. He will write a history of Lady Bruton's family when he is out of Parliament, and she assures him that the documents are ready for him at her estate "whenever the time came; the Labour Government, she meant" (p. 122). The Conservative Prime Minister who appears at Clarissa's party at the end of the book remained in office only until January 1924, when he was succeeded by the first Labour Prime Minister, Ramsay MacDonald. And though the new government lasted less than a year, the Labour Party has remained the ruling or opposition party ever since. Since *Mrs. Dalloway* was published in 1925, her readers would certainly have been aware of these crucial events.

These references suggest that the class under examination in the novel is living on borrowed time. Its values — "the public-spirited, British

Empire, tariff-reform, governing-class spirit" (pp. 85–86), in Peter's words—were very much under attack. Characters like Lady Bruton, Miss Parry, and Peter himself are identified with Britain's imperial mission, but the Empire was crumbling fast. In 1922, the Irish Free State government was proclaimed and the last English troops left Dublin; and when Lady Bruton cries in dismay, "Ah, the news from India!" (p. 122), she probably has in mind the beginnings of the agitation for independence in that country. The *Times* in June 1923 was full of "news from India" sure to agitate someone with her values: imperial police "overwhelmed and brutally tortured by the villagers" (2 June); "Extremists Fomenting Trouble" (23 June); "Punjab Discontent" (29 June). Peter Walsh goes to Clarissa's party not only to see her again but also "to ask Richard what they were doing in India—the conservative duffers" (p. 177).

As a class and as a force, then, the world to which the Dalloways belong is decadent rather than crescent. The party at the end of the novel, for all its brilliance, is a kind of wake. It reveals the form of power without its substance. When the Prime Minister finally arrives, he is described as looking "so ordinary. You might have stood him behind a counter and bought biscuits—poor chap, all rigged up in gold lace" (p. 189). And the imagery of the last section suggests rigidity, calcification, the exhumation of relics: "Doors were being opened for ladies wrapped like mummies in shawls with bright flowers on them" (p. 180); Clarissa's ancient aunt, whom Peter had mistakenly thought dead, appears at the party: "For Miss Helena Parry was not dead: Miss Parry was alive. She was past eighty. She ascended staircases slowly with a stick. She was placed in a chair. . . . People who had known Burma in the 'seventies were always led up to her" (pp. 195–96); and even the young people of the class, in Clarissa's words, "could not talk. . . . The enormous resources of the English language, the power it bestows, after all, of communicating feelings . . . was not for them. They would solidify young" (p. 195).

Solidity, rigidity, stasis, the inability to communicate feelings—these are central concepts in *Mrs. Dalloway.* As they apply to the governing class in the novel, they point to something inflexible, unresponsive, or evasive in their nature which makes them incapable of reacting appropriately to the critical events of their time or their own lives. The great contemporary event of European history had of course been the First World War, and it is no exaggeration to say with one critic that "deferred war-shock" is the major theme of *Mrs. Dalloway.*[11] Though the War had transformed the lives of millions of people, only one character in the novel—Septimus Smith—seems to have counted its cost, both to the victims of the slaughter and to the survivors. He does not, of course, belong to the governing class, whose way of responding to the War is crucially different. Woolf suggests that they are engaged in a conspiracy to deny its pain or its significance. Their ideal is stoicism, even if the price they pay is petrifaction. Clarissa consistently idealizes the behavior of

Lady Bexborough, "who opened a bazaar, they said, with the telegram in her hand, John, her favourite, killed." The sentence comes from one of several passages in which the War is mentioned, in a section in which Clarissa complacently muses, "For it was the middle of June. The War was over . . . thank Heaven — over. It was June. The King and Queen were at the palace" (pp. 6–7). The easy assumption that the War is a thing of the past and need no longer be a subject of concern is also voiced in Richard Dalloway's momentary thought for the "thousands of poor chaps, with all their lives before them, shovelled together, already half forgotten" (p. 127); or the words of "little Mr. Bowley, who had rooms in the Albany and was sealed with wax over the deeper sources of life": "poor women, nice little children, orphans, widows, the War — tut-tut" (p. 23).

Neither Virginia Woolf nor any of her Bloomsbury associates could have brought themselves to say "the War — tut-tut." "Curse this war; God damn this war!" the man in her story "The Mark on the Wall" cries out.[12] For all of them, pacifists by nature and conviction, the War was an unmitigated catastrophe that forced them to examine their consciences and make major ethical decisions — whether to declare themselves conscientious objectors, whether to participate in any form. As Woolf later recalls, "We were all C.O.'s in the Great war."[13] The War is an important theme not only in *Mrs. Dalloway*, but in *Jacob's Room* (1922) and *The Years* (1937); and the tension that dominates *Between the Acts* (1941) has a great deal to do with the imminence of the next global conflict. In *Jacob's Room*, Woolf had already described the slaughter of the young in a way that suggested the perversion of the cult of stoic impassivity:

> The battleships ray out over the North Sea, keeping their stations accurately apart. At a given signal all the guns are trained on a target which (the master gunner counts the seconds, watch in hand — at the sixth he looks up) flames into splinters. With equal nonchalance a dozen young men in the prime of life descend with composed faces into the depths of the sea; and there impassively (though with perfect mastery of machinery) suffocate uncomplainingly together. (p. 254)

If the War had any justification, it could only be as a liberating force likely to transform society and human relations. Perhaps the brave new world it might help to bring to birth could make one believe in its necessity. In *The Years*, this hope for the regeneration of humanity is expressed in the crucial air raid scene that takes place in 1917. Eleanor asks, with the ardor and desperation of a character in Chekhov, "when will this new world come? When shall we be free? When shall we live adventurously, wholly, not like cripples in a cave?"[14] But in *The Years*, as in *Mrs. Dalloway*, the hopes for a new society are betrayed by the return of the old. The sacrifice has been meaningless. As Clarissa Dalloway says in the short story out of which the novel grew, "Thousands of young men had died that things might go on."[15]

The sense of living in the past, of being unable to take in or respond to the transformations of the present, makes the governing class in *Mrs. Dalloway* seem hopelessly out of step with its time. Peter turns Miss Parry's glass eye into a symbol: "It seemed so fitting—one of nature's master-pieces—that old Miss Parry should turn to glass. She would die like some bird in a frost gripping her perch. She belonged to a different age" (pp. 178–79). Woolf gives us a picture of a class impervious to change in a society that desperately needs or demands it, a class that worships tradition and settled order but cannot accommodate the new and disturbing. Lady Bradshaw is described, in an extraordinary phrase, as feeling "wedged on a calm ocean" (p. 105). But the calm is only on the surface; there is turbulence beneath. The class, in fact, uses its influence to exclude and sequester alien or threatening forces—the Septimus Smiths, the Doris Kilmans—and to protect itself from any sort of intense feeling. It may well be this calculated emotional obtuseness that has kept it in power, since Woolf makes it clear (in the sky-writing scene) that many others in the society long for a restoration of the status quo ante. The political activities of the novel—Richard's committees, Lady Bruton's emigration project, Hugh Whitbread's letters to the *Times*, the ritual appearance of the Prime Minister—are all essentially routine in nature and suggest that it is only by ignoring the more devastating facts and deep scars of recent history that the "social system" has managed to keep functioning.[16] Perhaps Woolf saw a necessary connection in unstable times between traditional political power and the absence of empathy and moral imagination.

Certainly the governing class in the novel demonstrates these qualities. It worships Proportion, by which it really means atrophy of the heart, repression of instinct and emotion. A. D. Moody has pointed to the impulse in the class "to turn away from the disturbing depths of feeling, and towards a conventional pleasantness or sentimentality or frivolousness" (*Virginia Woolf*, p. 21). Richard Dalloway, for example, finds it impossible to tell his wife that he loves her or even, for that matter, to use the word "I": "The time comes when it can't be said; one's too shy to say it. . . . Here he was walking across London to say to Clarissa in so many words that he loved her. Which one never does say, he thought. Partly one's lazy; partly one's shy" (p. 127). When the desperate Septimus stammers "I—I—" in Dr. Bradshaw's consulting room, Sir William cautions, "Try to think as little about yourself as possible" (p. 109). That this repression of feeling is very much the product of upper-class training is suggested not only in *Mrs. Dalloway* but in a crystallizing minor incident in *The Years*: "Here a footman's white-gloved hand removing dishes knocked over a glass of wine. A red splash trickled onto the lady's dress. But she did not move a muscle; she went on talking. Then she straightened the clean napkin that had been brought her, nonchalantly, over the stain" (p. 274).

Such unruffled self-control has everything to do with the ability to
retain power and to stay sane. The characters in *Mrs. Dalloway* who
cannot learn to restrain their intense emotions (Septimus, Miss Kilman,
even Peter Walsh) are all in serious trouble. They are the outsiders in a
society dedicated to covering up the stains and ignoring the major and
minor tremors that threaten its existence. When such people become too
distressing, they are dealt with by the "authorities," agents of the governing class like the psychiatrist Sir William Bradshaw who "had to support
police and the good of society" to make sure that "these unsocial impulses
. . . were held in control" (p. 113). For the anesthesia of the governing
class must not be permitted to wear off. And so Sir William "made
England prosper, secluded her lunatics, forbade childbirth, penalised
despair, made it impossible for the unfit to propagate their views" (p. 100).
This whole section of the novel, in which Woolf comes closest to Lawren-
tian "preaching," makes us realize that the complacency of the governing
class is not a natural state but must be constantly defended by the
strenuous activity of people like Sir William. There is a conspiracy to keep
any kind of vividness, any intense life, at a safe distance. The doctor's gray
car is furnished in monotone, with gray furs and silver gray rugs "to match
its sober suavity" (p. 104).

This sense of living in a cocoon which protects the class from
disturbing facts and feelings is reiterated in the treatment of its relations
with its servants. Lady Bruton, for example, floats gently on "the gray tide
of service which washed round [her] day in, day out, collecting, intercept-
ing, enveloping her in a fine tissue which broke concussions, mitigated
interruptions, and spread round the house in Brook Street a fine net where
things lodged and were picked out accurately, instantly" (p. 119). Service
is assumed to be part of the natural order by the governing class,
dependable in its regular rhythms, creating an environment of basic
security by maintaining a predictable daily routine. The fact that the
entire system is based on the power and wealth of one class and the
drudgery of another is ignored by master and servant alike in an unending
ritual of deception and self-deception, as Woolf sarcastically suggests:

And so there began a soundless and exquisite passing to and fro through
swing doors of aproned, white-capped maids, handmaidens not of
necessity, but adepts in a mystery or grand deception practised by
hostesses in Mayfair from one-thirty to two, when, with a wave of the
hand, the traffic ceases, and there rises instead this profound illusion in
the first place about the food — how it is not paid for; and then that the
table spreads itself voluntarily with glass and silver, little mats, saucers
of red fruit; films of brown cream mark turbot; in casseroles severed
chickens swim; coloured, undomestic, the fire burns; and with the wine
and the coffee (not paid for) rise jocund visions before musing eyes;

gently speculative eyes; eyes to whom life appears musical, mysterious. (pp. 115–16)

It is a way of life that seems part of some eternal order, functioning without apparent friction or even choice. But Woolf makes us see the connection between the elegance and composure of the governing class and the ceaseless activity of the lower. Clarissa Dalloway, in a little hymn of praise to her servants, mentally thanks them "for helping her to be . . . gentle, generous-hearted" (p. 44). She sends her "love" to the cook, Mrs. Walker, in the middle of one of her parties; but we are given a vivid glimpse of the pandemonium belowstairs not visible to the guests pleasantly floating on "the grey tide of service":

> Did it matter, did it matter in the least, one Prime Minister more or less? It made no difference at this hour of the night to Mrs. Walker among the plates, saucepans, cullenders, frying-pans, chicken in aspic, ice-cream freezers, pared crusts of bread, lemons, soup tureens, and pudding basins which, however hard they washed up in the scullery, seemed to be all on top of her, on the kitchen table, on chairs, while the fire blared and roared, the electric lights glared, and still supper had to be laid. (pp. 181–82)

The relationship between master and servant in *Mrs. Dalloway* is typical of the gulf between all classes in the novel. Clarissa's party is strictly class-demarcated. No Septimus, no Rezia, no Doris Kilman could conceivably set foot in it. Miss Kilman, indeed, bitterly notes that "people don't ask me to parties" (p. 145). Even impoverished gentlefolk, like Clarissa's cousin Ellie Henderson, are invited only under pressure and out of habit. Clarissa defends her parties as an expression of her ideal of unity, the wish to bring together "So-and-so in South Kensington; some one up in Bayswater; and somebody else, say, in Mayfair" (p. 134), and critics have often stressed her ability to merge different worlds and create a feeling of integration.[17] But the London neighborhoods she mentions are upper-middle-class preserves, the residential areas where the members of the Dalloway set are likely to live (though Bayswater might require an ingenious explanation). Clarissa's integration is horizontal, not vertical.

Woolf is often treated as an upper-class writer who complacently accepted the fact that her own status protected her from intimate knowledge of how the rest of the world lived. Yet she herself felt that her class isolation was a kind of doom and knew that it was bound to have adverse effects on her work. In her essay "The Niece of an Earl" she laments the fact that the English novelist is "enclosed, and separate, and cut off . . . is fated to know intimately, and so to describe with understanding, only those who are of his own social rank."[18] And in a passage from her diary written in the year *Mrs. Dalloway* was published, she writes with scorn of the exclusive "fashion world at the Becks . . . where people secrete an envelope which connects them and protects them from others, like myself, who am outside the envelope, foreign bodies" (*A Writer's Diary*, p. 75).

It is notable that in this quotation Woolf thinks of herself as subtly excluded from the fashionable world rather than at home in it. For the Dalloways shut out not only the Septimus Smiths and the Doris Kilmans but the artists as well. The novel makes it clear that their world is consistently and uneasily philistine. Though a token poet makes an appearance at Clarissa's party, her set has a deep distrust of writers, precisely because they might disturb its complacency. Richard opines that "no decent man ought to read Shakespeare's sonnets because it was like listening at keyholes (besides, the relationship was not one that he approved)" (p. 84). Sally says of Hugh Whitbread that "he's read nothing, thought nothing, felt nothing" (p. 81); Sir William Bradshaw "never had time for reading" (p. 108); and Lady Bruton, though Lovelace or Herrick once frequented her family estate, "never read a word of poetry herself" (p. 116). This indifference or hostility to literature is symptomatic of the class's lack of curiosity about life outside its precincts. In the novel, an obsession with Shakespeare (as in the thoughts of Septimus and Clarissa) is a kind of shorthand indication that the soul has survived, that some kind of sympathetic imagination is still functioning.

Clarissa's instant empathetic feeling for Septimus when his suicide is mentioned at her party is in marked contrast to the way her set usually deals with outsiders. His death shatters her composure and touches her in a profoundly personal way. This is not at all the manner in which the rest of the governing class treats the threatening presences by which it is surrounded. Their method is rather to turn the individual into a "case," as Bradshaw does in mentioning Septimus in the first place: "They are talking about this Bill. Some case Sir William was mentioning, lowering his voice. It had its bearing upon what he was saying about the deferred effects of shell shock. There must be some provision in the Bill" (p. 201). In this way of treating alien experience, the living Septimus becomes a category, his life an "it" to be considered by government committees drafting legislation. The ability to translate individual human beings into manageable social categories is one of the marks of the governing-class mentality Woolf examines in the novel. They have learned to think and talk in officialese. Richard "championed the downtrodden . . . in the House of Commons" (p. 127). A young woman he passes in the park ("impudent, loose-lipped, humorous") immediately becomes an example of "the female vagrant" in a passage that perfectly suggests his need to keep people at a distance: "Bearing his flowers like a weapon, Richard Dalloway approached her; intent he passed her; still there was time for a spark between them—she laughed at the sight of him, he smiled good-humouredly, considering the problem of the female vagrant; not that they would ever speak" (pp. 128–29). Lady Bruton's emigration project is designed for "young people of both sexes born of respectable parents" (p.

120). Sir William sees Septimus as merely another of "these prophetic Christs and Christesses" (p. 110). These examples suggest that the governing class has remained unruffled by viewing all social problems as involving distinct categories of people different from themselves. Like all good administrators, they compartmentalize in order to control and make things manageable.

These managerial skills are used to keep the society stable and to retain power. Emigration is a way of handling the massive unemployment of the period;[19] benefits in cases of delayed shell shock will separate the lunatics who insist on flaunting their rage or guilt about the War from those who are trying to forget it; Richard's work on committees for "his Armenians, his Albanians" (p. 132) might defuse another explosive international situation. All the governing-class types in the novel think of themselves as progressive reformers, even the unctuous Hugh Whitbread, whose "name at the end of letters to the *Times*, asking for funds, appealing to the public to protect, to preserve, to clear up litter, to abate smoke, and stamp out immorality in parks, commanded respect" (p. 114). But behind the public concern and tradition of social service is the need to dominate, the habit of power. It is here that one can see the social system "at work, at its most intense." Its symbol is the figure of Sir William Bradshaw, preaching Proportion but worshiping Conversion, a Goddess who "feasts on the wills of the weakly, loving to impress, to impose, adoring her own features stamped on the face of the populace," a deity at work not only in Sir William's consulting room, but "in the heat and sands of India, the mud and swamp of Africa, the purlieus of London, wherever, in short, the climate or the devil tempts men to fall from the true belief which is her own" (pp. 110–11). The passage clearly connects the "case" of Septimus Smith with British imperialism and social repression and reveals the iron hand in a velvet glove. It is entirely appropriate that this psychiatrist-policeman and the Prime Minister should be invited to the same party.

The passages concerning Sir William Bradshaw are markedly different in tone from the rest of the book, but this is not simply because Woolf is writing out of her own painful experience of how mental derangement is handled by some professional therapists. Such "treatment" is itself a symptom of a disease in the social system — the easy assumption of the habit of command. It connects with Woolf's savage criticism of the patriarchy in A Room of One's Own and Three Guineas as well as with her satiric picture of the imperial policeman in Between the Acts, her symbol of Victorian England, who tells the audience:

> Go to Church on Sunday; on Monday, nine sharp, catch the City Bus.
> On Tuesday it may be, attend a meeting at the Mansion House for the
> redemption of the sinner; at dinner on Wednesday attend another —
> turtle soup. Some bother it may be in Ireland; Famine. Fenians. What
> not. On Thursday it's the natives of Peru require protection and

*correction; we give 'em what's due. But mark you, our rule don't end
there. It's a Christian country, our Empire; under the White Queen
Victoria. Over thought and religion; drink; dress; manners; marriage
too, I wield my truncheon.*[20]

"What right has Bradshaw to say 'must' to me?" Septimus demands (p.
162). Behind philanthropy and reform, industriousness, morality, and
religion there is the same impulse—telling others how to live, "forcing
your soul," as Clarissa puts it (p. 203). In a diary entry about Victorian
philanthropists, Woolf reveals how repugnant the easy assumption of
power in this class was to her: "More and more I come to loathe any
dominion of one over another; any leadership, any imposition of the will"
(*A Writer's Diary*, p. 10).

The fundamental conflict in *Mrs. Dalloway* is between those who
identify with Establishment "dominion" and "leadership" and those who
resist or are repelled by it. The characters in the novel can be seen as
ranged on a sort of continuum with Bradshaw at one end and Septimus at
the other. Thus far I have concentrated on the characters at the Establishment end of the scale: Sir William, Hugh Whitbread, Lady Bruton, Miss
Parry, and Richard Dalloway. Among the rebels (present or former) we
must count Septimus Smith, Doris Kilman, Sally Seton, and Peter Walsh,
though there are important distinctions among them. And in the center of
this conflict—its pivot, so to speak—stands Clarissa Dalloway.

Septimus Smith is instantly seen as a threat to governing-class values
not only because he insists on remembering the War when everyone else is
trying to forget it, but because his feverish intensity of feeling is an
implicit criticism of the ideal of stoic impassivity. In Woolf's preliminary
notes for the novel, she treats this as the essence of Septimus' character:
"He must somehow see through human nature—see its hypocrisy, &
insincerity, its power to recover from every wound, incapable of taking any
final impression. His sense that this is not worth having."[21] Septimus comes
through the War unscathed: "The last shells missed him" (p. 96), but
afterward discovers a psychic wound from which he has no wish to recover
because it is a badge of honor in a society that identifies composure with
mental health. The mark of his sensibility is perpetual turbulence, as in
this passage: "the excitement of the elm trees rising and falling, rising and
falling with all their leaves alight and the colour thinning and thickening
from blue to the green of a hollow wave. . . . leaves were alive; trees were
alive" (p. 26). It is as if Septimus were a repository for the suppressed
feelings of the rigidly controlled people around him, those like Mr. Bowley
"sealed with wax over the deeper sources of life." Far from being sealed,
Septimus is a seething cauldron of emotions constantly threatening to
overflow, a sacrificial victim or scapegoat who takes upon himself the sins
of omission rather than commission. Woolf planned that he "should pass
through all extremes of feeling."[22] Like Leontes in *The Winter's Tale*,
Septimus is "a feather for each wind that blows," but his emotional

instability is a compensation for his society's repression and can only be understood and judged in relation to it.

For Septimus was not always a rebel. He begins, indeed, like the classic ambitious working-class boy entering the Establishment: moving to the city from the provinces, "improving himself" by taking evening classes, impressing his superiors at work and in the army by his ability and detachment. He volunteers early in the War, and when his friend Evans is killed, he "congratulated himself upon feeling very little and very reasonably. The War had taught him. It was sublime. He had gone through the whole show, friendship, European War, death, had won promotion, was still under thirty and was bound to survive" (p. 96). But this mood of self-congratulation does not last and is suddenly displaced by the "appalling fear . . . that he could not feel" (p. 98). His stoic fortitude in the face of slaughter sends him into a panic incomprehensible to a society that idealizes Proportion. For his fear of emotional aridity is finally greater than his dread of insanity. And so he surrenders to the force of feeling in all its variety and intensity—guilt, ecstasy, loathing, rage, bliss. His emotions are chaotic because they are entirely self-generated and self-sustained; he becomes a pariah. That Septimus should have no contact with the Dalloway set is absolutely essential to Woolf's design, though it has often been criticized as a structural flaw of the novel.[23] And among the people in his own world, Rezia has no idea what goes on in his mind; Dr. Holmes recommends bromides, golf, and the Music Hall; Sir William orders seclusion and bed rest. His only companion is the dead Evans, whom he must resurrect in fantasy. He is alone.

It is no wonder that the resultant vision of the world is as distorted as the governing-class view. Where Richard complacently sees his times as "a great age in which to have lived" (p. 129), Septimus is conscious only of "the brute with the red nostrils" all around him (p. 103). In Shakespeare, in Dante, in Aeschylus, he can find only one message: "loathing, hatred, despair." His wife's innocent wish for a child is seen as an example of the "filth" of copulation, and the ordinary run of humanity at his office is "leering, sneering, obscene . . . oozing thick drops of vice" (pp. 98–100). All this is an obvious projection of his own guilt, which he feels simultaneously: "He had not cared when Evans was killed; that was worst; . . . was so pocked and marked with vice that women shuddered when they saw him in the street" (p. 101). These black feelings are unendurable and consistently alternate with their opposites, with pastoral visions of a world of eternal beauty and harmony. In his fantasy, Evans is brought back to life and the sparrows sing "how there is no crime . . . how there is no death" (p. 28). Though Septimus is intended to serve as an antithesis to the governing-class spirit, he is in no sense a preferable alternative to it. And he, too, is finally forced to pretend that the War's cost was not real, that death is an illusion. He is a victim not only of the War but of the peace, with its insistence that all could be forgotten and the old order reestablished. The pressure to do so is eventually too much for him, and he succumbs.

Like Septimus, Doris Kilman is a war victim. Dismissed from her teaching position because "she would not pretend that the Germans were all villains" (p. 136), she must earn her living by occasional tutorial instruction. The degrading poverty and isolation her dismissal brings about embitters her profoundly, making her despise herself and her society in alternate flashes of emotion. Like Septimus, she cannot control "the hot and turbulent feelings which boiled and surged in her" (p. 137). And also like him, she finds release in a quasi-mystical experience that momentarily assuages her distress. But her religious calm is temporary; her passionate nature continues to vent itself in unpredictable and uncontrollable surges — her murderous hatred of Mrs. Dalloway; her agonized love for Elizabeth: "If she could grasp her, if she could clasp her, if she could make her hers absolutely and for ever and then die; that was all she wanted" (p. 145). But what hope is there that the discreditable feelings Doris Kilman harbors — her lesbian attachment to Elizabeth, her class rage, her contempt for British jingoism during the War — could ever see the light of day? The lid of convention is heavy and firmly in place in the world around her; and so her intense emotional life must be lived entirely in her own mind, where it takes on a nightmare quality comparable to that of Septimus. She, too, is alone.

Between the extremes of Sir William Bradshaw and Hugh Whitbread on the one hand, and Septimus and Doris Kilman on the other, Woolf invents three characters who cannot be placed so easily: Sally Seton, Peter Walsh, and Clarissa. Though all belong to the upper middle class, all have gone through a passionate rebellious phase, rejecting what their world stood for — the worship of convention, the inevitability of the class structure, the repression of feeling. As young women, Sally and Clarissa planned "to found a society to abolish private property"; they read the utopian socialists and talked about "how they were to reform the world" (p. 38). Sally once radiated "a sort of abandonment, as if she could say anything, do anything" (p. 37), that made Clarissa fall passionately in love with her. The girlhood attachment is as intense as Miss Kilman's feeling for Elizabeth. Clarissa too had longed for a *Liebestod:* " 'if it were now to die 'twere now to be most happy.' That was her feeling — Othello's feeling, and she felt it, she was convinced, as strongly as Shakespeare meant Othello to feel it, all because she was coming down to dinner in a white frock to meet Sally Seton!" (p. 39). Sally's unconventional behavior and readiness to take risks strike Clarissa as wonderful and dangerous, bound "to end in some awful tragedy; her death; her martyrdom." The extravagant terms suggest Septimus' fate, but Sally's future course is anything but tragic; she marries "a bald man with a large buttonhole who owned, it was said, cotton mills at Manchester" and surfaces at Clarissa's party as the prosperous Lady Rosseter, the mother of five boys, her voice "wrung of its old ravishing richness" (pp. 199–200). Her rebellion is merely a youthful stage in the process that transforms "the wild, the daring, the romantic Sally" (p. 81) into a marginally acceptable adult member of her class.

Peter's rebellion is longer lived but no more dependable. He too revolts against convention in youth, becomes a socialist, defines himself as an outsider:

> He was not old, or set, or dried in the least. As for caring what they said of him — the Dalloways, the Whitbreads, and their set, he cared not a straw — not a straw (though it was true he would have, some time or other, to see whether Richard couldn't help him to some job). Striding, staring, he glared at the statue of the Duke of Cambridge. He had been sent down from Oxford — true. He had been a Socialist, in some sense a failure — true. Still the future of civilization lies, he thought, in the hands of young men like that; of young men such as he was, thirty years ago; with their love of abstract principles; getting books sent out to them all the way from London to a peak in the Himalayas; reading science; reading philosophy. The future lies in the hands of young men like that, he thought. (pp. 56–57).

The passage is a good example of Woolf's satiric exposure of her character's illusions. We come to know Peter better than he knows himself, can see through his heroic posturing ("striding, staring"), his rhetoric ("the future of civilization"), his verbal formulas and clichés ("he cared not a straw"). His whole personality in middle age is a flimsy construct designed to reassure himself that the passion and radicalism of his youth are not dead. At various moments in the novel he imagines himself a romantic buccaneer (p. 60), a solitary traveler (p. 63), and "as young as ever" (p. 178). He continues to patronize the conservativism of people like Richard Dalloway and the social conventions crystallized in Clarissa's role of hostess.

Nevertheless, he is as firmly a part of the Establishment by this time as Lady Rosseter. Though no great success, he is not a failure either, "had done just respectably, filled the usual posts adequately" (p. 171) as a colonial administrator, and expects to use the influence of the people he patronizes — Richard's, Hugh's — to find a position in England. The old school tie is fully exploited. The class conditioning he rejects so violently in youth returns in middle age almost against his will, makes him feel "moments of pride in England; in butlers; chow dogs; girls in their security" (p. 62), or turn the ambulance coming for Septimus into a symbol of British efficiency, "one of the triumphs of civilisation" (p. 166). This compromised rebellion or permanently inhibited aggression is epitomized in the pocket knife Peter carries and is forever opening and closing, a weapon that becomes a toy in his hands.

Yet a part of his youth has survived intact — his passion for Clarissa; the emotional anesthesia of his set has not managed to kill off the deepest attachment he has ever felt. He recalls every incident of their painful courtship in precise detail and can summon up the intense emotions of that time in all their power: "he had spoken for hours, it seemed, with the tears running down his cheeks" (p. 72). His susceptibility to sudden gusts of feeling "had been his undoing in Anglo-Indian society" (p. 167), Peter thinks, and it is true that he is in some sense an emotional exhibitionist. But in a world that penalizes despair and idealizes Lady Bexborough's ramrod bearing, the passions have no legitimate channel and will flow unpredictably. Peter's tears and moments of joy are paler variants of Septimus' rages and rapturous visions. What one sees throughout *Mrs. Dalloway* is a single disease that takes different forms. Peter's or Septimus' or Doris Kilman's emotional compulsiveness and display, their gaudiness or profligacy, are the antithesis of the denial of feeling in the governing class. But both are failures to maintain a natural flow of response commensurate with the occasion or situation, a failure that expresses itself variously as the inhibition or exhibition of emotion. Perhaps Woolf's complex attitude is paradoxically also rooted in an ideal of Proportion, though in a form very different from the goddess Sir William Bradshaw worships. In *Macbeth*, Macduff breaks down on hearing that his wife and children have been brutally murdered. When he is encouraged to "dispute it like a man," he replies, with great dignity, "I shall do so;/But I must also feel it as a man" (IV.iii. 219–20). It is precisely this dual commitment to self-control and to emotional expression that the characters in *Mrs. Dalloway* lack.

In the Establishment rebels, the failure is related to the passage of time. Peter notes that the "governing-class spirit" had grown on Clarissa, "as it tends to do" (p. 86); but the same could be said about Sally or Peter himself. Woolf was interested in the process through which an independent, responsive, emotionally supple young man or woman is gradually transformed into a conventional member of his class. She treats this theme not only in *Mrs. Dalloway* but in many other works. In *Jacob's Room*, as Jacob in a towering romantic passion rails against women, the narrator drily comments in a parenthesis: "(This violent disillusionment is generally to be expected in young men in the prime of life, sound of wind and limb, who will soon become fathers of families and directors of banks.)" — p. 247. And in *The Years*, North Pargiter reflects that his distinguished Uncle Edward had finally become "somebody who had an attitude fixed on him, from which he could not relax any longer" (p. 439). Woolf's interest in this change of human beings through time underlay what she called "my prime discovery so far" in writing *Mrs. Dalloway*: "my tunnelling process, by which I tell the past by instalments, as I have need of it" (*A Writer's Diary*, p. 61). As J. Hillis Miller has shown, *Mrs. Dalloway* "is a novel of the resurrection of the past into the actual present of the characters' lives"[24] (though for some of these characters the past can no longer be resuscitated: Lady Bradshaw, for example, had "gone under" fifteen years before, p. 111). Even Septimus is out of touch with his former self; his youthful passion for Shakespeare, for England, for Miss Isabel Pole is now utterly alien to him, dismissed by the narrator as "such a fire as burns only once in a lifetime" (p. 94).

In Sally, Peter, and Clarissa, Woolf traces the process of socialization from the extended moment in which each was intensely alive—young, brash, open, taking emotional risks—to the stage of conventionality. The class and set in which these characters find themselves, it is made clear, is not at all hospitable to such intense feelings. Gradually, it blunts, denies, trivializes, or absorbs them, transforming the young rebels into wooden creatures whose public lives no longer express their buried selves. The result is a failure of imaginative sympathy and emotional resonance, an absence of "something central which permeated," as Clarissa puts it in a highly critical summary of her own failings, "something warm which broke up surfaces and rippled the cold contact of man and woman, or of women together" (p. 36).

But Clarissa is harder on herself than her creator is. For *Mrs. Dalloway* is finally a sympathetic picture of someone who has surrendered to the force of conventional life and permitted her emotions to go underground. Woolf's decision to record Clarissa's thoughts and feelings as well as her words and actions is crucial and represents a deliberate change in her own attitude toward such people. For the Dalloways had made an extended appearance in Woolf's first novel, *The Voyage Out* (1915), where they were treated with unremitting satiric contempt and where their inner lives were kept dark. We can trace Woolf's conception of Clarissa Dalloway through several stages, from her first appearance in *The Voyage Out*, to her resurrection in the short story "Mrs. Dalloway in Bond Street" (1923), to her flowering in the novel that grew out of the story. In *The Voyage Out*, the Dalloways are simply caricatures of their class—worldly, jingoistic, snobbish, smug, philistine, and utterly devoid of inwardness. They exist in a self-contained satiric pocket of the novel and make no connection with the characters the author takes seriously. When Woolf decided to write about them again in the next decade, she must have felt that she had done them an injustice. But even in the short story "Mrs. Dalloway in Bond Street," in which something approximating stream of consciousness is first used to reveal Clarissa's inner life, the character who emerges remains a satiric object. She is utterly loyal to her country, her class, and its leaders. As she passes Buckingham Palace, she treats the monarch's ceremonial functions as an example of British "character": "something inborn in the race; what Indians respected. The Queen went to hospitals, opened bazaars—the Queen of England, thought Clarissa, looking at the Palace" (*Mrs. Dalloway's Party*, p. 21).

In the course of revising "Mrs Dalloway in Bond Street" to make it into the first section of the novel, Woolf modifies most of the cruder manifestations of Clarissa's snobbishness and complacency. For example, in the story she thinks, "It would be intolerable if dowdy women came to her party! Would one have liked Keats if he had worn red socks?" (*Mrs Dalloway's Party*, p. 26). But in the novel, a dowdy woman (Ellie Henderson) is invited to her party, though reluctantly; and the young poet Jim Hutton appears wearing red socks, "his black being at the laundry" (p. 194). In the course of the book Clarissa becomes less a typical member of her class and more an individual. This impression is reinforced by some of the titles Woolf apparently considered using—"The Life of a Lady," "A Lady of Fashion"—before she settled on *Mrs. Dalloway*.[25] She was convinced that the book would be an advance on her previous work because "the human soul will be treated more seriously."[26] Clarissa Dalloway became the first character in Woolf's fiction whose inner life is completely known to us.

Clarissa has troubled readers from the first. Woolf noted in her diary that Lytton Strachey complained of "some discrepancy in Clarissa herself: he thinks she is disagreeable and limited, but that I alternately laugh at her and cover her, very remarkably, with myself." And she recalls nearly abandoning the novel because she found the main character "in some way tinselly. Then I invented her memories. But I think some distaste for her persisted" (*A Writer's Diary*, pp. 78–79). This ambiguity of response is reflected in nearly all subsequent commentary on the novel, the attacks on or defenses of Clarissa determined in part by the critic's attitude toward convention and governing-class values. In one of the most interesting treatments of the novel, A. D. Moody insists that Clarissa is not an individualized character at all, but merely an embodiment of society's code, an "animated mirror" of the shallow world she reflects ("The Unmasking of Clarissa Dalloway," pp. 68–69). But other commentators have stressed Clarissa's progress to "the freedom of full maturity"[27] or her determination "never to bow to the laws of limitation set up in society, but instead to carry a sense of freedom and love into her world."[28]

What seems to me to account for such discrepancies is that Clarissa's is essentially a laminated personality made up of distinct layers that do not interpenetrate. Like Peter and Sally, she has both a conformist and a rebellious side, a public and a private self. But though it is true that the governing-class spirit has increasingly come to dominate her life, the stream of her thoughts and feelings shows us that the various strata of her personality are all intact and that the movement from rebellion to conformity is not necessarily inexorable or irreversible. Certainly convention dominates her words and actions. She has indeed become "the perfect hostess," as Peter predicted she would, with all the suppression of self that this ideal demands. She is proud that she is descended from courtiers and sees herself continuing a great tradition: "she, too, was going that very night to kindle and illuminate; to give her party" (p. 7). And like the other Establishment characters in the novel, she worships the stoical ideal and connects it with the War: "This late age of the world's experience had bred in them all, all men and women, a well of tears. Tears and sorrows;

courage and endurance; a perfectly upright and stoical bearing. Think, for example, of the woman she admired most, Lady Bexborough, opening the bazaar" (p. 12). The passage suggests an apparently inevitable sequence in Clarissa's mind from misery to endurance to rigidity. This ideal of conduct is manifested in her original decision to reject Peter Walsh, with all his emotional violence, and marry the stolid and reliable Richard Dalloway. When she tells Peter their affair is over, he recalls "She was like iron, like flint, rigid up the backbone" (p. 72).

But though the decision to give up Peter and Sally and identify herself with the governing-class spirit is never reversed, it is also never final, because Clarissa continually goes over the merits of the case thirty years later. This accounts for her obsession with the past, for her continued attraction to Peter and vulnerability to his criticism, decades after the issue was supposedly settled. At one point Peter thought he could write her obituary: "it was her manner that annoyed him; timid; hard; arrogant; prudish. 'The death of the soul.' He had said that instinctively, ticketing the moment as he used to do — the death of her soul" (p. 66). But Clarissa's soul is not dead, it has only gone underground. She has moments in which she feels herself "invisible; unseen, unknown," a mood she connects with her married state and public identity, "this being Mrs. Dalloway; not even Clarissa any more; this being Mrs. Richard Dalloway" (p. 13). In her world, the soul has no public function and can only survive in solitude. But even her marriage to Richard is not really a betrayal of self so much as a compact between two people to live together yet allow the soul a little breathing space: "And there is a dignity in people; a solitude; even between husband and wife a gulf; and that one must respect, thought Clarissa . . . for one would not part with it oneself, or take it, against his will, from one's husband, without losing one's independence, one's self-respect — something, after all, priceless" (p. 132). What Clarissa calls "the privacy of the soul" is one of her bedrock values, consistently connected in her mind with the old lady who lives in the house opposite hers, whom she has often observed but never spoken to (pp. 139–40).

In feeling this need for solitude, Clarissa is expressing one of Woolf's own cherished beliefs. In her essay on E. M. Forster, she describes a technique of his fiction that applies equally to her own: "he is always constrained to build the cage — society in all its intricacy and triviality — before he can free the prisoner."[29] Even Mrs. Ramsay in *To the Lighthouse*, one of Woolf's most social characters, can allow herself to think: "To be silent; to be alone. All the being and the doing, expansive, glittering, vocal, evaporated; and one shrunk, with a sense of solemnity, to being oneself, a wedge-shaped core of darkness, something invisible to others."[30] And in *The Years*, North Pargiter quotes a couplet from the only poem he has learned by heart, Marvell's "Garden":

> Society is all but rude—
> To this delicious solitude. (p. 365)

In her essay on Elizabethan drama in *The Common Reader*, Woolf suggests that a modern audience has an absolute need for some exploration of the private as against the public self. Immersed as we are in the "extravagant laughter, poetry, and splendour" of an Elizabethan play, we gradually become aware that there is something we are being denied: "It is solitude. There is no privacy here. Always the door opens and someone comes in. . . . Meanwhile, as if tired with company, the mind steals off to muse in solitude; to think, not to act; to comment, not to share; to explore its own darkness, not the bright-lit-up surfaces of others" ("Notes on an Elizabethan Play," p. 83).

There is an exact parallel here to Clarissa's withdrawal from the party at the climax of *Mrs. Dalloway* in order to reflect on Septimus's suicide. The little room is a solitary retreat where "the party's splendour fell to the floor, so strange it was to come in alone in her finery" (p. 202). And in this solitude, Clarissa allows herself to think about Septimus' death with full imaginative sympathy, understanding his feelings and situation instinctively with some part of her self that scarcely functions in the public world she normally inhabits. She realizes that Septimus had managed to rescue in death an inner freedom that her own life is constantly forcing her to barter away: "A thing there was that mattered; a thing, wreathed about with chatter, defaced, obscured in her own life, let drop every day in corruption, lies, chatter. This he had preserved" (p. 202). Septimus is Clarissa's conscience, is indeed the conscience of the governing-class, though only she is willing to acknowledge him. In doing so, she sees her acceptance of the governing-class code in a highly critical light: "She had schemed; she had pilfered. She was never wholly admirable. She had wanted success, Lady Bexborough and the rest of it. And once she had walked on the terrace at Bourton" (p. 203). This juxtaposition of present and past stresses the loss of the intense feeling of her youth, for it was on the terrace at Bourton that she had known "the most exquisite moment of her whole life," when Sally kissed her on the lips and released the torrent of Clarissa's first romantic passion (p. 40).

In feeling a sense of kinship with Septimus, Clarissa is crossing class lines in her imagination, for certainly he is beyond the pale of her set. Woolf moves in this passage from the traditional social satire of the English novelist of manners to what she called "The Russian Point of View" in *The Common Reader*. Unlike the class-obsessed English writer, Dostoevsky is indifferent to class barriers and social identity: "It is all the same to him whether you are noble or simple, a tramp or a great lady. Whoever you are, you are the vessel of this perplexed liquid, this cloudy, yeasty, precious stuff, the soul" (p. 228). Though they have never exchanged a word, on the deepest level Septimus and Clarissa are kin. And so, for all their mutual hatred, are Clarissa and Miss Kilman. Just before she withdraws to the little room, Clarissa has a moment of contempt for her social triumphs, which she feels "had a hollowness; at arm's length they were, not in the heart." At the same instant she recalls "Kilman her enemy. That was satisfying; that was real. Ah, how she hated her—hot, hypocritical, corrupt; with all that power; Elizabeth's seducer. . . . She hated her: she loved her. It was enemies one wanted, not friends" (p. 192). These reactions to Septimus and Doris Kilman (with their characteristic mixture of exalted and base feelings) together suggest that Clarissa's soul is far from dead, that she can resurrect the intense emotions of youth despite the pressure of a society determined to deny them quarter.

In such passages Woolf gives Clarissa her pivotal role, balancing the anesthesia of the governing class against the fervor of a Septimus Smith or Doris Kilman. At the same time, Peter Walsh is asking himself, "What is this terror? what is this ecstasy? . . . What is it that fills me with extraordinary excitement?" And replying, "It is Clarissa" (p. 213). These ardent feelings will probably never be translated into action, or even speech. It seems improbable that the outer life of Peter or Clarissa will change, for "the social system" Woolf describes in *Mrs. Dalloway* is not likely to be transformed soon enough to allow either of them to build their lives on the flow as well as the containment of emotion, especially since both must also be regarded as accomplices if not agents of repression. Woolf was too convinced of the fundamental inertia in human nature and institutions to imagine a radical transformation of either. But she was conscious of change, too, in both societal and individual values, even if such change sometimes appeared to be taking place in geological rather than human time. *Mrs. Dalloway* captures a moment in which the domination of the ideal of rigid self-control began to seem oppressive rather than admirable. In illuminating the price the characters in her novel have had to pay to live under the sway of this ideal, Woolf is not only fulfilling her ambition "to criticise the social system, and to show it at work, at its most intense," but contributing indirectly to its replacement by one less hostile to the buried life of feeling in every human being.

Notes

1. Virginia Woolf, *A Writer's Diary: Being Extracts from the Diary of Virginia Woolf,* ed. Leonard Woolf (London: Hogarth, 1972), p. 57.

2. Among the many studies of the novel, only two seem to me to deal seriously with Woolf's social criticism: Ralph Samuelson, "The Theme of *Mrs. Dalloway,*" *Chicago Review,* 11 (1958), 57–76; and A. D. Moody, "The Unmasking of Clarissa Dalloway," *Review of English Literature,* 3 (1962), 67–79. See also Moody's *Virginia Woolf* (Edinburgh: Oliver & Boyd, 1963), pp. 19–28.

3. E. M. Forster, *Virginia Woolf* (Cambridge, Eng.: Cambridge Univ. Press, 1942), p. 8; Guiguet, *Virginia Woolf and Her Works,* trans. Jean Stewart (London: Hogarth, 1965), pp. 71–72.

4. Woolf, *A Writer's Diary,* p. 188; Woolf, "The Novels of George Meredith," *The Common Reader: Second Series* (London; Hogarth, 1932), p. 234.

5. *Night and Day* (London: Hogarth, 1930), p. 279: *Mrs. Dalloway,* Uniform Ed. (London: Hogarth, 1968), p. 120.

6. *Jacob's Room* (London: Hogarth, 1929), p. 173.

7. See also her story "The Man Who Loved His Kind," *Mrs. Dalloway's Party: A Short Story Sequence*, ed. Stella McNichol (London: Hogarth, 1973), pp. 29–36.

8. "The Pastons and Chaucer," *The Common Reader* (London: Hogarth, 1925), p. 31.

9. *Howards End* (London: Edward Arnold, 1910), p. 172, Ch. XIX.

10. "The Intellectual Aristocracy," in *Studies in Social History: A Tribute to G. M. Trevelyan*, ed. J. H. Plumb (London: Longmans, Green, 1955), p. 244.

11. Bernard Blackstone, *Virginia Woolf: A Commentary* (London: Hogarth, 1949), p. 98.

12. *A Haunted House and Other Short Stories* (London: Hogarth, 1973), p. 48.

13. Quoted in Quentin Bell, *Virginia Woolf: A Biography* (London: Hogarth, 1972), II, 258; see also pp. 30–31 of the same volume for Bell's account of Bloomsbury reaction to the War.

14. *The Years* (London: Hogarth, 1972), p. 320.

15. "Mrs. Dalloway in Bond Street," *Mrs. Dalloway's Party*, p. 28.

16. Compare the assessment of the interwar governments in Charles Loch Mowat's *Britain between the Wars 1918–1940* (London: Methuen, 1962): "adequate discharge of routine duties, complacency, the failure of imagination and will" (p. 144).

17. Jean O. Love, e.g., writes that the party is an "indiscriminate mingling and, finally, fusion into a single whole of persons from different social strata" in her *Worlds in Consciousness: Mythopoetic Thought in the Novels of Virginia Woolf* (Berkeley: Univ. of California Press, 1970), p. 158.

18. *The Common Reader: Second Series*, pp. 214–17. For other treatments of this idea in her work, see "Street Haunting" and "Three Pictures," in *The Death of the Moth and Other Essays* (London: Hogarth, 1942), pp. 19–29, 14–17; "Lady Dorothy Nevill," in *The Common Reader*, pp. 248–54; and the account of the excursion to Whitechapel in *Flush: A Biography* (London: Hogarth, 1968), pp. 89–92.

19. See A. J. P. Taylor, *English History 1914–1945* (Harmondsworth: Penguin, 1970), pp. 194–95.

20. *Between the Acts* (London: Hogarth, 1969), p. 190.

21. MS Notebook dated Nov. 9, 1922–Aug. 2, 1923, p. 12, Berg Collection, New York Public Library.

22. MS Notebook dated Nov. 9, 1922–Aug. 2, 1923, p. 4.

23. See, e.g., J. K. Johnstone, *The Bloomsbury Group: A Study of E. M. Forster, Lytton Strachey, Virginia Woolf, and Their Circle* (London: Secker & Warburg, 1954), pp. 340–41.

24. "Virginia Woolf's All Souls' Day: The Omniscient Narrator in *Mrs. Dalloway*," in *The Shaken Realist: Essays in Modern Literature in Honor of Frederick J. Hoffman*, ed. Melvin J. Friedman and John B. Vickery (Baton Rouge: Louisiana State Univ. Press, 1970), p. 113.

25. Quoted in Wallace Hildick, *Word for Word: A Study of Authors' Alterations with Exercises* (London: Faber & Faber, 1965), p. 185, from the British Museum MS of *Mrs. Dalloway*.

26. MS Notebook dated Nov. 9, 1922–Aug. 2, 1923, p. 2.

27. Isabel Gamble, "The Secret Sharer in *Mrs. Dalloway*," *Accent*, 16 (1956), 251.

28. Alice van Buren Kelley, *The Novels of Virginia Woolf: Fact and Vision* (Chicago: Univ. of Chicago Press, 1973), p. 104.

29. "The Novels of E. M. Forster," *The Death of the Moth*, p. 106.

30. *To the Lighthouse* (London: Hogarth, 1930), p. 99.

"No More Horses": Virginia Woolf on Art and Propaganda   Jane Marcus*

"If we use art to propagate political opinions," wrote Virginia Woolf in *Three Guineas*, "we must force the artist to clip and cabin his gift to do us a cheap and passing service. Literature will suffer the same mutilation that the mule has suffered; and there will be no more horses."[1]

If art is a splendid and noble horse and propaganda a baser beast of burden, a donkey, their coupling is implied in sexual terms but also in class terms. The mule which is produced, a stubborn creature, and sterile to boot, lacks its father's dash and daring, its mother's patient persistence. When propaganda propagates with art as its partner, Woolf warned in 1938 (after England had seen almost a decade of political poetry, painting, and prose), then artists may degenerate into mute, brute mules. The gentle brays of the donkeys, the high whinnies of the horses will be lost to history.

The argument is, I think, historical. Woolf means that if the artist sacrifices his freedom for the momentary historical cause, he will be doing a disservice to the past and future history of art. Once "indifference," "disinterestedness," "impersonality," those qualities she valued so highly, are given up, then art loses its fertility.

Worried as she was over the health of poetry and its young practitioners in the thirties, one wonders how she would have felt about Auden's later change of heart, his praise of Yeats, his assertion that "poetry makes nothing happen." And what do we think now of the poetry of Auden and his fellows in the anti-Fascist thirties? Was their collective voice mulish? Woolf objected to the "enterprising book-fed brains" of the young poets, and to their "uni-sexual bodies," and she captures the 30's poet's egotism brilliantly in his appearance at the last party in *The Years*.

But Virginia Woolf was no more certain of what the proper relations between art and propaganda should be than she was ready to dictate what exact proportions of "truth of fact" and "truth of fiction" would make a good biography. A case in point occurs in the note I have just quoted. *Three Guineas* is itself an extremely polemical work, and the point in the note comes as an afterthought about a rather interesting propagandistic act. Woolf has been comparing Mrs. Pankhurst, leader of the English suffragette movement, to Antigone. She goes on to apply the comparison to Frau Pommer, the wife of a Prussian mines official at Essen who was to be tried (it was 1938) for the act of slandering the state and the Nazi movement by saying, "the thorn of hatred has been driven deep enough into the people by the religious conflicts, and it is high time that the men of today disappeared" (*TG*, 169). Virginia Woolf argues here that *Antigone* could be made "into anti-Fascist propaganda," that Creon, tyrant

*Reprinted from *Women's Studies*, 4 (1977), 265–89.

and patriarch, resembles Hitler and Mussolini — even though Sophocles in the end is such a great artist that he makes us sympathize "even with Creon himself." The plot and the "buried alive" theme of *Antigone* form the mythology and structure of *The Years* and as a *novelist* Woolf makes her reader sympathize with her English Creons. It is only as a "pamphleteer" that she chooses between good and evil.

Why does she then describe the coupling of art and propaganda as "mutilation," having just done rather a good job of coupling them in her own note and in *Three Guineas* as a whole? Perhaps there are good mules and bad mules, some less mutilated than others? We know that Woolf believed that women and the working classes would produce great works of art when their historical identity and continuity were once accomplished and several generations of women and workers had laid claims to their own history and their own literature. She also believed, genteel Marxist that she was, that each individual work of art was the product of collective historical consciousness, that the writing of women and workers would improve through the ages. "For masterpieces are not single and solitary births," she wrote in *A Room of One's Own* (68–69), "they are the outcome of many years of thinking in common, of thinking by the body of the people, so that the experience of the mass is behind the single voice." She was by no means uncritical of the individual artist, nonetheless, and felt that any woman writer would have difficulty "flying" free, with the "shoddy fetters of class on her feet" as well as the socially determined limitations on any open discussion of sexuality. Working-class writers, she felt, had an unfortunate habit of imitating the mincing speech of the middle class, rather than celebrating the traditional rich vitality of their own culture.

The mule who stops the fertile flow of literary history is suspiciously like the "middlebrow," neither upper class nor working class, who writes and teaches for money and fame. The mule is suspiciously like the "unisexual" and egotistical young poets who take up "the masses" as a cause in poems which their subjects cannot read, ignoring what she felt was their real mission, to persuade men of their *own* class to give up their privileges.

That Virginia Woolf used her own art for propagandistic purposes is a fact. *Three Guineas* is a socialist, pacifist, and feminist polemic. Perhaps she felt because her cause was just and her point of view unheard in the daily press that it did not fall into her own category. Or perhaps she felt that Fascism had already had such a pernicious effect on art and artists that she was justified in producing another mule for her side (since she did very vociferously take sides), hoping that a few well-placed kicks from its sterile and mute body would serve the cause of political justice and intellectual freedom.

In "Middlebrow"[2] Woolf defined the highbrow as "the man or woman of thoroughbred intelligence who rides his mind at a gallop across country in pursuit of an idea," and a lowbrow as "a man or woman of thoroughbred vitality who rides his body in pursuit of a living at a gallop across life." As for middlebrows, they are not capable of riding at all, and the sight of them on horseback is ridiculous. Horses represent both art and sexuality, but the middlebrow is a prostitute in both areas: ". . . how can you let the middlebrows teach *you* how to write?" she asks the lowbrows, "you, who write so beautifully when you write naturally, that I would give both my hands to write as you do — for which reason I never attempt it, but do my best to learn the art of writing as a highbrow should." "What will become of us," Woolf asked, her mind mating class conflicts with artistic conflicts, "men and women, if Middlebrow has his way with us, and there is only a middle sex but no husbands or wives?" The androgyny she approves is in the artist's mind, not his body. High and lowbrow horses obviously can stomp out the middlebrow, for in the last line of the essay, he is reduced to a "half-crushed worm."

The figure of the horse and the mule continued to work in Virginia Woolf's mind as she wrote *Three Guineas*, her great book on woman as the scapegoat of history. She described in her diary two kinds of writing, "donkey-work" and "galloping," as earlier she had described "stonebreaking" and "flying"; writing was to her always divided into two categories, one of hard work and one of speed and release. "After a most dismal hacking got into a little canter," she wrote in February 1937, and later, "once I get into the canter over *Three Guineas* I think I shall see only the flash of the white rails and pound along to the goal" (*AWD*, 266).[3] "I've been having a good gallop at *Three Guineas*" (267). "So now I'm straining to draw that cart across the rough ground . . . one always harnesses oneself by instinct" (268). "Oh how violently I have been galloping through these mornings! It [the book] has pressed and spurted out of me" (276).

It is interesting that Virginia Woolf imaginatively divides herself into artist and pamphleteer, horse and donkey (in a new metaphor for the androgynous mind of the artist), yet at the same time criticizes the union of art and propaganda, even in *Three Guineas* itself, for sterile progeny. In the course of composition she noted that we really need two separate languages, one for fact and one for fiction. For words, like artists, need privacy. "Why?" she asked, and answered herself in sexual terms: "For their embraces, to continue the race" (*AWD*, 268). But in *Three Guineas* she urges, not the fertility of language but the purge of language of its obsolete words, like "feminism," which is dramatically burned in her book. And she wishes for the day when words like "tyrant" and "dictator" may also be purged from the language.

"Feminism," by the way, is obsolete because the only freedom and equality that matters, the economic, has been achieved. (This was rather premature and optimistic, one thinks.) Quentin Bell asserts that Virginia Woolf was "amazed" at his "socialist" analysis of the world crisis as economic. Now it is true that Virginia Woolf was not in the habit of using the rhetoric of vulgar Marxists. But any reader of her political essays and pamphlets knows full well that the weight of the argument always rests on economics. Women's oppression is economic, she argues in *A Room of One's Own*, and art is determined by the class origins of the artist, she argues in "The Niece of an Earl." Art is part of the superstructure, she argues in "The Artist and Politics"; its flourishing and failure depend most certainly on the economic and political conditions of the state. All through her own writings she identified herself as artist and worker, and defined the necessity of the artist's involvement in politics (not that he write at the dictates of the politician but that he must be politically active to insure his own survival and that of his art). "Art is the first luxury to be discarded in times of stress; the artist is the first of the workers to suffer" (*Essays*, III, 231).[4]

"The rose and the apple have no political views," she states in the same essay; but the artist who contemplates them must be both economically and politically free to do his work. She does not call for a political bias in the work of art, but in the artist himself. This essay was written for the *Daily Worker* in order to explain why artists in the thirties were forming political organizations. Just as Leonard Woolf (in an impulse of whitewash?) forgot to tell the reader the essay's source when he compiled the *Collected Essays*, the editors of the *Daily Worker* had been anxious to tell their readers that they did not agree with her views.

She was truly an "outsider," for this is a complex position she expounds, although her lack of rhetoric makes her sound uncommitted.

Virginia Woolf took her leftist politics very seriously. She was very upset by the criticism of her politics by Wyndham Lewis, a serious rightist, but not in the least upset by the scurrilous personal attack of Queenie Leavis on *Three Guineas* in *Scrutiny*. For she realized that the "scrutineers," as she called them, had no serious political ideas at all, and didn't understand hers.

Modern readers have been led to believe that Virginia Woolf's acute sex and class consciousness derived from a Victorian virginal and "lady-like" misunderstanding of politics (Leavis, Forster, Bell) or, more recently, were part of her "madness." But Woolf's socialism and feminism were very much a response to nineteenth- and twentieth-century experience. It was the *timing* of her publication of polemical views which disturbed the critics. What was the use of being a feminist after women had the vote, they asked in 1929? What was the point of being a pacifist in the face of Hitler and Mussolini, they asked in 1939? Woolf had a particularly acute sense of history and an international distrust of local patriotism; these large ideological attitudes produced her self-definition as "outsider." She had seen the suffragettes under Emmeline Pankhurst and her daughter Christabel turned into warmongers overnight. She knew that one could be female and fascist, despite the contradictions. She knew that the vote had not been "won" by women after more than fifty years of agitation but had been granted, along with full manhood suffrage, when the government could no longer deny the claims of returning soldiers and sailors. Ever since the 1832 Reform Bill had first deprived women of what citizens' rights they had, women had fought bits and pieces of battles with patchwork ideologies to fit local and particular fights. Virginia Woolf, like her heroine Mary Datchet, flew her feminist and pacifist colors under the banner of international socialism. Only Wollstonecraft, Olive Schreiner, and Sylvia Pankhurst, as her literary feminist forebears, held such clear and consistent convictions.

The timing of the publication of *A Room of One's Own* is a case in point. In 1928 women could vote and feminism was unfashionable. In that essay Virginia Woolf braced herself against what Rebecca West called "an invisible literary wind."[5] West called the book "an uncompromising piece of feminist propaganda," "the ablest yet written," and remarked on the courage which "defied a prevalent fashion among the intelligentsia, which is particularly marked in the case of her admirers." The argument is inflexible and "all the more courageous because antifeminism is so strikingly the fashion of the day among intellectuals," Rebecca West explained. "Before the war conditions were different. The man in the street was anti-feminist, but the writers of quality were pro-suffrage." She explained the change as "due to the rising tide of effeminacy which has been so noticeable since the war. The men who despised us for our specifically female organs chastised us with whips; but those to whom they are a matter for envy chastise us with scorpions." West saw Woolf's honesty to be as remarkable as her sensibility because she was willing to risk losing by expressing her politics to those who most admired her art.

"It is a fact," Woolf explained, "that the practice of art, far from making the artist out of touch with his kind, rather increases his sensibility. It breeds in him a feeling for the passions and needs of mankind in the mass which the citizen whose duty it is to work for a particular country or a particular party has no time and perhaps no need to cultivate" (*Essays*, III, 231–32). The artist is a worker; as such he must defend his position economically and politically. But his product, which is limited enough by his class and determined by his origins, must be consciously free from the desire to preach and teach. As she told the young poets, "then you become a biting and scratching little animal whose work is not of the slightest value or importance to anybody" (III, 184).

I think the complexity of this carefully worked out theory about art and politics was a little difficult for some of her critics to follow. Much to the annoyance of Quentin Bell, and, one thinks, Leonard Woolf, she defended her pacifist position in 1936, allying herself with Aldous Huxley, even though her husband and most active socialists were forming a united front against fascism.

"But were we then to scuttle," protested Bell, "like frightened spinsters before the Fascist thugs?" He tried to account for her advocacy of peace, when for him the only thinkable stand was for war, by arguing that she was out of touch. "She belonged, inescapably, to the Victorian world of Empire, Class and Privilege. Her gift was for the pursuit of shadows, for the ghostly whispers of the mind and for Pythian incomprehensibility, when what was needed was the swift and lucid phrase that could reach the ears of unemployed working men or Trades Union Officials."[6]

Quentin Bell seems to have felt that while he was trying to do something "urgent, vital and important" his aunt was only interested in gossip. She happened in truth to have spent some of her formative years teaching working men at Morley College; she knew them well enough to be aware that they could write their own manifestoes—furthermore that they despised meddling missionaries. She had led meetings of her local branch of the Women's Cooperative Association for years and was, at the time Mr. Bell wanted to pass his "United Front" resolution, secretary of the Rodmell Labour Party—scarcely a shadowy voice of Empire and Privilege. Did he quite fail to realize that her "gossip" was something hardly to be dismissed as feminine silliness—that it might have been a conscious political maneuver by a committed Pacifist?

The pacifism of *Three Guineas* is probably the most difficult position for modern readers to accept, even those who appreciate the socialism, feminism, and anti-fascism of the essay. The origins of her abhorrence of violence, I suspect, are to be found in the ethics of her ancestors, in the Clapham Sect and her Quaker family. Christopher Caudwell saw pacifism as the strongest of the liberal bourgeois illusions because it pretends that violence is an ethical problem rather than a political problem, and thus allows the pacifist to avoid the idea of the revolutionary attack on private property.[7] Woolf knew that wars were fought essentially over property, but she could not quite bring herself to urge women and workers to any violence stronger than that of "trespassing" on the property of patriarchal culture.

Were Bell's allusions of sex and class intentionally diversionary? "Spinster" and "Victorian" make her not only older than she was and more upper class, but frigid. When Quentin Bell disapproves of his aunt's politics, he attacks her womanhood and her birth. Virginia Woolf may have been more sexually serious and active, more politically serious and active, than any nephew can ever conceive in his aunt.

Mr. Bell could not accept the connection between feminism and anti-fascism in *Three Guineas*. He wanted a simple description of what should be done: "true criticism of *Three Guineas* came from events; for the events of 1938 did not turn upon the Rights of Women but upon the Rights of Nations" (Bell, II, 205). Quentin Bell, I think, disliked the anti-patriotic tone of *Three Guineas*, its "international" outsider's stance. Virginia Woolf did, of course, offer a course of action: fight English tyranny and chauvinism at home.

But it was to "daughters of educated men," women of her own class and profession that she addressed the pamphlet. Hence its title. Only luxuries are sold in guineas; the words and the coin have a ring of obsolescence and gentility whose effect is carefully calculated; the reader thinks the writer can afford the "luxury" of anti-patriotic views. (Who would read a book entitled *Three Pounds*?) Her "Outsiders' Society" would "consist of educated men's daughters working in their own class—how indeed can they work in any other?—and by their own methods for liberty, equality and peace" (*TG*, 106), because "as a woman, I have no country. As a woman I want no country. As a woman my country is the whole world" (109). They are to reform themselves first: "the glamour of the working class and the emotional relief afforded by adopting its cause, are today as irresistible to the middle class as the glamour of the aristocracy was twenty years ago (see *A La Recherche du Temps Perdu*). Meanwhile it would be interesting to know what the trueborn working man or woman thinks of the playboys and playgirls of the educated class who adopt the working-class cause without sacrificing middle-class capital, or sharing working-class experience" (*TG*, 177). Woolf directs her reader to Margaret Llewelyn Davies' *Life As We Have Known It* and to *The Life of Joseph Wright*, for first-hand accounts of working-class life not seen through "pro-proletarian spectacles." Readers objected then and still object to the exclusiveness of her audience, but Woolf's logic is inescapable; "our ideology is so inveterately anthropocentric," she asserted, "that it has been necessary to coin this clumsy term—educated man's daughter. . . . Obviously, if the term 'bourgeois' fits her brother, it is grossly incorrect to use it of one who differs so profoundly in the two prime characteristics of the bourgeoisie—capital and environment" (146).

The revolutionary artist is revolutionary in form, wrote Christopher Caudwell. We are by now well aware of Virginia Woolf's formal rebellions in the shape and design of her novels. Her political works can be considered even more revolutionary by these same standards, because they are radical in both form and content.

"Oh it pleased me," she wrote in her diary after *Three Guineas* was published, "that the *Lit. Sup.* says I'm the most brilliant pamphleteer in England" (*AWD*, 284). It mav well be argued that *A Room of One's Own* and *Three Guineas* are in the first rank of English literature in their mode. The Milton of *Areopagitica* and the Swift of *A Modest Proposal* were her models, and her essays rank with theirs as passionate polemic enhanced by innovative technical genius. *A Room of One's Own* argues that women artists need time, money, and privacy, as well as an establishment of alternate female institutions of power in order to produce great works of art. The analysis combines a Marxian economics with Freudian psychological insights and Wollstonecraft's revolutionary feminism. What marks the essay as a work of genius, aside from the avoidance of the rhetoric of her distinguished forbears, is a fictional narrative technique which demands open sisterhood as the stance of the reader. This technique not only puts

the male reader on guard and makes him feel "other," alien; it reminds
him quite forcibly how "other," how alien, women must feel while reading
most of literature. The female reader, while she delights in being so
directly addressed, realizes how often she has been excluded and alienated. The conversational intimacy of the tone, the invented narrator and
fictional characters, the sharing of specific insults and pleasures, and the
sharpness of the intellectual assault on patriarchal institutions, are audacious in their breaking of the formal conditions of the essay.

Although what *Three Guineas* says is why we read it, its extraordinary use of form assures its place on the shelf of English literature in the
satiric mode. The stance of "daughter of an educated man" responding by
letter to requests for donations to Good Causes is itself a radical reflection
of women's powerlessness. The writing of letters had been, after all, the
approved and often the only means of expression for middle-class women.
That Woolf should choose the epistolary mode, almost two centuries after
Clarissa, was a matter of deliberate strategy. Her anger and hostility at the
exclusiveness of male institutions are all the more effective because
"cabin'd and cribb'd" in limited and limiting letters. Like prison journals
and letters, read while we know the author is in jail, they serve their cause
not only by what they say but by their very form.

In its original form *Three Guineas* included several photographs of
men in patriarchal garb. Beribboned, bemedaled, begowned, and be-
wigged, they exhibit the author's sharp eye for how the powerful assert
their power. The message is very clear, as clear as the photograph of white
men leering at the hanging bodies of blacks with which the South African
feminist Olive Schreiner introduced her brilliant anti-Boer War pamphlet,
Trooper Peter Halkett. Women, as Woolf noted, have a good eye for the
obvious.

"I strike the eye," she wrote in 1920, after the publication of *Night
and Day*, "and elderly gentlemen in particular get annoyed" (*AWD*, 25).
Three Guineas' anti-Fascist theme is derived from photographs of dead
children and ruined houses in Spain. What is the connection she was
trying to make? She refers several times to these photographs of fascist
atrocities, but the photographs before us as readers are of men in their
garb of power. We are meant to put the patriarchal horse before the
Fascist cart. It is a very clever device.

Although Woolf's nearest literary ancestor is Swift, given the difference in political attitudes she might prefer to be compared to Swift's
spiritual heir of the opposite side, the witty Sydney Smith. In April 1940,
she wrote to the composer, Dame Ethel Smyth, "I'm reading Sydney
Smith—his life—with only one wish in the world: that I'd married him.
Isn't it odd when the rumble tumble of time turns up some entirely
loveable man?"[8] Sydney Smith's causes were the emancipation of slaves
and of Catholics, but he preached them with humor, wit, and style and
with a lack of that egotistic patronizing tone, that smug holier-than-thou

Puritanism, which Virginia Woolf felt characterized reformers of her own and Victorian times. Smith's gay, elegant eighteenth-century detachment, so effective in propaganda, did not prevent him from being the kind of man who put antlers on his donkeys' heads, to please a lady visitor who complained that he had no deer. Virginia Woolf, "brilliant pamphleteer," was not above renting a donkey's head to take her bows for her play *Freshwater*, to show that she considered it to be "donkeywork."

After hearing Annie Besant lecture at the 1917 Club, Virginia Woolf wrote: ". . . the only honest people are the artists . . . these social reformers and philanthropists get so out of hand and harbour so many discreditable desires under the disguise of loving their kind. . . . But if I were one of them?" (*AWD*, 17). Of course the men of her circle did think she was one of them. One makes worse enemies out of one's colleagues who share *some* of one's views than out of those on the opposite side.

"Art is being rid of all preaching," she wrote later (*AWD*, 183). The preacher's tone was wrong, she felt, not only for fiction but for pamphlets — *Three Guineas* gestated for six years as *On Being Despised*, a draft inspired by personal insults, salt in her wounds, from Yeats, Huxley, E. M. Forster, and others. But all of the personal lamentation and the preaching were removed to make the essay grow into *Three Guineas* as we have it, from what she called in her diary "this little piece of rant" (*AWD*, 236). "Truth is only to be spoken by those women whose fathers were pork butchers and left them a share of the pig factory" — an example of the "rant" that did not survive her final test (*AWD*, 236). (This may refer both to Arabella's familiarity with the "pig's pizzle" in *Jude the Obscure* as well as to Jane Austen's letter about pork while the battle of Waterloo was being fought.)

In commenting on the chips on Ethel Smyth's shoulders in her published memoirs, Virginia Woolf wrote in 1933: "I hate personal snippets more and more. And the mention of 'I' is so potent — such a drug, such a deep violet stain — that one in a page is enough to colour a chapter" (*Ethel Smyth*, 228). Woolf explained that she was often tempted to do the same thing but was restrained by the large, ugly "I":

> I didn't write "A Room" without considerable feeling even you will admit; I'm not cool on the subject. And I forced myself to keep my own figure fictitious, legendary. If I had said, "Look here, I am uneducated because my brothers used all the family funds" — which is the fact — "Well," they'd have said, "she has an axe to grind"; and no one would have taken me seriously, though I agree I should have had more of the wrong kind of reader, who will read you and go away and rejoice in the personalities, not because they are lively and easy reading; but because they prove once more how vain, how personal, so they will say, rubbing their hands with glee, women always are; I can hear them as I write. (*Ethel Smyth*, 229, 230)

Virginia Woolf did of course grind her own axe in *Three Guineas*, so much so that she feared criticism of its autobiographical stance. Her mental life was so much a part of her identity that she did not realize that the exposure of her intellectual self was not considered "autobiographical" by others. She needn't have feared exposure. What is interesting is that while Woolf chastized Ethel Smyth for complaining as a feminist at actual injustices and prejudices against her as a woman composer, she wanted a fuller and more honest account of Dame Ethel's bisexuality:

> I was thinking the other night that there's never been a woman's autobiography. Nothing to compare with Rousseau. Chastity and modesty I suppose has been the reason. Now why shouldn't you be not only the first woman to write an opera, but equally the first to tell the truth about herself? But the great artist is the only person to tell the truth. I should like an analysis of your sex life as Rosseau did his. More introspection. More intimacy. (*Ethel Smyth*, 232–233)

Both the great artist and the pork-butcher's daughter tell the truth; perhaps Virginia Woolf felt she was neither. But she tried. The simultaneous "truth of fiction" and "truth of fact" about women of her own generation and her own class in *The Years* and *Three Guineas* ("one book," she called them) made her feel that she had spoken as plainly as possible on all the subjects which concerned her most — feminism (and sexual relations), pacifism (and anti-fascism), and socialism (the importance of recognition of the class struggle, the role of the female intellectual in the class struggle). "One can't propagate at the same time as write fiction," Virginia Woolf admonished herself in the *Diary*, "and as this fiction is dangerously near propaganda, I must keep my hands clear." As *The Years* and *Three Guineas* show us, she could and did, but only at the expense of a terrific struggle. The *Diary* records that Leonard felt that art and politics should not be mixed, but it also provides evidence that Woolf was uncertain about this. The early manuscript of *The Years* shows us that she had alternated each chapter, at the beginning, with an historical essay; had she dared to publish these we might have had one of the first modern "documentary" novels. Ironically *The Years* has seemed to be the least experimental in form of her novels and consequently is not beloved by modern critics. It was a bold plan; one wishes that Leonard Woolf had had the taste and lack of timidity to encourage its boldness.[9]

But *Three Guineas* is not the same kind of propaganda as *A Room of One's Own*. In fact, I think one might make a distinction here between the propaganda of hope and the propaganda of despair. *Three Guineas* is not in the least amusing. Her friends who did not share her views could not single out passages of wit and fine writing while ignoring or deprecating her arguments, as E. M. Forster had done with *A Room of One's Own*. She herself felt that *Three Guineas* was better written because it had less of the "egotistic flaunting" of *A Room* (*AWD*, 279). "The more complex a vision the less it lends itself to satire," Woolf told herself; "the more it understands the less it is able to sum up and make linear" (236). *Three Guineas* documents this more complex vision; the feminism-and-art problem of *A Room* is only part of the serious intellectual grasp of the political problems of the twentieth century — *Three Guineas* was to be her last work as civilization destroyed itself; it was "a moth over a bonfire" (*AWD*, 282). "For having spat it out, my mind is made up. I need never recur or repeat, I am an outsider" (282).

Three Guineas is for modern readers neither as indigestible as the second figure suggests, nor as frail as the first. Aptly named, it is about the relation between money and property and conflicts between the sexes, the classes, and the nations. The essay "tunnels" back, as Woolf's novels do, to first causes. Fascism is derived from patriarchy; patriarchy is defined as power chasing itself in vicious circles around "the mulberry tree of property." Woolf demanded that women crush shoots of incipient fascism in all the men around them, the "caterpillars of the commonwealth." She met with a reply even angrier than she expected, led by Queenie Leavis,[10] to unite those very caterpillars, in the name of *real* wife and motherhood.

How many professional women, writers and teachers — for it is to us that Virginia Woolf speaks here — have been able to meet her rigorous demands? We are the guardians of culture and its future promise, *if* we do not join the professions on the same terms as men, but remain in poverty, intellectual chastity, and "freedom from unreal loyalties."[11] The terms are hard: do not teach literature to middle-class students; do not lecture, write, or speak for money on any subject you do not believe; do not allow any publicity which capitalizes on your personal charm; do not have anything to do with "the pimps and panders of the brain-selling trade." Woolf insists: "do all in your power to break the ring, the vicious circle, the dance round and round the mulberry tree, the poison tree of intellectual harlotry." What would happen if women followed her advice?

> . . . the slaves who are now kept hard at work piling words into books, piling words into articles, as the old slaves piled stones into pyramids, would shake the manacles from their wrists and give up their loathsome labour. And "culture," that amorphous bundle, swaddled up as she now is in insincerity, emitting half truths from her timid lips, sweetening and diluting her message with whatever sugar or water serves to swell the writer's fame or his master's purse, would regain her shape and become . . . muscular, adventurous, free. (*TG*, 99)

Three Guineas is a final declaration of independence from patriarchal values pushed to the extreme, which Woolf believed had produced Fascism. It is a long, agonized, rational argument, unemotional and impersonal, defining the role of the outsider — with Coleridge, "to find a form of society according to which each one uniting with the whole shall yet obey himself only and remain as free as before" — and with Walt Whitman, "of Equality — as if it harm'd me, giving others the same chances and rights as myself—as if it were not indispensable to my own rights that others possess the same." These are not the words of an elitist or a snob or a "fragile middle-aged poetess, a sexless Sappho—a distressed gentlewoman caught in a tempest and making little effort either to fight against it or to sail before it." This judgment is Quentin Bell's. He continues: "She made far less of an attempt than did Forster to contribute something to the debates of the time, or rather, when she did, it was so idiosyncratic a contribution that it could serve no useful purpose" (Bell, II, 185).

E. M. Forster asserted that Virginia Woolf was not a great writer because she had "no great cause at heart" (Joan Noble, 187). He meant that he did not share her cause, the brilliant and sustained attack on private property as the foundation of corrupt capitalist England, which she makes in *Three Guineas*, the devastating rationality of the argument that fascism is simply a natural result of an extremely patriarchal value system, the impassioned cry to women to remain indifferent to war and warmakers and the capitalist greed which would begin to corrupt them as they entered the professions on equal terms with men.

Forster obviously felt that feminism was a social disease. "There are spots of it all over her work," he says, hardly concealing his distaste. But distaste is different from dishonesty, in a critic and a friend. Class was a more touchy subject than sex, and here Forster declares to posterity that Virginia Woolf was a snob, a lady, and was detached from "the working class and Labour." He must have known better. He dedicated the Rede Lecture to Leonard Woolf, which suggests that Leonard approved of his estimate. Leonard Woolf *certainly* knew better.

Snobbery, elitism, hatred or distrust of the working class—not true. What her enemies have in common is that they are liberals, that they mistake Woolf's honesty about the working class for snobbery. Because they dislike the rationality, the inescapable logic of *Three Guineas*, they declare it frivolous. The liberal imagination is infuriated with her logic; in the person of Queenie Leavis they call her "silly," "ill-informed," "emotional," and "dangerous." They accuse her of lacking "mind," when it is her rational arguments and brilliant analysis which so disturb them. The liberal likes to be first in the cause of freedom; often enemies to the left can be put down by attacking their class or sex or by declaring that they are not really democratic socialists at all.[12]

Unfortunately this has been the fate of Virginia Woolf's political ideas. And Leonard Woolf has contributed to this vision of her. In 1927 (in *Essays on Literature, History, Politics*, N.Y., Harcourt, 1927) Leonard Woolf wrote:

> . . . in classes the mentality at the top—i.e. in Royalty & the uppermost aristocracy—is exactly what it is at bottom—i.e. in the basement. . . . My theory is that the minds of a Duke and butler, of a Countess & a kitchen maid, have a natural affinity, and at certain

periods of the world's history become indistinguishable. Whether the
Duke becomes more like the butler, or the butler more like the Duke, is a
nice question; probably the influence is reciprocal. But whenever in
history the moment comes at which the mentality of the Duke and
Countess is absolutely indistinguishable from that of the butler and the
kitchen maid, there is an elementary catastrophe — not indeed a confla-
gration of the earth, but a revolution. (p. 299)

Now Leonard Woolf's words do not betray a particularly socialist sympathy for the working class, and this is certainly not a serious Marxist's view
of the making of a revolution. Some critics of Virginia Woolf have felt that
while they do not share Forster's view of her complete lack of political
sense, they will allow the influence of Leonard's politics. Frankly, it seems
to be the other way round. She was often considerably to the left of
Leonard, and remained a pacifist despite his arguments; he maintained
that art and politics should never be mixed.[13] Clearly her views upset him
enough to cause him to leave out, for example, the fact that she had
written some of her essays for the *Daily Worker* and, in his selection of
texts for the *Collected Essays*, to remove some of her views altogether.

The most pronounced editorial bias appears in his choice of the text
of her essay on the Women's Cooperative Guild. It concerns a meeting
held in June, 1913, but was heavily revised for publication in 1931 as the
Introduction to Margaret Llewelyn Davies' *Life As We Have Known It, By
Cooperative Working Women*, a book the Woolfs printed at the Hogarth
Press.[14] Most of Virginia Woolf's revisions were of a political nature and
were meant to clarify her opinions about the relation of class to art. She
printed the original in the *Yale Review* in 1930 but revised it with the help
of Margaret Llewelyn Davies and the working women writers themselves
for publication in England; in choosing the unrevised first draft for the
Collected Essays Leonard Woolf was acting politically. The Davies book
was not exactly a bestseller, predictably, and is not commonly found on
library shelves.

In the revised essay Virginia Woolf changed the meeting place from
Manchester to Newcastle and included a photograph of the cooperative
Women's conference in session. She brought her original fictional charac-
ters, Miss Wick and Miss Erskine, out of the parsonage and down to earth
giving them back their real names, Miss Kidd and Miss Harris. Lilian
Harris is brought to life with an actual photograph, next to one of
Margaret Llewelyn Davies herself.

Originally Virginia Woolf had written of the agitation at the conference that their reforms "would not matter to me a single jot." In the book
she changed this to read, "If every reform they demand was granted this
instant it would not touch one hair of my capitalistic head." The earlier
essay contains a passage which describes what seems to be rather frivolous
and pointless housekeeping on the part of the women. She revised it to
show both their collective consciousness and their politics: "the world was

to be reformed, from top to bottom, in a variety of ways . . . after seeing Cooperative jams bottled and Cooperative biscuits made." The added words "Cooperative" transubstantiates the biscuits and jam.

Woolf had at first created a rather sinister and bored figure in Miss Erskine, smoking a pipe and reading a detective story. The revision shows the sure hand of the novelist and more sympathy than cynicism. Here Miss Harris, "whether it was due to her dress which was coffee coloured or to her smile which was severe or to the ashtray in which many cigarettes had come amiably to an end, seemed the image of detachment and equanimity." The first essay said it was "bad manners" for working women to imitate the mincing speech of ladies; the revision called it "foolish." The first essay had described all working people as servants, "those who touch their foreheads with their fingers." Her revision recognized the proletariat as well: "And they remain equally deprived," she wrote. "For we have as much to give them as they to give us — wit and detachment, learning and poetry, and all the good gifts which those who have never answered bells or minded machines enjoy by right." Most importantly, Virginia Woolf removed the offending sentence, "It is not from the ranks of working-class women that the next great poet or novelist will be drawn." Her revision reads: "The writing, a literary critic might say, lacks detachment and imaginative breadth, even as the women themselves lacked variety and play of feature. Here are no reflections, he might object, no view of life as a whole, and no attempt to enter into the lives of other people. . . . And yet, since writing is a complex art, much infected by life, these pages have some qualities even as literature that the literate and instructed might envy." These qualifications are important ones for those still troubled about the relations between class, sex, and art.

The most significant change Woolf made was in tone. The *Yale Review* essay is narrated in the voice of an "irritable" middle-class visitor. She is annoyed by what seems to be waste of all that working-class energy, suspicious of full-time organizers of the cooperative women, and confident that the scraps of writing are not literature. While Woolf remains as scrupulous as ever in the new essay, the cynicism is gone. She has become both more politically committed to the cooperative cause and more artistically Woolfian. She names names in the new essay, recording the reality of the "lives of the obscure," and her storyteller's art rejects the earlier cynical adjective "squat" for "sombre," as in the end she describes Lilian Harris' reason for dedication to the cause: Woolf respectfully records the secretary's dry and reserved tale of her rape by "a gentleman," "At eighteen, I was a mother." What Virginia Woolf did in her revised essay was to make another contribution to the propaganda of hope.[15]

Virginia Woolf's editor[16] and her biographer have, it seems to me, for whatever reasons of their own, wished Virginia Woolf to appear as a thoroughbred horse. They have attempted to remove for posterity the donkey of hard work and of fun from her own image of herself. They were also, it seems, quite seriously troubled by Virginia Woolf's confirmed pacifism during the last years of her life, as many of her readers are. The image of someone silly and apolitical is less threatening than the image of someone as sure of her intellectual position as the Virginia Woolf who wrote *Three Guineas*. It is easy to see why *Three Guineas* makes people uncomfortable. One can hardly argue with its logic or its morality. Pacifism is to me an ethical luxury, a self-indulgence at some historical moments, but in Woolf it is understandable.

The declaration that "There will be no more horses" was not so much a criticism of the coupling of art and propaganda in the age of Fascism as a facing of the facts. Her novels were as thoroughbred a stable as any noble Englishwoman could wish. But Woolf could see the necessity for donkeys and "donkeywork" as well. In *Three Guineas* she produced her own mule. Perhaps it was sterile, but it did kick and it did bite.

She repeated, in August, 1940, her advice to women in "Thoughts on Peace in an Air Raid." A "mind-hornet," this advice is called, meant to sting her sisters into consciousness: "We must create more honorable activities for those who try to conquer in themselves their fighting instinct, their subconscious Hitlerism. We must compensate the man for the loss of his gun" (*The Death of the Moth*, p. 247). But it would not be much use for women and workers, outsiders all, to beat the dead horse of society as the poets of the thirties had done. If "commoners and outsiders like ourselves," she said to the Workers' Educational Association in May, 1940, are to be the artists of the future, they must take advantage of the war to prepare themselves for the task. "Let us trespass at once," she demanded, on the grounds of English Literature as patriarchal private property. "Literature is no one's private ground; literature is common ground. It is not cut up into nations; there are no wars there. Let us trespass freely and fearlessly and find our own way for ourselves."[17]

Virginia Woolf declared herself an "outsider" in *Three Guineas*. The official guardians of her image, it seems, preferred a view of Virginia Woolf as another kind of outsider, a class snob and an artist alienated from ordinary people. Any bourgeois husband, one feels, would be disturbed if he felt he had treated his wife as a sensitive, blueblooded, elegant race-horse, only to find that she saw part of herself as a hard-working donkey. Woolf, on the other hand, saw part of herself as Miss LaTrobe, the lonely artist, preserver of culture, allied with the people who keep history and art alive while the upper classes ignore or destroy civilization. In *Between the Acts*, Miss LaTrobe leaves her bits of property at the big house, where they care about such things, but she takes her lonely, misunderstood, awkward, visionary self down to the local pub. This view of the alienated artist allied with ordinary people to educate the middle and upper classes is consistent with Woolf's view of herself as an "outsider," a feminist, socialist, artist, and worker.

Acknowledgements

I am grateful to David Erdman and Margaret Comstock for the criticism of this essay, and especially to Tillie Olsen who demanded that this work be done. A version of this paper was read at the Virginia Woolf seminar, MLA, New York, 1974. The issues raised in this paper were also raised at the Princeton Virginia Woolf conference, April 1975, and I am grateful to the other participants for raising interesting questions, particularly on Woolf's pacifism. The question we debated, on how much she knew about the persecution of the Jews may be answered by seeing Leonard Woolf's biography, and Nigel Nicolson's edition of his father's diaries and letters 1930–1939.

Notes

1. Virginia Woolf, *Three Guineas* (New York: Harcourt Brace, 1973, Harbinger Paperback), 170 — hereafter *TG*. First published by Hogarth, London, and Harcourt Brace, New York, in 1938. The paperback does not reprint the photographs from the original editions, which were so central to the book's argument. In May and June, 1938, the *Atlantic Monthly* published a condensed version under the title "Women must weep — or unite against the war," which clearly identified it as an anti-fascist document written from a feminist and pacifist point of view. The contributors' column stated that "her essays, especially *A Room of One's Own*, have endeared her to all militant members of the gentle sex."

2. "Middlebrow" — letter written but not sent to the *New Statesman*; in *The Death of the Moth* (New York: Harcourt Brace, 1942), 176–186.

3. *A Writer's Diary*, Leonard Woolf (Ed.) (New York: Harcourt Brace Jovanovich, 1954).

4. Virginia Woolf, *Collected Essays*, 4 vols., Leonard Woolf (Ed.) (New York: Harcourt Brace, 1967). Since, in the cases noted in this essay, the editor did not always choose to reprint the last revised version of the author's essays nor to supply the necessary information about original publication, the reader is advised to check earlier collections of essays as well as the periodical in question.

5. Rebecca West, "Autumn and Virginia Woolf," 208–213 in *Ending in Earnest* (New York: Doubleday, 1931).

6. Quentin Bell, *Virginia Woolf: A Biography* (New York: Harcourt Brace Jovanovich, 1972), II, 186.

7. See *Pacificism and Violence. A Study — in Bourgeois Ethics* (New York: Oriole Chapbooks). Quentin Bell in *Bloomsbury* sees pacifism as an aesthetic as well as an ideology as the one defining characteristic of the group. See also H. B. Parkes, *Scrutiny*, 1936, "The tendencies of Bergsonism," 407–424 for a discussion of Bergsonism as a philosophy which may be used to justify withdrawal from life; the discussion is of Proust, and Bergsonism as "the philosophy of an invalid," but as Woolf was much influenced by this philosophy through her reading of Jane Harrison, this study is applicable.

8. Christopher St. John, *Ethel Smyth* (London: Longmans Green; 1959), 233. In *The Fortnightly Review*, 1891, 677, Millicent Garret Fawcett in "The Emancipation of Women," an answer to Frederick Harrison's earlier essay which had called for better educated housewives, wrote: "In the time of Mrs. Hannah More, it was unwomanly to learn Latin; Sidney Smith tried to reassure the readers of the *Edinburgh* eighty years ago that the

womanly qualities in a woman did not really depend on her ignorance of Greek and Latin, and that a woman might even learn mathematics without "forsaking her infant for a quadratic equation."

9. See the Winter, 1977, complete issue of *The Bulletin of the New York Public Library* for revaluations of *The Years* by several critics including two whose work is collected here [in this issue of *Women's Studies*] as well as Woolf's galleys of the novel cancelled at the last moment and an essay on "The Pargiters," the unpublished first version of the novel with the interspersed documentary chapters.

10. The "snub" to Queenie Leavis ascribed to Woolf in *AWD* as the cause of her vicious personal attack on *Three Guineas* and its author, was Woolf's refusal to answer Mrs. Leavis' letter praising her introduction to *Life As We Have Known It* and enclosing a copy of a review in *Scrutiny*. Woolf sent it to Margaret Llewelyn-Davies on September 6, 1935, saying "I don't know her, but am told that she and her husband represent all that is highest and dryest at Cambridge. So I rather feel from reading her article; but I suppose she means well, and I'm glad that she should feel sympathetic in her high and dry way to our book." (Manuscripts of V. W.–M. Llewelyn-Davies correspondence, Sussex University Library, courtesy of Quentin Bell, Nigel Nicolson, Lord Llewelyn-Davies and A. N. Peasgood). In "Lady Novelists and the Lower Orders," *Scrutiny*, 1935, 112–132, Queenie Leavis asks why books about the working class haven't "resulted in technical originality and locally authentic writing?" "No amount of observation of the district-visiting kind, however conscientious and however creditable to the industry and heart of the novelist, will produce a convincing substitute for adequate response to the quality of working-class life." She praises Grace Lumpkin's 1933 *To Make My Bread* as "better propaganda because better literature" and compares the novels under review with passages from the cooperative working women's letters. The novels have a "nauseating sentimentality" because they only see the workers as symbols of capitalist exploitation while Woolf as an artist responded to the quality of life in the writing of real workers. She praises Woolf for recognizing the rich language and culture of the British working class but like Woolf in *The Years* she sees the dangers which threaten it in the cinema and the loudspeaker. Later that year, reviewing Dorothy Richardson (p. 330) Mrs. Leavis called Woolf's feminism dated and *A Room of One's Own* crude. "The demand for mass rights" she wrote "can only be a source of embarrassment to intelligent women, who can be counted on to prefer being considered as persons rather than as a kind. . . ." The Leavises and *Scrutiny* have been responsible for forming the taste of several generations of readers. The false choice demanded by pitting Lawrence against Woolf, the reiteration of Woolf's snobbery and elitism and denial of her appeal to ordinary readers on the basis of her birth has deprived many of the experience of finding pleasure in the radical politics, moral strength and aesthetic experimentation of Woolf's fiction.

11. "By freedom from unreal loyalties is meant that you must rid yourself of pride of nationality — religious pride, college pride, school pride, family pride, sex pride — Directly the seducers come with their seductions to bribe you into captivity, tear up the parchment; refuse to fill up the forms" (*TG*, 80). Woolf also demands "that you help all properly qualified people, of whatever sex, class or colour, to enter your profession" (*TG*, 80). Some things will take care of themselves, for "we can scarcely doubt that our brothers will provide us for many centuries to come, as they have done for many centuries past, what is so essential for sanity, and so invaluable in preventing the great modern sins of vanity, egoism and megalomania — that is to say ridicule, censure and contempt." (*TG*, 82). She warns women of the dangers of professional life: loss of the senses, competition, greed. The professional who has lost his humanity is "only a cripple in a cave." Woolf describes with an outsider's knowledge what "uneasy dwelling places," what "cities of strife" are the old and rich universities for both women and the working class. *Their* new college should teach "Not the arts of dominating other people; not the arts of ruling, of killing, of acquiring land and capital" (*TG*, 34). See *The Workingmen's College 1854–1904*, J. Llewelyn-Davies (Ed.) (London: Macmillan, 1904) for similarities between Woolf's ideas on education and those of F. D. Maurice.

12. Contemporary reviews of *Three Guineas* are worth a study in themselves. I quote in full *Time and Tide*'s defense, because Woolf wrote to Margaret Llewelyn-Davies that it had saved her the trouble of preparing her own response. (June 25, 1938, 887–888):

"Mrs. Woolf's best-seller, *Three Guineas*, descending on the peaceful fold of reviewers, has thrown them into that dreadful kind of internal conflict that leads to nervous breakdown. On the one hand there is Mrs. Woolf's position in literature: not to praise her work would be a solecism no reviewer could possibly afford to make. On the other hand there is her theme, which is not merely disturbing to nine out of ten reviewers but revolting. There are things which should be ignored and she has not ignored them. There are faces that should remain behind a veil – or at any rate a yashmak – and she has dragged the veil away. A terrible sight. Indecent, almost obscene.

The appalling struggle of most of the reviewers to combine respect and loathing is only too evident in their phrases. On the whole, I award the palm to Mr. Graham Greene for his review in *The Spectator*. While paying all the obligatory lip service to Mrs. Woolf's genius, he contrived to slip in a suggestion that her thesis was out of date, her voice shrill, her outlook provincial and her experience over sheltered.

The only reviewer, as far as my reading goes, who gave up the struggle and frankly went all out in two columns of sheer passionate exasperation was Mr. G. M. Young in the *Sunday Times*. Mr. Young's exasperation was buttressed by page references calculated to induce readers to believe that he could substantiate each point of his attack in detail. Well – I looked them all up. Inaccurate, said he, quoting Mrs. Woolf as making statements she never could or would have made, besides perverting into literalness flights which were obviously intended to be figurative and symbolic. "Belated sex-egoism," he exclaimed, "a pamphleteer of 1905; agnostic, radical, pacifist and feminist," He, at least, has got it out of his system. I should think he is in no danger of a nervous breakdown."

Graham Greene (*The Spectator*, June 17, 1938, 112) pokes fun at Woolf's analysis of "woman's influence" as a refined form of prostitution, saying "It is all a little reminiscent of that good man who would rather have given his daughter poison than a copy of *The Well of Loneliness*." He is absolutely mystified by the fact that she does not regard chastity as woman's highest virtue and is genuinely dismayed by a woman's refusal to see that physical chastity is her real virtue. More interesting to modern readers, however, are the responses of women, to whom the book is addressed. K. John ("The New Lysistrata," *New Statesman* and *Nation*, June 11, 1938, 995–996) praises the book but feels that most women don't "deserve all these bouquets" and that many women are not pacifists by nature; some have the violence of Queen Victoria in them and some are even fascists. "There is no questioning the justice of Mrs. Woolf's demands, or the beauty of her gospel," she writes but feels that she is too bitter on lecturers as "personal charm" is one of Woolf's own best qualities. Louise Bogan (*New Republic*, September 14, 1938, 164–165) titles her piece "The Ladies and Gentlemen" and noble as Woolf's motives are, the elegance of style and class of the writer are to be questioned. "Upper-middle-class Englishwomen, thus fenced off, are to erect, upon the class-consciousness and class education dinned in to them from the first moment they were dandled before the nursery fire, a moral pattern so severe that it has never been adhered to by anyone who was not by nature an artist or a saint." She asks Woolf to forget that she is a lady and "go on being an artist," for her position has allowed her, unlike the rest of us, to concentrate on pure ends, not means.

13. Virginia Woolf's own attitude toward revolution may be found in a review of T. D. Beresford's novel *Revolution* in *TLS*, January 27, 1921, 58, which is not in *Collected Essays*. "If the reader finds something amiss – he will probably blame the subject. He will say that revolutions are not a fit subject for action. And there he will be wrong – He means that to write a book about what is going to happen in England when Isaac Perry proclaims a general strike and the army refuses to obey its officers is not a novelist's business – Yet the fault cannot lie with revolutions. Tolstoy and Hardy have proved, revolutions are fine things to write about if they have happened sufficiently long ago. But if you are impelled to invent your own revolution, half your energy will be needed to make sure it works. . . . We find ourselves

tempted to suggest alternatives, and seriously wish to draw Mr. Beresford's attention to the importance of the cooperative movement which he appears to overlook. . . . As Lady Angela plays we cannot help thinking about a possible policy for the left wing of the Labour Party. We want Mr. Beresford to turn his mind to that problem, directly the Chopin is over. In short, we want him to give us facts, not fiction."

14. London: L. & Virginia Woolf, 1931; with introduction by Virginia Woolf. The editor of the *Yale Review* (xliv) describes Woolf as the author of *A Room of One's Own* who "turns her mind here to women of the working class." In a footnote he gives the membership of the English Women's Cooperative Guild in 1930 as 70,000.

15. Woolf praises the working class women in her introduction, "not downtrodden, envious and exhausted, they are humorous and vigorous and strongly independent." In the Woolf-Davies correspondence cited above, Woolf's concern, politically and morally with the Cooperative Women's Guild is demonstrated. She arranged lectures on venereal disease, wondering to her friend why some working women objected and some wept since they were the class most affected by it. Woolf explained her "impertinence" in writing *Three Guineas* to her fellow feminist (July 4, 1938) "to sit silent and acquiesce in all this idiotic letter signing and vocal pacifism when there's such an obvious horror in our midst – such tyranny, such Pecksniffism – finally made my blood boil into the usual ink-spray." She answered Miss Davies' objection to "verbosity"; "One has a secrete a jelly in which to slip quotations down people's throats – and one always secretes too much jelly." She was glad she roused G. M. Young's rage and said the book was for the "common" "reluctant" and "easily bored" reader, not for the convinced. She praised the Coop women for a much more radical stance than the Labour Party. As early as 1920 Woolf read Mrs. Layton, one of the writers in *Life As We Have Known It*, praising the style except when it was "too like a book" and a feeling that "she hushes things up a little." (July 21, 1920). In July 1930 she still had grave doubts about her own paper on the Guild being suitable for an introduction to the book. She asked for permission to change the names to make it fictional for the *Yale Review* since the editor had said Americans were "in the dark" about cooperation. "Can you trust me to make the thing blameless? I don't suppose any Guildswoman is likely to read the *Yale Review*." On July 27 she wrote that Leonard had given his oath that "it will be quite all right about America," that she would rewrite the essay for the book and asked what the women felt, "Do they want their things to appear in print? Are they all alive?" On September 14 she sent a revised version back to Miss Davies, saying that she would withdraw her essay if it would "give pain and be misunderstood;" "The difficulty with impressions is that if you once start altering from the best of motives everything gets blurred and out of proportion." On October 10 she responded to the working women's criticism of her essay: "Vanity seems to be the same in all classes. But I swear that Mrs. Burton shall say exactly what she thinks of the appearance of me and my friends and I wont [*sic*] think her unsympathetic. Indeed I wish she would – what fun to hand her a packet of our letters and let her introduce it." Woolf was appalled by "the terrific conventionality of the workers. "I don't think they will be poets or novelists for another hundred years or so. If they can't face the fact that Lilian smokes a pipe and reads detective novels, can't be told that they weigh on an average 12 stone – which is largely because they scrub so hard and have so many chilidren [*sic*]" then, Woolf felt, they weren't facing reality. She was depressed that the workers were taking on the "middle class respectabilities" which artists had worked so hard to throw off. "One has to be 'sympathetic' and polite and therefore one is uneasy and insincere." In February 1931 she offered her royalties to the Women's Guild as the *Yale Review* had paid her "handsomely"; "I should only feel I was paying my due for the immense interest their letters gave me." Most importantly, she confessed that she had now when reading proof, come round to Miss Davies' view that she had "made too much of the literary side" of her interest. "I tried to change the tone of some of the sentences to suggest a more human outlook," and she added the sentence about cigarettes, "a little blue cloud of smoke seemed to me aesthetically desirable at that point." In June Woolf wrote that she was relieved by the "generous" and "appreciative" letters of the working women but she agreed with Margaret Llewelyn-Davies' sister-in-law that she was the wrong person as a writer to

"get people interested in the women's stories." The Yale Press rejected the book for America as "rather far from the experience and interest of possible readers here," but Woolf said that young English intellectuals found the letters "amazing." She reported much later (July 1937) that there were 395 copies left, "I wish we could bring out another volume. The young are all on the side of the workers, but naturally know nothing whatever about them." Leonard Woolf may perhaps have only remembered the fuss and printed the first version of the essay, but I think it may be argued that the essay itself became a cooperative venture and the last version was Virginia Woolf's own best version.

16. Perhaps Leonard Woolf was leaving some clues behind him when in *A Calendar of Consolation* (London: Hogarth, 1967) he quoted the proverb, "Go down the ladder when you choose a wife, up when you choose a friend," and Gorky on Tolstoy's determination to tell the truth about women only when he had one foot in the grave.

17. "The Leaning Tower," in *The Moment and Other Essays* (New York: Harcourt Brace, 1948), 154.

St. Ives and Kensington

Phyllis Rose*

Her earliest memory was of red and purple flowers on a black dress. She was sitting on her mother's lap, returning from St. Ives, in Cornwall. Then, the sound of waves breaking on the beach as she lay in the nursery.

She was Adeline Virginia Stephen, third child, second daughter of Leslie and Julia Stephen, born 25 January 1882. She shared the nursery with her older sister and brother, Vanessa and Thoby, and later with her brother Adrian, born a year after she was. Since each of her parents had been married before and widowed, it was a household crowded with children: Leslie's daughter, Laura, who would turn out to be retarded, and Julia's children, George, Stella, and Gerald Duckworth, who were twelve, thirteen, and fourteen when Virginia was born.

Her parents were solid members of upper-middle-class late-Victorian society, not rich, but well-to-do and well connected. Leslie Stephen was an intellectual, but not a bohemian. He observed the bourgeois pieties. Tea was served formally in the afternoon, great men like Henry James were entertained with dignity, and in the evening one dressed for dinner. Neither the informal lifestyle of intellectuals today nor their modest birth rate had come to prevail, so that the quantity of emotion generated by so many people living in the same house was kept in check by strict rules of behavior. It is hard to over-emphasize the repressive force of the world Virginia Woolf was born into.

On the other hand, it was an extremely literate, verbal, and articulate world. Reading and writing were the center of Leslie Stephen's life. Giving up the quiet life of a don at Cambridge because of religious doubt, Stephen had moved to London in his mid-thirties and had begun turning

*Reprinted from Phyllis Rose, *Woman of Letters: A Life of Virginia Woolf* (New York: Oxford Univ. Press, 1978), pp. 3–29, 271–72.

out literary journalism with the characteristic energy of the great Victorians. As editor of *The Cornhill Magazine*, he worked with the leading writers of his time, maintaining his own output all the while. His monumental *History of English Thought in the Eighteenth Century* thrust him to the summit of English literary life, and, more or less as respite from his serious labors, he contributed to the English Men of Letters Series volumes on Pope, Swift, Johnson, George Eliot, and Hobbes. In 1882, the year Virginia was born, he resigned as editor of the *Cornhill* and undertook the production of the *Dictionary of National Biography*, that vast collection of biographical essays of which he himself wrote 378. For the next ten years, this enormous project of writing and editing was being conducted in, was to some extent dominating, the house in which Virginia Woolf was growing up. By the time Stephen was forced to abandon it, worn out by the writing, the working over of copy, the correcting of proofs, leaving it to someone else to push on through Q, R, and S to Z, he had established himself as the leading man of letters of England, the successor to Matthew Arnold,[1] and had imprinted on the mind of his youngest daughter a heroic impression of literary activity.

Naturally, her father's friends were writers, too: George Meredith, Henry James, J. A. Symonds, John Morley, and James Russell Lowell, a frequent visitor to the Stephen house in the early eighties, when he was American ambassador to the Court of St. James. He was also Virginia's godfather. Such men, along with many bores, no doubt (for even as children the Stephens made such distinctions), would gather in the drawing room. Less palpably, a great Victorian novelist haunted the house in the person of Laura Stephen, for her mother Minny, Leslie's first wife, had been one of Thackeray's daughters. His other daughter, the children's aunt, Anny Ritchie, was a popular novelist in her own right. For the young Virginia Woolf, all this was enabling. It doesn't hurt a writer to be born into a family where writing is a normal human activity.

If there was a family tradition of Talent, there was also a family tradition of Beauty. Julia Stephen's mother was one of seven sisters, the Pattles, six of whom were famous for their looks. The seventh, Julia Margaret Cameron, the photographer, was to become famous for her talent. The breathtaking beauty of the Pattles (it has not dated, as beauty can do) may be seen in Mrs. Cameron's photographs of Julia Stephen, the magnificent structure to her face highlighted against and seeming to emerge from the dark like a crescent moon.

Virginia inherited this beauty, but from early on her relationship to it (for her beauty seems, as she talks of it, a thing detached from her) was complex and difficult. She could not simply accept it or rest easy with it. Another of her early memories focuses on the looking-glass in the hall at the house in St. Ives. She was six or seven, and already she could scarcely bring herself to look in the mirror. Why? She offers explanations: she was a tomboy, and it violated the tomboy code. More searchingly, she says that something in her made her reject whatever in herself gave her pleasure. Her paternal grandfather, Sir James, smoked a cigar, liked it, and so threw it away, vowing never to smoke another. She treasures that example of the puritanical streak, the strain of spartan asceticism, which she thinks she inherited from her father, which made her shy and self-conscious when she looked in a mirror, and which kept her from taking pleasure in her beauty.[2] One may think that at her birth some malicious fairy gave Virginia the distressing compulsion to see dualities. Beauty and talent are not necessarily immiscible, but Virginia seems to have perceived them as such and from the earliest of ages to have chosen to enroll herself under the standard of talent.

What she called "looking-glass shame" lasted all her life, making everything to do with dressing her body painful and sometimes terrifying. She hated shopping, being fitted for clothes, wearing a new outfit. She could hardly bear to be photographed. She enjoyed beauty intensely but it had to be beauty of nature—of a nature outside of herself; anything connected with her body carried a burden of shame.

Partially, confusedly, she associates a sordid childhood episode with this "looking-glass shame." When she was six or seven, again at Talland House in Cornwall, her handsome, eighteen-year-old half-brother, Gerald Duckworth, placed her on a ledge outside the dining room and explored her body as she sat there. She said in later years she could recall the feel of his hand going lower and lower and hoping he would stop. She stiffened and wriggled as his hand approached her private parts and went on to explore them, too. Her feelings? Resentment, dislike, and shame, a shame she didn't later understand. Why, she wondered, should she have felt shame at the age of six? She concluded that certain parts of the body must not be touched, that it is wrong to allow them to be touched, and that this feeling is instinctive, inherited at birth.

Her memoirs present the story of Gerald's assault as confirming a sexual reticence already established rather than traumatically provoking it. With the experience she associates a dream: she is staring into the mirror when a hideous face, the face of an animal, appears over her shoulder, the very face of sex. When Woolf writes about sex in her novels, the elements present in this childhood episode are usually repeated—male advances as aggression and exploitation, the woman's chief response a fear of violation and a desire not to be touched, the shame and disgust represented by an animal. The animal, that curiously Victorian image, suggests that at least some of her disgust is culturally conditioned. Ladylike Kensington had bred reticence, a reluctance to deal with things of the body, which Virginia Woolf was later to acknowledge as the chief flaw of her writing, as it was the chief distortion and diminishment of her life.[3]

One thing that makes us pause at this remembrance is that, by Woolf's account, something so similar happened to her later. Some time after her mother's death in 1895 probably when she was twenty, her other half-brother, George Duckworth, began making advances which seemed to her distinctly sexual.[4] Her description of these events is vague: George kissed her, George embraced her, George leapt upon her in bed. He was a sloppily emotional sort of man, particularly maudlin about family ties, but he was also the soul of propriety, a believer in dressing for dinner, a social climber. His physical gestures seemed to him, no doubt, proper expressions of family feeling, but not to Virginia. Although she never accused him of anything more than ambiguously erotic gestures, never, that is, accused him of actually raping her, she regarded his behavior as sexually criminal and called him (with relish) her "seducing half-brother."

Gerald's sexual tampering left nowhere near the same residue of bad feeling that George's did, and George Duckworth, not Gerald, came to symbolize sexual perfidy to Virginia. Throughout her adult life, with some intervals of pity, benign contempt, and even, occasionally, mild affection, she regarded George as a nasty creature and talked of him spitefully to her friends. In her memoirs, George is a fully developed character, a villain, albeit faintly comic, whereas Gerald is rarely mentioned. He is a Duckworth, which is to say well-dressed, good-looking, largely philistine; but in contrast to George's frenetic pursuit of social success, Gerald seems to have gone about his business quietly and with self-restraint, never bullying Virginia and Vanessa as George did. He set up a publishing house and was, in fact, the publisher of Virginia's first two novels. She never, so far as I can tell, mentioned the incident on the slab outside the dining room of Talland House until quite late in her life, in "A Sketch of the Past," which she wrote in 1939–40, and in a letter to Ethel Smyth of 1941.

Her mother, who holds her in her lap in her earliest memory, continues to dominate Virginia's memories of childhood, whether in her own person or in her more diffused embodiment in the landscape of St. Ives. Of the family's two houses, Virginia vastly preferred Talland House at St. Ives, where the entire menage relocated for the summer, to the gloomy town house at 22 Hyde Park Gate, Kensington. As with most children, the country made a deeper impression on her than the city. Twice-daily walks in Kensington Gardens could not compare to sailing, digging, and scrambling over rocks at the beach, or playing in the gardens of the house overlooking the bay and the Godrevy lighthouse. Still, there is more to it than a simple preference for country over city. Most of Virginia's early memories are of St. Ives, warm and sensual memories, full of light and color, and the place is intimately connected in her imagination with her mother, who was the altarpiece, the center of the cathedral space of her childhood.

She recalled her mother's rings, one diamond, one emerald, one opal, and the twisted silver bracelets James Russell Lowell had given her, which tinkled as she walked, remembered particularly when she came into the nursery to say goodnight, her hand shading a candle. Very early she became aware, through servants and visitors, that her mother was considered very beautiful.

Julia Jackson Duckworth, when she married Leslie Stephen in 1878, was a young widow of astonishing beauty, and, by all accounts, a remarkable person. Her beauty made people think of Greek goddesses and the Elgin marbles; her character made them think of madonnas and saints. She had three children by her first marriage and four more with Leslie, and she was, it would seem, a splendid mother. According to Leslie's reverential account of her, to love was her essence, and all her energies were spent in caring for other people. She possessed instinctively the art of soothing, of ministering to needs almost unspoken, and naturally enough people were always falling in love with her. In a backhanded tribute to Leslie Stephen after his death, George Meredith told Virginia Woolf, "He was the one man to my knowledge worthy to have married your mother."

Julia Stephen had spent much time in her youth at Little Holland House, the home of her aunt, Mrs. Prinsep, a Pattle sister who had married a retired Indian official and who turned her home into a gathering place for artists. G. F. Watts was given a studio at Little Holland House, and the Prinseps also cared for Burne-Jones occasionally. Tennyson might turn up for croquet on Sunday afternoons. It was a hothouse of aestheticism, where, according to Ellen Terry, another habituée, all the men were gifted and all the women were graceful.[5] The women, scorning the crinolines of the day, walked about in Venetian draperies and offered strawberries and cream to artists they were taught to revere. Julia Jackson was used to admiration: Woolner, the sculptor, and Holman Hunt, the painter, are said to have proposed to her when she was in her teens. She chose to marry instead a man with no pretensions to art or intellectuality, the handsome, wealthy, and respectable barrister Herbert Duckworth, by whom she had three children and with whom she was exquisitely happy, until one day, reaching up to pluck her a fig, he burst an abscess and died.

What was Julia besides beautiful? Quick, direct, practical, amusing, says Virginia. She liked simplicity, disliked affectation. She struck people as a combination of madonna and woman of the world. With no waste motion, she managed the business of a large household. Something of a matchmaker, she liked bringing people together. Virginia uses metaphors of weaving and connection in describing her. She supported the fabric of their lives, but living on such an extended surface, she had no time to concentrate on any one of them, unless they were ill, or unless, perhaps, it was Adrian, her youngest and favorite child.

From very early, verbal facility was Virginia's principal weapon in the nursery battle for place and for identity. She used it to hold her own against an older sister and brother who had been close before she arrived on the scene, and it was also her chief way of winning the approval of adults, who liked her because she made them laugh more than the other children. In 1891, the children, with Virginia as chief writer, began producing a family newsletter, the *Hyde Park Gate News*. Vanessa remembers, as typical of her sister's sensitivity to the good opinion of adults, a particular day when they laid a copy of the paper on the table next to their mother's sofa while she was at dinner and then crept into another room to watch her response. As they looked, Virginia trembling with excitement, they could see their mother's lamplit figure sitting near the fire, their father on the other side, both reading. Then Mrs. Stephen saw the paper, picked it up, began to read. Virginia and Vanessa listened greedily for comment. "Rather clever, I think," she said. Without seeming much excited, she put the paper back down, but this was, according to Vanessa, enough to thrill Virginia.[6] What is striking is how Leslie Stephen fades into the background and this scene about the need for approval is dominated by Julia.

Virginia presents her childhood as radiantly happy, merry, lively, filled with people, and the center of it all was Julia. When Julia died in 1895 — worn out, some said, by her demanding husband and family cares — the joyful days were over. A palpable black pall seemed to settle over the family. The children had to wear mourning clothes. Even their small pleasures were curtailed. Their greatest pleasure, the house at St. Ives, where they had spent thirteen summers, had to be given up, because Leslie associated it too painfully with his dead wife. A regime of sorrow, solemnity, and heavy emotion was enjoined upon them by the grief-struck widower and a wailing chorus of female relations. It was unnatural for children, and they resented it almost as much as they were pained by their mother's death. "The shrouded, cautious, dulled life took the place of all the chatter and laughter of the summer. There were no more parties; no more young men and women laughing. No more flashing visions of white summer dresses and hansoms dashing off to private views and dinner parties, none of that natural life and gaiety which my mother had created." No more of those "snatched moments that were so amusing and for some reason so soothing and yet exciting when one ran downstairs to dinner arm in arm with mother; or chose the jewels she was to wear. There was none of that pride when one said something that amused her."[7] Leslie presided over the replacement of gaiety and laughter by foolish sentimentality, hypocritical solemnity, and all the conventions of sorrow. They had lost, in a way, not one parent but two, for their father in his assertive and coercive grief had suddenly become hateful.

Woolf's memoirs shape her life before the move to Bloomsbury in 1904 as a two-act drama with a brief entr'acte. The long first-act idyll of childhood happiness, starring her mother, ends with her mother's death. In the entr'acte, spanning the years from 1895 to 1897, Stella Duckworth, Virginia's half-sister, inherits Julia's place, running the household and trying to wrest it from despair. Stella, almost as beautiful as her mother, shared her mother's early preference for gentlemen over artists and intellectuals, and she fell in love with a simple, honest, affectionate, well-dressed young solicitor named Jack Hills. Jack brought some of the healthy openness of country life to the Kensington household. It was he, for example, who much later explained sex, in a relaxed and humorous way, to Virginia. Incredibly innocent, she had thought that all men loved only one woman, as her father did, and were "dishonourable" if "unchaste," as much as women were. Jack was a breath of fresh air in Virginia's book-centered world.

The marriage of Stella and Jack, which seemed so good and so natural, was taken as a personal blow by Leslie Stephen. Virginia was to say later that if only her father could have said "I am jealous" rather than "You are selfish," the whole family atmosphere would have been lightened. But he chose to take the tack that Stella, in marrying, was selfishly abandoning him, although she was moving only three doors away and he was to enjoy daily visits. In an atmosphere of pain and gloom he consented to the marriage, a marriage which opened up vistas of renewed joy to Vanessa and Virginia. Stella, married, would launch them on the sea of life, love, and womanhood. But Stella returned from her honeymoon suffering from the infection of which, a brief three months after her wedding, she was to die. So the entr'acte, promising a happy ending, closed with a tragedy which recapitulates the tragedy at the end of Act I.

In describing this period (1895–97), Virginia barely touches upon the fact that her mother's death was followed by her first mental breakdown, but Stella's death forced her to recall the earlier one and to feel consciously, perhaps for the first time, its full impact.

> Anyone whether fifteen or not, whether sensitive or not, must have felt something very acute, merely from the pressure of circumstance. My mother's death had been a latent sorrow. How at thirteen would one feel it fully? But Stella's death two years later fell upon a different substance. . . . The glooms, the morbidity, the shut bedrooms, the giving up of St. Ives, the black clothes — all this had found my mind and made it apprehensive: made it I suppose unnaturally responsive to Stella's happiness and the promise it held out for us and for her — when once more, unbelievably, catastrophically, I remember saying to myself, this impossible thing has happened: as if it were unnatural, against the law, horrible, as a treachery, a betrayal, — the fact of death. The blow, the second blow of death struck on me; tremulous, creased, sitting with my wings still stuck together on the broken chrysalis.[8]

This double blow conditioned her to perceive happiness and beauty as a fragile fabric containing a much more substantial world of chaos and pain, explosive, always threatening to break out. If she connected her mother's death with the demands of marriage, Stella's death so soon after her wedding must have confirmed the yoking of the ideas of death and sex.

Contrasts had dominated her childhood: the beauty of the Pattles and the talent of the Stephens, the self-absorbed energy of her father versus her mother's diffused concern for others, restricted London winters and golden summers at St. Ives, nondescript days of cotton-wool well-being and periodic outbreaks of violence. Three miniature epiphanies prefigured the double blows of death, moments when a hidden enemy emerged from the haze of daily life and startled her consciousness. First, she and her brother Thoby were having a fight when, suddenly overwhelmed by her own powerlessness, Virginia dropped her fists and let Thoby beat her. Second, she heard that a man who had stayed with them at St. Ives had killed himself. Third—and this is the odd element in this series of memories—she perceived a flower rooted in the earth. The discrepancy between flower and earth seemed to bother her as had the suicide against a background of placid contentment, until she recognized that "that is the whole," earth and flower.[9] So fundamentally was the world divided into the threatening and the non-threatening that even a flower could be disturbing unless you recognized that it emerged naturally from the mothering earth and was a part of it. Virginia connects her deepest impulse as a writer with this attempt to see the intruding, destructive, assertive elements of life as a part of a whole. Constructing such "wholes" would be her equivalent of sexual activity.

Even before the blows began to fall, she had been fearful. In the nursery at night, she would check to see if the fire was low. She dreaded its burning after they had gone to bed, frightened of the flickering shadow on the wall. Adrian, on the other hand, who shared the nursery with her, liked the flickering flame-light. To compromise, the nurse would put a towel over the fender, muting the shadows. (In *To the Lighthouse* the shadows cast by the night light on a boar's skull nailed to the wall terrify Cam, but James cannot go to sleep without a light and will not let the skull be touched. Mrs. Ramsay, the peacemaker, wraps her shawl around the skull, softening the shadow, so Cam sees mountains and bird's nests and gardens instead of the face of death.) Tempering the wind to the shorn lamb, Woolf's art, too, softens the harsh angularities of fact by placing them in a context of affective perception. Even a puddle of water must be seen in connection to something else, placed into a context, or it becomes unbearable. Rigid boundaries between perceived and perceiver, rigid boundaries between one part of reality and another are abhorrent to her. *The Waves*, her most ambitious novel, seeks to portray six individuals as aspects of one being; seeking continuity is her hallmark as a writer.

Her mother's death, reinforced by Stella's death two years later, was the cataclysmic disruption of her childhood, its major discontinuity, the blow from the hidden enemy which made everything else seem insubstantial. It was decades before she could fit this violence into an artistic whole. In the meantime, until she was forty-four, she was haunted by her mother. She could see her, hear her, imagine her responses as she went about her day. Invisible presences like that of her mother, she writes, tug us this way and that in daily life, luring us one way, deflecting us into different paths, yet how seldom are they described. Woolf, lover of memoirs, says that most memoirs and biographies, in ignoring such invisible presences, describe the fish, but not the stream which holds them in place.[10] Her mother was the current of her life. She was obsessed by her "unhealthily," as she says in her diary, until she finished *To the Lighthouse*, and then the obsession ceased—she no longer heard her voice or saw her. "I suppose that I did for myself what psychoanalysts do for their patients. I expressed some very long felt and deeply felt emotion. And in expressing it I explained it and then laid it to rest."[11]

"A Sketch of the Past," the memoir in which Woolf describes her early childhood, is of extraordinary interest, not only because it was written by a connoisseur of memoirs, adept at the art, and a reader of Proust, who enjoyed the chance to savor the interactions of past and present, of memory and consciousness, but also because it was written late in her life by a recent reader of Freud, one who had at least a passing knowledge of the theory of psychoanalysis.[12] Free association only loosely linked to chronology provides the structure for the essay, so that she begins—as I have done—not with her background and birth but with her first and most important memories, and if, as self-analysis, "A Sketch of the Past" is the merest beginning, still it is a beginning.

If we step back and adopt a more analytic view of her recollections, what strikes us first is their well-bred, repressed, but unmistakable eroticism. She remembers a time of "raptures" and "ecstasies," of intense shame about her body which suggests an intense awareness of her body. Woolf herself found the clue to the identity of these opposites when she thought of her grandfather, who enjoyed his cigar and so threw it away. Sensitive to pleasure, she prohibited it to herself, or sanitized its source by acknowledging only her responses to nature and impersonal things. In her first recollection she sits on her mother's lap; in the second, the maternal presence is the sea and the rhythmic sound of the waves and of the acorn on the window shade being drawn by the wind across the floor which lulls her to sleep. This displacement onto nature of the sources of her childhood pleasures is the next striking feature of her memoirs. Her third early memory provides an even better example of this. It is a highly sensual remembrance of the garden at St. Ives—bees murmuring, flowers in bloom—fairly bursting with fertility. "It still makes me feel warm; as if everything were ripe; humming; sunny; smelling so many smells at once; and all making a whole that even now makes me stop—as I stopped then going down to the beach."[13] Later in "A Sketch of the Past" she wonders, without answering her own question, why she should remember the hum of bees as she walked to the beach and forget being thrown naked into the sea by her father, an event brought to mind only because it was mentioned in the memoirs of a St. Ives acquaintance. Woolf goes out of her way in "A Sketch of the Past" to prove that she was frigid from birth, telling about

Gerald Duckworth's exploration of her and her response to it to assert the myth of her congenital asexuality. She protests, one feels, rather too strongly, and the sensual texture of her recollections belies her point. This was not an anaesthetic childhood.

In the second act of the drama, which opens after Stella's death in 1897 when Virginia is fifteen years old, Leslie Stephen emerges as a full-fledged villain and the heroine's role is thrust upon Vanessa. The pattern had been set earlier, of course. In their afternoon walks at St. Ives, one of the children had always to accompany their father. Julia was too concerned with his pleasure and his health and seemed, to her children, willing to sacrifice them on the altar of his needs. How much better for everyone if he could have taken his walks alone and overworked if he chose to, but instead this "legacy of dependence" survived Julia and became a terrible burden for her daughters — one of whom, at least, couldn't help noticing that Julia, so concerned about her husband's health, had died of fatigue at forty-nine while cancer found it very hard to kill Sir Leslie at seventy-two.

When Vanessa took over from Stella the running of the household, she had to endure not merely his screams and rages, his sighs and groans, at the weekly presentation of the account books, but the demand to satisfy all his emotional needs, needs for flattery, sympathy, and consolation. His daughters witnessed histrionics and attitudinizing such as his friends would never have believed possible in him, for such scenes were saved for women. With men, he was rational and analytical. Women, creatures of emotion as the Victorian myth had it, were for Leslie emotional wastebaskets. Afraid of having failed as a writer and thinker, he could not confess his failure to men, so he turned to his daughters for reassurance. Virginia Woolf would come to think of egotism as an exclusively masculine trait, and when one glimpses the monumental egotism of the principal man of her childhood, it seems less implausible.

Woolf's family experience reinforced the Victorian polarity of the intuitive sympathy of women and the rational, analytic understanding of men. In Virginia's opinion, Leslie was unrelentingly, repellently analytical, and underdeveloped emotionally. Give him an idea to analyze, let us say the philosophy of Hobbes, and he was clear, concise, shrewd: a splendid example of the Cambridge analytic spirit. But give him a character to discuss and he was cruder than a child. Virginia attributed this to Cambridge, whose overemphasis on intellection she found crippling. Leslie so ignored, disguised, covered up, suppressed his own emotions during his life, that by the age of sixty-five he was completely isolated, with no conception of what he felt himself or what others felt. The powerful example of her father planted in her mind the notion that men were emotional cripples, having sacrificed feeling to thought, a perception which has come to many but which few have stated as strongly as Woolf. Part of her defense against the prestige of an education she could not have would be to say that the education was sterile and draining.

To his two remaining daughters Leslie Stephen seemed a Bluebeard, a devourer of women. They remembered how he had tasked Stella's fragile strength, made her few months of joy bitter and difficult, and had not seemed unhappy enough after her death. He was more vigorous than any of them, and now it seemed he was going to make Vanessa his next victim. No woman of character could listen to him carry on without getting angry. Vanessa got angry but fought him in silence. They made him the type of everything they hated. He was a tyrant, a monster of selfishness. Writing later, Virginia could say that she had been extremely harsh and to some extent unjust—but not altogether so.

Vanessa was well suited for her central role. With a great deal of the beauty and much of the character of her mother and half-sister, she was thought worthy to carry on their tradition, and in their morbid state, "haunted by great ghosts," the Stephen children told themselves that to be like Julia or like Stella was to "achieve the height of human perfection." Everyone turned to Vanessa. Enormous demands were made on her, and she moved like a young queen weighted down by the pomp of her ceremonial robes. "It was in a sense, so easy to be what was expected, with such models before her, but also it was so hard to be herself."[14] She was acclaimed by all as the inheritor of all womanly virtures, yet she managed to keep something of herself intact: she mounted her bicycle and went off every day to study art.

There were, of course, other men in the household in those unhappy years from 1897 to 1904. Virginia's favorite was her brother Thoby, a year and a half older than she. He was not outstandingly clever, but he liked people, got along well with them, and took the lead out of a kind of natural ascendancy. Virginia's favorite image of him was from the St. Ives days, steering their sailboat around the point as he strained to keep the sails from flapping. During London winters, they argued about Shakespeare, and she was an eager listener to his stories about school, with no experience of her own with which to cap his. She imagines he found her a sheltered little creature, studying Greek and writing essays for only herself in her room at the top of the house at Hyde Park Gate, while he wrote essays for prizes at Trinity. When he went to Cambridge she missed him and envied him his freedom. She pictured him sitting of an evening by the fire with Lytton Strachey, smoking a pipe, carrying on fascinating discussions denied her in her solitary Kensington study. He was the man of the world—the intellectual world she longed for—while she was the immured maiden.

She defined herself by contrasts, and if Leslie Stephen was an eminent Victorian remnant against whom the more up-to-date daughters longed to rebel, if Thoby enjoyed a masculine freedom which Virginia envied, the Duckworths represented a conventional society which she loathed, but whose power over her was in some ways more real, more insidious than Leslie's melodramatic tyranny.

Up in her room, Virginia could spend the mornings reading, writing, translating Greek, but towards four-thirty she had to transform herself into a well-bred young lady and participate in the rites of polite society, dressing up and chatting at the tea table in the proper Victorian manner. The ability to make small talk and to respond in the manner spoken to did not come naturally to Virginia and Vanessa, but they had learned it from their mother. Rereading some of her early reviews, she would blame their politeness, their lack of bite, on her tea-table training. Her father trained her, in reading books, to state her reactions clearly and candidly, but the lesson of the tea table was precisely the reverse—to flatter, to sympathize, to console.

At seven-thirty the young ladies changed clothes again and scrubbed their necks and arms, for at eight they had to enter the drawing room in evening dress, arms and neck bare. Down Virginia came in a green dress—made of curtain fabric, partly to save money, partly for the adventure of it—to face George Duckworth in black tie and evening jacket, sitting in a chair by the fire with all the lights in the room up. He inspected her dress, he looked her up and down as he might have a horse, and then a look of sullen disapproval came over his face, a disapproval not merely aesthetic, for he recognized hints of more serious insurrection, moral and social. He told her to go and rip the dress up.

That he was thirty-six and she was twenty, that he had a thousand pounds a year and she had fifty made it difficult to disobey George. But there was more to it—he made her feel like an outsider, a tramp or gypsy peering into the tent in which the spectacular Victorian circus was in full swing. Virginia and Vanessa had a good view of the show and could see all the acrobats, George among them, jumping through hoops, winning themselves headmasterships, judgeships, cabinet posts, but they were not allowed to take part. She was amused, cool, detached, but still George, with the force of wealth, tradition, and power behind him, was not to be defied.

George made even Leslie look a little better, for the Duckworth suppression of natural feeling was in the service of nothing more than propriety, polite appearances. The old man, upstairs in his study, now deaf and completely cut off, devoted himself to the life of the mind. George ruled a world of convention in the drawing room, and no one cared less for convention than Leslie Stephen. Virginia would leave the gossip in the drawing room to return a book to the library, find her father there absorbed in a book, becoming only slowly aware of her presence, and feel a flash of love for this unworldly, lonely old man.

George was the perfect social being, eagerly trying to please, buying umbrellas for the servants at Christmas, giving Virginia a looking-glass to encourage her vanity, calling cabs in the rain, attending funerals, remembering aunts' birthdays, sending turtle soup to the afflicted—a kind of male Mrs. Dalloway. His style more than anything else offended Virginia, and the way he insisted on imposing his philistinism on his sisters. Why would he insist on dragging them with him on his relentless climb up the social ladder? Handsome, rich, private secretary to Austen Chamberlain, he had London society before him. "He believed that aristocratic society was possessed of all the virtues and the graces. He believed that his family had been entrusted to his care. He believed that it was his sacred duty—and when he reached that point his emotions overcame him; he began to sob; flung himself on his knees; seized Vanessa in his arms; implored her in the name of her mother, of her grandmother, by all that was sacred in the female sex and holy in the traditions of our family to accept Lady Arthur Russell's invitation to dinner, and to spend the weekend with the Chamberlains at Highbury."[15] Vanessa did not want to go out to be bored by young men in the Foreign Office and condescended to by ladies with titles. Every morning the post brought new invitations for Mr. Duckworth and Miss Stephen, and every evening they fought.

When Vanessa refused finally to accompany George, he turned his attentions to Virginia, who was not as resolute in her opposition to society as Vanessa. For Virginia it had charms—glamor, brightly lit rooms, beautiful clothes. But she was not a social success. She was not asked to dance, hid, was discovered, was given by a kindly peeress a piece of cake. On the evening that epitomized for Virginia the whole disastrous social enterprise, George took her to dine with Lady Carnarvon and her sister, and Virginia proceeded to shock them by talking of Plato. Later, before leaving for the theater, Virginia heard George and Lady Carnarvon kissing passionately, and yet, on the principle that one might do such things but never talk about them, Lady Carnavon felt obliged to lead her little group away from the play when it turned out to be a racy French comedy. Afterwards, she could not even bring herself to mention the distressing episode at the theater. In the cab, she took Virginia's hand and said in a tremulous voice, "I do hope, Miss Stephen, that the evening has not tired you very much." Bloomsbury's social radicalism was to consist not so much in novel and shocking behavior as in talking openly about the things people had been doing all along in private.

The account of her evening out with George ends with a vignette intended to be offhandedly shocking: Virginia has taken off her white satin dress, her long white gloves, her white silk stockings and is lying in bed, almost asleep, when the door opens stealthily, and George, telling her not to be frightened and not to turn on the light, flings himself onto the bed and takes her in his arms. "Yes, the old ladies of Kensington and Belgravia never knew that George Duckworth was not only father and mother, brother and sister to those poor Stephen girls; he was their lover also."[16] George's behavior was of a piece with the larger Victorian coverup, the disguising of all real emotion in a veil of propriety, sentimentality, and polite conversation. Elsewhere Virginia might blame George's disgusting advances for warping her sexuality, but in the context of her memoirs, the affair is presented as the final and most grotesque example of the cleavage between appearances and reality which so distressed her about the world of fashion.

This is the view of polite society one gets when Virginia, in her later memoirs, is developing the myth of a repressed, constricted childhood, a kind of imprisonment in Kensington, which ends when the ogre dies, the spell is broken, and the enchanted maidens are freed to live in Blooms-bury. But she has another myth of society, developed in her diaries of the time and one which will inform *Mrs. Dalloway:* society is a heroic endeavor, social life a holding action against chaos and despair. This view enables Virginia to watch with some delight the social game which otherwise caused her such pain. "Major so and so laughs as though he hadn't a care in the world; we know he can't pay his butcher's bill. Mrs. Thingamagig is more amusing than ever tonight—didn't she lose an only son in the war?"[17] A moralist, she writes, might find this artificial and conclude that society is hollow and heartless, but the other side is this—doesn't Mrs. Thingamagig do better making the world laugh than by sitting home crying over her sorrows? To be a social success one has to have the courage of a hero. There is a certain amount of irony in all this, yet a residue of sincerity remains: Mrs. Thingamagig, transformed, filled out, sobered up, and elevated to the nobility, will become Lady Bexborough whom Mrs. Dalloway so admires, who opens a bazaar still holding the telegram announcing her son's death in World War I.

In mapping the social landscape of Virginia's youth, one must mention, too, the world of artists to which she was allied because of her mother's Little Holland House connections. After leaving Lady Carnarvon that scandalous evening, she and George continued on to a party at the Holman Hunts', where the painter sipped cocoa and discoursed to his admiring guests on the symbolism of *The Light of the World.* Virginia felt no more at home in the world of artists than she did in the world of fashion and high society, and she was keenly aware before she was twenty that there was nothing in Philistia to equal the snobbery of Bohemia. "I am always impressed," she wrote mockingly in her 1903 diary, "by the splendid superiority of these artist men and women over their Philistine brethren. They are so thoroughly convinced that mankind is divided into two classes, one of which wears amber beads and low evening collars—while the other follows the fashion. Each thanks God it is not the other—but the artist is the more intolerant."[18]

In Virginia's personal myth of liberation, the world of art could be as much of a threat as the world of bourgeois conventionality. Later she would write a little play called *Freshwater,* to be acted by members of the family at a family party. Intended as a joke, this comic sketch of life at the home of her great-aunt, Mrs. Cameron, features Tennyson always reading "Maud" and complaining about the prevalence of sibilants in the titles of Watts' paintings, Watts turning his wife into a model of Modesty trampled on by Mammon, Mrs. Cameron always about to leave for Ceylon but in the meantime using her cook as a model for Guinevere, and Ellen Terry, Watts' wife, sick of being given perfect white roses instead of kisses, sick of Art, a lusty young woman married to an old man. "Nothing ever changes in this house," she says. "Somebody's always asleep. Lord Tennyson is always reading Maud. The cook is always being photographed. The Camerons are always starting for India. I'm always sitting to Signor." Out of this atmosphere of stifling, didactic aestheticism, out of this enchanted sleeping-beauty world, Ellen Terry escapes, running off (disguised as a boy) with Edward Gordon Craig to 46 Gordon Square, Bloomsbury, precisely where the Stephen sisters went when they left Hyde Park Gate.[19]

Bloomsbury makes no sense in Woolf's personal mythology without 22 Hyde Park Gate preceding it. In telling the story of her own life, when she comes to the Bloomsbury years, she doubles back and describes again the house in Kensington from which in 1904 she and Vanessa freed themselves. In the symbolic landscape of her youth, it is the principal monument, embodying the claustrophobia of Victorian family life. This tall half-brick, half-stucco structure, covered with vines, so close to its neighbor you could see Mrs. Redgrave across the way washing her neck, generated gloom and darkness. Eleven people between the ages of eight and sixty were thrown together inside, waited upon by seven servants. Three families dwelt there—Stephens, Duckworths, and the retarded girl Laura. You never knew, Virginia says, if you would stumble across Herbert Duckworth's barrister's wig, Leslie's discarded clergyman's collar, or sheets of drawings by Thackeray.[20]

If ages and families were conflated at 22 Hyde Park Gate, everything else presents itself to Virginia's recollection as rigidly segregated. It was a house divided. The drawing room was divided by black folding doors, on one side of which (when Julia was still alive) ladies would tell dark and troubled stories about husbands accidentally poisoned or discovered in bed with the maid, while on the other side the men discussed India and botany. Even when the sexes converged, their roles were clearly defined, and when Leslie got irritated and with the privilege of an elderly masculine eccentric groaned "Oh Gibbs, what a bore you are!" his wife would throw a pretty young woman his way to charm him back to good humor, just as Mrs. Ramsay uses Minta Doyle to keep her husband happy. Mrs. Stephen's favorite for this purpose was Kitty Lushington (later Kitty Maxse). "Kitty wants to tell you," she would say to Leslie, "how much she loved your lecture."

Virginia's only refuge from family life was her own room, which so strongly suggested to her a symbol of psychic space that it deserves some attention. It had been the night nursery, shared with Vanessa, until 1897 when Stella married, freeing her room for Vanessa. The nursery was done over (at George Duckworth's expense) into a more grown-up space for Virginia, a combination bedroom and sitting room. On one side was her bed, flanked by the washstand and the looking-glass. On the other side was the wicker chair in which she read, a writing table inherited from Stella, made by the St. Ives carpenter and stained green and brown with a leaf pattern by Stella herself, and, on top of it, her Greek lexicon, always open — also, inkpots and manuscript books in which she was constantly working. This "literary" side of the room contained Virginia's icons of selfhood, and it was to this side that she escaped, reading in the hours between tea and dinner, writing whenever she could. She began keeping journals in her teens, sporadic notations of events, but by 1903 her diary consisted of a series of attempts to write fully modeled essays. In these notebooks, too, she practised descriptive writing. Already she was training herself to be a writer, finding in writing a happier reality, an alternative to family life.

In the other half of her room not much went on. She remembers herself listening to traffic, to dance music, to cats wawling, as she waited for Vanessa to come home. She makes a great deal of the division of the room into writing part and sleeping part, as though they were in conflict and represented a conflict in herself:

> Which would I describe first — the living side or the sleeping side? They could be described separately. Yet they were always running together. And how they fought each other: how often I was in a rage and in ecstasy, torn between all the different forces that entered that room, whether one calls them the living side or the sleeping side. . . . But I was thinking, feeling, living there two lives that the two parts of the room symbolize with the intensity which the butterfly or moth feels when with sticky tremulous legs and antennae it pushes out of its chrysalis and emerges; waits beside the broken shell for a moment; damp; its legs still creased; its eyes dazzled; incapable of flight.[21]

She is one-half well-bred young lady, a body to be dressed up and put on display for the marriage market, and one-half intellectual, a mind to be nourished and trained. Life at Hyde Park Gate was, for the most part, focused on preparing her for marriage and a social role. Furtively, in her own room, she carried on her insurrectionary labors of the mind, engaged, in a small but determined way, in overturning the established order of things. Her pleasures in life were almost all to come from being a mind — her miseries from having that mind housed in a body.

Notes

1. See Noel Annan, *Leslie Stephen: His Thought and Character in Relation to His Time* (Cambridge: Harvard University Press, 1952).

2. This chapter relies heavily on "A Sketch of the Past," in *Moments of Being.*

3. See "Professions for Women," in Virginia Woolf, *Collected Essays*, 4 vols. (New York: Harcourt, Brace & World, 1967), II, 287–88.

4. Virginia's memoirs place George's aggressions around 1904, although it's possible they had started earlier and Leonard Woolf believed they dated from much earlier indeed — around 1895, just after Julia's death. See Bell, I, 44n.

5. See Virginia Woolf's introductory essay about Julia Margaret Cameron in *Victorian Photographs of Famous Men and Fair Women*, ed. Tristram Powell (Boston: David R. Godine, 1973), p. 14. This is a reissue of a volume of Cameron's photographs originally published by the Hogarth Press in 1926, with introductions by Woolf and Roger Fry.

6. Vanessa Bell, *Notes on Virginia's Childhood* (New York: Frank Hallman, 1974), unpaged.

7. *Moments of Being*, pp. 94–95.

8. Autobiographical fragment, written 1940, beginning "The tea table was the centre of Victorian family life," Berg Collection, New York Public Library.

9. *Moments of Being*, p. 71.

10. *Ibid.*, p. 80.

11. *Ibid.*, p. 81.

12. She was reading Freud in 1939–40, the same period at which she was writing "A Sketch of the Past." See *A Writer's Diary*, ed. Leonard Woolf (London: The Hogarth Press, 1969), pp. 322, 326. The Hogarth Press was Freud's English publisher, but that does not mean Virginia necessarily read Freud's works as they were published. When Freud moved to Hampstead at the start of World War II, the Woolfs went to visit him. Freud gave Virginia Woolf a narcissus (which need not have been meant as a comment on her character).

14. "Reminiscences," in *ibid.*, p. 54.

15. "22 Hyde Park Gate," in *ibid.*, p. 148.

16. *Ibid.*, p. 155.

17. "Thoughts on Social Success," in 1903 Diary, Berg Collection.

18. "An Artistic Party," 1903 Diary. For an interesting analogue to Woolf's experience, see Diana Holman-Hunt's memoir, *My Grandmothers and I* (New York: Norton, 1961), which tells of her dual Victorian heritage: one grandmother was the wife of a retired K.C., the other was the widow of the pre-Raphaelite painter.

19. A first version of *Freshwater* was written in 1923; the final version was written and performed in 1935. Vanessa Bell played Mrs. Cameron and Leonard Woolf played her husband.

20. "Old Bloomsbury," in *Moments of Being*, pp. 160–61.

21. Autobiographical fragment, 1940, "The tea table. . . ," Berg Collection.

The Problem of the Fiction   Michael Rosenthal**

It is only relatively recently that Virginia Woolf seems to have emerged from the limbo of polite esteem in which she has generally been held into the forefront of the contemporary social and literary scene.

*Reprinted from Michael Rosenthal, *Virginia Woolf* (New York: Columbia Univ. Press, 1979), pp. 35–48.

Having languished for decades in the shadow of her august fellow modernists like Joyce, Lawrence, and Conrad, Woolf appears at last to have secured for herself the stamp of the authentic classic that had previously managed to elude her. The obligatory if slightly stale respect invariably accorded her by readers has now given way to a passionate, searching interest in every aspect of her life. The torrent of Newsletters, Quarterlies, Miscellanies, English Institute Conferences, and Modern Language Association Sessions, among other forms of tribute, attest to her arrival. Virginia Woolf is a very hot literary property indeed.

The impulses behind this adulation are worth exploring, particularly as they tell us a good deal more about our world than they do about Woolf. To begin with, it is clear that the rediscovery of Woolf is part of the larger phenomenon of the canonization of Bloomsbury which has been in process for the past ten years. It is a marvelous irony of social history that Virginia Woolf's Bloomsbury associations, which for years had damned her in the earnest eyes of the Leavises and others, now constitute one of her strongest sources of appeal. Riding the crest of the Bloomsbury mania, Woolf has become a cult figure in a way that would certainly have amazed her. It is probably fair to say that the renewed interest in Woolf on the part of the general reader is more a result of her role in the chic, provocative Bloomsbury way of life than of any developing awareness of the inherent merit of her fiction.

If sheer titillation accounts for much of the public's attention, the gradual realization that Virginia Woolf was, in fact, a woman writer (or at least not a man, the androgynous theory having its own advocates) has also played a substantial role. The polemical grinder of the feminist movement has greedily devoured Woolf, spewing her forth as the appropriately committed feminist whose preoccupation with the cause is somehow the key to her fiction. Such a view of Woolf is not particularly useful. It is of course true that she was very much concerned with the economic and social plight of women, and deeply sensitive to the pyschic crippling inflicted on them by a male dominated world. *Orlando*, *A Room of One's Own*, *Three Guineas*, and assorted essays eloquently testify to her involvement in these issues, as well as to the deft way she can expose the absurdities of our culture. But to focus on her fiction through any sort of politicized feminist lens is seriously to distort it. Woolf herself deplored novels that preach, and hers are conspicuously free from the proselytizing that frequently occupied her when she was not at her desk struggling with her fiction. This is not to argue that Woolf was not conscious of the assumptions of an environment which held for example, that Virginia's brothers, but not Virginia, should go to university; it is simply to protest against the reductionist view, in vogue today, that Woolf's novels speak in some essential and exclusive way to feminist preoccupations. Woolf, in fact, hated the word "feminist" altogether—"What more fitting than to destroy an old word, a vicious and corrupt word that has done much harm

in its day and is now obsolete? The word 'feminist' is the word indicated"
(*Three Guineas*, 184), finding it divisive and inimical to the overall unity
of civilized people she so desired.

The feminist claim on Woolf has lately been joined by the androgynist, which sees Woolf's novels as endorsing the splendors of the
androgynous mind as a palliative to all our ills. Taking as a seminal
passage Woolf's discussion in *A Room of One's Own* of the flourishing
artistic imagination being able to transcend any narrow sexual role, the
hunters of androgyny doggedly chase the metaphor through all of Woolf's
fiction, hacking out new patterns of meaning as they go. But metaphors
are better left in peace to illuminate the specific contexts in which they
appear. The illustrative use of anydrogyny to represent the kind of wide-
ranging, non-dogmatic, resonant intelligence Woolf finds admirable — and
capable of producing great art — cannot be generalized into establishing
Woolf's "androgynous vision." To discover that Woolf believes that men
and women should share a complex view of reality, one as free as possible
from the parochialisms of any single sex, is not to discover anything very
new about her work.

If Woolf is to survive as other than a precious oddity of the modernist
movement, it will be neither as a member of a coterie, a radical feminist,
nor a prophetic androgynist. Sexual ideologies and exotic ambiences aside,
Woolf's fiction must be able to meet the reservation still shared by many
and most recently expressed by Elizabeth Hardwick: acknowledging the
richness of Woolf's language and the glow of her genius, Hardwick goes on
to say, "yet in a sense, her novels aren't interesting."[1] Whatever else novels
are, they should at least be interesting, and it is a fact that hers have not
always been thought so. Woolf was herself aware that her work posed
more than the usual difficulties for readers. Her diary notes with sympathy (and some irritation) the puzzled efforts of critics to comprehend what
she is doing. The problems are real, and a passage from *Between the Acts*,
her last novel, suggests what they are: "Did the plot matter? She shifted
and looked over her right shoulder. The plot was only there to beget
emotion . . . Don't bother about the plot: the plot's nothing" (*Between
the Acts*, 109). Isa's reflection on the meaning of Miss La Trobe's pageant
at once describes Woolf's own art and points out the greatest obstacle to its
appreciation. For plot is indeed nothing in Woolf's fiction, and character,
Isa might have gone on to say — or character traditionally conceived — not
much more. Novelists who dispense with both of these staples are going to
have difficult times, and Woolf has received her share of critical abuse for
writing novels in which, it is argued, nothing happens.

Not, of course, that she is the sole practitioner of the twentieth-century
novel to have abandoned established notions of plot and character; the
modern novel clearly developed through precisely such liberties, but in
many ways her work is the most radical. For despite the formal break-
throughs made by Conrad, Ford, Lawrence, Joyce and others, their work

still exhibits a basic narrative interest (perhaps *Finnegans Wake*, a fictional cosmos unto itself, could be considered an exception) which is almost entirely lacking in Woolf's. However complicated the point of view and richly patterned the symbolic structure, their novels essentially remain part of a story-telling tradition from which Woolf dissociated herself. We are impelled through *Ulysses* less by its dazzling virtuosity than its abiding concern for Leopold and Stephen and what befalls them, just as we are absorbed in the destinies of Paul Morel or Decoud or Lord Jim or Benjy or even Winnie Verloc as they go about their muddled business. Although they do so in a variety of innovative ways, the great modern novels of the twentieth century implicate the reader in the lives of their characters as they confront experience, and in the problems of choice and self-definition that confrontation engenders. "Yes — oh dear yes," E. M. Forster writes in *Aspects of the Novel* with bemused resignation, "the novel tells a story" (*Aspects of the Novel*, 27). Subtilized and internalized though it is, the primitive energy of the story animates most of modern fiction.

Woolf's novels, however, contain no substantial narrative impulse. In a very real sense it is true she does write novels in which nothing happens. It would be impossible, for example, to speak in any serious way about the sustained "action" of *The Waves* or *Between the Acts*, or even of a more manageable novel like *To the Lighthouse*. Her work contains little humor, passion, or particular dramatic or even ideological tension. Demanding everything and making few concessions to readers, it seems to many hermetically sealed in its austerity and fragility from the vital currents of life. Woolf recognized, of course, that in writing novels that lacked any strong narrative thread she was cutting herself off from one of the enduring appeals of fiction, but she had no difficulty making this choice.

For as an artist Woolf was obsessed with what we can call formal rather than thematic concerns, with finding ways of embodying, as she says, "the exact shapes my brain holds" (*A Writer's Diary*, 176). That Woolf was absorbed primarily in creating shapes is what makes her such an utterly original voice in modern literature. It is also what makes her such a difficult writer to talk about, for her work does not readily lend itself to critical analysis of character or theme or philosophy. The difficulties are not simply ours: certainly Woolf's own language fails when she tries to formulate for herself her fictional intentions. Reflecting in her diary on Arnold Bennett's criticism that *Jacob's Room* doesn't have characters that survive, Woolf agrees that she hasn't "that reality gift. I insubstantiate willfully to some extent, distrusting reality — its cheapness. But to get further. Have I the power of conveying the true reality?" (*A Writer's Diary*, 57). If distinctions between "reality" and "true reality" are seldom satisfying, this at least has the virtue of suggesting what one should *not* expect from a Woolf novel. Other attempts to state positively what she wants her fiction to achieve are no more successful (*A Writer's Diary*, 132).

That is one of the experiences I have had here in some Augusts; and got
there to a consciousness of what I call "reality": a thing I see before me,
something abstract but residing in the downs or sky . . . in which I shall
rest and continue to exist. Reality I call it. And I fancy sometimes this is
the most necessary thing to me; that which I seek. But who knows—
once one takes a pen and writes? . . . Now perhaps this is my gift: this
perhaps is what distinguishes me from other people. I think it may be
rare to have so acute a sense of something like that—but again, who
knows? I would like to express it too.

The reality Woolf wants her fiction to express cannot easily be
formulated apart from the particular way it inheres in each novel. It is not
a substantive vision of the sort J. Hillis Miller finds in Conrad's fiction,
whose "aim is to make the truth of life, something different from any
impression or quality, momentarily visible. Not colors or light but the
darkness behind them is the true reality."[2] Woolf's reality has nothing to do
with stripping away illusion or penetrating surface phenomena to unearth
the grim darkness beneath, but resides in a form which makes comprehen-
sible the way the various impressions and colors and darkness together
constitute the texture of human life. It is something which is communicated emotionally rather than intellectually. Woolf writes (*Collected
Essays*, vol. 2, 129):

When we speak of form, we mean that certain emotions have been
placed in the right relations to each other; then that the novelist is able
to dispose these emotions and make them tell by methods which he
inherits, bends to his purpose, models anew or even invents for himself.

Endlessly evolving new techniques to dispose these emotions, Woolf
succeeds in making out of the chaos and disharmony she found in the
world marvelously coherent shapes. One of the best descriptions of what
she tries to do in her novels was written by Roger Fry, not about Woolf at
all but about the Post-Impressionist painters he so loved. Interestingly,
Woolf quotes the passage herself in her biography of Fry (*Roger Fry*,
177–8):

Now these artists . . . do not seek to give what can, after all, be but a
pale reflex of actual appearance, but to arouse the conviction of a new
and definite reality. They do not seek to imitate form, but to create
form, not to imitate life, but to find an equivalent for life. By that I
mean that they wish to make images which by the clearness of their
logical structure, and by their closely knit unity of texture, shall appeal
to our disinterested and contemplative imagination with something of
the same vividness as the things of actual life appeal to our practical
activities.

The center of a Woolf novel, then, does not reside in any of those
several themes frequently singled out for critical investigation—the workings of consciousness, the perception of time, the quality of personal

relationships — but in her effort to orchestrate these in such a way as to make us feel how together they constitute part of the experience of living. The quest is always for the form that will embody Woolf's sense of what that experience is. From *Jacob's Room* to *Between the Acts*, every one of Woolf's novels originated not with any notion of theme or character but with some notion of the form the novel might take. As she indicates in her diary, *Jacob's Room* developed out of three short pieces she was working on even as she was struggling through to the end of her second novel, *Night and Day (A Writer's Diary,* 23):

> I'm a great deal happier . . . today than I was yesterday having this afternoon arrived at some idea of a new form for a new novel. Suppose one thing should open out of another — as in an unwritten novel — only not for 10 pages but 200 or so — doesn't that give the looseness and lightness I want . . . Conceive(?) "Mark on the Wall," "K. G." ["Kew Gardens"] and "Unwritten Novel" taking hands and dancing in unity. What the unity shall be I have yet to discover; the theme is a blank to me; but I see immense possibilities in the form I hit upon more or less by chance two weeks ago.

Similarly, her first intuitions about *The Waves* were purely formal ones (*A Writer's Diary,* 104):

> Why not invent a new kind of play; as for instance:
>
>> Woman thinks . . .
>> He does.
>> Organ plays.
>> She writes.
>> They say.
>> She sings.
>> Night speaks.
>> They miss.
>
> I think it must be something on this line — thought I can't now see what. Away from facts; free; yet concentrated; prose yet poetry; a novel and a play.

Or consider her early sense of *Between the Acts (A Writer's Diary,* 287):

> Will another novel ever swim up? If so, how? The only hint I have towards it is that it's to be dialogue: and poetry; and prose all quite distinct. No more long closely written books. . . . It came over me suddenly last night as I was reading . . . that I saw the form of a new novel. It's to be first the statement of the theme; then the restatement; and so on: repeating the same story: singing out this and then that, until the central idea is stated.

Before there is theme there is already a vision of form, and even after the substance of the novel has been thought out the commitment is always to the design.

Such a comitment does not make her, as many have claimed, a theoretician of the novel. Intuitions about form affect her in much the same way as a fresh image will stimulate a poet's creative process. Neither an abstract nor purely intellectual fascination, formal considerations provide Woolf with the emotional and imaginative impetus for each new book. Her absorption with formal problems makes the thematic content of her novels relatively unimportant to her fictional inspiration, and it is a fact that such content does not alter radically over the course of her lifetime. Although intended somewhat flippantly, her note that *To the Lighthouse* contains "all the usual things I try to put in — life, death, etc." (*A Writer's Diary*, 76-7) — is very much to the point and might well have been written about any of her works. It is less the things themselves than the different patterns they achieve in each novel, the relationship she fashions between them that matters. The challenge in every work is always to find a new method for rendering her sense of experience: once a form has been fully worked out, Woolf moves on to a different attempt. Each experiment is "a shot at my vision — if it's not a catch, it's a cast in the right direction" (*A Writer's Diary*, 173) — and represents a shot she will not repeat a second time. A London day in the life of Clarissa Dalloway, the passage of ten years on an island in the Hebrides, the makeshift, harried performance of Miss La Trobe's pageant — each constitutes a unique version of Woolf's remarkably steady perception of the world. The extraordinary structural diversity of *Jacob's Room, Mrs. Dalloway, To the Lighthouse, The Waves, The Years,* and *Between the Acts* paradoxically attests to the underlying singleness of purpose Woolf held to throughout her career.

Woolf's own quest as an artist — to create shapes that will make lasting sense of the fluidity of life — is reflected within her novels by people who are engaged in the same kind of search. "Odd how the creative power at once brings the whole universe to order," she notes in her diary (*A Writer's Diary*, 220), speaking to the impulses both behind and within her fiction. In so far as it is possible to generalize about the meaning of the human activity in Woolf's fictional world, we can say that the characters in her novels constantly try, through widely different means, to establish for themselves from the chaos around them a coherent grasp of their world. What Woolf attempts to accomplish through her fiction, that is, Lily Briscoe attempts with her painting, Bernard with his novel, Miss La Trobe with her pageant. And although these are the specific aesthetic endeavors which most closely approximate to Woolf's own, the instinct to bring things together is not limited to painters and writers. Certainly it is the animating principle behind the soliloquies of all the voices in *The Waves*, not just Bernard's, and is what impels that superficially least creative of souls, Clarissa Dalloway, to give her parties. Most memorably, of course, it is Mrs. Ramsay's particular genius, possessing as she does the ability to "choose out the elements of things and piece them together and so, giving them a wholeness not theirs in life, make of some scene, or meeting of people (all now gone and separate), one of those globed compacted things over which thought lingers and love plays" (*To the Lighthouse*, 295–6).

The workings of the creative imagination shaping different visions of order, then, is the single great theme which appears in Woolf's fiction. The importance of that imagination in her work comes directly out of the overwhelming sense of human isolation in which every novel is steeped. Whether it is Jacob searching for himself, or Septimus and Rezia unable to talk to each other, or Giles and Isa struggling in their tempestuous marriage, or even Mrs. Ramsay, giving of herself to exhaustion, the people in Woolf's fiction invariably feel cut off, not only from other human beings but from the world around them. The fact of isolation and the possibility of fleeting transcendence and communion—these are the two poles of Woolf's fictional universe. Rooted in one, characters can earn, through their own arduous efforts, brief contact with the other. Scratching out its monotonous "Unity-Dispersity . . . Un . . . dis," the gramophone of *Between the Acts* (235) actually lays out the psychic contours of all of Woolf's mature work. "Scraps, orts, and fragments," (*Between the Acts*, 220), as Miss La Trobe's pageant insists, the isolated selves in Virginia Woolf's world grapple not only with their own inadequacies and fears but with the uncertainty of personal relationships, the intractableness of language, the fact of death, to achieve their completed visions. The battle is difficult—filled with the same kind of loneliness and pain Woolf experienced in her own life as she fought her way through the demons of madness and despair that constantly assailed her to the lucid forms of the fiction—and the successes transient, but there is nothing else. Whatever the suffering involved, all the novels from *Mrs. Dalloway* on manage to end on a final note of affirmation: a party is given, a lighthouse reached, a pageant produced. Such accomplishments, however trivial they might appear, suggest the basic commitment to living made by the fiction. As Lily Briscoe understands after she has finished her painting, it does not matter in the least whether the canvas is ultimately destroyed or rolled up in some dusty attic. In Woolf's universe to be able to say, "I have had my vision," is the consummate human achievement, and Lily's words, which close *To the Lighthouse*, speak not only to her particular feat in complet- ing her canvas but to the successes of the other protagonists as well and finally, of course, to those of Woolf.

They could not be reasonably applied, however, to Woolf's first two novels, *The Voyage Out* (1915) and *Night and Day* (1919). If D. S. Savage is perhaps unduly harsh in finding *Night and Day* to be the dullest novel in the English language, it is nevertheless true that her first two books are not particularly distinguished. Lacking any kind of formal originality, both are lamentably tedious, dragging on far longer than they should in a thoroughly pedestrian manner.

Although Terence Hewet's notion in *The Voyage Out* that he would like to write a "novel about silence," about "the things people say," seems to anticipate Woolf's later development, neither of these initial efforts suggests the unique things to come. What they do make clear is how uncongenial the realistic—or what Woolf might call the Edwardian—method of fiction was to her genius. For Woolf, conventional techniques could produce only conventional fiction. It was not until the publication of *Jacob's Room* in 1922 that she felt, as she notes in her diary, that she has finally learned "how to begin (at 40) to say something in my own voice" (*A Writer's Diary*, 47). Irrevocably turning away with *Jacob's Room* from the established tradition within which *The Voyage Out* and *Night and Day* were written, Woolf devoted the next nineteen years of her life to exploring the different possibilities of that newly discovered voice.

Jacob's Room is the first of her novels which tries to dispense with what Woolf calls the "appalling narrative business of the realist: getting on from lunch to dinner." Her well-known rejection of the realist method—enunciated most emphatically in two essays, "Mr Bennett and Mrs. Brown" and "Modern Fiction"—claims that in its attention to the superficial and mundane, realism fails to catch the vital experience of living itself. Trotting out her favorite trio of Edwardian villains—Wells, Bennett, and Galsworthy—in both essays, Woolf demonstrates how they frittered away their talent "making the trivial and the transitory appear the true and the enduring" (*Collected Essays*, vol. 2, 105). In a word, they are *materialists*, devoting themselves with varying degrees of success to the pursuit of the unimportant. Opposed to these are writers who, like Joyce, are spiritual, who understand that life is a far more curious and fluid affair than the stolid materialists would have us believe. The mind does not function according to rigidly defined patterns, Woolf declares, but rather receives "an incessant shower of innumerable atoms" (*Collected Essays*, vol. 2, 106), so that if a writer were not constrained by convention and forced to follow prescribed directions, "if he could base his work upon his own feeling . . . there would be no plot, no comedy, no tragedy, no love interest or catastrophe in the accepted style, and perhaps not a single button sewn on as the Bond Street tailors would have it." Neither unique to Woolf nor by any means a theoretical principle she holds to in her own criticism, such an argument is primarily an intensely personal assertion of what her own fiction will be. Implicitly, we cannot help but feel, it is also a way of absolving herself from continuing to labor in the direction that the rather dismal *Night and Day* and *The Voyage Out* suggest she could not manage very happily.

Employing techniques of point of view and organization in *Jacob's Room* that she had tentatively experimented with in "Mark on the Wall,"

"Kew Gardens," and "Unwritten Novel"—three short pieces she published between 1917 and 1920—she attempts to embrace the "unknown and uncircumscribed spirit" of life by writing a novel that steadfastly avoids much of the prosaic connective tissue necessary to narrative fiction. *Jacob's Room* is technically very different from *The Voyage Out* and *Night and Day*. Instead of the consecutive narrative movement of these books, it progresses by a series of discrete jumps through Jacob's life. Moving without apology—or much serious transition—from incident to incident, the novel is compounded of specific, isolated moments strung together relating to Jacob, his friends, his family. But if Woolf manages to liberate herself from some of the formal conventions under which she wrote her first two novels, such liberation is not in itself a recipe for fictional success. A freer form is not necessarily a fully expressive form, and while *Jacob's Room* has been purged of narrative dross, the result is not altogether satisfying. The novel's episodic organization does not find in the discontinuities of existence significant patterns that imprint themselves on the imagination. If the novel succeeds in documenting the isolation and the fragmentariness of existence, at the same time it does not embrace them in an affecting, substantial form. An important new direction which helped Woolf break free from the confines within which she had been working, *Jacob's Room* is finally a sterile form, one not capable of the resonance of her mature work.

But Woolf learned her lessons well and her next effort, *Mrs. Dalloway*, achieves a formal coherence and power altogether absent from *Jacob's Room*. In place of the flaccid chronological organization covering all of Jacob's life, *Mrs. Dalloway* effectively focuses on the events of one day in the lives of Clarissa Dalloway and Septimus Smith. Digging "caves and tunnels" beneath her characters, Woolf creates a densely structured texture in which a June day in London is constantly informed by pressures and vestiges of the past. The novel is complexly organized both spatially and temporally. Physical meetings of characters in the street—and finally in Clarissa's home—merge with a web of intersecting memories and reveries to create a form that succeeds brilliantly in conveying Woolf's sense of the isolation, ironies, and ecstasies of life. Implacably tolling out the passage of time throughout the book, Big Ben punctuates the reflection of individual characters with its unyielding insistence on the passage of time. In addition to the mundane purpose of announcing a shift of narrative focus from one character to another, the gonging serves to emphasize the restricted framework of a single day which Woolf's imagination exploited continually during her career for her best work. It is significant that Woolf's four most distinguished novels—*Mrs. Dalloway*, *To the Lighthouse*, *The Waves*, and *Between the Acts*—essentially take place, either metaphorically or actually, within a twenty-four hour period. *Mrs. Dalloway* and *Between the Acts*, of course, do so explicitly. Although ten years elapse between parts One and Three of *To the*

Lighthouse, the novel imagistically follows the movement of an entire day from the late afternoon of the first part, through the dark night of the second, to the early morning which opens the third section. And the nine poetic interludes of *The Waves*, describing the progression of the sun across the sky, clearly set the different dramatic soliloquies within the natural rhythm of a single day. However startlingly varied in form they are, the fact that all four play variations on the basic structure of a day indicates the degree to which Woolf's imagination flourished within the security of strict limitations. When she deserts these confines, as the difficulties of *Jacob's Room* and *The Years* reveal, her work loses considerably in power.

Woolf's feelings about *Mrs. Dalloway* as she was still completing it in 1924 — "if this book proves anything, it proves that I can only write along those lines [of *Jacob's Room*] and shall never desert them, but explore further and further and shall, heaven be praised, never bore myself an instant" (*A Writer's Diary*, 63) — were prophetic about the course all of her fiction was to follow. The process of formal exploration, haltingly begun in *Jacob's Room*, continues until her death in 1941. It is an open-ended search, each new novel struggling with formal problems totally alien to everything preceding it. For too long it has been a critical commonplace to see *The Waves* as the teleological fulfillment of Woolf's genius. Such a view not only leaves critics hard pressed to explain what came after — *The Years* and *Between the Acts* — it seriously distorts the nature of what came before. For Woolf's novels do not follow a linear path, the discoveries of one leading to the production of the next, but rather constitute a series of discrete forays in altogether different directions into unknown territory. *The Waves* no more represents a culmination of her work than does *Orlando* or *To the Lighthouse*. Even *The Years*, with its superficially realistic trappings is not, as frequently thought, a renunciation of experiment. Moving from the sustained internality of *The Waves* to the strict "externality" of *The Years*, from the novel of vision to the novel of fact, was as daring an innovation for Woolf as was the extraordinary conception of *The Waves* itself. What matters in each novel is that Woolf was able to force herself "to break every mould and find a fresh form of being, that is of expression, for everything I feel or think" (*A Writer's Diary*, 220). Just as *The Waves* is an entirely different book from *Orlando*, published three years earlier, so with *The Years*, Woolf comments in her diary, "I am breaking the mould made by *The Waves*."

Common to all her novels is the attempt to create a texture for them of the sort Lily Briscoe seeks for her painting (*To the Lighthouse*, 264):

> Beautiful and bright it should be on the surface, feathery and evanescent, one colour melting into another like the colours on a butterfly's wings; but beneath the fabric must be clamped together with bolts of iron. It was to be a thing you could ruffle with your breath; and a thing you could not dislodge with a team of horses.

The centrality of such a conception for Woolf is also suggested, in language strikingly similar to Lily's, by a 1925 diary entry. Musing on the greatness of Proust, Woolf praises him for qualities she unmistakably wants to achieve in her own work: "The thing about Proust is his combination of the utmost sensibility with the utmost tenacity. He searches out those butterfly shades to the last grain. He is as tough as catgut and as evanescent as a butterfly's bloom" (*A Writer's Diary*, 72).

The delicacy of her sensibility, of course, is granted her even by her most vehement detractors; indeed, it is frequently used as a reason for dismissing her as a serious artist, on the grounds that her exquisiteness (the epithet most generally attached to her) leads only to sterile exercises in preciosity. In fact, highly patterned and sensitive though the surface of her novels is, there is nothing exquisite in the least about her fiction. From the bewildered Mrs Flanders, standing dumbly in Jacob's room after his death, holding out his shoes, to the curtain rising at the end of *Between the Acts* on the confrontation between Isa and Giles, her work deals with enduring human concerns without solace of illusion or sentimentality. Woolf looks unflinchingly at a world that offers very little in the way of easy gratification. Death and the anguish of isolation are the inescapable pressures felt in every book; it is always in the face of these that her characters attempt to fashion their precarious visions of order, and their fleeting successes never obscure our sense of the difficulty of the battle or the knowledge that the dangers remain. In affirming the possibility of order, she never falsifies the chaos threatening it. "Nothing was ever one thing," *To the Lighthouse* (286) insists, and James's discovery as he nears the lighthouse that it is not just the "silvery, misty-looking tower" (*To the Lighthouse*, 286) that gleamed at him when he was a child, but also something stark, solid, and forbidding, is precisely the kind of complex view Woolf holds to throughout her life.

Despite her tough-mindedness and complexity, it is still not clear that Woolf will ever quite luxuriate in the unquestioned eminence accorded a Conrad or a Joyce or a Faulkner. As long as the cult of Bloomsbury worship flourishes, of course, Woolf's reputation will continue to grow. But even Bloomsbury's mythic stature will one day erode and we will once again have to confront an enigmatic writer whose novels lack the narrative interest and overt social and psychological concerns of the other great twentieth-century writers. Such a confrontation will always be difficult for a large number of readers. Woolf's uncompromising effort to convey "the exact shapes my brain holds" is an enterprise whose basically subjective character has frequently been thought to ensure its ultimate insignificance. As I have tried to indicate, however, the explicitly personal nature of her attempt is neither precious nor self-indulgent. Developing out of Woolf's urgent need to get to the heart of the reality she felt was somehow available to her, the novels are at the same time informed by a strict artistic integrity which prevents them from degenerating into the narrowly private. In rendering that vision of reality, Woolf provides us with a rich variety of compelling shapes that speak in immediate ways to all of us, revealing her special truth that[3]

> behind the cotton wool [of daily life] is hidden a pattern; that we — I mean all human beings — are connected with this; that the whole world is a work of art; that we are parts of the work of art. *Hamlet* or a Beethoven quartet is the truth about this vast mass that we call the world. But there is no Shakespeare, there is no Beethoven; certainly and emphatically there is no God; we are the words; we are the music; we are the thing itself.

Notes

1. *Seduction and Betrayal* (Vintage, 1974), 141.

2. *Poets of Reality* (Harvard University Press, 1966), 27.

3. *Moments of Being: Unpublished Autobiographical Writings*, ed. J. Schulkind (Harcourt Brace Jovanovich, 1976). 72.

Hunting the Moth: Virginia Woolf and the Creative Imagination

Harvena Richter*

I

At the end of section V of *Jacob's Room*, the narrator assumes the guise of a hawk moth, hovering "at the mouth of the cavern of mystery" (JR, 120). What is Jacob like, the moth — an insect which is a member of the sphinx moth family and should certainly know the answer to all riddles — seems to ask. But the moth can only make up stories. "What remains," the narrator continues, "is mostly a matter of guesswork. Yet over him we hang vibrating" (JR, 121).

Jacob's Room was published in 1922, Virginia Woolf's third novel, and the first in which she introduces a specific symbol to represent the questing creative mind. The symbol is also a feminine one, for the sphinx is mistress of silence, mystery, the underground. Following that novel, over a period which embraces Woolf's finest work, the figure of the moth grows in importance and meaning. It becomes not only an emblem of her writing self, but of the act of imagination; in other words, not only the

*Reprinted from *Virginia Woolf: Revaluation and Continuity*, ed. Ralph Freedman (Berkeley: Univ. of California Press, 1980), pp. 13–28.

mind which creates but also the very process of creating. In the novel *The Waves*, which climaxes her concern with this theme, the public and private meanings of the moth symbol are fused, and the writer and her work become one.

The search for the meaning of the moth symbol leads into a labyrinth, a "cavern of mystery" which includes Virginia Woolf's childhood, her illnesses and personal relationships, and her scientific determination to understand her own creative process. *The Waves*, originally titled *The Moths*, is a little-explored section of the cavern. But as the thread of the moth symbol is followed, certain areas of the novel spring into light. This essay will attempt to hunt the sources of the symbol, trace its development through Woolf's writing, and show how the original vision of moths flying through a window turned into a book which deals, on one level, with the creative imagination. Finally, it will explain the connection between Rhoda, the "beautiful single moth" who metamorphoses into a girl, and Virginia Woolf herself.

Perhaps the best introduction to the complexity of the moth image occurs in Virginia Woolf's essay "Reading," which was begun about the time she started *Jacob's Room*. In the center of that essay—one which concerns the relation of both the writer and the reader to their own pasts, as well as to the literary work itself—there is a brilliant description of hunting moths.[1] It seems at first to have no relation to the essay. The narrator, the young Virginia Stephen, shuts the book she is reading on the Elizabethans. Grown-ups come in from the tennis court; the "swift grey moths of the dusk" come out; and a group of young people, armed with lantern, poison jar, and butterfly nets, go into the woods. As they leave the road for the forest, the narrator remarks that "it was the last strip of reality . . . off which we stepped into the gloom of the unknown."[2] The reader has the sense of entering some strange underworld in which everything is seen with heightened emotion and the vivid perception with which Orlando, in the later novel, glimpses the world "as if she had a microscope stuck to her eye" (O, 320). The light of the lantern alters the forest; everything looks different from by day. As the reader experiences its depths—the insects moving through the grass like "creatures crawling on the floor of the sea,"[3] the lantern flashing this way and that in the magic circle, the moths, lured by pieces of flannel soaked in sugar and rum, quivering their wings in ecstasy as they drink up the sweetness, and the final appearance of the great moth, the crimson underwing—the reader realizes that it is not only the forest, it is his own imagination. Even further, it is the mind of the writer, searching to pin down words and ideas that flit in the dark places of the brain—" 'the silver-grey flickering moth-wing quiver of words,' " as they are described in *The Waves*.

A third level of meaning hovers ominously at the edge of the scene. The great moth with the scarlet underwing is captured, subjected to the poison pot, imprisoned in glass. He composes himself "with folded wings."

At the moment of death, a "volley of shot" rings out; it is a tree, fallen in the forest.[4] The reader is aware that there has been a subtle change, a shift in focus from the hunter to the hunted, to the great moth itself, a victim in its search for sweetness and for light. There seems no rational explanation for "the little shock" the reader feels, the "queer uneasy movement" when the moth is taken and the tree falls. As T. S. Eliot has said of Hamlet's grief, the emotion is in excess of the fact. Several pages later, after a discussion of Sir Thomas Browne and his exploration of the soul, "the microcosm of my own frame," as he puts it, the narrator comments on the "importance of knowing one's author." "Somewhere, everywhere, now hidden, now apparent in whatever is written down is the form of a human being."[5] Somewhere in the essay, Virginia Woolf is trying to say, is the presence of herself. She is not simply the young girl reading the Elizabethans or Sir Thomas, not only the grown writer searching in the forest of the unconscious; she is the crimson underwing.

If we search for the origin of the moth symbol, we can find it, at least in part, in the many butterfly- and moth-hunting expeditions which Quentin Bell, in his biography of Virginia Woolf, describes the Stephen children as taking until they were quite grown.[6] Although perhaps dramatized for the essay, the reminiscence seems genuine. However, it is doubtful that the young Virginia Stephen would have felt the symbolic relationship between the death of the moth and the fall of the tree. Something intervened between the years of hunting moths and the writing of the essay, something which made the synchronicity of the two events significant to her. For the young Virginia, the moth hunt must have embodied a sense of exploration, excitement, penetration into the unknown. For Virginia Woolf, writing in 1919, it involved a sense of being pursued, being destroyed by unknown and hostile forces.

One thing that intervened was a series of five mental breakdowns between 1895 and 1920–1922 when *Jacob's Room* was written. Another, perhaps closely related, was the death of her brother Thoby. There are three novels in which the tragic aspect of the moth occurs, and in all three it is connected with her grief over Thoby's death. The first is *The Voyage Out*, in which Rachel, the heroine, dies from typhoid fever as did Thoby. The moth appears in the center of the book soon after Rachel and Terence have discovered they were in love — a love which is doomed — and later, in a nearly duplicate image, at the end of the book after Rachel dies.[7]

The Voyage Out may have been an attempt by the then Virginia Stephen to accommodate herself to the reality of her brother's death. Virginia is Rachel, but also the dying Thoby. In the jungle scene, which foreshadows the dreamy deep-sea atmosphere of the night forest in "Reading," crimson and black butterflies circle near the lovers, and one is reminded of the crimson underwing.

In *Jacob's Room*, the death of the moth and the fall of the tree are linked directly with Jacob. Jacob collects *lepidoptera;* at least eleven varieties of butterflies and four of moths are mentioned in the novel, including the death's-head moth. Another is a mysterious moth which Jacob discovers at midnight in the forest and cannot accurately identify in Morris' book on moths. That same night "the tree had fallen," sounding like "a volley of pistol shots." A brief reprise of the longer scene in the essay is given, together with a mention of the red underwing which, however, "flashed and had gone" and Jacob never saw it again. In the following chapter the images of the death of the tree and the volley of pistol shots recur, a sound echoed just before Jacob dies (JR, 32, 33, 49, 300). Jacob, it should be noted, travels to Greece, where Thoby had contracted the fatal typhoid. But unlike Thoby, Jacob Flanders is killed in World War I and is ironically "collected," like one of the specimens in his butterfly box, in Flanders Field, where so many perfect specimens of young manhood were gathered.[8]

In *The Waves*, in which the unseen character Percival is modeled after Thoby, a similar image occurs. Rhoda, who loves him, feels after his death that " 'an axe has split a tree to the core' " (W, 162). The image of the death of the tree, refined and synthesized over the years, suggests both Percival's death and the grief which Rhoda feels, an axe which "splits" the core of her being.

There is another possible source for the moth symbol, one which again lies at the heart of Virginia Woolf's childhood. It is her sister Vanessa, whose name signifies a genus of butterfly. That Virginia Woolf knew this is obvious from the number of butterflies mentioned in her works which belong to the tribe Vanessidi. They include red admirals, tortoiseshells, commas, the peacock butterfly, and one which must have seemed particularly to belong to Vanessa, who was an artist: *Vanessa cardui*, the painted lady.[9] Although the relationship between the sisters was unusually affectionate, Quentin Bell notes a touch of rivalry. Virginia, for example, competed with Vanessa to the extent of having a desk made where she could stand erect to write as Vanessa did at her easel to paint.[10] If Vanessa had a butterfly of her own, as it were, it should not be surprising that Virginia would then adopt the image of the butterfly's nocturnal sibling, the moth.

It had been decided quite early between them that Virginia would be a writer, Vanessa a painter.[11] In other words, Virginia would be concerned with what went on in the dark forest of the imagination, Vanessa with light, color, and shape. In the early novels especially, certain men and women characters tend to come under either the moth or butterfly rubric. Katherine Hilbery in *Night and Day*, Rachel of *The Voyage Out*, and Rhoda of *The Waves* closely resemble their author and are moth or night people, connected to intuition and darkness. Characters associated with light, such as Jacob, Ralph Denham of *Night and Day*, and Lily Briscoe and Mr. Ramsay in *To the Lighthouse*, are butterfly or day people, concerned with the search for knowledge and outward form. Lily Briscoe, the painter, who like Vanessa was absorbed in light and color, twice expresses her vision of color as the "light of a butterfly's wing" (L, 75, 255). As Virginia Woolf's work develops, the concern with the outer or butterfly aspect of art drops away and a concentration on questions of inward form and the creative imagination becomes apparent.

II

So far, certain sources for the moth symbol have been suggested which have their genesis in Virginia Woolf's childhood. But the allusion has been mainly to outer events. There were also the inner happenings: " 'the presence of those enemies who change, but who are always there; the forces we fight against,' " to quote Bernard (W, 240).

A symbol for oneself is not arbitrarily chosen. It appears to rise spontaneously from some deep inner necessity, as images arise in dreams, and it tends to change or develop as the needs of the self change. After *Jacob's Room* and the essay "Reading," the moth symbol appears to lie quiescent. Then, as Woolf is finishing *To the Lighthouse*, she refers in her diary to "tapping my antennae in the air vaguely" before getting down to work each morning. Twenty-five days later her diary records, "an impulse behind another book," one which would, several years later, become *The Moths* or *The Waves*.[12]

An undated entry just before the "antennae" note may reveal a possible cause for the surfacing of the moth symbol: it tells of experiencing "a whole nervous breakdown in miniature." But the connection between her illness (one of " 'those forces we fight against' "), the moth symbol, and her writing is not given until September 10, 1929, when she looks back on the long illness which followed the completion of *Mrs. Dalloway* five years before:

> These curious intervals in life—I've had many—are the most fruitful artistically—one becomes fertilised—think of my madness at Hogarth— and all the little illnesses—that before I wrote the *Lighthouse* for instance. Six weeks in bed now would make a masterpiece of *Moths*.

In February of the following year, 1930, the connection between illness and the "chrysalis stage" of the moth is made:

> Once or twice I have felt that odd whirr of wings in the head, which comes when I am ill so often . . . If I could stay in bed another fortnight . . . I believe I should see the whole of *The Waves* . . . I believe these illnesses are in my case—how shall I express it?—partly mystical. Something happens in my mind. It refuses to go on registering impressions. It shuts itself up. It becomes chrysalis. I lie quite torpid, often with acute physical pain . . . Then suddenly something springs . . . Two nights ago . . . I felt the spring . . . and all the doors opening; and this is I believe the moth shaking its wings in me. I then begin to make up my story whatever it is.

In the essay "On Being Ill" — published in the same year, 1930, by Hogarth Press — a similar image appears of a creature with wings rising out of bodily pain, followed by a reference to a sedative as "that mighty Prince with the moths' eyes and feathered feet."[13] With these might be placed a sentence from *Orlando* which occurs just before Orlando is delivered of her child: ". . . sleep, sleep . . . water of dimness inscrutable, and there, folded, shrouded, like a mummy, like a *moth*, prone let us lie on the sand at the bottom of sleep" (O,295, italics mine).

Illness, the unconscious, dreams, the waters of sleep — taken together they suggest the period of gestation necessary for the birth of an idea, the waiting time during which the concept develops in the waters of the unconscious. With Virginia Woolf's dramatization of this period as the chrysalis stage, the final synthesis of the moth symbol is complete. What began as a persona or mask of her own difficult artistic self has widened into a symbol representing the cycle of the creative imagination: conception, gestation, birth. Or, in metaphorical terms, the creative trinity of larva, chrysalis, and winged moth.

This widening of the symbol into what might be called a reproductive cycle implies certain things about the creative imagination: that it is not merely an isolated process occurring within the mind but one bound up with natural biological rhythms, alternating cycles of energy and fatigue, differing body temperatures (Mrs. Woolf had long periods of fever while writing), states of physical and mental hiatus which have their meaning even as does the dormant period for a seed.

In *The Waves* a good deal of attention is given to this aspect of the imagination, a procreative and re-creative element common to all living things which, in the last analysis, is mystical rather than scientific. Mrs. Woolf continually used the term "mystical" in her diary when speaking about both her illness and the projected novel (that is, *The Moths* will be a "mystical eyeless book . . . if I write *The Moths* I must come to terms with these mystical feelings").[14] Two major themes in the novel are related to this "mystical" sense. One is the archetypal pattern of death and rebirth or resurrection, carried out in the many mythical allusions to the vegetation gods of the ancient Middle East, and imaged in the moth cycle with the womb or tomb of the chrysalis and the ascended moth. A second theme is the eternal struggle of the mind to bring ideas to light, just as the moth reaches toward the flame. The yearning of the six friends for Percival (who represents a mystical sense of consciousness or light); the many references to the tearing of the veils; Bernard's search for words or phrases to reveal the reality of things — all are variations of the striving of the creative mind to express itself.

III

The years over which the moth symbol became synthesized are those, significantly, in which Virginia Woolf's works concerned with the creative imagination were written. The first glimpse of *The Waves* came, as mentioned earlier, while she was finishing *To the Lighthouse,* which deals with the need for the creative feminine element within the artistic mind. At that time, sensing an idea about to surface, Mrs. Woolf wrote that she wanted to watch "how the idea at first occurs. I want to trace my own process"—in other words, watch her mind as it is making up a book. Some eight months later (June 18, 1927) images are set down for a possible opening for this book, which she calls *The Moths:* a man and a woman, night, "the arrival of the bright moths," and the woman letting in "the last great moth."

Two years later there appears to be little progress; the diary gives much the same image: "a current of moths," a woman opening a window and letting in a "beautiful single moth."[15] But in the meantime Virginia Woolf had written *Orlando* and *A Room of One's Own,* both of which deal with the creative feminine imagination. And the image of the moth has kept haunting Mrs. Woolf's diary. She speaks of her mind as "the most capricious of insects—flitting, fluttering." She refers to "some nervous fibre, or fanlike membrane in my species" which records sensory impressions. When, she finally asks, will she begin *The Moths?* "Not until I am pressed into it by those insects themselves."[16] It is not until the symbol is complete toward the end of 1929 that, after several false starts on the novel, she is somehow free to write. Interestingly, at this time the waves— which, like the moths, suggest the unconscious and creativity—take over the book. The title changes. And the moths retreat into the background.

But they have not entirely disappeared, they have merely changed shape. The current of moths, "flying strongly this way," has become the motion of the "phantom waves," as they are at first called. And of those moths, six have remained to become the characters of the novel.

Briefly, *The Waves* is the story of these six characters, carried out in nine sections that go from the dawning of consciousness to death. The events of their lives are interior rather than exterior and belong more to the dark forest than to the lantern which goes exploring. The lantern itself to which the six are attracted is an unseen character, Percival—the mystical seventh—around whom the friends hover like moths about a flame. He is a transfiguring element, and as such unifies the six friends, three men and three women, who appear to represent different aspects of a single androgynous being.[17] They also suggest various facets of the imagination, its diverse processes, its conscious and unconscious areas. Passing through stages of mental development, Bernard, Neville and Louis, Susan, Jinny, and Rhoda illustrate collectively the struggle of idea from conception to birth. Seen in Jungian terms, they may be said to symbolize the individuation of the creative self.

Of these six friends whose soliloquies make up the novel, two represent conscious aspects of creativity, four unconscious; thus two-thirds of the creative process is placed in the "under-mind," as Mrs. Woolf called it in "The Leaning Tower," or in her diary referred to as "the deep water of my own thoughts navigating the underworld."[18] Bernard and Neville belong in the conscious realm, though not exclusively so. Bernard, the phrase-maker, is involved with words that " 'bubble up,' " indicating their origin in those deep waters. Neville, in love with Percival, is clarity, one of the properties of light; he expresses the ordering power of the imagination. Louis, the Australian, who symbolically comes from the continent "down under," is the male counterpart of the feminine unconscious. His roots go down; he sees women " 'carrying red pitchers to the Nile.' " (W, 66, 95). Thus he is the sense of history and time from which the creative imagination draws images, as he himself draws from those deep levels of the Nile whose rising and falling waters figure in the fertility myths.

The three women are involved mainly in nonconscious aspects of the creative imagination. Jinny is sexual force, her " 'imagination is the bodies' " (W, 128). She creates on the sensory and motor level and is associated with fire, energy, and especially dance, the last being an analogy of the act of creation.[19] She does not dream. Susan is the earth mother who croons "sleep." Her nurturing qualities are shown in the way she is " 'spun to a fine thread round the cradle, wrapping in a cocoon made of my own blood the delicate limbs of my baby.' " (W, 171). She nets over the strawberry beds, stitches " 'the pears and the plums into white bags to keep them safe.' " She may be called the gestation or chrysalis period of the creative cycle. As such, she loves Bernard, whose emblems of bee, seed, and grain link him to the fertilizing force. The emblem of the dove (the Holy Spirit) belongs to them both.

It is Rhoda, whose " 'shoulder-blades meet across her back like the wings of a small butterfly,' " (W, 22) and whose movement is always described in terms of flight, who is the "beautiful single moth" of the diary notes. Her body " 'lets the light through' "; her " 'spine is soft like wax near the flame of the candle.' " A girl in a white dress who cries to a star, " 'Consume me,' " she flutters against a background of dark like a white moth against the night forest. With her echoing " 'I dream, I dream,' " her eyes like " 'pale flowers to which moths come in the evening,' " she is related to the Egyptian Isis, goddess of the moon.[20] Water and moonlight are associated with her, and the swallow sacred to Isis; she sees " 'pools on the other side of the world reflecting marble columns' " — " 'dark pools' " in which " 'the swallow dipped her wings.' " Her emblems are the tree, cavern, and fountain; her leitmotif " 'the nymph of the fountain always wet.' " Thus she is the dreaming imagination as well as the psychic springs of creativity to which Mrs. Woolf refers in her diary.[21] She and Louis, of time and the Nile, are conspirators, but she is closest to Percival. The tone of her elegy upon his death in section V is somehow the narrating tone of the novel, the endless feminine mourner, the prophetic invisible chorus.[22]

For Rhoda has " 'no face.' " The reader sees her always from the back (traditionally her unconscious), gazing toward the other side of the world, as if Virginia Woolf, who admitted her close connection with this character, did not wish to reveal herself and hid in Rhoda's " 'clumsy . . . ill-fitting body.' "[23] Rhoda is the unstable element in the imagination: her mind leaves her body; solid objects fall apart, distorting her perceptual world. Totally of the mind, the physical is repugnant to her; she leaves Louis, with whom she is having an affair, and finally kills herself. Bernard, speaking of her death, could " 'feel the rush of the wind of her flight as she leapt.' " In several ways she is related to Septimus Smith, the schizophrenic sufferer in *Mrs. Dalloway* whom Virginia Woolf admitted patterning after herself and who also leaps to his death.[24]

The problem of writing about oneself, even by "distancing," as Woolf did through the character of Septimus, is evident in the difficulty she had with the mad scenes in *Mrs. Dalloway*. The difficulty seemed to recur with *The Waves*, whose notebooks appeared to her at times like "a lunatic's dream."[25] If one looks at Rachel, the unconscious suicide of *The Voyage Out*, then at Septimus (whose hawklike image is related to the hawk moth), then at Rhoda, one sees a serial depiction of her destructive double which comes progressively closer to, and finally merges with, her own theriomorphic symbol.[26] In *The Waves*, Rhoda's mental deterioration is shown when the six friends meet, in late middle age, at Hampton Court — mirroring perhaps the author's own fear, as she approached fifty, of being engulfed by mental illness.

Although Rhoda appears as the lone surviving moth of the early version, other characters have clinging to them shreds of the original image. Bernard, in the final chapter, sees himself as " 'a little stout, grey, rubbed on the thorax.' " Memories of friends who are part of himself flit through his mind " 'like moths' wings' " or send him " 'dashing like a moth from candle to candle' " (W, 242, 268, 293).

Two aspects of the moth survive in Louis, one connected with the laughter of imagination and fantasy glimpsed in " 'his laughing eye, his wild eye' " (W, 92). This meaning is suggested by the curious passage in the preceding novel *Orlando*, in which the moths say, "Laughter, Laughter!" and breathe "wild nonsense" in listening ears when they come at evening (O, 271). The second aspect of the moth connected with Louis is concerned with the mythic imagination, a sense he shares with Rhoda and which is illustrated in the dinner for Percival when he and Rhoda see the celebration in terms of the mystic meal observed in the rites of Attis. Louis describes the other diners as having " 'become nocturnal, rapt. Their eyes are like moth's wings moving so quickly that they do not seem to move at all' " (W, 140). This level of the imagination — seeing mythically — seems to draw on archetypes of the collective unconscious, on mental processes of transformation and time manipulation.

Another attachment of Louis to this mythic level appears in the nightmare image of anxiety which haunts him long after his childhood: the sound of the beast's foot *stamping* on the beach. The beach, the no-man's area between land and water, may be analogous to the state of consciousness between waking and sleeping. Although the beast is identified on the following page as an " 'elephant with its foot chained' " (W, 10), perhaps a symbol of racial memory forcibly separated from its source, there is another more ancient image from Teutonic mythology which hovers around it, the nightmare figure cited by Jacob Grimm as the *Stempe*, or stamper, which tramples children to death. The movement of stamping or treading is traditionally connected with nightmares, and Jung notes the word's supposed derivation from the Old English *mara*, or "ogress, incubus, demon."[27] Whatever the private source of Louis' nightmare image, it appears obscurely linked to what might be termed certain perils of the imagination. Virginia Woolf in her diary (September 5, 1925) mentions her life as "hag-ridden . . . by my own queer, difficult, nervous system." A similar fear of the dangers of the creative unconscious is reflected in Faust's dread of going to the realm of the Mothers, the guardians of forms and images in the "cavernous deep" — a place reached only by the act of *stamping*.[28]

Even closer than Louis to the world of nightmares is his conspirator Rhoda, who comes at midnight to his attic rooms (as dreams come to the mind), who rides the darkness as do the nightmare and hawk moth. " 'I sink down on the black plumes of sleep; its thick wings are pressed to my eyes. Travelling through darkness I see the stretched flower-beds' " (W, 27) — the same gardens where earlier in the chapter Bernard, Jinny, Neville, and Susan (but not Louis and Rhoda) have been skimming their butterfly nets. Always feeling pursued, by people, by nightmares, by unknown fears, Rhoda can be seen, together with Louis, as involved in the darker, myth-haunted precincts of the imagination.[29]

As to the association of the moth with the remaining characters, the chrysalis has been connected with Susan, and one of the first things Susan notices as a child is " 'a caterpillar . . . curled in a green ring' " (W, 9). Percival is remembered by Bernard from their schooldays " 'burrowing' " in his blanket " 'like some vast cocoon' " (W, 84). Neville spins thoughts into a cocoon of meaning.[30] The relation of Jinny to the moth image had always eluded me, save for the fact that her affairs are consummated at night — " 'night traversed by wandering moths' " — just as the creative mind, which contains both the masculine and the feminine, "celebrates its nuptials in darkness," as Virginia Woolf writes in *A Room of One's Own*.[31] The most puzzling part was that the name Jinny is a diminutive of Virginia; no character in *The Waves* is less like her author. It was not until the section on the essay "Reading" was studied that the relationship became clear.

Crimson is Jinny's main color. Operating at night, signaling with a " 'moth-colored scarf,' " she is the restless search of the feminine imagination to find union in darkness (that is, union with the masculine element of the mind), to take pleasure from the moment as the moth lights in ecstasy on the sugared flannel. In section IV of *The Waves* Jinny says: " 'My body goes before me, like a lantern down a dark lane, bringing one thing after another out of darkness into a ring of light' " (W, 129), a description reminiscent of the moth-hunters in the forest. If Rhoda metamorphosed from the "beautiful single moth," so did Jinny from the crimson underwing with which Virginia Woolf identified herself in the earlier essay. Jinny is the joyful eye, the necessary sensory link with the world of objects which furnish images to thought. And being the crimson *under*wing, she suggests that hidden aspect of the unconscious or "undermind" which comes into play only in flights of imagination.

Still another aspect of Jinny connects her to the crimson underwing, and coincidentally to the fall of the tree. She represents sacrifice. The act of the harlot or Magdalen is traditionally sacrificial, an earthly parallel of Christ's self-sacrifice on a tree (or Attis' sacrifice beneath it). The giving of the body is an act of love, like creation; and creation is not possible without sacrifice. The ancients sacrificed people, then animals, to insure the fruitfulness of their fields — and Jinny refers to herself as " 'Little animal that I am.' " The mother, as Susan makes clear, gives her blood and body to her unborn child. Virginia Woolf experienced illness and pain during the creation of her work; after each novel was published she suffered a breakdown, which can be likened to postpartum depression.

Curiously, after *The Waves* the moth image disappears from Virginia Woolf's writing. Perhaps the sacrifice of the moth was necessary to the creation of the work. But the death of the symbol so closely related to herself signaled the beginning of her decline as a writer.

To sum up the meaning of the moth, it is not merely a symbol of the creative process; it is both the imagination and what it feeds upon — fears and anxieties, emotional relationships, pains and joys — that piece of sugar-and-rum-soaked flannel. In an allegorical sense, it is the moth brought back from the forest who "composed himself" within the glass "with folded wings": it is the *completed work*.[32] So the moth symbol includes not only the subjective cycle of creation but its object, the work of art. It is probably not accidental that the verb to *compose* also means to create a musical or literary work, as well as to set type. And having founded the Hogarth Press with her husband Leonard, Virginia Woolf was especially familiar with that later extension of the creative process.

The moth, then, like other symbols in Virginia Woolf's writing, assumed many roles. For her, it was the means by which she managed to wring survival out of disaster. For the reader, it is a way of suggesting the very motion of creativity, the stirring of ideas as they rise into consciousness, the sense of sudden discovery as the mind's lantern peers into dark areas of the forest and glimpses objects of creation never seen before. In a more general manner, the moth embodies the continuous struggle of the mind to bring form out of chaos: the universal and often desperate condition of the artist. In Virginia Woolf's essay "The Death of the Moth," a simple account is given of that struggle to formulate and understand in the figure of a small day-moth which battles out its life against a windowpane. An "insignificant little creature," it is nevertheless a "bead of life," a "vital light," heroic in its role. When one remembers that the mind for Virginia Woolf was the room, the window, and the moth, asking for more light (as did Goethe on his deathbed), one can feel the power of the image which was not only to aid its author but to open, for the reader, a window on the creative mind.

Notes

1. The date 1919 appears in the essay as if set down at the moment of writing *(The Captain's Deathbed)*. See *Collected Essays* (London: Hogarth Press, 1966), II, 26.

2. Ibid., p. 22.

3. Ibid., p. 23.

4. Ibid., p. 25.

5. Ibid., pp. 28–29.

6. Quentin Bell, *Virginia Woolf: A Biography* (New York: Harcourt Brace Jovanovich, 1972), I, 33–34.

7. ". . . a large moth which shot from light to light . . . causing several young women to raise their hands nervously and exclaim, 'Someone ought to kill it!' " (VO, 183). "A young woman put down her needlework and exclaimed, 'Poor creature! It would be kinder to kill it' " (VO, 370).

8. "The battleships ray out over the North Sea . . . With equal nonchalance a dozen young men in the prime of life descend with *composed* faces into the depths of the sea; and there impassively . . . suffocate *uncomplainingly* together" (JR, 265, italics mine here and below). Compare with the crimson underwing who "*composed* himself . . . with folded wings" or the small day-moth in the essay "The Death of the Moth," who "now lay most decently and *uncomplainingly composed*"; *Collected Essays*, I, 361.

9. E. B. Ford, *Butterflies* (London: Collins, 1945), p. 76.

10. Bell, *Virginia Woolf*, I, 22–23, 73.

11. Ibid., p. 23.

12. *A Writer's Diary* (New York: Harcourt, Brace, 1954). Entries dated Sept. 3, 5, and 30, 1926, pp. 98, 100; Apr. 29, 1930, p. 155.

13. *Essays*, IV, 194–195.

14. *A Writer's Diary*, Nov. 7, 1928, p. 134.

15. We might stop for a moment and see what, in terms of the creative imagination, this means. A man and a woman: the two sexes in the mind necessary for the creative act (cf. *A Room of One's Own*); night: the unconscious; the bright moths: creative ideas; the woman letting in the "beautiful single moth": Mrs. Woolf herself and the concept of a book; the open window: the mind open to reality and the imagination.

16. *A Writer's Diary*, Feb. 18, 1928, p. 121; Aug. 12, 1928, p. 128; Sept. 22, 1928, p. 131. See also Feb. 11, 1928, pp. 120–121; Nov. 7, 1928, pp. 132–135.

17. See my *Virginia Woolf: The Inward Voyage* (Princeton: Princeton University Press, 1970), pp. 120–121 and appendix.

18. *Essays*, II, 166; *A Writer's Diary*, June 27, 1925, p. 78.

19. J. E. Cirlot, *A Dictionary of Symbols* (New York Philosophical Library, 1962), p. 73.

20. The opening sentence of the first ms. notebook of *The Waves* (New York Public Library, Berg Collection) is: "An enormous moth had settled on the bare plaster wall. As the wings quivered, the purple crescent in the dark border made a mysterious hieroglyph, always dissolving." The crescent is the young moon, symbol of Isis. The "mysterious hieroglyph," an attempt at communication, is related to the hawk moth at the cavern of mystery.

21. "After 6 weeks influenza my mind throws up no matutinal fountains" (*A Writer's Diary*, Feb. 18, 1922, p. 45). "I have been for the last six weeks rather a bucket than a fountain" (*A Writer's Diary*, March 22, 1928, p. 122). Note also Mrs. Ramsay as fountain.

22. In a small notebook Woolf kept while writing *The Waves*, which can be seen in the Berg Collection, she wrote: "Rhoda has the entirely visionary or ideal sorrow."

23. *A Writer's Diary*, March 17, 1930, p. 153; also May 28, 1929, pp. 139–140.

24. Both Rhoda and Septimus are sexually cold, exhibit perceptual distortion, fear falling into gulfs of fire, tend toward dehumanization (i.e., Rhoda hears voices "like trees creaking in the forest"). See also my *Virginia Woolf*, p. 88.

25. *A Writer's Diary*, final entry of 1929 (Rodmell – Boxing Day), p. 147.

26. The images of the hawk and the sun, used with Septimus, suggest the Daedalus/Icarus legend which mythicizes the artist and his soaring flights of imagination. Icarus flying near the sun is parallel to the moth attracted by the light.

27. Jung also notes that in the Czech language the word *mura* stands for both nightmare and hawk moth, so called because they come in the darkness; C. G. Jung, *Symbols of Transformation: An Analysis of the Prelude to a Case of Schizophrenia*, trans. R. F. C. Hull (New York: Harper, 1962), I, 249–250.

28. Mephistopheles to Faust: "Bear down with might and main: Stamping you sink, by stamping rise again"; Johann Wolfgang von Goethe, *Faust*, pt. 2, act 1, "Dark Gallery," lines 6303–6304, trans. Philip Wayne, ed. E. V. Rieu (Baltimore: Penguin, 1962), p. 79.

29. The small *Waves* notebook suggested dreams for both Rhoda and Louis.

30. "This room to me seems central . . . outside lines twist and intersect, but round us, wrapping us about . . . Thus we spin round us infinitely fine filaments." Compare with what she says of Henry James's characters, who "live in a cocoon, spun from the finest shades of meaning"; "Phases of Fiction," *Essays*, II, 81.

31. *A Room of One's Own* (New York: Harcourt, Brace and World, 1929 [paperback edition]), p. 108.

32. Can we not follow the allegory further and see in the "folded wings" the image of a book, open at the center?

The Politics of City Space in *The Years*: Street Love, Pillar Boxes and Bridges

Susan Squier*

I

In *The Years*, as in so many of her novels, Virginia Woolf presents a politics of space. Focusing on the urban experience, she guides her readers to an awareness of the female experience, both as it is and as it may be. The speech she gave in January 1931 to the London National Society for Women's Service reveals her keen understanding of the difficulty a woman writer encounters if she tries to tell the truth about her experiences.[1] In order to practise her profession, she points out, the woman writer has to give in to some impulses and to deny others. She must kill the Angel in the House, who coaxes her to flatter and to defer to men, and she must let "her imagination sweep unchecked round every rock and cranny of the world that lies submerged in our unconscious being" (*P*, p. xxxviii). Yet those fishing trips of the creative imagination are often disrupted, Woolf tells us, to the fisherwoman's dismay. Either the line of her imagination floats "limply and dully and lifelessly upon the surface" of her mind, for want of experience, or the reason reels it in, because "men would be shocked" by the "very queer knowledge" it has hooked "about womens [*sic*] bodies . . . their passions" (*P*, pp. xxxviii–xxxix). Not only the more common problem of a limited experience hampers the woman novelist. The male taboo against free speech concerning sexuality, which women have internalised, also checks the free movement of the female writer's mind.

What Woolf described, in her speech to the London/National Society for Women's Service, is the allegorical "watcher at the gates" that Friedrich Schiller playfully evoked in his letter to a friend suffering from writer's block:

> In isolation, an idea may be quite insignificant, and venturesome in the extreme, but it may acquire importance from an idea which follows it. . . . In the case of a creative mind, it seems to me, the intellect has withdrawn its watchers from the gates, and the ideas rush in pell-mell, and only then does it review and inspect the multitudes. . . . You are ashamed or afraid of the momentary and passing madness which is found in all real creators, the longer or shorter duration of which distinguishes the thinking artist from the dreamer. . . . You reject too soon and discriminate too severely.[2]

Schiller understood that, although an excessively strict watcher at the gates could curtail a writer's creativity by inhibiting promising ideas, at

*Reprinted from *New Feminist Essays on Virginia Woolf*, ed. Jane Marcus (Lincoln: Univ. of Nebraska Press, 1981), pp. 216–37.

the proper time and place the watcher played a useful role. In contrast, Woolf's watcher quite literally barred the gate to the outside world for women writers. To outwit the watcher, she wrote "at a rapid and haphazard gallop" in her diary; she also wrote at unexpected times and in unexpected places.[3] For her, as for all women writers, the watcher was on the alert for more than bad art. As the protector of the patriarchal castle, he was on the alert for subversive material as well: for shocking sexual candour or that partisan anger and special pleading which, Woolf felt, were more threatening to the castle of the traditional canon even than candour about female sexuality.[4]

Woolf outwitted her watcher by modifying not just where and when she wrote, but also what she wrote: she learned to use a modern descendant of the patriarchal castle to disguise and to embody the truth of her experience as a woman. For this, she turned to London, which "takes up the private life and carries it on, without any effort" (*WD*, p. 61). The watcher, surveying the view from the castle gates, would fail to recognise subversive topics because they were mingled with their urban surroundings, the tune of a barrel organ or the puzzle of a street crowd. An examination of the image and experience of the city in *The Years* reveals both the process and the product of Woolf's vision of woman's experience, then: not just what that truth was that she fought the watcher at the gates to express, but what the creative strategies were that enabled her to achieve that expression.

II

Woolf's working title for the early drafts of *The Years* was *The Pargiters*. Published in 1977 by the New York Public Library, *The Pargiters* reveals Woolf's awareness of the woman novelist's difficulty in writing about her experience. Since Jane Marcus's exciting finding of the resemblance between the book's title (and surname of the novel's family of protagonists) and "pargeters," an entry in Joseph Wright's *English Dialect Dictionary* meaning to cover up, whitewash or lie, and to patch up, build and beautify, critics have explored the ways in which the word "Pargiter" evokes the creative struggle of *The Years*.[5] The negative and positive connotations of "pargeter" echo the tension Woolf struggled with in her work. Concerned to tell the truth about "the sexual life of women" (*WD*, pp. 161–2), a truth which reflected their political and social oppression, she turned to the technique of "pargeting" to express her vision. Both meanings of "pargeter" are thus crucial to an understanding of *The Years*. Woolf built up her picture of women's lives in the experience of the city itself. Thus, she used the constructive technique of the "pargeter" to convey the destructive truth, that male oppression causes women to cover up, whitewash, or lie about the truth of the female experience in order to avoid alienating their male audience. "Pargeting," building the truth of women's experience into the setting itself, she used the city to embody her ideological perspective.

Woolf had first intended to combine fact and vision in the "novel-essay" *The Pargiters*. As she envisioned it, the essay part of the book would explore the sexual, economic and social forces affecting the lives of those characters whose experiences she would dramatise in the fictional sections. Her fear that anger could distort a work of art was marked in her approach to fiction. However, both *A Room of One's Own* and *Three Guineas* use the essay form strongly to express Woolf's feminism.[6] Therefore it is not surprising that she was able to express her vision of woman's experience more fully in the essay chapters of *The Pargiters* than in the later, fully fictional manuscript of *The Years*. In those essay sections, Woolf connects the urban and the female experiences: the war for sexual equality is fought in the battlefield of London, where men and women struggle with each other for control of the streets. She shows us a city "artificially partitioned off" into sex-linked zones, each with its own form of "love" (*P*, p. 36).[7] To women and children belongs the drawing room, with its varied forms of open and concealed love. The largely male force Woolf calls in contrast, street love, which seems "different from all the other loves inside the drawing room," controls the streets, and besieges the private home "on all sides" (*P*, pp. 35, 37). In her discussion of street love, Woolf focuses on the question central to the novel as she first envisioned it: "I have this moment, while having my bath, conceived an entire new book — a sequel to *A Room of One's Own* — about the sexual life of women" (*WD*, pp. 161-2). Woolf did not produce the exposé one might expect from such a description of her subject, however. Instead, she turned the topic inside out, to show how the sexual life of women, or rather their lack of sexual freedom, was a result of the restrictive structure of their lives. Woolf's analysis of street love uncovers the powerless situation of the Pargiter women in 1880; the politics of city space suggests the underlying sexual politics which was the novel's theme.

The fact of street love, Woolf tells us, had a far greater influence upon the women of the time than upon the men. Although it affected women in all areas of life, the social effects of street love were undoubtedly the most blatant, for by street love Woolf meant the frank, aggressive, in many cases hostile, display of male sexuality, like that which Rose Pargiter experiences one evening when she disobeys the rules and ventures out to Lamley's. As she hurries to the shop to buy a box of ducks and swans for her bath, she passes a man whose face frightens her. "The enemy — the enemy!" Rose cried to herself, . . . playing the game" (*P*, p. 42). On her return trip, there is nothing playful about the encounter. "When she reached the pillar box there was the man again. He was leaning against it, as if he were ill, Rose thought. . . . There was nobody else anywhere in sight. As she ran past him, he gibbered some nonsense at her, sucking his lips in & out, & began to undo his clothes . . ." (*P*, p. 43).

Because of the threat of such incidents, Rose Pargiter and her sisters were virtually confined to their home in Abercorn Terrace. They could not go for a walk alone except in the streets right around their house, and then only during the daylight hours. Expeditions to other parts of London were impossible unless they had a brother or a matron to chaperone them. Street love made the simplest form of meeting impossible for the Pargiter girls: they could not move freely from one part of London to another.

The social limitations which street love enforced upon the Pargiter girls had psychological effects as well, Woolf explains, for, since they were spirited children, they did not always obey the rules. Occasionally they did the forbidden; went to Bond Street or the Burlington Arcade alone, and then, to make matters worse, lied about it to their father. The restrictions on their physical and social liberty thus resulted in limitations upon their psychological freedom as well, manifest in the need to cover up, to lie to others about their activities. So Rose was unable to tell Eleanor what she had seen that had frightened her so much, following her confrontation with the man at the pillar box.

Not only was communication between siblings, or between parent and child, affected. Soon the self could not communicate with itself, with the discouraging effects which Woolf described in her speech to the London/National Society for Women's Service. In fact, the interruption of self-awareness which street love created was far more damaging than the frightening incidents which resulted from it: "not only did it restrict their lives, [but] to some extent it [poisoned] their minds — lies of all sorts undoubtedly having a crippling and distorting effect, and none the less if the liar feels that his lie is justified" (P, p. 52). The guilt and confused pleasure which the girls felt when they saw one of the taboo scenes of street love woke them in the night with strange feelings and disturbing dreams, reactions to the cloistered, sexually straitened atmosphere in which they lived. The shock and guilt provoked in Rose by the man's frightening act of exhibitionism at the pillar box was accompanied, Woolf explains, by her sudden awareness of an untapped fund of feeling inside her which the experience identified and even seemed to elicit. Woolf calls it "a rage of emotion,"[8] and the ambivalence of the term is appropriate, for Rose finds now that her sexuality, like her anger, is difficult to express. Both emotions were taboo for women in a patriarchal society, as Woolf pointed out in "Women and Fiction" (1929) and her speech of 21 January 1931.

City experience and female experience are interrelated in The Pargiters. The effect of the restrictions street love placed on the Pargiter girls was to alienate them from two of their fundamental experiences as human beings: to turn to ugliness their own sexual feelings by overlaying them with guilt, and to defuse anger at their oppression by confusing it with guilt and hence robbing it of legitimacy. Such repression in the mind of a child could have lasting effects on the adult as well. Kitty Malone, for instance, who was sexually sheltered throughout adolescence, lost contact not only with the outer world from which she had to be protected to preserve her innocence, but with her inner world as well, with her feelings as a woman. Since restraint was the first lesson she had been taught, she felt little, even when proposed to. Like many Victorian women, Woolf explains, Kitty's sexual response had been muted by the restrictions placed upon it.

Since sexual response is dependent upon that escape into freedom which each longed to make, the women in *The Years* paradoxically directed their sexual energy towards those qualities of life which would liberate it. "[They] are drawn to women who (erroneously) seemed to have escaped the tyrannies and repressions endured by most of their sex and whose lives as a consequence seem more romantic, less constricted, more autonomous, freer, and bolder than their own."[9] Thus Kitty Malone loves Lucy Craddock's passion for knowledge, for "things in themselves" (*P*, p. 112). Her love expresses her mingled longing to break free of all her oppressions: free play of the mind is at least as important, if not more, as sexual freedom in motivating her love. The women of *The Years* eroticise liberty because for them liberty *is* sexuality. The oppression of the former results in the denial of the latter.

Cut off from both the outer world of the city streets and from the inner world of their female experience, the Pargiter girls also suffered from a diminished sense of life's possibilities. Because they had to be protected from street love, they could not go to parties or even visit friends without a chaperone. Thus their chance for enjoyment or occupation was reduced to finding the one socially acceptable route out of their father's home into a less straitened existence: marriage. Woolf's comments in the interpolated essays shed more light on the hostility Eleanor senses between Delia and Milly in "1881," when Colonel Pargiter mentions that he "met old Burke at the Club," who asked him to bring "one of them to dinner because his son Robin was 'back on leave.' "[10] Rivalry between sisters inevitably resulted from such a restricted, competitive social environment: the economics of marriage settlements and dowries added a further complication. So later, in *The Years*, North Pargiter considers Eleanor's spinsterhood. "She had never married. Why not? he wondered. Sacrificed to the family, he supposed — Old Grandpapa without any fingers" (*Y*, p. 372).

Since in most cases women were unable to earn a living wage, a single life posed a grim threat to a woman. Competition in the marriage market was intense. Quentin Bell seems to miss the point of the conversation to which he alludes in his biography. As Woolf described the conversation in her essay "Leslie Stephen," Lady Ritchie's tendency to exaggerate was provoked by Stephen's own "sobriety." " 'There are 40,000,000 unmarried women in London alone!' Lady Ritchie once informed him. 'Oh, Annie, Annie!' my father exclaimed in tones of horrified but affectionate rebuke."[11] Bell overlooks Lady Ritchie's playfulness, revealed in this scene;

instead, he calls her "hardly aware" of facts and "unabashedly sentimental."[12] His view of her conflicts markedly with Woolf's description in her essay "The Enchanted Organ" (1924). There, Lady Ritchie is neither sentimental nor dreamily vague. Although "she said things that no human being could possibly mean; yet she meant them" (*M*, p. 195). Her instinct for truth was profound: "if her random ways were charming, who, on the other hand, could be more practical, or see things, when she liked, precisely as they were" (ibid.). That irrepressible honest ability to see things as they were and to express what she saw was captured for Woolf in a scene from Lady Ritchie's childhood, a scene which provides a surprising analogue to Rose Pargiter's night-time escapade, yet which, unlike the episode of exhibitionism at the pillar box, has a happy ending.

> The enormous respectability of Bloomsbury was broken one fine morning about 1840 by the sound of an organ and by the sight of a little girl, who had escaped from her nurse and was dancing to the music. The child was Thackeray's elder daughter, Anne. For the rest of her long life, through war and peace, calamity and prosperity, Miss Thackeray, or Mrs. Ritchmond Ritchie, or Lady Ritchie, was always escaping from the Victorian gloom and dancing to the strains of her own enchanted organ. (*M*, p. 193)

Woolf's description of Lady Ritchie's moment of freedom from the respectable Victorian home has a curiously fitting *double-entendre* which reveals the true extent and significance of such an escape. In freeing herself from the "Victorian gloom" which Woolf described so thoroughly in the interpolated essays of *The Pargiters*, woman frees her sexuality from repression as well. Lady Ritchie's dance seems to celebrate her female sexuality itself, "her own enchanted organ" to which she dances.

The free celebration of female sexuality which Lady Ritchie's dance suggests was also disbarred by street love.

> The question of chastity was therefore complicated in the extreme, since it was influenced by so many feelings that could not be discussed and by so many facts that might be resented but could not possibly be altered. Had not the demand for the vote, which might ultimately lead to some right to earn one's living, been again defeated in the House of Commons? (*P*, p. 53).

The effect of that dismissal was maddeningly circular. The vote was denied women, Woolf implies, to protect their chastity: female chastity was essential because women did not have the vote, and hence could not change the law which disabled them from earning enough money to support the children which might result from sexual freedom. The ultimate effect of street love in the 1880s, Woolf argues, was to keep from women economic, social and legal equality. Women were denied the vote, and hence denied the opportunity for education and a profession, because their chastity must be protected. And from what? From assertive male sexuality: street love. And so street love reveals the relationship between the urban experience and the female experience, a relationship Woolf went on to explore, implicitly rather than explicitly, in *The Years*.

III

Woolf revised the manuscript of *The Pargiters* in 1933, and the revision was sweeping. "Today I finished — rather more completely than usual — revising the first chapter. I am leaving out the interchapters — compacting them in the text. . . ."[13] Abandoned along with the essay portions of the novel was Woolf's explicit consideration of the experience of women, contained in her analysis of street love. Instead, Woolf presented her vision implicitly, moving towards "that aesthetic tension which is generated from documented vision in union with poeticised truth."[14] Two urban objects, the pillar box and the bridge, suggest in microcosm how Woolf uses the whole city experience implicitly to convey the truth of women's experience in *The Years*. The pillar box appears in Woolf's speech to the London/National Society for Women's Service, which was the origin of *The Years*.[15] There, it marks the boundary between the private and public worlds, between the dependence of a woman in the patriarchal home and the freedom of money and a room of one's own. To the difficulty that many women, among them the composer Dame Ethel Smyth, faced in finding a place in the professions, Woolf contrasts her own relative ease at becoming a writer: the result, she claims with tongue in cheek, of "the cheapness of writing materials" (*P*, p. xxviii). All a woman need do to become a writer, she tells her audience, is to follow the example of the girl in the story, who is, of course, Virginia Woolf herself.

> my story is compared with Dame Ethel's a very tame one. You have only got to figure to yourselves a girl [sitting and writing] / in a bed-room with a pen in her hand / a girl who had plenty of pens and paper at command. Then it occurred to her to do what again only costs a penny stamp — to [send] / slip / an article [on to a newspaper / into a pillar box /; and to suggest to the editor of that newspaper that she might be allowed to try her hand at reviewing . . . a book. (*D*, p. *xxix*)

"Hence I became a reviewer," Woolf tells her audience. Yet in her speech she goes on to describe how something which seems so simple, that walk to the pillar box with envelope in hand, is actually fraught with difficulties for women. The pillar box is first associated with work, and with the oppression which makes work so difficult for women.

In *The Years*, the pillar box besides marking the boundary between the private home and the professional world, marks other thematic boundaries. "That red box at the corner" first teaches Rose Pargiter the distinction between male and female sexuality.[16] In *The Years*, as in *The Pargiters*, Rose eludes her nurse and sneaks out of the house one night in

1880, drawn to Lamley's shop by the box of toy ducks in the window. The forbidden jaunt is an adventure to Rose at first; in a strikingly militaristic and masculine fantasy, she imagines herself a brave rescuer of besieged British troops. Yet, when the mewing, pock-marked man by the pillar box exposes himself to her, her fantasy world is shattered and she flees for home. Even when she is safely in bed, the experience continues to affect her, troubling her sleep with fear and guilt.

The exhibitionist episode links the pillar box to the social oppression of women which Woolf saw was a product of street love. As she rode down Melrose Avenue with the dash of a man, imagining herself to be "Pargiter of Pargiter's Horse" (Y, p. 27), and enjoying therein feelings of competence and adventure, Rose was confronted by an experience which sharply redefined her sexual role and limited her appropriate feelings. "She was herself again, a little girl who had disobeyed her sister, in her house shoes, flying for safety to Lamley's shop" (Y, p. 28). The man's exhibitionism drove Rose from the streets back to the nursery in the private home. So the pillar box also marks the boundary between the world of sexuality, which men have annexed for themselves despite Rose's heroic attempt to liberate it, and the world of the private home, where women live in cloistered, pre-sexual retreat. The experience at the pillar box also cloisters off certain areas of Rose's mind. She cannot tell Eleanor what she saw — the man's genitals, presumably. Woolf has now added another association to the pillar box. While in her talk of 21 January 1931 it was an emblem of woman's freedom of speech, in The Years it is associated with prohibitions against speech, especially speech about sexuality. In fact, Rose herself lives in the "besieged garrison" of her fantasy. The man at the pillar box, whom she rightly knows to be "the enemy," now not only holds her captive at home, but has invaded her mind. The consequences for Rose can be disastrous, for it is "hard to fight an enemy with outposts in your head."[17]

To the pillar box's two associations of work and sexuality, Woolf adds a third: education. That theme is embodied in a ritual which Eleanor remembers, the night her life changes forever with the death of her mother. She writes a letter to her brother Edward about her mother's condition, and Morris offers to post it for her.

> He got up as if he were glad to have something to do. Eleanor went to the front door with him and stood holding it open while he went to the pillar box. . . . Morris disappeared under the shadows round the corner. She remembered how she used to stand at the door when he was a small boy and went to a day school with a satchel in his hand. She used to wave to him and when he got to the corner he always turned and waved back. It was a curious little ceremony dropped now that they were both grown up. (Y, p. 41).

One wonders if the ceremony has been dropped because it has served its purpose. After years of training, Eleanor has accepted her place in the private home; that night, with her mother's death, she will take on the role of housekeeper for her father. The "suppressed emotion" which Morris feels "cooped up with all these women" is the product of that obsolete little ceremony (Y, p. 44). That ceremony is responsible, too, for the distance which has grown up between Eleanor and Morris. Here the pillar box marks another barrier, between the education available to women and that given to men. Eleanor's sketchy self-education prevents her from communicating with Morris; she no longer asks questions about his work, for fear of seeming silly, and he, in turn, no longer shares his thoughts with her.

> Ought she not to have said Lord Chief Justice? She never could remember which was which; and that was why he would not discuss Evans v. Carter with her.
> She never told him about the Levys, either, except by way of a joke. That was the worst of growing up, she thought; they couldn't share things as they used to share them. When they met they never had time to talk as they used to talk — about things in general — they always talked about facts — little facts. (Y, p. 34).

When Morris disappears under the shadows round the corner, he crosses another boundary marked by the pillar box, the boundary of education. Morris receives the education of a man — Eleanor, of a woman. As Woolf writes of this distinction in *Three Guineas*, it is a "precipice, a gulf so deeply cut" between the female and the male that she wonders whether "it is any use trying to speak across it" (*TG*, p. 4). Education permits Morris to enter the world of the Bar; without it, Eleanor must stay in the home or do volunteer work with the Levys. The gulf which separates them affects communication; it discourages the speaker and lessens the receptivity of the listener. So the pillar box embodies the demarcation Woolf deplored between the male, public world (where educational and sexual experiences are allowed men) and the female, private world (where both educational and sexual experiences are strictly controlled, by rationing money and interactions).

The triple associations of the pillar box, then, characterise the Victorian era's oppression of women. Woolf does not express her subversive vision directly. Instead, she conveys it through the image of the pillar box, which embodies and connects the different episodes of oppression (societal, sexual, psychological) she presents. So, in "Present Day," Eleanor and Peggy Pargiter pass Abercorn Terrace as they take a taxi to a family party. As they both look at the "imposing unbroken avenue with its succession of pale pillars and steps" Eleanor thinks of her childhood. " 'Abercorn Terrace,' said Eleanor. 'The pillar box.' " Peggy wonders why Eleanor makes the association, but soon she seems to have made the same one. "Was it that you were suppressed when you were young?" she asks Eleanor. In an image which combines the three associations of the pillar box, Eleanor remembers "a picture — another picture — [which] had swum to the surface": "There was Delia standing in the middle of the room; Oh my God! she was saying; a hansom cab had stopped at the house next door; and she herself was watching Morris — was it Morris? — going down the street to post a letter" (*Y*, pp. 335-6).

Although Eleanor had no way of knowing the pillar box's associations for her sister Rose, the picture of her repression as a young girl includes these limitations which the division of social life into male and female zones, the boundary marked by the pillar box, places upon women.[18] Woolf elaborated upon Delia's feelings during this scene in *The Pargiters*. There, sexual, social and psychological freedom are linked. Delia, despairing, says "Oh, my God!" because she sees a woman wheeling a baby carriage; that image of her own probable future makes her realise she will never be allowed to travel to Germany to study music. Eleanor's memory of watching Morris post the letter recalls the same triad of restrictions which settled upon her with the death of her mother. While that event freed Delia and her sisters from the private home, as Eleanor promised it would, it left Eleanor as the spinster housekeeper for her father.

IV

While the picture of London which Woolf's use of the pillar box paints in *The Years* is a grim one, it is important to emphasise that Woolf is not suggesting that the oppression of women is a result of the urban environment. Far from it; in fact, here as in her other works, Woolf's treatment of the city setting stresses the interaction of urban environment and the structure of human society. In her use of the pillar box she explores the way in which oppressive human societies shape, even distort, the urban environment; she uses the bridge image in *The Years* to explore the opposite interaction: the city's effect on human behaviour. The bridge image, which Woolf drew on to suggest her sense of the positive future for women, is deeply rooted in the past — both in the history of the Pargiter family within the novel, and in the history of the novel itself. In fact, the two histories are mingled; an understanding of their interrelationship illuminates the significance of the bridge image in the novel. *The Years* grew out of the speech which Woolf gave to Pippa Strachey's society, the London/National Society for Women's Service. There, she analysed the obstructions to a career as a writer which she had faced as a young woman. Woolf celebrated the accomplishments of Dame Ethel Smyth, the preceding speaker, who "built bridges and thus made a way for those who came after her" (*P*, p. xxviii):

> we honour her not merely as a musician and a writer, but also as a blaster of rocks and the maker of bridges. It seems sometimes a pity that a woman who only wished to write music should have been forced also to make bridges, but that was part of her job and she did it. (Ibid.)

As in her talk, so in *The Years* Woolf analyses woman's situation in society; yet she uses the novel's background, both physical (the city setting) and historical (the characters' memories) to present her message. Woman's talent — and her job — is "bridge building."

A memory of Eleanor Pargiter's, of a curious little song her nurse-maid Pippy used to sing her, possesses significance which radiates throughout the novel's thematic exploration of oppression, "Sur le pont d'Avignon," Pippy sang; as the song continues, "l'on y danse, tout en ronde" (Y, p. 91). Metaphorically, that bridge presents the experience of the women in *The Years*. There, on the bridge between the private home and the professions, the women dance — sometimes a dance of liberated sexuality, like Rose's lesbianism or Maggie's happy marriage, and sometimes a dance of death. That such an important image of woman's future should appear in the nursery rhyme Pippy sings prompts a re-examination of those songs to uncover the primal self-definitions they instil.

Just as the novel was nursed to life by *Pippa* Strachey's request for a talk by Woolf, so the vision which the novel explores, that complex interaction between women, men, and the space in which they live, is revealed through memories of the songs sung by the Pargiters' nurse, *Pippy*. Although several critics have mentioned the evocative quality of those songs Pippy sang to her small charges, no critic has realised that Pippy sings a different tune depending upon the sex of her listener.[19] Pippy is, in fact, something of a sociological oracle. To Martin Pargiter, who will grow up to be a wealthy businessman, Pippy sings, "The King of Spain's daughter came to visit me/All for the sake of my silver nutmeg tree" (Y, p. 227). The song suggests Martin's role of sexual and economic superiority; in it he commands the attention of the King of Spain's daughter because of his wealth, embodied by a silver nutmeg tree. The curious image is revealing: the nutmeg tree, called the pasha of spices, grew in rows like a harem, one male tree for every ten female trees. Male sexual and political domination are both associated with the nutmeg tree, for many (male) wars were fought for possessions of lands planted with those valuable spice harems.[20] While Martin's exotic possession thus defines his economic, political and sexual dominion, the woman in the nursery rhyme is defined by her powerful male relative, the King of Spain. In the fantasy world of the nursery rhyme, as in reality, the role of the woman is ancillary; the excitement of being visited by the King of Spain's daughter, one assumes, lies in the political implications of such a visit.

Pippy may be an oracle, but she is not Fate herself; we see Martin's own influence shape the meaning of the song, and of his life. In his youth, the song was part of a ritual of release in which Martin, unafraid, abandoned his sense of safe continuity to an exciting discontinuity. "She used to take him on her knee and croak out in her wheezy rattle of a voice, 'The King of Spain's daughter came to visit me, all for the sake of . . .' and then suddenly her knee gave and down he was tumbled onto the floor"

(*Y*, p. 226). However, as he grows up, Martin comes to use the song for an opposite purpose, to support his ego when he feels threatened. Martin has turned his song into a private incantation, a type of personal hymn to money and power.

While the song Pippy sings Martin evolves from a celebration of exciting discontinuity to a retreat into stability and stasis, the song she sings Eleanor instead emphasises the qualities of discontinuity, change and movement.[21] The bridge image of that song is developed further in *Three Guineas*, where it takes on an ironically pessimistic tone:

> We, daughters of educated men, are between the devil and the deep blue sea. Behind us lies the patriarchal system; the private house, with its nullity, its immorality, its hypocrisy, its servility. Before us lies the public world, the professional system, with its possessiveness, its jealousy, its pugnacity, its greed. The one shuts us up like slaves in a harem; the other forces us to circle, like caterpillars head to tail, round and round the mulberry tree, the sacred tree, of property. It is a choice of evils. Each is bad. Had we not better plunge off the bridge into the river; give up the game; declare that the whole of human life is a mistake and so end it? (*TG*, p. 74)

Woolf's angry, ironic tone emphasises the difficulties of change. If the professional system oppresses women through jealousy, pugnacity and greed, that transition from the private to the public world may well seem like a move from one form of stasis to another. Then, instead of dancing on the bridge, women will be tempted to plunge from it into the river.

What Woolf states directly in *Three Guineas*, she expresses through her use of the urban setting in *The Years*. If human life is not all to seem "a mistake," the oppression of women must cease; human beings must learn to respond positively to people and experiences which are alien to them. That single quality of otherness is central to urban experience, of course; it gives the city that exciting sensation of change and discontinuity anatomised by writers and social theorists.[22] Woolf's striking insight lies in her awareness that in responding to the urban experience, whose main quality is otherness, men are suggesting the way they respond to women as well—women, who have cross-culturally and throughout history been seen as the "Other."[23] Martin Pargiter's transformation of his song from a celebration of discontinuity to a reinforcing personal hymn echoes that sultan-like sexual, political and economic dominion he establishes as part of the patriarchal system. That system is threatened by otherness, change, discontinuity: all qualities which Woolf knew were characteristic both of the urban and the female experiences. The pillar box and the bridge represent two responses to that experience of otherness which *The Years* explores; the former, denial and retreat; the latter, affirmation and connection.

V

As *The Years* moves from 1880 to 1937, the novel shows a changing city and a change in the situation of women. The fellowship enjoyed by women in 1880, brought about by street love, is the fellowship of oppression, of what Lillian Robinson has called the "sexualization of women's experience." Robinson evokes that fellowship in her essay "Who's Afraid of a Room of One's Own?": "It occurred to me that even Virginia Woolf on an omnibus was exposed to the same possibility of insult, the same hint of danger. She could not be 'just' a brilliant novelist observing a segment of London life; she was also a piece of female flesh experiencing it."[24] We can accept Robinson's description of the oppression of women — even famous and creative women — in the patriarchal city. In *The Years*, as in Robinson's New York, the city streets reflect both woman's role and her potential for the future. Either her surroundings allow her an identity which transcends her physical capabilities — allow her to dance across that bridge between the private and the public realms — or they relegate her to immanence as a "piece of female flesh," restricted from the world beyond the pillar box by the masculine tyranny of street love.

Yet, when we accept Robinson's insight, we do so with an understanding that the city she describes is a patriarchal one, an identity Woolf showed changing in *The Years*. If we reflect on the interaction between self or society and city revealed there, we see that Woolf would be unlikely to affirm or advocate a role as serene, uninvolved and static as that of a "brilliant novelist" and observer. Rather, in *The Years* Woolf used the changing city to affirm a more engaged, active relationship to the urban environment. She used the image and the experience of the city to make a point implicitly which she felt she could not make explicitly, and so to outwit the watcher at the gate. In her use of pillar box and bridge imagery, she incorporated both the positive and negative connotations of "pargeter," she both covered up and built up the truth of female experience.

Virginia Woolf created a politics of space in *The Years*. In her use of those two urban objects she showed two responses to otherness, whether it be the otherness of the woman or the otherness of the city. The pillar box embodies the first response: denial and retreat, and an attempt to protect the *status quo*. The phenomenon of street love is an aspect of that response to otherness; it limits the woman's freedom geographically and socially. The spatial enactment of the other response to otherness is embodied by the bridge image; like a bridge itself, it affirms and unifies.

Finally, like Robinson's New York, the London of *The Years* mirrors the "sexualization of women's experience," the oppression which Woolf saw as characteristic of the "sexual lives of women" (*WD*, pp. 161–2). Women do find their treatment as women embodied in the geography of the city. However, Woolf moves beyond that view of the city as image for the political and social situation of women at present to consider its role in affecting the future. Vivid and vital embodiment of otherness and change, by the end of *The Years* the city confronts the characters with an experience to which they must respond. As Woolf shows, their response will determine not just the way the sexes will live together, but the possibility of international coexistence as well. Discontinuity and otherness are the challenges the city presents in *The Years*. The response of the pillar box, that impulse to retreat and deny those threatening alien qualities, will result in what Woolf called "subconscious Hitlerism," totalitarianism at home and abroad.[25] Woolf explores that totalitarian response fully in the novel through her use of the urban setting.

Yet she conducts an equally thorough exploration of the other response in *The Years* as well — of that bridging impulse which affirms change and unifies the discontinuous. We see that affirmative response to otherness in one striking episode at the end of the novel. Two Cockney children, representatives of the inscrutable, alien future generation of city dwellers, sing their discordant and jarring song to the gathered Pargiter family. "The grown-up people did not know whether to laugh or cry. . . . Nobody knew what to say. There was something horrible in the noise they made. It was so shrill, so discordant, and so meaningless" (*Y*, p. 430). Patrick acts the privileged and removed spectator, thanking them genially; Martin slips coins into their hands. But Eleanor takes neither the stance of the removed observer nor of the powerful patron. Humble and interested, Eleanor responds affirmatively: she asks a question. " 'Beautiful?' she said, with a note of interrogation" (*Y*, p. 431). *The Years* ends there, having presented both a model of woman's situation at present and a vision of the possibilities for men and women in the future — a vision of an affirmative response to otherness and change enacted by Eleanor Pargiter's final words to her brother Morris. " 'And now?' she asked, holding out her hands to him" (*Y*, p. 435).

Notes

1. Virginia Woolf, "Speech Before the London/National Society for Women's Service, 21 January, 1931," in *"The Pargiters": The Novel — Essay Portion of "The Years,"* ed. Mitchell A. Leaska (New York: New York Public Library and Readex Books, 1977) pp. xxvii–xxxiv. Further references (to *The Pargiters* proper and to the speech) are to this edition, cited as *P*.

2. Friedrich Schiller, cited in Sigmund Freud, *The Interpretation of Dreams* (New York: Avon Books, 1965) p. 135.

3. Virginia Woolf, *A Writer's Diary*, ed. Leonard Woolf (New York: Harcourt, Brace, 1965) p. 7. Further references are to this edition, cited as *WD*.

4. In "Women and Fiction," Woolf argued that such partisan anger and special pleading in the works of George Eliot and Charlotte Brontë resulted in the "consciousness of a woman's presence," which by her aesthetic standards, distorted the work's style and point of view — "Women and Fiction," *Granite and Rainbow* (New York: Harcourt, Brace and World, 1958), p. 79.

5. Jane Marcus, "*The Years* as Greek Drama, Domestic Novel, and *Götterdämme-*

rung," *Bulletin of the New York Public Library*, Winter 1977, pp. 280–1. See also Mitchell A. Leaska, "Virginia Woolf, the Pargiter: A Reading of *The Years*," ibid., pp. 172–210.

6. Virginia Woolf, *A Room of One's Own* (New York: Harcourt, Brace and World, 1957), and *Three Guineas* (New York: Harcourt, Brace and World, 1966). Further references to the latter are to this edition, cited as *TG*.

7. "Love, then, whether of the drawing room or of the street variety, affected the lives of the Pargiter sisters profoundly . . . it restricted them to certain quarters of London, and was perpetually impeding their freedom of movement" (*P*, p. 52).

8. I disagree with Mitchell Leaska's transcription of this phrase in his edition of *The Pargiters*. He transcribes it as "a range of emotion," which, while it captures the same sense of untapped and unrecognised feelings, neither has the lovely metaphoric sweep of Woolf's phrase nor, more practically speaking, seems to be what Woolf actually wrote. Repeated readings of the holograph manuscript of *The Pargiters* have convinced me that there is no 'n' in the word Woolf wrote. The phrase appears at *P*, p. 50.

9. Sallie Sears, "Notes on Sexuality: *The Years* and *Three Guineas*," *Bulletin of the New York Public Library*, Winter 1977, p. 217.

10. Virginia Woolf, *The Years* (New York: Harcourt, Brace and World, 1965) p. 15. Further references are to this edition, cited as *Y*.

11. Virginia Woolf, "Leslie Stephen," *The Captain's Death Bed and Other Essays* (New York: Harcourt, Brace and World, 1950) p. 71. Woolf also writes of Lady Ritchie in "The Enchanted Organ," *The Moment and Other Essays* (New York: Harcourt, Brace, Jovanovich, 1974). Further references are to this edition, cited as *M*.

12. Quentin Bell, *Virginia Woolf: A Biography*, 2 vols (New York: Harcourt, Brace, Jovanovich, 1977) vol. I, p. 63.

13. Mitchell A. Leaska, Introduction, *P*, p. xvii.

14. *P*, p. xviii.

15. *P*, p. xv.

16. The phallic overtones of the pillar box are inescapable. The *Bulletin of the New York Public Library*, Winter 1977, p. 251, has a picture of an unmistakably phallic pillar box. Jane Marcus points out that not all pillar boxes were so distinctly phallic, however: "they were red and, in shape, ambivalently male/female; they bore the King's [or Queen's] initials." Yet, if the suffragists saw the pillar boxes they blew up as "symbols of the state," we might assume they were not unconscious of the pillar boxes' equal role as symbols of the phallic power which Woolf called "street love" (ibid., p. 284).

17. Sally Kempton, "Cutting Loose," *Liberation Now* (New York: Dell, 1971) p. 55.

18. Here I disagree with Mitchell Leaska, who sees it this way: "They pass Abercorn Terrace, . . . and Eleanor murmurs '. . . the pillar box' . . . ; and again we are in 1880 recalling Rose's horrifying experience which Eleanor has somehow assimilated" — in *Bulletin of the New York Public Library*, Winter 1977, p. 192.

19. In Woolf's essay "A Sketch of the Past," we learn that the model for Pippy was Justine Nonon. Unlike Pippy, however, Justine Nonon sang both the "male" and the "female" songs to her young charge, Virginia Stephen. "I used to sit on her knee; and her knee jugged up and down; and she sang in a hoarse cracked voice 'Ron ron ron et plon plon plon' — and then her knee gave way and I was tumbled onto the floor." Woolf's memory unifies Eleanor's song ("Sur le pont l'Avignon") and the tumbling game Pippy played with Martin (*Y*, p. 226). See *Moments of Being, Unpublished Autobiographical Writings of Virginia Woolf*, ed. Jeanne Schulkind (New York: Harcourt, Brace, Jovanovich, 1976), p. 74.

20. I am grateful to Jane Marcus for this information. The sultan theme also appears in the episodes excluded from *The Years* during the final revision; there, Kitty Lasswade's retreat from the new freedom of her widowhood is "chaperoned" by her big dog, Sultan. Oppressed by the patriarchal property laws which have evicted her from the home and the

land she loves, Kitty has responded by identifying with her oppressors. So, in her response to the city, she resembles the sultan-like Martin Pargiter. Overwhelmed by disappointment and pessimism, Kitty can only imagine one option for her own life, a regression to the past and an identification with the sex and class which is responsible for her present powerlessness. So, she adopts mannish gestures, eats "like a school boy," and stands "in front of the fire with her arms behind her like a country gentleman." With her dog, Sultan, she will retreat to a "Tudor manor house" in the north of England to live the life of feudal isolation which befits her nickname, "The Grenadier." See Grace Radin (ed.), " 'Two Enormous Chunks'; Episodes Excluded During the Final Revisions of *The Years*," *Bulletin of the New York Public Library*, Winter 1977, pp. 221–51.

21. The nursery rhyme may even contain a concealed allusion to a change in the locus of power, appropriate to the unifying, affirmative response to otherness Woolf anticipates in the "New World" of the future (Y, p. 297). Avignon was the papal residence from 1309 to 1377; then the seat of spiritual power shifted to Rome. We can imagine Woolf's ironic enjoyment of such an undercurrent to her subversive vision of the future, embodied in the "innocent" nursery rhyme.

22. See, for example, Paul J. Tillich, "The Metropolis in Modern Times: Spiritual Aspects," in *The Metropolis in Modern Life*, ed. Robert Moore Fisher (New York: Russell and Russell, 1955) pp. 346–8; Richard Sennett, *The Uses of Disorder: Personal Identity and City Life* (New York: Knopf, 1970); Virginia Woolf, *The London Scene* (New York: Frank Hallman, 1975); and Walter Benjamin, "On Some Motifs in Baudelaire," *Illuminations*, ed. Hannah Arendt (New York: Schocken Books, 1969) pp. 154–200.

23. Simone de Beauvoir, *The Second Sex*, trs. H. M. Parshley (New York: Vintage Books, 1974) p. xix.

24. Lillian D. Robinson, "Who's Afraid of a Room of One's Own?," in *The Politics of Literature: Dissenting Essays in the Teaching of English*, ed. Louis Kampf and Paul Lauter (New York: Random House, 1973) pp. 354–409; cited in Madeline Moore, "Virginia Woolf's *The Years* and Years of Adverse Male Reviewers," *Women's Studies*, IV (1977) p. 249.

25. For a further discussion of this phenomenon, see Virginia Woolf, "Thoughts on Peace in an Air Raid," *The Death of the Moth and Other Essays* (New York: Harcourt, Brace, Jovanovich, 1970) pp. 243–8; and Margaret Comstock, "The Loudspeaker and the Human Voice: Politics and the Form of *The Years*," *Bulletin of the New York Public Library*, Winter 1977, pp. 252–75. For an analysis of the relationship between subconscious Hitlerism and woman-only mothering in the works of Woolf, see my "Mirroring and Mothering: Reflections on the Mirror Encounter Metaphor in Virginia Woolf's Works," *Twentieth Century Literature*, forthcoming.

Androgynous Vision and Artistic Process in Virginia Woolf's *A Room of One's Own*   Ellen Carol Jones*

"Think of things in themselves," Virginia Woolf exhorts her reader in *A Room of One's Own*.[1] It is only by doing so that one can come within the "presence of reality." The precise nature of that reality Woolf can never

*This essay was written specifically for this volume and is published here for the first time by permission of the author. © Ellen Carol Jones, 1984.

quite define; she can only suggest its nature through images — images which, significantly, are similar to the ones she creates to suggest the nature of fiction and the nature of truth:

> What is meant by "reality"? It would seem to be something very erratic, very undependable — now to be found in a dusty road, now in a scrap of newspaper in the street, now in a daffodil in the sun. It lights up a group in a room and stamps some casual saying. It overwhelms one walking home beneath the stars and makes the silent world more real than the world of speech — and then there it is again in an omnibus in the uproar of Piccadilly. Sometimes, too, it seems to dwell in shapes too far away for us to discern what their nature is. But whatever it touches, it fixes and makes permanent.[2]

Woolf believes that the artist, especially the writer, has the chance "to live more than other people in the presence of this reality. It is his business to find it and collect it and communicate it to the rest of us" (p. 114). What Woolf herself communicates in *A Room of One's Own* is the process of artistic creation: the process of finding, of collecting, of creating. T.E. Hulme describes the process of artistic creation as one of "discovery and disentanglement."[3] For Woolf, it is always "the process of discovering" that is essential, "not the discovery itself at all."[4] She emphasizes the process, the quest, in *A Room of One's Own* as she tells her reader: "I am going to do what I can to show you how I arrived at this opinion" — that "a woman must have money and a room of her own if she is to write fiction" (p. 4); here the very telling of that process of discovery becomes the art itself. She is careful not to let her reader forget that she is telling a story, creating a fiction: "I need not say that what I am about to describe has no existence," she says nonetheless; "Oxbridge is an invention; so is Fernham; 'I' is only a convenient term for somebody who has no real being" (p. 4). That the reader immediately recognizes Oxbridge as a thinly disguised Oxford and Cambridge, Fernham as Newnham and Girton, and Mary Beton, Mary Seton, and Mary Carmichael — figures from both history and art — as representatives of the twentieth-century woman, particularly the woman artist, and most particularly Woolf herself, accounts for much of the irony of her "story" and much of the force of her social and political statements. But in emphasizing the fictive nature of her work, Woolf asks her reader to consider her essay not only as a statement of her social and political beliefs, but also as it is in itself: a creation, a fiction, a work of art.

The process of artistic creation is also one of disentanglement, of freeing the mind from all impediments. The artist must be able to emancipate herself from the molds of conventional perception and language, to see things as they "really" are and to communicate that vision in a language free of any bias. To perceive things as they really are and to express that perception is to redefine our ideas about reality. Central to Woolf's purpose in *A Room of One's Own* is the concept of the process of artistic creation as such a process of redefinition: as she explores, within the dialectics of content and of form, the relationships of men and women, of fiction and life, of fiction and truth, she redefines the nature of the artist, the nature of fiction, the nature of truth.

Virginia Woolf's vision of reality in *A Room of One's Own* is ultimately an androgynous one, reflecting an androgyny which extends far beyond the metaphorical fusion of the male and the female into a "unity of the mind" (p. 100). The creative act is, for her, a movement towards androgyny, a process which entails a synthesizing of subject and object into an artistic whole. It is the reciprocal action of the imagination of the artist impinging on the world, the world impinging on the imagination of the artist; the imagination invests an ordinary occurrence with order and meaning, and yet it does so only because that occurrence has "the power to communicate" something to it (p. 100). Essential to Woolf's conception of artistic creation is that of epiphany; the moment of vision is reflected in and extended by the creative process: "it is or will become a revelation of some order; it is a token of some real thing behind appearances; and I make it real by putting it into words."[5]

Woolf's method in her essay is to set up dialectics both of content and of form, the argument itself and the way in which it is presented. The argument's ideal synthesis of the male and the female into a transcendent "unity of the mind" is mirrored in the form's synthesis of two disparate modes of discourse into a creative whole. Like the writer she describes in "The Narrow Bridge of Art," Woolf, in addressing the question of women and fiction, brings to bear upon her "tumultuous and contradictory emotions the generalizing and simplifying power of a strict and logical imagination."[6] Ever conscious of the need to find the form which can contain easily and naturally the meaning that the work attempts to express, she creates in *A Room of One's Own* a form which is at once fragmented and unified, the product of an imagination that can be simultaneously creative and "strict and logical." She presents the argument of the essay through two modes of discourse: the first mode, the "story" Woolf tells, is that of the rambling, digressive, associative account of the process by which she has arrived at her "opinion" (p. 4). The second mode of discourse is that of the formal rhetorical argument itself: clear and ordered, it is a product of a "strict and logical imagination."[7]

Woolf's "opinion," that a woman must have money and a room of her own if she is to write fiction, asserts symbolically her thesis that the state of mind necessary for artistic creation is inextricably connected with the conditions of the artist's life. She believes that it is impossible for the imaginative act to sustain itself without a secure foundation of tradition, history, and especially material necessities:

> fiction is like a spider's web, attached ever so lightly perhaps, but still attached to life at all four corners. . . . these webs are not spun in midair by incorporeal creatures, but are the work of suffering human

> beings, and are attached to grossly material things, like health and money and the houses we live in. (pp. 43–44)

The syllogism informing her argument begins with the premise that "intellectual freedom," the ability to think of things in themselves, "depends upon material things." And poetry, *all* art, "depends upon intellectual freedom" (p. 112). Therefore, art depends upon material things. The corollary to this argument is that because women are poor, they have no intellectual freedom and, consequently, cannot create art.

The argument follows the classical five-part sequence which Woolf mocks even as she carefully calls it to our attention just before the *peroratio*:

> Here I would stop, but the pressure of convention decrees that every speech must end with a peroration. And a peroration addressed to women should have something, you will agree, particularly exalting and ennobling about it. . . .
>
> How can I further encourage you to go about the business of life? Young women, I would say, and please attend, for the peroration is beginning, you are, in my opinion, disgracefully ignorant. (pp. 114–16)

In the *exordium*, or introduction, Woolf presents a variety of perspectives on and interpretations of the words "women" and "fiction," sets up her argument, and informs her readers — obliquely, to be sure — of the object of the argument. The *narratorio* is the symbolic "statement," the "opinion" that "a woman must have money and a room of her own if she is to write fiction . . ." (p. 4). The *confirmatio*, the proof of the argument, begins with the introduction of the persona: "Here then was I (call me Mary Beton, Mary Seton, Mary Carmichael or by any name you please . . .)" (p. 5). In the course of the *confirmatio* itself, the argument is expanded to encompass a variety of problems dealing with women and fiction. The *refutatio* begins as Woolf resumes her "own voice" and answers objections to her argument. And, of course, she announces her own *peroratio*.

Yet, although the basic argument of *A Room of One's Own* adopts a traditional structure — that of the Aristotelian syllogism — and the presentation of that argument follows a traditional sequence — that of the Ciceronian rhetoric — the essay itself is most unconventional. Woolf claims to give the reader her thoughts as they come to her; like her own creation, Mary Carmichael, who has broken the traditional sentence and the traditional sequence, she may be "merely giving things their natural order, as a woman would, if she wrote like a woman" (p. 95). She is redeveloping for her audience, as fully and as freely as she can, the train of thought which led to her "opinion" about women needing financial independence and privacy to be able to write fiction. The narrative of her "story" slowly, meticulously traces the growth and development of this opinion; it follows the lives and the careers of female writers — both fictional and historical — through five centuries, defining a tradition; it allows the audience to observe "the limitations, the prejudices, the idiosyncrasies of the speaker" (p. 4), to follow her "flying into the arms of a Beadle, lunching here, dining there, drawing pictures in the British Museum, taking books from the shelf, looking out of the window" (p. 109). The qualities of her narrative, like those most characteristic of the novel, are "the very qualities that are most incompatible with design and order."[8] By blending fiction with traditional structures and sequences from logic and rhetoric, by devising "some entirely new combination of her resources" to absorb "the new into the old without disturbing the infinitely intricate and elaborate balance of the whole," Woolf creates a new form, a synthesis of disparate modes of discourse and of thought into an artistic whole (p. 89).

This blend of fact and fiction gives *A Room of One's Own* much of its richness and charm. But it is the very necessity to create art out of the dearth of facts, out of the void of history, that gives the essay much of its relevance and power. In pointing out the disjunction between the artistic portrayal of women by men and the position of women in history, Woolf suggests that in order to comprehend the true nature of women, one must "think poetically and prosaically at one and the same moment, thus keeping in touch with fact . . . but not losing sight of fiction either" (p. 46). Yet this method fails when there is a scarcity of facts. Neither history nor biography has adequately recorded the experience of being a woman: she cannot be brought to life because one knows "nothing detailed, nothing perfectly true and substantial about her" (p. 46). History does not need to be rewritten; it needs to be recreated. The intersection of history and art is the cross-roads where Judith Shakespeare lies buried.

Out of the void of history, Woolf creates Judith Shakespeare and Mary Carmichael, the fictional first and last members of a tradition she is trying to trace through history. She redefines history in terms of fiction; her portrayal of the Elizabethan woman who had had Shakespeare's genius

> . . . may be true or it may be false — who can say? — but what is true in it, so it seemed to me, reviewing the story of Shakespeare's sister *as I had made it*, is that any woman born with a great gift in the sixteenth century would certainly have gone crazed, shot herself, or ended her days in some lonely cottage outside the village, half witch, half wizard, feared and mocked at. (p. 51; my emphasis)

The fiction underlying Woolf's own, the Scottish balad "Mary Hamilton," tells the story of a woman who defies the restrictions imposed on her sex and is condemned to die for doing so. Mary Hamilton — one of the "Queen's Maries," ladies-in-waiting to Mary, Queen of Scots — "gangs wi bairn / To the hichest Stewart of a'."[9] Refusing to be burdened with a child, she throws the baby into the sea, saying: "Sink ye, swim ye, bonny wee babe! / You'l neer get mair o me." The Queen, discovering the infanticide, instructs Mary Hamilton to put on her robes of black or of brown, for she must go with the Queen to Edinburgh. Mary defiantly refuses to put on clothes which would symbolize either mourning or guilt, effecting a kind of triumph in her downfall:

> 'I winna put on my robes o black,
>   Nor yet my robes o brown;
> But I'll put on my robes o white,
>   To shine through Edinbro town.'

In some versions of the ballad, she even rejects the mercy the king extends, reminding him of his own responsibility in her guilt:

> 'Hold your tongue, my sovereign leige,
>   And let your folly be;
> An ye had a mind to save my life,
>   Ye should na shamed me here.'[10]

Mary Hamilton, her heart "caught and tangled in a woman's body" (p. 50), is condemned to die because the means by which she chose to remain free were drastic and ultimate. The ballad asks — as Woolf herself asks — if a woman can attain freedom only by refusing to raise children; the woman's very decision to have children is out of her hands: the male imposes his power. And the power of society — the power of the male — condemns a woman for refusing to accept what it has imposed. Mary Hamilton becomes Woolf's paradigm for the woman refusing to accept the bonds of male domination. Woolf represents the women Mary Hamilton leaves behind as women not yet entirely free of the restrictions which a male-dominated society has imposed:

> 'Last nicht there was four Maries,
>   The nicht there'l be but three;
> There was Marie Seton, and Marie Beton,
>   And Marie Carmichael, and me.'

The artist too is not free of the restrictions of heritage: she is "an inheritor as well as an originator" (p. 113). What Woolf finds reprehensible, then, is that women have such a scanty intellectual and artistic tradition upon which they can build: "since freedom and fullness of expression are of the essence of the art, such a lack of tradition, such a scarcity and inadequacy of tools, must have told enormously upon the writing of women" (p. 80). A long tradition of economic and intellectual freedom for women must be established before any woman can hope to produce the great art that depends so completely on that freedom. The "dead poet who was Shakespeare's sister" will then be able to draw her life "from the lives of the unknown who were her forerunners, as her brother did before her," and write her poetry (p. 118). Without that preparation, without that tradition sustaining her, she will be unable to create her art:

> For masterpieces are not single and solitary births; they are the outcome
> of many years of thinking in common, of thinking by the body of the

people, so that the experience of the mass is behind the single voice. (pp. 68–69)

Woolf recognizes, however, that the "experience of the mass" has been until the twentieth century largely that of the male. Women have shared little or no part of that experience; they have been denied by men the "power to move on equal terms."[11] Rather than being the natural inheritor of her civilization, the woman is "outside of it, alien and critical" (p. 101). Woolf is uncomfortable with that position for women, although she later embraces it in *Three Guineas* as a kind of counter-elitism to the elitism of a patriarchal society.[12] But in *A Room of One's Own* she finds such a position, whether consciously adopted or not, to be in itself repressive and unnatural. It alters the woman's perspective of the world; it tampers with the integrity of her vision. Any alternation of one's vision, whether in reaction to oppression and injustice or in deference to convention, impedes the process of artistic creation, distorts the aesthetic truth of the thing created: "The vision becomes too masculine or it becomes too feminine; it loses its perfect integrity and, with that, its most essential quality as a work of art."[13] Woolf claims that in order to create art, all "desire to protest, to preach, to proclaim an injury, to pay off a score, to make the world the witness of some hardship or grievance" must be "fired out" of the mind of the artist and "consumed" (p. 58). The artist's mind, Woolf believes, must be unimpeded, "resonant and porous," "naturally creative, incandescent and undivided" (p. 102). The mind of the artist must be androgynous. Such a mind comprehends and transcends the feelings of both sexes; it is able to see "human beings not always in their relation to each other but in relation to reality" (p. 118).

Implicit in the very concept of androgyny, of course, is the presupposition of the difference between the male and the female. Although her argument itself is social rather than biological, Woolf describes the "fully fertilized" mind of the androgynous artist in sexual metaphors (p. 102):

> Some collaboration has to take place in the mind between the woman and the man before the act of creation can be accomplished. Some marriage of opposites has to be consummated. . . . The writer, I thought, once his experience is over, must lie back and let his mind celebrate its nuptials in darkness. (p. 108)

That men and women perceive the world differently, pursue knowledge differently, and create art differently is essential to Woolf's vision.[14] These differences result from the interaction of psychological and social conditions, conditions which have profoundly affected the perspective of the artist, the nature of art. Woolf is not calling for the kind of union of the sexes, the superficial equality, that comes from the belief that the two sexes must be alike in order to be equal: "It would be a thousand pities if women wrote like men, or lived like men, or looked like men, for if two sexes are quite inadequate, considering the vastness and variety of the world, how should we manage with one only?" (p. 91). Rather, she is calling for an androgynous artistic vision which encompasses both sexes but is itself unconscious of either sex. To be a woman and to create, Woolf believes, one must "devise some entirely new combination of her resources . . . so as to absorb the new into the old without disturbing the infinitely intricate and elaborate balance of the whole" (p. 89). The woman writer must find a language and a style to express her vision of the world with integrity. Yet she must write "as a woman who has forgotten that she is a woman," not thinking specially or separately of her sex, not allowing a consciousness of the injustices her sex has endured to interfere with the integrity of her vision, but rather holding fast to the thing as she sees it (pp. 96, 102–03, 77).

To attain the freedom and fullness of expression which are of the essence of art, both language and style must stretch, expand, transcend their present use if they are to portray adequately the experience of women. Mary Carmichael — the contemporary woman writer Woolf creates as both part of and separate from her persona, "the descendant of all those other women whose circumstances [she has] been glancing at" (p. 84) — breaks the traditional sentence and the traditional sequence. Woolf sees this break with tradition as necessary and inevitable if a female writer is to preserve the integrity of her vision, if she is to break the bonds of chastity. Modern women writers, like the contemporary artists she envisions in "The Narrow Bridge of Art," are

> . . . writers who are trying to work themselves free from a bondage which has become irksome to them; writers who are trying to readjust their attitude so that they may once more stand easily and naturally in a position where their powers have full play upon important things.[15]

There is for Woolf a clear connection between the thought and the expression of it — and between the creator and his or her creation. To find the form which best suits the thought involves not only a consideration of the nature of the thought itself, but also a consideration of the nature of the creator. Woolf asserts that the traditional shape of the sentence and the traditional structure of sentences within a book have been formed by men "out of their own needs for their own uses" (p. 80). They are inadequate for a woman's artistic use. She must so alter and adapt these shapes and structures that they take "the natural shape of her thought without crushing or distorting it."[16] Woolf believes that, as far as women are concerned, physical conditions must play a great part in the future of fiction (p. 81). Not only must a woman win her right to tell "the truth about [her] own experiences as a body" from the restrictions masculine beliefs about feminine chastity have placed upon her,[17] but she must also win her right to tell the truth about her own experiences as an intellect and as a spirit and to express these truths in a form which is natural to her.

Chastity, Woolf claims, has had in the past, as it has even now, "a religious importance in a woman's life, and has so wrapped itself round with nerves and instincts that to cut it free and bring it to the light of day demands courage of the rarest" (p. 51). Because she believes that the body and the mind are inextricably connected,[18] any violence done to the body — and Woolf considers male-imposed chastity a violence — is a violence done to the spirit, especially to the artistic spirit. To say that a book must somehow be "adapted to the body" is to imply an intrinsic relationship between the artist and her creation. Art comes out of and reflects the artist. The artifact itself originates from the "body" of the artificer. The male's insistence on female chastity, then, prevents the woman artist from creating because it denies her the freedom to write fully and honestly about her passions and her body, and, more important, it ultimately denies her the very right to create, to "give birth" to a work of art.

For Woolf, style and meaning are inextricably connected: the style reflects and extends the argument; the meaning can be discovered in the presentation itself. Woolf assures her readers that although she will not immediately disclose the thought informing her essay, "if you look carefully you may find it for yourselves in the course of what I am going to say" (p. 5). She claims that lies will flow from her lips, "but there may perhaps be some truth mixed up with them; it is for you to seek out this truth and to decide whether any part of it is worth keeping" (p. 4). The way in which Woolf demonstrates the process of her imaginative act forces her reader to participate in a parallel process. The act of reading the essay thus also becomes a process of discovery and disentanglement. In seeking for the thought, the truth embedded in the presentation of the argument, the reader must distinguish the truth entangled with the "lies."

One of the processes of artistic creation Woolf demonstrates in her essay is the progression from the making of scenes to the creating of fiction, complete with characters, setting, dialogue, and even a fictional author, the movement from meaning imposed on the scenes to meaning expressed by the fiction. Another is the transformation of self-expression into art, as Woolf illustrates the transformation she hopes to find in the writings of her female contemporaries. Woolf laments that in showing her reader how she arrived at her "opinion," in revealing the complete process of her artistic creation, she leaves "the great problem of the true nature of woman and the true nature of fiction unsolved" (p. 4). Yet it is in the personae she envisions — Mary Beton, Mary Seton, Mary Carmichael, personae in whom "woman" and "fiction" are inextricably mixed together — and in the very fiction she creates that she suggests what the true natures of woman and fiction may be. In "making use of all the liberties and licenses of a novelist," Woolf hopes to create in A Room of One's Own a fiction "likely to contain more truth than fact" (p. 4). And in shifting to fiction, Woolf shifts the meaning of truth.

Woolf mocks conventional notions of truth: one cannot receive from any lecture "a nugget of pure truth" to wrap up between the pages of one's notebook and "keep on the mantlepiece for ever"; one cannot find truth on the shelves of the British Museum or extract it from the biased opinions of others (pp. 3–4). One cannot hope to tell the truth, she contends, when a subject is as highly controversial as that of sex: "One can only give one's audience the chance of drawing their own conclusions as they observe the limitations, the prejudices, the idiosyncrasies of the speaker" (p. 4). It is the task of the audience to seek out the truth. Woolf's refusal to come to conclusions about many of the questions she raises forces her readers into imaginative acts of their own, acts which are cut off by the intrusion of material considerations, of time and of history, in much the same way that she claims a woman's imaginative acts are disrupted. Throughout her essay, Woolf gives her readers a second sight, asking them to reconsider art and life, and all they entail, from a different perspective, with a new complexity. Her "new philosophy calls all in doubt,"[19] but it does so not only to destroy, but also to create. Out of the lies of art she creates a truth that transcends that of the mere fact.

Woolf asks if a novelist "might not capture fuller and finer truths" if he were to stand back from life, "draw a little apart, see people in groups, as outlines," as significant forms:

> Then it is not the actual sight or sound itself that matters, but the reverberations that it makes as it travels through our minds. These are often to be found far away, strangely transformed; but it is only by gathering up and putting together these echoes and fragments that we arrive at the true nature of our experience.[20]

To see things as significant forms, the artist must alter "slightly the ordinary relationships," shift "the values of familiar things" in accordance with one's vision.[21] Such a process of redefinition is necessary for the artist to be able to free "whole and entire the work that is in him" (p. 58). Woolf claims to be unable to come to any conclusions, but she does reach two that are essential to her vision of women and of fiction. The state of mind "most propitious for creative work," she decides, must be "incandescent": "There must be no obstacle in it, no foreign matter unconsumed" (p. 58). It must be resonant, unimpeded, androgynous (p. 102). Can a woman's writing attain that incandescence? Can a woman yet transform self-expression into art? Or would the fact of her sex — the impediments of her own suppression and that of her mother and her grandmother before her — interfere with her integrity as an artist? Woolf suggests that among the new novels "one might find an answer to several such questions" (p. 83). To discover her answer, she creates a fiction within a fiction, Mary Carmichael's *Life's Adventure*. But although Mary Carmichael writes without any consciousness of her sex, without any fear or hatred towards men or any perceptible restriction on her art, still her first novel does not succeed. She cannot sustain her vision unbroken against the tide of "the bishops and the deans, the doctors and the professors, the patriarchs and the pedagogues all at her shouting warning and advice" (p. 97). As the female writer makes the attempt to look "beneath into the depths," she fights centuries of overwhelming prejudices, of values and traditions not her own. The lack of a tradition of her own upon which she can build her art, the lack of the material and intellectual security necessary to found that tradition, ensure the failure of Mary Carmichael's first novel; and here Woolf reaches her second conclusion:

> Give her another hundred years, I concluded, reading the last chapter . . . give her a room of her own and five hundred a year, let her speak her mind and leave out half that she now puts in, and she will write a better book one of these days. She will be a poet, I said, putting *Life's Adventure*, by Mary Carmichael, at the end of the shelf, in another hundred years' time. (p. 98)

The telling of her process of discovery, the story of how she reaches her "prosaic conclusion" about the room and the money, becomes in itself a revelatory process: "in a question like this truth is only to be had by laying together many varieties of error" (p. 109). One may not be able to hope to tell the truth, but one may hope to suggest its nature within the very context of the question. The only way for the artist to portray the thing in itself is to allow that portrayal to arise, barely articulated in words "hardly syllabled yet," out of the portrayal of something entirely different (p. 88). One can only capture those "fuller and finer truths" by describing the context; one can only reveal "the inner life of things" by suggesting "things that speech is not calculated to express."[22] The artist must not skim the surfaces merely, but must look "beneath into the depths" to "show the meaning of all this" (p. 97). And that revelation of truth would come through the artist's power of suggestion:

> And she would begin — how unmistakable that quickening is! — beckoning and summoning, and there would rise up in memory, half forgotten, perhaps quite trivial things in other chapters dropped by the way. And she would make their presence felt while some one sewed or smoked a pipe as naturally as possible, and one would feel, as she went on writing, as if one had gone to the top of the world and seen it laid out, very majestically, beneath. (p. 97)

It is this power of suggestion that Woolf believes is the most essential attribute of androgynous writing. Without it, a book cannot penetrate beyond the surface of the mind. With it, a book can reveal all the truth of life: "one sees more intensely afterwards; the world seems bared of its covering and given an intenser life." In calling for that power of suggestion, Woolf invokes it; in suggesting the nature of reality, she creates it; in defining the mind of the androgynous artist, she embodies it. Her vision of art and her expression of it within the fiction and the argument of her essay give *A Room of One's Own* the "secret of perpetual life" (p. 105) found only in androgynous art.

Notes

1. *A Room of One's Own* (1929; rpt. New York: Harcourt Brace Jovanovich, 1957), p. 115. References to this essay will be cited hereafter in the text. I am indebted to Charlotte Frascona, University of Wisconsin, for her sensitive reading of an earlier version of this essay, and for her willingness to share with me her ideas about *A Room of One's Own*.

2. *A Room*, pp. 113–14. T. E. Hulme, in "Bergson's Theory of Art," *Speculations: Essays on Humanism and the Philosophy of Art*, ed. Herbert Read (1924; rpt. London: Routledge & Kegan Paul, 1936), pp. 150–51, uses similar language to describe the function of the artist and of art:

> It is as if the surface of our mind was a sea in a continual state of motion, that there were so many waves on it, their existence was so transient, and they interfered so much with each other, that one was unable to perceive them. The artist by making a fixed model of one of these transient waves enables you to isolate it out and to perceive it in yourself. In that sense art merely reveals, it never creates.

3. *Speculations*, p. 149.

4. *Night and Day* (1919; rpt. New York: Harcourt Brace Jovanovich, Inc., 1948), p. 135. See Fyodor Dostoevsky, *The Idiot*, trans. Constance Garnett, III, 5 (New York: Modern Library, 1935), p. 375.

5. Woolf, *Moments of Being: Unpublished Autobiographical Writings*, ed. Jeanne Schulkind (1976); rpt. New York: Harcourt Brace Jovanovich, 1978), p. 72. Clive Bell describes the essential reality of a thing as "that which lies behind the appearance of all things—that which gives to all things their individual significance, the thing in itself, the ultimate reality." *Art* (London, 1913; rpt. New York: G. P. Putnam's Sons, 1958), p. 54.

6. Woolf, "The Narrow Bridge of Art," in *Collected Essays*, II (London: Hogarth Press, 1966), p. 228.

7. Thomas J. Farrell also argues that Woolf uses two modes of rhetoric, alternating between the "male" mode of formal rhetoric and the "female" mode of "indirection," consciously combining a discussion of exposition and fiction. But Farrell relates the two modes of rhetoric to the Jungian conception of the development of the human psyche: the male mode with the development of "personalized ego-conscious" and the female mode with the "'sublimation' of the ego and the transformation of consciousness into a new unity of the self." "The Female and Male Modes of Rhetoric," *College English*, 40 (April 1979), 909–21; see p. 919.

8. "Phases of Fiction," in *Collected Essays*, II, p. 101.

9. "Marie Hamilton," *Sharp's Ballad Book*, 1824, p. 18; quoted in *The English and Scottish Popular Ballads*, ed. Francis James Child, 5 vols. (Boston: Houghton, Mifflin, 1983; 1888), III, No. 173, A, pp. 384–85.

10. "Mary Hamilton," Motherwell's MS., p. 337; quoted in Child, *English and Scottish Popular Ballads*, III, No. 173, B, p. 386.

11. "George Eliot," in *Collected Essays*, I, p. 199.

12. *Three Guineas* (1938; rpt. New York: Harcourt Brace Jovanovich, 1966), p. 82. Compare her claim in *The Letters of Virginia Woolf*, VI (New York: Harcourt Brace Jovanovich, 1980), p. 303: "I can't myself conceive any position more positive than an outsider's, if one could put it into practise. One can't—that's the difficulty. . . ." Waiting for the publication of *Three Guineas*, Woolf reflects in her diary: "For having spat it out, my mind is made up. I need never recur or repeat. I am an outsider. I can take my way:

experiment with my own imagination in my own way." *A Writer's Diary: Being Extracts from the Diary of Virginia Woolf*, ed. Leonard Woolf (New York: Harcourt Brace Jovanovich, 1953), p. 282.

13. "Women and Fiction," in *Collected Essays*, II, p. 145.

14. This conception of men and women, so graphically portrayed in *A Room of One's Own*, especially in the scene in the British Museum, is corroborated in "Women and Fiction": "both in life and in art the values of a woman are not the values of a man"; "a woman's book is not written as a man would write it" (*Collected Essays*, II, pp. 146, 147).

15. "The Narrow Bridge of Art," in *Collected Essays*, II, p. 229.

16. "Women and Fiction," in *Collected Essays*, II, p. 145.

17. "Professions for Women," in *Collected Essays*, II, p. 288.

18. Woolf makes this point with great humor in *A Room of One's Own*: "The human frame being what it is, heart, body and brain all mixed together, and not contained in separate compartments as they will be no doubt in another million years, a good dinner is of great importance to good talk. . . . The lamp in the spine does not light on beef and prunes" (p. 18).

In "On Being Ill," Woolf claims that "literature does its best to maintain that its concern is with the mind; that the body is a sheet of plain glass through which the soul looks straight and clear, and, save for one or two passions such as desire and greed, is null, and negligible and non-existent. On the contrary, the very opposite is true." *Collected Essays*, IV (London: Hogarth Press, 1967), p. 193. Woolf's concept of the androgynous mind of the artist emphasizes this interdependence of the mind and the body.

19. John Donne, "The First Anniversary," in *Renaissance England: Poetry and Prose from the Reformation to the Restoration*, ed. Roy Lamson and Hallett Smith (New York: W. W. Norton, 1956), p. 816.

20. "Impassioned Prose," in *Collected Essays*, I, p. 172.

21. "Impassioned Prose," p. 172.

22. Hulme, *Speculations*, pp. 152–53.

Objects of Vision: Women as Art in the Novels of Virginia Woolf   Barbara Hill Rigney[*]

Clarissa Dalloway pauses for a moment in a doorway, aware of the excitement her entrance creates; Mrs. Ramsay sits framed in a window, accepting the homage of passing spectators; Jinny in *The Waves* enters a candle-lit room, seats herself in a gilt chair and arranges her dress so that it billows around her. Unlike other of Virginia Woolf's heroines, who are painters, writers, or musicians making art into life, these characters make life into art, creating of *themselves* "objects of vision." Losing subjectivity and identity as they assume the traditionally male-defined role of art object, they are a testament to Woolf's political consciousness and to her concern for the social situations and psychological conditions of women; as

[*]This essay was written specifically for this volume and is published here for the first time by permission of the author. © Barbara Hill Rigney, 1984.

embodiments of an aesthetic ideal, they also represent one aspect of Woolf's exploration into the ways in which art is both perceived and created.

In *Ways of Seeing,* John Berger also discusses the manner in which art objects are perceived, and particularly the ways in which women as art objects are perceived both by male spectators and by themselves:

> . . . *men act* and *women appear.* Men look at women. Women watch themselves being looked at. This determines not only most relations between men and women but also the relation of women to themselves. The surveyor of woman in herself is male: the surveyed female. Thus she turns herself into an object — and most particularly an object of vision: a sight.[1]

And, Berger continues, this rendering of the self into art object is the very mechanism by which women have survived in a patriarchal society, although the cost is inevitably a kind of doubleness in which a woman's self is split into two:

> A woman must continually watch herself. She is almost continually accompanied by her own image of herself. Whilst she is walking across a room or whilst she is weeping at the death of her father, she can scarcely avoid envisaging herself walking or weeping . . . And so she comes to consider the *surveyor* and *surveyed* within her as the two constituent yet always distinct elements of her identity as a woman.[2]

Similarly, Simone de Beauvoir in *The Second Sex* describes that moment in puberty in which the young girl first discovers the unknown figure in the mirror, the "she-as-object": "For the young girl, erotic transcendence consists in becoming prey in order to gain her ends. She becomes an object, and she sees herself as object; she discovers this new aspect of her being with surprise: it seems to her that she has been doubled; instead of coinciding exactly with herself, she now begins to exist *outside.*"[3] Caught and imprisoned thus in "the motionless silver trap,"[4] women, according to de Beauvoir, are rendered into the passivity of immanence, killed, as it were, into art.

Woolf's Jinny, for example, is always an observer of herself, split between her mirror and reality. In fact, her mirror-identity is perhaps her only reality other than that which exists in the consciousness of Bernard in whose androgynous soul she represents one aspect of the female. Continually, Jinny searches in her mirror, surveying her face "like an artist,"[5] intent upon the picture of herself she will present:

> I have sat before a looking-glass as you sit writing, adding up figures at desks. So, before the looking-glass in the temple of my bedroom, I have judged my nose and my chin; my lips that open too wide and show too much gum. I have looked. I have noted. I have chosen what yellow or white, what shine or dullness, what loop or

straightness suits. I am volatile for one, rigid for another, angular as an icicle in silver, or voluptuous as a candle flame in gold. (pp. 221–22)

A dancer in her youth, and thus a literally moving picture, Jinny arranges the composition which is herself, how she will tie her hair in a white ribbon so that "when I leap across the court the ribbon will stream out in a flash, yet curl round my neck, perfectly in its place" (pp. 42–43). Repeatedly, she imagines herself seated in a lamp-lit room full of admiring men, any one of whom might answer her mysterious summons to accompany her that evening to her home which is itself a stage setting, the vases filled ". . . with lavish, with luxurious, with extravagant flowers nodding in great bunches" (p. 195). Nor does the identity of the man matter to Jinny, whether he is Bernard or a stranger observed on a train, for he is necessary merely as an anonymous audience; as with Berger's women described above, Jinny by herself is both spectator and spectacle, artist and art object.

Jinny, of course, ages with the other characters, but her artistry nevertheless preserves her; it is only for a moment that she quails before her mirror, ". . . catching sight of myself before I had time to prepare myself as I always prepare myself for the sight of myself . . ." (p. 193). Jinny's obsession with her reflected self might be explained as narcissism, as de Beauvoir describes that pathology in *The Second Sex:* the narcissist seeks to divide herself into "male subject and female object," thus holding an "affectionate dialogue between self and self."[6] Yet, in another sense, Jinny has no self for she has suspended subjectivity in the interest of art; nor, as Bernard perceives her at the end, has she "future, or speculation." Paradoxically, however, she possesses a quality of dignity, she is worthy of our admiration, as Bernard also observes, because, like the artist, she has "respected the moment with complete integrity . . . for which I loved her . . . for which I honored her" (p. 265).

Mrs. Ramsay in *To the Lighthouse* is also, like Jinny, an artist of the self. She, too, as Lily Briscoe perceives, is capable of "making of the moment something permanent (as in another sphere Lily herself tried to make of the moment something permanent) — this was the nature of a revelation. In the midst of chaos there was shape. . . ."[7] Perhaps with less deliberate consciousness than Jinny, but with equal dedication, Mrs. Ramsay creates herself and allows herself to be created by others as an object of vision. She needs no looking glass, however, for her mirror is in the faces of spectators whose reactions constitute the greater part of the novel. Lily Briscoe, Mr. Ramsay, Mr. Bankes, and the rest, in fact, form a kind of parade, a moving line past the window where Mrs. Ramsay sits for the first part of the novel, framed and enshrined, her son by her side; here she is a Renaissance Madonna, an icon, an art object. She is, at some points depending on the viewer's perception, doubly framed, for, directly behind the window seat is "an authenticated masterpiece by Michael

Angelo," and its gilt frame, over which Mrs. Ramsay has tossed her green shawl, outlines her head (p. 48). Similarly, Charles Tansley recalls her at an earlier moment, descending a stair and pausing; she ". . . stood quite motionless for a moment against a picture of Queen Victoria wearing the blue ribbon of the Garter; when all at once he realised that it was this: it was this: — she was the most beautiful person he had ever seen" (p. 25).

Each character, then, projects his or her own idiosyncratic aesthetic framework upon the image of Mrs. Ramsay. An obscure poet of forgotten identity has seen in her the classic beauty of the Greeks and inscribed his book to "the happier Helen of our days" (p. 43). William Bankes, who also reads the classics, sees her in terms of Greek sculpture: "Nature has but little clay . . . like that of which she moulded you," he silently addresses her, for "He saw her at the end of the line very clearly Greek, straight, blue-eyed . . . The Graces assembling seemed to have joined hands in meadows of asphodel to compose that face." Further, Mr. Bankes seems actually to be creating Mrs. Ramsay as one composes a picture, for he recognizes ". . . something incongruous to be worked into the harmony of her face . . . one must remember the quivering thing, the living thing . . . and work it into the picture" (pp. 46–47).

It is Mrs. Ramsay's beauty, then, which mystifies the observer, eludes definition, provides the mask or facade which protects the enigma and defies artistic interpretation. But Lily Briscoe's actual painting of Mrs. Ramsay (which provides the ostensible reason for Mrs. Ramsay's posed attitude in the early pages, a fact which she periodically recalls by attempting to keep her head in the same position) is the most revealing of all previous interpretations: Lily's is the creative force which renders Mrs. Ramsay in her essence as a triangular purple shape, an image seen by Mr. Bankes as reductive, but which, of course, corresponds so exactly with Mrs. Ramsay's view of herself as "a wedge-shaped core of darkness . . . it was thus that she felt herself" (p. 95).

Lily's image of Mrs. Ramsay is, quite obviously, a death image which denotes an absence of personality or a loss of individuality, a death into art which prefigures Mrs. Ramsay's actual death and her abstracted and disembodied presence in the "Time Passes" section of the novel. As Elaine Showalter concludes in A Literature of Their Own, Mrs. Ramsay is in fact guilty of a kind of suicide: "In one sense, Woolf's female aesthetic is an extension of her view of women's social role: receptivity to the point of self-destruction, creative synthesis to the point of exhaustion and sterility . . . For Mrs. Ramsay, death is a mode of self-assertion. Refined to its essences, abstracted from physicality and anger, denied any action, Woolf's vision of womanhood is as deadly as it is disembodied."[8]

Certainly, it is Mrs. Ramsay's passivity which the reader at times finds so irritating and which Showalter criticizes so severely. And yet, paradoxically, Mrs. Ramsay is extremely powerful, creating her beautiful moments from the material of domestic inanity, managing her husband

and children, manipulating her world, arranging marriages even though these might prove disastrous. In a sense, she chooses even her own annihilation, which, in overtly sexual images, is described as an "exquisite abandonment to exhaustion . . . the rapture of successful creation" (p. 61). Mrs. Ramsay herself is her greatest creation, her very clothing being a testament to her conscious creation of herself as art object: the soft greys and greens she wears so flatteringly, the shawls she drapes about herself, even the fisherman's hat she so whimsically places on her head—all serve to present her in pictorial terms. Mrs. Ramsay believes that Mr. Carmichael alone suspects her artifice (and thus she explains in her own mind his resistance to her charm):

> She bore about with her, she could not help knowing it, the torch of her beauty; she carried it erect into any room that she entered; and after all, veil it as she might, and shrink from the monotony of bearing that it imposed on her, her beauty was apparent. She had been admired. She had been loved . . . That was what she minded . . . the sense she had now when Mr. Carmichael shuffled past, just nodding to her question, with a book beneath his arm, in his yellow slippers, that she was suspected; and that all this desire of hers to give, to help, was vanity. For her own self-satisfaction was it that she wished so instinctively to help, to give, that people might say of her 'O Mrs. Ramsay! dear Mrs. Ramsay . . . Mrs. Ramsay, of course!' and need her and send for her and admire her? Was it not secretly this that she wanted . . . (pp. 64–65)

If, as Oscar Wilde once maintained, art is the "telling of beautiful untrue things,"[9] then Mrs. Ramsay is a consummate artist, for lies are part of her stock in trade. She placates her son James by telling him that the weather will be fine on the following day so that he can go to the lighthouse; she covers the boar's skull with her shawl and tells her children that it is a bird's nest, a garden, something harmless and beautiful; she advises young girls, particularly Minta Doyle, that marriage will make them happy. Mrs. Ramsay is, above all, a male-identified woman, and it is to men that she lies most readily, as she smooths the ruffled feelings of Charles Tansley or as she reaffirms Mr. Ramsay's belief in his own superior intelligence. Mrs. Ramsay is clearly aware that ". . . she had the whole of the other sex under her protection; for reasons she could not explain, for their chivalry and valour, for the fact that they negotiated treaties, ruled India, controlled finance; finally for an attitude towards herself which no woman could fail to feel or to find agreeable, something trustful, childlike, reverential. . ." (p. 13).

As art object, and thus as a reflector of the perceiver's self, Mrs. Ramsay quite consciously serves the traditional function of women which Woolf describes in A Room of One's Own: that of liar, flatterer, and looking glass ". . . possessing the magic and delicious power of reflecting the figure of man at twice its natural size."[10] John Berger's Ways of Seeing also documents the historical male ownership of art objects, including women, and notes that one function of art is its testament to the owner's power or wealth: ". . . the essential way of seeing women, the essential use to which their images are put, has not changed. Women are depicted in a quite different way from men — not because the feminine is different from the masculine — but because the 'ideal' spectator is always assumed to be male and the image of the woman is designed to flatter him."[11]

It cannot be surprising, then, that Mrs. Ramsay avoids her own mirrored reflection (p. 121) and sees her own beauty as a curse. The price of survival in this male world, however, is for Mrs. Ramsay to serve in her capacity as both mirror and art object, to lose, ultimately, her sense of self and finally her life. Sandra Gilbert and Susan Gubar in *The Madwoman in the Attic* describe the fate of female literary characters who define their existences according to a male construct of beauty: like the archetypal Snow White in her glass coffin, they surrender identity to become objects, "to be displayed and desired, patriarchy's marble opus."[12]

Similarly, Mrs. Ramsay cannot be said to exist as a self; the mirrored reflection becomes the only reality, and the external object, Mrs. Ramsay herself in this case, comes to be interpreted solely as reflector. Similarly, in Woolf's short story, "The Lady in the Looking Glass,"[13] Isabella Tyson is described as though she had no existence beyond that perceived by a nameless spectator (whose sex is also unidentified) who watches her through a mirror as she walks in her garden. The spectator's imagination, inspired by the reflection, provides the only knowledge we have of Isabella Tyson's life. Harvena Richter in *The Inward Voyage* sees this set of images as a stylistic device to explore and to render modes of perception: "What Mrs. Woolf seems to imply is that, since the mind-eye is a camera lens in which the image is reflected, the picture in the mind (the way we know the object) is the reality, rather than the object itself."[14] James Naremore in *The World Without a Self* has a similar idea in mind when he discusses the "disembodiment" or feeling of selflessness which Woolf's characters so frequently experience and which her narrators often manifest.[15] In this sense, Lily Briscoe has quite perceptively and truthfully painted Mrs. Ramsay as "the semblance of the thing," not as the thing itself, thus calling into question the problem of identity and the nature of reality.

Using Woolf's image of "the angel in the house," Gilbert and Gubar attribute what they see as an almost universal failure of identity in women to the internalization of an aesthetic ideal imposed from without: "Whether she becomes an *objet d'art* or a saint, however, it is the surrender of her self — of her personal comfort, her personal desires or both — that is the beautiful angel-woman's key act, while it is precisely this sacrifice which dooms her both to death and heaven. For to be selfless is not only to be noble, it is to be dead."[16] Certainly, Mrs. Ramsay is "the angel in the house," the passive receiver of others' impressions, art object and aesthetic ideal. Her presence persists after death simply because, even when alive, she did not possess a reality or a subjective existence. Perhaps, then, Woolf did not envision Mrs. Ramsay as a positive illustration of "the female aesthetic" in the sense that Elaine Showalter indicates, but rather as a tragic figure, doomed by her assumed role as an object of vision and by her social circumstances to an existence devoid of identity. Woolf herself, as she writes in her essay "Professions for Women," struggled to kill the angel in the house, that part of the self which would have killed the artist in her and "plucked the heart out of my writing."[17]

In Mrs. Ramsay's case, as with other of Woolf's heroines, however, truth is not so simple, for it may reside solely in the perception of the moment. The enigma of Mrs. Ramsay remains secure, for at the same time that we declare her to be a nonentity, a mere object without a soul, we also find ourselves attracted to her in much the same way that Lily is attracted, seeking to determine that essence, that meaning: "What art was there, known to love or cunning, by which one pressed into those secret chambers?" (p. 79). As Carolyn Heilbrun says in *Toward a Recognition of Androgyny*, "Mrs. Ramsay has thrust herself into the midst of our impoverished world and seduced us into worshipping her."[18]

But perhaps our fascination is not inspired so much by "the mother goddess" aspect of Mrs. Ramsay which Heilbrun describes[19] nor by the Demeter symbolism which Joseph L. Blotner suggests,[20] but rather by that quality in Mrs. Ramsay which might be likened to the integrity of the artist. Like Jinny, who is honored for her devotion to the moment, so Mrs. Ramsay creates islands of perfection with her own presence. Her very position in the window might indicate that her relationship to the world is that of the artist. As Naremore states, the metaphor of the window is a recurrent image in Woolf's work which indicates creativity, the merging of individuality with an anonymous life outside.[21] Mrs. Ramsay is certainly the creator of illusion, but she is also perhaps the ultimate realist, knowing that life is the "old adversary," that "there is no reason, order, justice . . . There was no treachery too base for the world to commit; she knew that. No happiness lasted; she knew that" (p. 98). In the face of her knowledge, then, Mrs. Ramsay's creation of the moment is an act of existential heroism, an affirmation rather than a negation, a declaration of meaning in the face of the absurd, a creation of "shape out of chaos."

Unlike Mrs. Ramsay, Woolf's Clarissa Dalloway does not literally die into her role as art object, partly, perhaps, because she is less beautiful. Small and birdlike, she cannot be compared to Greek sculpture or to a Renaissance madonna. And yet, wearing her sea-green dress the color of a mermaid's, standing at the head of the stairs or in a doorway, Clarissa, too, is a work of art. As Peter Walsh perceives her, she is

> . . . purely feminine; with that extraordinary gift, that woman's gift, of making a world of her own wherever she happened to be. She came into a room; she stood, as he had often seen her, in a doorway with lots of people round her. But it was Clarissa one remembered. Not that she was striking; not beautiful at all; there was nothing picturesque about her;

she never said anything specially clever; there she was, however; there she was.[22]

Clarissa's gift, like Mrs. Ramsay's and Jinny's, is to make of the moment something beautiful and memorable; her parties, for example, are, like Mrs. Ramsay's dinner, ". . . an offering; to combine, to create . . ." (p. 185). Clarissa's presence alone is her contribution as she moves through a room: "Lolloping on the waves and braiding her tresses she seemed, having that gift still; to be; to exist; to sum it all up in the moment as she passed. . ." (p. 264).

Clarissa, too, pays a price for her gift, and that price is the doubling and splitting of the self. Her obvious double is, of course, Septimus Warren Smith, but even within her actual self, her identities are multiple. She recognizes this fact as she sits before her looking glass, attempting to compose the fragments of self into wholeness:

> How many million times she had seen her face, and always with the same imperceptible contradiction! She pursed her lips when she looked into the glass. It was to give her face point. That was her self — pointed; dartlike; definite. That was her self when some effort, some call on her to be her self, drew the parts together, she alone knew how different, how incompatible and composed so for the world only into one centre, one diamond, one woman. . . . (p. 55)

Clarissa watches herself walking in Piccadilly, and is "at the same time . . . outside, looking on. She had a perpetual sense . . . of being out, out, far out to sea and alone. . ." (p. 11). For Clarissa, it is the other and public self, that aspect of her personality which Woolf portrays in *The Voyage Out* and in the short stories, that self as art object, which has become the reality, while an actual self has somehow become disembodied, dispossessed, ". . . invisible; unseen; unknown; . . . this being Mrs. Dalloway; not even Clarissa anymore; this being Mrs. Richard Dalloway" (p. 14). Perhaps, in Woolf's view of female existence, such a loss of self comprises the actual and irrevocable "death of the soul" (p. 88).

In her depictions of Clarissa, Mrs. Ramsay and Jinny, Woolf seems to suggest that there exists a kind of bargain, a pact that women make, not with the devil but with the self: in order to control their worlds, they forfeit identity; to create the self after an image, they surrender the reality and the value of that image to the establishment of others. And, in this exploration of what constitutes "the feminine ideal," Woolf also radically re-defines the very meaning of "art," of "reality," and of the relationship of the individual to both.

Notes

1. John Berger, *Ways of Seeing* (London: Penguin, 1977), p. 47.
2. Berger, p. 46.

3. Simone de Beauvoir, *The Second Sex*, trans. H.M. Parshley (New York: Bantam, 1961), p. 316.

4. Beauvoir, p. 594.

5. Virginia Woolf, *The Waves* (New York: Harcourt Brace Jovanovich, 1978), p. 226. All subsequent references are to this edition.

6. Beauvoir, p. 593.

7. Woolf, *To the Lighthouse* (New York: Harcourt, Brace & World, 1927), p. 241. All subsequent references are to this edition.

8. Elaine Showalter, *A Literature of Their Own: British Women Novelists From Bronte to Lessing* (Princeton: Princeton Univ. Press, 1977), p. 296.

9. Oscar Wilde, "The Art of Lying," *Selected Writings* (London: Oxford, 1961), p. 37.

10. Woolf, *A Room of One's Own* (New York: Harcourt Brace Jovanovich, 1981), p. 34.

11. Berger, p. 64.

12. Sandra M. Gilbert and Susan Gubar, *The Madwoman in the Attic: The Woman Writer and the Nineteenth Century Literary Imagination* (New Haven: Yale Univ. Press, 1979), p. 41.

13. Woolf, "The Lady in the Looking Glass," *A Haunted House and Other Short Stories* (New York: Harcourt Brace Jovanovich, 1972), pp. 87–93.

14. Harvena Richter, *Virginia Woolf: The Inward Voyage* (Princeton: Princeton Univ. Press, 1979), p. 100.

15. James Naremore, *The World Without a Self: Virginia Woolf and the Novel* (New Haven: Yale Univ. Press, 1973).

16. Gilbert and Gubar, p. 25.

17. Woolf, "Professions for Women," *The Death of the Moth and Other Essays* (New York: Harcourt Brace Jovanovich, 1974), p. 238.

18. Carolyn G. Heilbrun, *Toward a Recognition of Androgyny* (New York: Knopf, 1973), p. 156.

19. Heilbrun, p. 159.

20. Joseph L. Blotner, "Mythic Patterns in *To the Lighthouse*," *Virginia Woolf: To the Lighthouse*, ed. Morris Beja (London: Macmillan, 1970).

21. Naremore, p. 243.

22. Woolf: *Mrs. Dalloway* (New York: Harcourt, Brace & World, 1925), pp. 114–15. All subsequent references are to this edition.

INDEX